D1082928

From Philosophy
to Philology

HARVARD EAST ASIAN MONOGRAPHS
110

Source: Seal calligraphy by Cheng Mingshi of the Shanghai Museum, through the arrangement of Tang Zhijun of the Shanghai Academy of Social Sciences. *Shih-shih ch'iu-shih* (to search for the truth in actual facts) was a Han dynasty expression used widely as a slogan for impartial scholarship during the eighteenth century. The phrase is again in vogue as part of the post-Cultural Revolution mood that energizes China today.

From Philosophy
to Philology

Intellectual and Social Aspects of Change
in Late Imperial China

• • •

Benjamin A. Elman

Published by COUNCIL ON EAST ASIAN STUDIES, HARVARD
UNIVERSITY and distributed by HARVARD UNIVERSITY
PRESS, Cambridge (Massachusetts) and London   1984

Library of Congress Cataloging in Publication Data

Elman, Benjamin A., 1946-
  From philosophy to philology.

  Includes index.
  Bibliography: p.
  1. China—Intellectual life—1644-1912.   2. Learning
and scholarship—China—History.   I. Title.
DS754.14.E44 1984   001.1   84-12862
ISBN 0-674-32525-7

To the memory of my grandfather,
Wolf Gryczak, for his courage and
perseverance. Without his efforts, my
family would not have survived
the second world war.

Acknowledgments

There are many to thank for the research and writing of this book. First and foremost, Nathan Sivin and Susan Naquin guided the preparation of the dissertation at the University of Pennsylvania upon which this work is based. Their encouragement and support after the dissertation was completed have been a major factor in the completion of the present project. Thanks are also due members of the Oriental Studies Department at the University of Pennsylvania for their instruction and guidance. These include Allyn and Adele Rickett, Hiroshi Miyaji, and, more recently, Derk Bodde. The reader will note very quickly the debt I owe to Japanese scholarship. It is an understatement to say that without the latter my own work would not have taken the shape that it has. In particular, I would like to acknowledge the generous aid I have received from Yamanoi Yū, Hamaguchi Fujio, and Kawata Teiichi during my stays in Tokyo and Kyoto between 1978 and 1982. My initiation in Ch'ing intellectual history began in Taiwan at the Stanford Center. Ch'en Shun-cheng and Liu Chi-hua were my initial guides through a body of research material that ultimately proved so fruitful and exciting. In addition, Yü Ying-shih's recent research on Ch'ing thought, particularly his work on Chang Hsueh-ch'eng and Tai Chen, has been a model for my own writings.

Numerous colleagues and friends also made substantial contributions to the present book. Kent Guy and John Henderson graciously shared their ideas and findings with me, and I thank them for allowing me to read the drafts of their dissertations while I was completing my own. My research should be viewed as a complement to their forthcoming studies of important aspects of Ch'ing intellectual history. Many of the ideas and analyses formulated below first were articulated in discussions

Acknowledgments

with Peter Bol, Al and Peg Bloom, Willard Peterson, Lee Feigon, and Charles Le Blanc. Portions of previously published work included in the journals *Ch'ing-shih wen-t'i*, *Journal of the American Oriental Society*, and *T'oung Pao* appear in the present work with the permission of the editors involved.

Preparation of the manuscript was aided by a humanities grant from Colby College for which I am grateful. During the final stages, the manuscript received a careful reading from Benjamin Schwartz, Tu Wei-ming, and Philip Kuhn, each of whom suggested many useful changes. Mary Ann Flood proved to be a rigorous editor for a manuscript that contained more technical deficiencies than she deserved. A special measure of gratitude is due Edwin Lee and Russell Blackwood of Hamilton College. They were responsible for my own turn from Western philosophy to Chinese studies as an undergraduate. Moreover, their considered advice helped me through the trying years of the Vietnam War period, when it appeared that my interests in China would be stillborn.

Contents

Contents

Contents

Tables, Maps, Figures

Foreword

It is hard to think of any idea responsible for more fuzziness in writing about China than the notion that Confucianism is one thing. The word is used freely to lump together any number of quite different things: the teachings of Confucius and of the many intellectuals who claimed to elucidate his ideas; the imperial rituals, most of which originated in the upper levels of popular religion; the texts and doctrines promulgated by the State to be taught in schools; the officialdom of the empire, although only a small fraction of its members could be considered intellectuals; conventional landowners, scholars, or aristocrats, regardless of whether they aspired to official careers; in much recent historical writing, members of these elite groups who opposed new ideas or new policies, in contrast to innovators who, although they belonged to the same classes, are usually identified with "the people," "Taoism," and so forth. To those who disapprove of it, "Confucianism" often stands for convention, reaction, and high-minded cant—in short, what is unpalatable about the Establishment (although this British notion fits China even more oddly than it does the United States).

These Confucianisms are not, despite the widespread practice, interchangeable. If we want to understand main currents of thought, lineages of teaching are no doubt the most profitable Confucianism to consider. Such lineages at least produced philosophy as well as consumed it.

Even so, that does not mean that we have settled upon one thing. A "school" (*chia*) in China is not a fixed historical entity, but a claim made by individuals or groups about their connections to forebears. Schools were not defined primarily by statutes, places, or participants, but by the intact transmission of authoritative written texts over generations, generally accompanied by personal teaching to ensure that the texts would be correctly understood so that their accurate reproduction and transmission could continue. The teachings were in principle peripheral to the central act of passing on the text. Years of preparation might be required to ensure that the disciple was spiritually, morally, and intellectually qualified to receive the canon—that is, to memorize or copy it. Most traditions in China, from Confucian movements to mathematics or architecture, were built around writings of sacred character, revealed by legendary or more-than-human figures. Because of this origin in an ideal order of reality, such "classics" contained all knowledge pertinent to the field of endeavor, in a form that in a degraded age only an intact line of teachers could make comprehensible to carefully prepared disciples. The Chinese word for a canonical scripture (*ching*) originally meant the warp threads in a fabric, an apt metaphor for the continuity of transmission.

Confucian teachers have always seen their task essentially as education for orthodoxy. All agreed that orthodoxy is essential, for moral judgment cannot be arbitrary. There have been disagreements and major shifts, of course, in views about what orthodoxy ought to be. These changes of conviction reflected changes in society, as teachings of the various schools were transmitted under state patronage from about 200 B.C., as this support was largely restricted to the Confucian canon from about 100 B.C. on, as the centrality of Confucianism diminished until it was competing unsuccessfully with Buddhism and Taoism for the power to form thought, and as from the eighth century on it gradually regained its moral, social, and intellectual authority. These new Confucian teachings, reshaped by interaction with Taoism and Buddhism, began to center on the realization of the individual's humanity, on what W. T. de Bary has called "the morally responsible self and spiritual self-determination." The pupil's guided self-cultivation, culminating in a personal experience of unity with Heaven, Earth, and all things, became the foundation for an activism meant to renew every level of society. The charismatic texts were still there—many in fact originated in the eleventh and twelfth centuries—but the focus was on living them.

As this intellectual tradition developed it gradually bifurcated. The power of the new teachings to engage the minds and imaginations of the elite came from the sense of urgent individual quest, the dedication to a social good, the promise of realizing millenary goals. To the state the new doctrines offered an unprecedentedly effective tool for ensuring the loyalty of the educated. Activism, with its threat of disturbance to the established order, could be transmuted into the conformist zeal of the good bureaucrat. Access to the civil service examinations could be based on an idealistic standardized indoctrination that exalted the servitor's duty to his emperor.

By the last stage of paralysis in the Ming polity (roughly 1600), public Confucianism had become a prop for an increasingly authoritarian monarchy that had largely done away with traditional checks on its power. Like modern totalitarian states, the Chinese government tolerated individual corruption in return for complicity in its larger corruption of ideals. To put it less abstractly, honest officials were tolerated and even admired by colleagues, but those who demanded honest and responsible behavior of their equals or betters posed an unacceptable threat, and were usually ruined. Private Confucianism had become a profusion of lineages pursuing their quests in many directions, variously emphasizing self-cultivation, world-ordering, and concern even among quietists about the growing disorder of the realm. Some of these schools even nurtured individualists unwilling to tolerate the rampant corruption and influence-mongering. The Ming debacle was a debacle for public and private Confucianism alike. The anticlimax of the Manchu invasion put in place a new order from which to reassess the Confucianisms of the past and sort through them for the true teachings of Confucius. Only by rediscovering that authentic original impulse was a new beginning orthodoxy possible.

Benjamin Elman's book is about that last new beginning, imperial China's final great intellectual shift. The self-cultivation and world-ordering of the sixteenth century seemed to some even before the collapse of the Ming too little rooted in what Confucius had said and done. The "model teacher for a myriad generations" was obscured behind Taoist images of man as mediator between cosmos and society, and Buddhist versions of the mystical unity of all experience. The only sure way back to what the classics really said and meant seemed to be a winnowing of the sources of discourse, using the classicist's techniques of systematic critical inquiry.

These tactics of rediscovery widely used at the end of the Ming (but none entirely new even then) became in the early Ch'ing a strategy for rebuilding shattered confidence. For more than a century after 1650 the whole canon about which elite intellectual life pivoted was gradually reevaluated. The tools were rigorous philology and mathematical astronomy (the latter provided objective tests of date and authenticity).

The outcome was irresistible in its rigor; it was also as sharply biased by its powerful methodology as the outcome of cost-benefits analysis today. What was ignored by this expanding program in its first century was its ostensible goal, philosophical reconstruction. A viewpoint began finally to emerge from its results in the mid-eighteenth century. The evidential scholars' willingness to accept the consequences of testing left this movement more open to the unexpected than previous Confucianisms. As the balance began to swing back in the direction of philosophy, the last of all Confucianisms—the "New Text" movement of the eighteenth and nineteenth centuries—turned out to be disturbingly compatible with new ideas from the West and ultimately with radical politics. This was radical conservatism, for Confucians can have faith only in what persists. But by the end of the empire, Neo-Confucianism as it unraveled had provided an ideology for destroying the traditional monarchic world order built about the image of Confucius. What the conventional elite over 2500 years had come to consider a creed meant for every civilized person—its acceptance the test of civilization—now suvives as merely one force among many available to those doing philosophy worldwide.

Elman has reconstructed the remarkable story of Confucianisms in late imperial China, centering his book on the reorientation from philosophy to philology. Parts of the story have been told over nearly a century by Chinese and Japanese scholars from Liang Ch'i-ch'ao (1873-1929) on, with notable recent contributions by their colleagues in the West. Elman's intense labor of research has filled in many gaps, and has thus led him to see a larger pattern than his predecessors have encompassed.

Benjamin Elman stands out among young scholars who are unwilling to follow the Sinological fashion and choose between intellectual and social history. His work carries conviction because he situates each transformation of ideas in people, and people in institutions. It is not that the ideas cause institutional change, or that institutions determine intellectual change; both are aspects of one reality.

The unprecedented autonomy of exact research was accomplished in unprecedented social circumstances: a new community of scholars widespread in the lower Yangtze and the capital. It spanned a range from coteries to academies that no longer aimed at official careers and did not base their curricula on the state examinations. It rewarded intellectuals according to the rigor and boldness of their scholarship. What made the research possible was made possible by the research. The logician may find that circular, but that is the way the world works.

Along the way Elman clears up many familiar muddles. He does not analyze the retreat from Confucian philosophy, which had always had political consequences, to apolitical philology as the simple matter of Manchu repression and literatus timidity that the textbooks make it. For another example, Elman and his contemporary John Henderson have come to grips with the pervasive knowledge of European mathematics and mathematical astronomy among Ch'ing philologists and other Confucians from 1600 on, a topic sedulously avoided by many "experts" who find themselves acutely uncomfortable in the presence of numbers. Less enterprising Sinologues are still writing biographies of major figures without so much as reading their scientific works. Again, Elman has avoided assuming fallaciously that the transformations he studies must be *either* China's response to the West *or* an internal readjustment in which foreign influence played no essential part. His account of how Western influence operated, and to what extent, is both clearer and subtler than any before it.

For three hundred years the great challenge of historiography in the European and American tradition has been finding the right relation between detailed research and conclusions about the flow of events. All too often we have been left with research results that are never incorporated in our general knowledge, and generalizations that do not display a decent regard for the facts. Elman demonstrates that one need not choose. I hope that this book will hearten other young scholars to ignore the advice they hear so frequently from their elders to concentrate on the details and leave the larger picture to someone else, someday. The result of this advice has been, in historical writing on China, a singular dearth of synthesis useful to intelligent readers who are not interested in becoming specialists. The scholar who knows the fine texture is likely to have the soundest instinct for overall pattern, if only he will learn to incorporate it in his findings. There is much to be learned about the necessary skills from this book.

N. Sivin
Chestnut Hill
8 June 1984

Preface

In one of the most penetrating probes into the boundaries of modern Chinese history, Philip Kuhn has explained that a perplexing problem for historians of modern China is "how to distinguish between the decline of the Ch'ing regime [1644–1911] and the decline of traditional Chinese society as a whole." If China was not on the eve of decisive changes before the nineteenth century, then, according to Kuhn, "one must assume that it was the Western intrusion that transformed a dynastic decline of a largely traditional type into a social and intellectual revolution in which nearly the whole of the old culture was swept away." Employing a sociological analysis, Kuhn has stressed that, after the middle of the nineteenth century, the social authority, power, and cohesion of the Confucian elite began to crumble.[1]

If instead of social relations we consider intellectual currents during the Ch'ing period, the drama of literati disenchantment with the imperial orthodoxy had already climaxed in the eighteenth century. The reaction of many Ch'ing literati against the unquestioned authority of the Confucian Classics was evident in their interest in precise and critical scholarship in linguistics, astronomy, mathematics, geography, and epigraphy. Eighteenth-century scholars applied these fields of research to verify or controvert important elements of the Confucian legacy. They were dissatisfied with the empirically unverifiable ideas that had pervaded Sung (960–1279) and Ming dynasty (1368–1644) interpretations of classical Confucianism. This change in outlook was most obvious in the application of systematic doubt to the ageless Classics

---

1. Philip Kuhn, *Rebellion and Its Enemies in Late Imperial China* (Cambridge, Mass., 1970), pp. 1–10.

and their historicization, that is, demotion to the status of historical sources.[2]

To understand the pervasive influence of the Ch'ing evidential research movement (*k'ao-cheng hsueh*), it is necessary to look at the intellectual community in which it took hold. One of the principal conclusions we will reach below is that during the Ch'ing dynasty a unified academic community existed in the Lower Yangtze Region of China before its dissolution during the Taiping Rebellion (1850–1864). To be sure, not even a majority of Ch'ing scholar-officials participated in or promoted evidential studies. A significant portion of the scholarly elite (whom we will call "literati"), as distinct from the political elite, did. Hence, this scholarly community, which included the greatest scholars of the age, should be understood as a subsection of the total pool of degree-holders, most of whom were not active participants in the scholarly currents we will explore. Members of this community of scholars were bound together by associations and institutions for the propagation of knowledge. A consensus of ideas about how to find and verify knowledge was the result.

To clarify the unified aspects of this academic community, we will make frequent use of Thomas Kuhn's pioneering analysis of the relationship between discrete bodies of technical writings and the community of specialized scholars who produce them. In particular, the internal and external aspects of Ch'ing intellectual history will be stressed. We will also find it useful to employ Michel Foucault's notion of a "discourse" as described in his *The Archaeology of Knowledge*. We will argue that evidential scholarship was such a discourse: a system of scholarly articulation and meaning. The formation of a shared epistemological perspective in seventeenth- and eighteenth-century China reveals dramatic changes in the uses and meanings of language. As conceptual events, the gradual articulation of the parameters of empirical philological discourse represented a fundamental pattern of intellectual change, which in turn led to an even more fundamental alteration of

2. Ibid., p. 6. Using a formulation that Kuhn himself entertained but ultimately rejected, we could perhaps hypothesize "that the West was impinging, not upon a dynasty in decline, but upon a civilization in decline: a civilization that would soon have had to generate fresh forms of social and political organization from within itself." Cf. John Henderson, "The Ordering of the Heavens and Earth in Early Ch'ing Thought" (PhD dissertation, University of California, Berkeley, 1977), pp. 98, 117.

traditional concepts and attitudes. The previous norms of acceptable knowledge were decisively challenged.[3]

In chapter 1, we will explore this revolution in discourse by focusing on the intellectual context within which it occurred. Beginning with chapter 2, we will evaluate a wide variety of scholarly writings from seventeenth- and eighteenth-century China, outline the nature of the intellectual order within those materials, and finally discuss the specialized textual, historical, and scientific studies that were produced. In chapters 3 and 4, in particular, we will describe the social and institutional patterns of organization that made a specialized research community possible. The institutional and historical context for the emergence of exact scholarship in Lower Yangtze urban centers marked what we will call the "professionalization" of academics in late imperial China. In these chapters, the roles of scholarly patronage, schools and academies, and the publishing industry will be given special attention.

The individual research scholar was by the eighteenth century part of a dynamic and evolving scholarly environment, which we will describe in chapter 5. Through the concentrated efforts of trained specialists, who employed precise procedures of inquiry, an almost autonomous subsystem of Ch'ing society with its own rubrics of status evolved in the Lower Yangtze Region. Although this academic community perished during the Taiping Rebellion (described in chapter 6), its intellectual legacy did not. The turn to empirical methods of exact scholarship initiated the unraveling of the orthodox Confucian tradition in late imperial China.

We should note at the outset, however, that until quite recently the eighteenth century in China, that is, "High Ch'ing," has been inadequately studied. Although there have been major exceptions, most scholars of late imperial China or modern China have stressed the seventeenth and nineteenth centuries in their efforts to reconstruct the perilous journey by which China entered the modern world. We will

3. Michel Foucault, *The Archaeology of Knowledge*, tr., A. M. Sheridan Smith (New York, 1972), *passim*. See also Thomas Kuhn, "Second Thoughts on Paradigms," *The Essential Tension: Selected Studies in Scientific Tradition and Change* (Chicago, 1977), pp. 293–319. Cf. Tetsuo Najita, "Method and Analysis in the Conceptual Portrayal of Tokugawa Intellectual History," *Japanese Thought in the Tokugawa Period: Methods and Metaphors*, Najita and Irwin Scheiner, eds., (Chicago, 1978), pp. 3–23, H. D. Harootunian, "The Consciousness of Archaic Form in the New Realism of Kokugaku," ibid., pp. 63–84, and Hayden White, "Foucault Decoded: Notes From Underground," *History and Theory* 12:23–54 (1973).

demonstrate below that eighteenth-century China should be grasped in part as a product of seventeenth-century political and conceptual events, which peaked in the late eighteenth century, but had enough staying power to influence the nineteenth and twentieth centuries. The eighteenth century in China, we will contend, cannot be grasped in isolation, especially because it is bounded by two centuries of momentous events: the Manchu triumph in the seventeenth and the Western impact in the nineteenth.

Much of what we will say about the eighteenth century will by necessity be preliminary remarks about a century of change too long underestimated by modern historians. The markers we will try to provide for those scholars whose attentions are increasingly being drawn to this understudied period in Chinese history will over the long run need to be revised and emended. We are hopeful, however, that the broader conclusions drawn and the general guidelines erected will continue to play a useful and stimulating role in helping to bring the eighteenth century to the forefront of our academic disciplines. At the same time that we try to tie together many of the loose ends in our understanding of this period, we will also stress those loose ends that still remain and urge more focused exploration than we will be able to engage in here. In short, our account does not presume to be definitive. Our first forays into this important century can only claim to clear away some of the obstructing brush, so that others who follow can penetrate even further down the road of scholarly evaluation.

Explanatory Notes

(1) Dates have not been included for well-known historical figures, e.g., Confucius and Mencius. Dates for all persons, excepting the above, will be given on their first appearance in each chapter. Chinese characters for all names, book titles, and terms will be included in the bibliography or glossary.

(2) The term "rubbing" for copies of texts taken from carved surfaces of either stone or wood is used below instead of "ink squeeze" because it has become the conventional term. The process of applying a wad of silk soaked with ink to the paper surface was actually a process of patting or tamping.

(3) In the discussion of libraries in chapter 5 and elsewhere, it would be preferable to give the number of titles contained in a particular collection. Because such information is not readily available for many of the libraries discussed below, our account for the most part will give approximate figures for the total number of *chüan* (scrolls, i.e., text divisions that were originally a scroll but later more or less a chapter) in Ch'ing libraries. These numbers will at least be useful for general comparisons.

(4) In order to forestall misunderstanding over the content and nature of *k'ao-cheng* (evidential research) studies in China, we will describe such research as "empirical" rather than "empiricist." Empiricism is usually thought of in relation to the British philosophers John Locke, George Berkeley, and David Hume, who stressed that all knowledge was presupposed by sense experience. Ch'ing evidential scholars were not empiricist in this strict philosophic sense, although the discussion in chapter 3 will show that evidential scholars were moving toward an empiricist position. By "empirical" is meant an epistemological position

that stresses that valid knowledge must be corroborated by external (textual or otherwise) facts and impartial observations. Hence, *k'ao-cheng* scholars were empirically oriented because they searched for an external source for the legitimation of their knowledge. Reason was regarded as a limited measure of knowledge, especially as it was used in the speculative conclusions debated by Neo-Confucian philosophers. Evidential scholars opposed forms of inquiry not reducible to the standards of verification used in *k'ao-cheng* discourse.

(5) The term "Neo-Confucianism" (*hsin Ju-hsueh*) will be used below to refer to the schools of Confucianism that developed in the Sung, Yuan, and Ming dynasties. Ch'ing dynasty Confucians referred to these disparate schools as "Studies of the Way" (*Tao-hsueh*). Unfortunately, there has been a tendency to use Neo-Confucianism to cover all Confucian intellectual currents from the T'ang dynasty (618–906) until the fall of the last dynasty in 1911. Our use here will be limited to the pre-Ch'ing period, and the reader should guard against the tendency to assimilate Neo-Confucianism to the broader amorphous designations that have been attached to it. Using the Ch'ing perspective as our framework for analysis, we will equate *Tao-hsueh* with Neo-Confucianism throughout the pages that follow. We should add, however, that the Ch'ing perspective on the Neo-Confucian tradition was by no means definitive. Recent research by Hoyt Tillman and Peter Bol, among others, has revealed that the definition and content of *Tao-hsueh* were as debatable during the eleventh and twelfth centuries as they were in the seventeenth and eighteenth. For our purposes, the Ch'ing standpoint provides us with historical markers within the Confucian tradition that enable us to see how seventeenth- and eighteenth-century Confucians evaluated their Neo-Confucian predecessors. Whether they were right or not, of course, is another matter. The term "Neo-Confucian orthodoxy" will refer specifically to the imperially sanctioned Chu Hsi school of interpretations to the Confucian Classics. These were officially accepted beginning in 1313 and remained the basis of the Confucian civil service examinations until 1905.

(6) The word "academics" in this work will refer specifically to intellectual activities within a community of scholars during the Ch'ing dynasty. Included in the meaning of this term will be the activities of scholars and students in academies, literary projects, and private research, that is, an academic community.

Explanatory Notes

(7) The bibliography includes all primary and secondary sources cited specifically by page number in the notes. Titles of works that are merely mentioned or referred to in the text but not in the notes are not cited in the bibliography. Chinese characters for the latter occur in the glossary. Translations into English for such titles occur after their first appearance in the text.

. . .

I, too, aspire to see clearly, like a rifleman, with one eye shut; I, too, aspire to think without assent. This is the ultimate violence to which the modern intellectual is committed. Since things have become as they are, I, too, share the modern desire not to be deceived.

Philip Rieff

One

A Revolution in Discourse in Late Imperial China

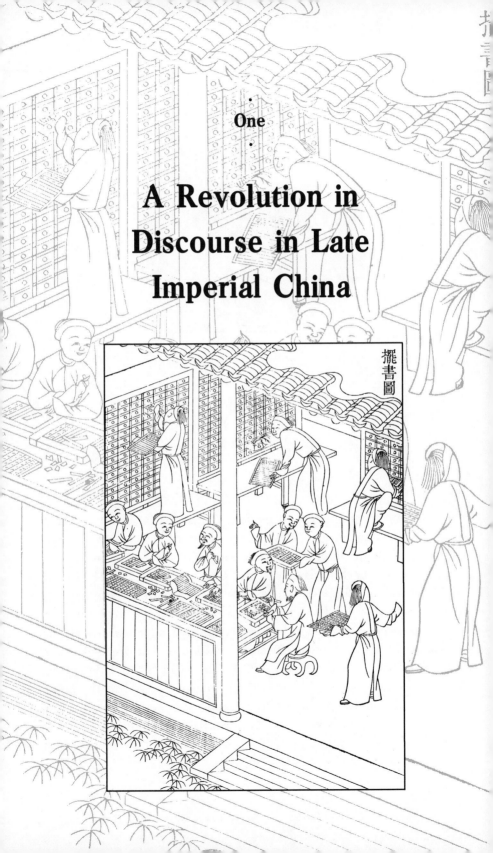

The transition from imperial to modern China was far less simple than we are inclined to imagine it. Western historians have tended to treat the history of late imperial China as a period of fading and decay. Usually viewed backwards, from the Opium War (1839–1842) and Taiping Rebellion (1850–1864), events in the eighteenth century and before often seem to have left China unprepared for modernity. In contrast to a powerful and industrialized Europe, China was weak and backward. Such impatient perspectives of China's past overlook, however, the crucial role the Sung (960–1279), Yuan (1280–1368), Ming (1368–1644), and Ch'ing (1644–1911) dynasties played in the emergence of early modern China and the decline of imperial Confucianism. The present work deals with the seventeenth and eighteenth centuries by considering them not as a prelude to the end of Confucian China but rather as a harbinger of things to come.

Figure 1 Setting Type
Source: *Ch'in-ting Wu-ying-tien chü-chen-pan ch'eng shih* (Peking, 1776).

By the seventeenth century, Confucian literati had outgrown earlier forms and modes of Confucian thought. Their decisive break with the imperial orthodoxy entrenched in official life initiated a turn toward a "search for evidence" as the key to the retrieval of China's past. Remarkably, they resembled Lorenzo Valla (1407-1457) and Desiderius Erasmus (1466?-1536), perhaps the greatest Latin philologists of the Renaissance. Like their European counterparts, Ch'ing dynasty philologists favored linguistic clarity, simplicity, and purity. This endeavor led them to expose inconsistencies in contemporary beliefs and forms of expression. Like Valla and Erasmus, Ch'ing philologists were prototypes of the modern philologist as moral reformer. They were scholarly iconoclasts who, in the interest of a higher consistency, hoped to eliminate linguistic confusion and thereby locate a bedrock of timeless order. The formally pure language of classical antiquity, if properly studied and reconstructed, would yield that order.[1]

Historians gradually have recognized that an important shift in intellectual and philosophic orientation began in seventeenth-century China. The decisive impact of the fall of the Ming dynasty to Manchu "barbarians" in 1644 confirmed, rightly or mistakenly, for many Chinese literati who experienced it, the sterility and perniciousness of recent Confucian discourse. They vigorously attacked the heterodox ideals of their predecessors, which had betrayed the true teachings of Confucius and thus had brought on this debacle.[2]

Before the fall of the Ming dynasty, the most compelling ideal that motivated the greatest Chinese scholars was sagehood. Among Sung, Yuan, and Ming dynasty Confucians, emphasis therefore was usually placed on the cultivation of moral perfection. In Western scholarship, this mode of philosophy is called "Neo-Confucianism." Only if every literatus was an exemplar of virtue could Confucian society survive and prosper. Knowledge and action were equated. Political and cultural stability depended on the moral rigor of each individual.

To buttress their moral claims, Sung and Ming Confucians developed an elaborate and often systematic account of the interaction between the heavens and earth. Through their meditations on the role of cosmological patterns of differentiation and organization in the creation of all things in the world, they thought they finally understood the place of man, and of his mental capacities, in a world of orderly and determinable change. To become a sage was to achieve a vision of the highest,

Map 1   Physiographic Macroregions of Agrarian China
in Relation to Major Rivers

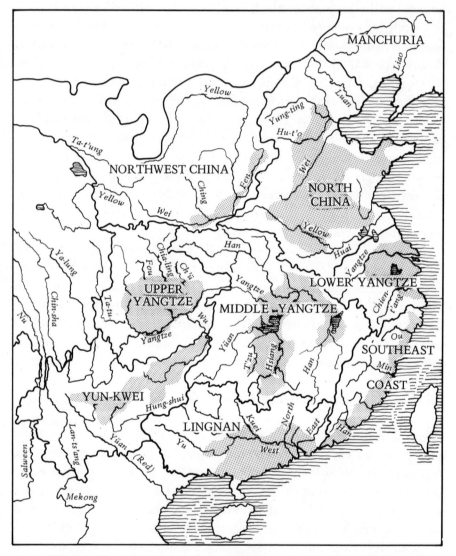

Map 2   China: Administrative Map

a vision of the cosmos in which man was a pivotal factor in a morally just and perfectly rational universe.

By 1750, however, the Ch'ing heirs of the Neo-Confucian legacy had become members of a secular academic community, which encouraged, and rewarded with livelihoods, original and rigorous critical scholarship. In contrast to their predecessors, Ch'ing literati stressed exacting research, rigorous analysis, and the collection of impartial evidence drawn from ancient artifacts and historical documents and texts. Abstract ideas and emphasis on moral values gave way as the primary objects of discussion among Confucian scholars to concrete facts, documented institutions, and historical events. Personal achievement of sagehood, by now an unrealistic aim for serious Confucians, was no longer their goal.

Ch'ing dynasty scholarship represented a new and highly important transition in traditional Chinese intellectual history. Through the revolution in scholarly discourse that took place during this time, we can observe the creation and evolution of a distinguished academic community, which represented the last great tradition of Confucian thought. Moreover, we can perceive the role these fresh intellectual impulses played in recasting the social role of the Confucian scholar in late imperial China. The philological tradition of evidential research (k'ao-cheng, lit., "search for evidence") created and maintained by these scholars will be the topic of our inquiry.

The major figures for the most part resided in the wealthy and sophisticated provinces located in the lower basin of the Yangtze River: Kiangsu, Chekiang, and Anhwei. There and in the imperial capital of Peking, as a result of their labors to uncover the roots of Confucian culture, they established the foundations for our knowledge of ancient China. Their efforts brought to completion one of the most prolific movements in scholarly research seen in Chinese history. They received, rediscovered, and transformed the Confucian tradition of learning and scholarship. Their approach still dominates Sinology.

. . .

The Context of Lower Yangtze Academics

. .

Internal and External History

To understand the syntax of events that produced a community of research scholars and an academic world of increasing specialization in the Lower Yangtze Region, we will investigate the complicated network of personal and institutional relations that mediated between individual textual scholars and the larger social milieu. The transformation of scholarly discourse during the Ch'ing dynasty was a complicated process. This process included an intellectual revolution and a change in the institutional conditions within which serious research and writing were produced.[3]

We will not rely on any single conceptual scheme to illuminate our study. As much as possible, we will borrow, whenever appropriate, from the work of Western scholars such as Michel Foucault and Thomas Kuhn to suit the Chinese case. Both the intellectual breakthroughs internal to the changes in academic discourse we will describe, and the social and political events external to but necessary for scholarly consensus, will demand our attention. The historical course of this dramatic change in discourse rested on institutions that rendered its vocabulary, concepts, and academic program available to those who would employ them. Accordingly, we will stress throughout our account the interaction of internal and external history.

The Lower Yangtze community is best discovered by examining patterns of education and scholarly communication that were shared by members of that community. Evidential scholarship was a group enterprise. Neither its empirical orientation, nor the manner in which it developed, can be properly understood without reference to the special characteristics of the groups of scholars who produced it. Empirical criteria for ascertaining all knowledge were championed by seventeenth-century scholars who were subjected to the decisive social, political, and cultural upheaval that accompanied the fall of the Ming dynasty. Many of the social and intellectual choices made by members of the eighteenth-century k'ao-cheng movement, as well as their research strategies, were in turn dictated by the shared epistemological perspective formed in the previous century.[4]

The intellectual revolution that started in seventeenth-century China could not have had the impact that it did in the eighteenth century without the formation of scholarly institutions appropriate for the propagation of the new discourse that was taking shape. Although the majority of degree-holders during the Ch'ing dynasty were not *k'ao-cheng* scholars, through their patronage and financial support they helped promote the new discourse. The society at large secured the viability of the academic community within. Our first priority, then, is to address the nature of the society at large.

· ·

The Lower Yangtze Connection

Since the medieval economic revolution that began in China in the middle of the T'ang dynasty (618–906), intellectual life was dominated by "men from the South." North China, although still the setting for important political events, no longer took the lead in the cultural life of the country. Literati from the South initiated most of the great movements in art, letters, and scholarship during the Sung, Yuan, and Ming dynasties. After the Manchu takeover in 1644, southern literati led the way in coming to grips with the dilemmas posed by the collapse of Ming rule. Their turn away from moral cultivation to precise scholarship was a key element in the Chinese response to the Ming collapse.

We now recognize that the Lower Yangtze River Basin was the hub of commerce and communication in late imperial China. Ch'ing dynasty cultural life was concentrated in the provinces known collectively as Kiangnan (lit., "South of the Yangtze," that is, the most important parts of Kiangsu, Anhwei, and Chekiang). The emerging centrality of Kiangnan had been preceded in earlier dynasties by a shift in the location of the majority of China's population from the northern plain to the valleys and slopes of the mountainous south (Kiangnan) and southeast coast (Lingnan, that is, Kwangtung and Fukien). New recruitment procedures initiated in the Northern Sung (960–1127), in addition to opening a government career to larger numbers of people than before, helped to break the power monopoly of northern aristocratic families.

Beginning in the late T'ang and Sung periods, but accelerating during the Ming and Ch'ing dynasties, the provinces in Kiangnan became a huge, interregional trading area based on an elaborate network of rivers, canals, and lakes. Within this region, the degree of urbanization was markedly higher than in other regional systems. Urban centers in the Lower Yangtze Region flourished as important cogs in trade and commerce.[5] The cities of Soochow, Nanking (one of two Ming dynasty capitals), Yangchow, and Hangchow were situated at the apex of the most commercialized macroregion in late imperial China. Set in the heartland of Kiangnan, one of China's best rice-, tea-, and fruit-growing areas, Soochow by the Yuan dynasty already had become a center for scholars and literary men. A leading producer of silk and cotton goods that supplied luxury items of many kinds for export and domestic markets, Soochow was a cosmopolitan city where the arts flourished alongside commercial activity. Soochow's literati remained influential in literature, music, theater, calligraphy, and painting until the twentieth century.

Because Kiangnan was both the southern terminus of the Grand Canal and the outlet to the sea for the Yangtze River, the local and regional market systems that developed there were centers for the grain, salt, and textile trade throughout the empire. During the Ming and Ch'ing dynasties, merchants from as far away as Shansi and Shensi in the northwest moved into Kiangnan to participate in the profitable trade of Kiangsu and Chekiang. The favorable commercial position of these provinces enabled Huai-an and particularly Yangchow to become important centers for the imperial government's salt monopoly and marshaling depots for grain shipments to Peking. With headquarters in Yangchow, at the junction of the Grand Canal and the Yangtze and Huai rivers, the Liang-Huai Salt Administration (serving the provinces of Kiangsu, Anhwei, Honan, Kiangsi, Hunan, Hupei, and Kweichow) easily outstripped all other areas in production, sales, and revenue. Shensi, Shansi, and Anhwei salt merchants were attracted to Yangchow both for business and pleasure, and these visitors gave the city a cosmopolitan flavor. Moving out of Kiangnan, many merchants left their home towns for other parts of China in order to carry on trade. Merchants from Huichow in Anhwei were scattered all over the empire.[6]

The Lower Yangtze merchants who managed the salt trade possessed the largest capital of any commercial group in late imperial China

Map 3   The Kiangnan Region

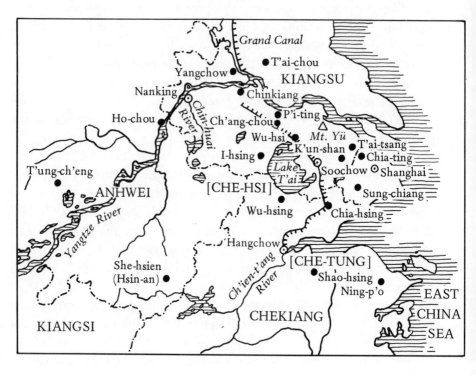

Map 4   The Soochow Region

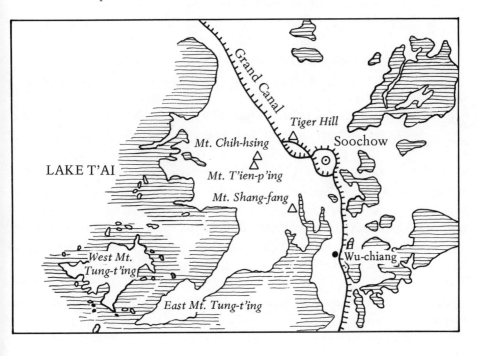

before the nineteenth century. Yangchow merchants, for example, were known as great patrons of scholarship, the theater, and the arts. Numerous scholars who participated in the evidential research movement frequently spent time as guests of Kiangnan salt merchants. In addition, there was considerable merchant support for the growth of schools and academies in the Kiangnan region. The result was a merging of literati and merchant interests.[7]

A close overlap existed between the book trade in China and the high level of cultural achievement in Kiangnan. Cities such as Soochow, Ch'ang-shu, Sung-chiang, and Wu-hsi had all been book-collecting and printing centers in the Lower Yangtze for centuries. *Chin-shih* (presented scholars, that is, highest examination graduates) in Kiangnan were urbanized to a much higher degree than in any other region. Figures for the distribution of *chin-shih* degree-holders during the Ch'ing period also reveal that Kiangsu and Chekiang ranked first and second for all of China. Academic success in turn led to high political position for many Lower Yangtze literati.[8]

The diversity of ideas current during the Ch'ing dynasty usually was classified by relation to schools of scholarship that centered on Kiangnan. School divisions were taken for granted as evidence of the filiation of scholars, who through personal or geographical association, philosophic or literary agreement, or master-disciple relations could be linked together into specific groups. Cross-fertilization of ideas and shared research methods among members of the Kiangnan schools of learning allow us to recognize that there were definite unifying features, which transcended individually defined schools. Despite obvious differences in focus and interest, most schools during the Ch'ing dynasty defined themselves according to shared criteria. These criteria in turn allowed each school to emphasize its unique characteristics.

Local schools of scholarship actually represented distinct subcommunities within specific urban areas in the Lower Yangtze macroregion. The larger academic community encompassed these distinct subcommunities of scholars, which we have usually characterized as schools. The schools of learning that emerged in Fukien, Kwangtung, and Hunan in the late eighteenth and nineteenth centuries were in many ways tributaries of or reactions against the dominant scholarly trends that developed in Kiangnan urban centers.

Functioning as a "national elite," literati from the Lower Yangtze

Region were also able to transmit much of the verve and flavor of Kiangnan academics to the capital in Peking. This transmission was accomplished through a network of vertical patronage that ran through the official projects sponsored by the imperial government, as well as through the Ch'ing academic system in which Kiangnan scholars excelled. Many of the most prominent scholars chosen to work on the imperially sponsored *Ssu-k'u ch'üan-shu* (Complete collection of the four treasuries) project completed in the 1780s were drawn from Kiangnan. The staffs of many national figures were filled with scores of dependent Lower Yangtze scholars, as was the Hanlin Academy in Peking. Kiangnan trends in scholarship, art, and literature were transmitted throughout China because of these patronage networks.[9]

These currents of thought took place, however, at a time when China was ruled by a foreign people. Consequently, the freedom with which Ch'ing philologists advanced and chose research problems generally has been ignored, the evidence buried under an accumulation of essays and monographs that seek to demonstrate that Manchu policies in China led to an era of intellectual sterility and stagnancy. In order to elicit the broader political implications of the *k'ao-cheng* movement, we will reconsider this unfortunate perspective.

· · ·

Politics and Scholarship in the Manchu State

The triumphs of Ch'ing philology have been dismissed as the "vice of the Confucian intellectual." Many modern scholars have assumed that Ch'ing literati diverted their attention from significant ethical and political issues by whiling away their hours in barren textual studies. We have been quick to accept this point of view because of prevailing scholarship that stresses the negative impact of ideological control by foreign Manchu rulers on Chinese literati after 1644 and the constraining effect literary persecutions during the Ch'ing dynasty had on intellectual inquiry.[10]

Manchu policies toward Chinese intellectuals are best evaluated, however, in light of earlier persecutions of literati for their political beliefs. The claim that Manchu inquisitions were largely responsible for the rise of evidential research overlooks the implications of similar policies during earlier dynasties. Neither the Sung nor the Ming dynasties, for example, were havens for free expression of political sentiments. Moreover, the ruthlessness and terrorist tactics that the eunuch Wei Chunghsien (1568–1627) employed to liquidate his opposition among the Tung-lin Academy partisans in the seventeenth century surpass the Manchu inquisitions in scope and violence.[11]

We are discovering, meanwhile, that Ch'ing philologists complemented their textual interests with concern for practical problems in astronomy, mathematics, water control, and land reclamation. John Henderson has shown that Confucian and technical studies were reunited as legitimate concerns for Chinese literati in the seventeenth century. In fact, the peril of discussing the Confucian tradition without an awareness of the astronomical and mathematical content of Confucian texts was more apparent to eighteenth-century *k'ao-cheng* scholars than to many twentieth-century historians, for whom a commitment to humanistic scholarship seems to justify ignorance of science.[12]

Manchu Policy and Evidential Research

Although the Manchus provided a stable social and economic framework for the institutions within which apolitical *k'ao-cheng* scholarship flourished, they did not dictate the forms that such research would take. The growth of philology and ancillary disciplines during this period was in some ways dependent on and in some other ways independent of the sociopolitical conditions for scholarly work and research created by Manchu policies toward intellectuals. Many seventeenth-century literati, for instance, were horrified by the partisan politics that had plagued the late Ming and blamed its fall on the bitter factionalism among Ming Confucians. Revulsion from political involvement is a frequently overlooked legacy of the Ming debacle. A life of scholarship appeared by contrast to be a welcome alternative.

The imperial government's large-scale intervention in academics in the seventeenth and eighteenth centuries aimed to depoliticize Chinese literati and mobilize them in support of the state. Chinese scholars living under Manchu rule were exposed, however, to a selective form of literary censorship. They had a considerable amount of freedom to advance and choose research problems. Scholars could say and write what they pleased about the Classics, but if one word was discovered that described the Manchu court or Mongols disrespectfully, they were pounced upon with a vengeance.[13]

Manchu censorship in China was political and rarely entered into the realm of doctrines and ideas. For example, Yen Jo-chü (1636–1704), a leader in the seventeenth-century turn to precise empirical scholarship, decisively demonstrated that a portion of an imperially sponsored and hitherto sacred Classic (sheng-ching) was spurious. Although Yen's findings evoked heated literati debates pro and con, his arguments were never taken up by the imperial court, even when there were calls for the elimination of the Old Text chapters of the Documents Classic from the official text used for the examination system.

The Ssu-k'u ch'üan-shu project, often described as an "inquisition," had of course its darker side. Over two thousand works, a large portion of which were late Ming writings, were destroyed as part of the Ch'ien-lung Emperor's (r. 1736–1795) efforts to weed out anti-Manchu sentiments in books and manuscripts. Officials ordered to invite book collectors to lend or sell rare books to the project were also required to search out and demand volumes containing material thought to be against the dynasty's best interests. Kent Guy has demonstrated, however, that the course of censorship and book suppression was more complicated than we have hitherto thought. Guy has shown how "the inquisition grew through the interaction of gentry, bureaucratic, and imperial interests, shaped by all but dominated by none." All had political axes to grind. Because the campaign went beyond its limited goals, the imperial court finally stepped in to mitigate its effects.

Manchu policies toward Chinese literati had a double edge. Although Ch'ing emperors tried to prevent overt political behavior by intellectuals, the Manchu court also actively encouraged Chinese scholars in their use of empirical and inductive methods of research. The sponsoring of numerous literary projects (described in chapter 3) requiring k'ao-cheng expertise and the prodigious publishing carried out by the

Imperial Household (described in chapter 4) attest to this support. Hence, an account of Ch'ing scholarship based on external, political events alone overlooks the historical roots and development of *k'ao-cheng* discourse during the Ming-Ch'ing transition period.[14]

As Guy has noted, the degree to which contemporary academic opinion influenced scholarly evaluations in the *Ssu-k'u ch'üan-shu* project reflects the considerable influence and remarkable independence Ch'ing literati had in enunciating values and expressing opinions. Sensitivity to the latest trends of scholarly opinion and demand for intellectual consistency on the part of the research scholars working on the project shaped to a considerable extent the way an imperially sponsored academic enterprise adopted the positions laid down by the most influential private Kiangnan scholars of the day.

Evidential research as an academic enterprise was not perceived as a threat by the imperial court. According to Guy, "the evaluation of texts, collation of variant versions, rectification and verification of errors was what the *Ssu-k'u ch'üan-shu* project was all about." The Ch'ien-lung Emperor and his editors felt, after all, that in preparing an accurate and permanent copy of the most important writings over millennia, they were making a highly significant contribution to Chinese letters. The editors were themselves imbued with a group consciousness that all texts, historical or classical, were bound by the same standards of proof and verification. In the political culture of Ch'ien-lung's China, the state had for all intents and purposes thrown its backing behind the evidential research movement. Polity and scholarship were wedded to a massive academic project that would show the dynasty in tune with the major intellectual movements of the day.

At the same time, the emperor supported projects that would focus on Manchu, Mongol, and Tibetan history and language. Even before the *Ssu-k'u ch'üan-shu* project, evidential scholars from Kiangnan had been commissioned to compile a dictionary of the languages of the Eleuths, Muslims, Tibetans, and natives of Kokonor. As a result of working on projects like these celebrated evidential scholars such as Wang Ch'ang (1725–1806) and others were able to compare Mongol and Manchu to Chinese in their studies of phonology and ancient rhymes (see chapter 5). When the dictionary project was concluded in 1766, Wang and others were commissioned to collect all incantatory formulas in the Buddhist Tripitaka. These formulas were edited subsequently in Manchu, Chinese, Mongolian, and Tibetan. The evaluative procedures used to authenticate Chinese materials could also be used by an alien dynasty to reconstruct its own historical pedigree.

What we see in the eighteenth-century inquisitions is the dark side of an education policy in which tuition support, academic prizes, and scholarly recognition reinforced the status-conferring function of education and rewarded scholarship. By providing the institutional preconditions for the growth of philology into an exact discipline, Manchu policies in fact made *k'ao-cheng* research possible on a large scale.

Ch'ing scholars turned to precise scholarship for a variety of reasons. One reason certainly was the fact that Manchu policies prohibited political discussions that might prove detrimental to the state. All dynasties, particularly foreign conquest dynasties, had shared this concern, however. Evidential research did not emerge after Mongol forces destroyed the Sung dynasty. Moreover, precise scholarship did not become popular when Ming rulers bullied Confucian literati into submission. We will have to look elsewhere for the exact reasons why an academic community devoted to evidential research emerged in eighteenth-century Kiangnan. Nor can we assume that *k'ao-cheng* discourse lacked political overtones.[15]

· ·

Tai Chen As Social Critic:
From Philology Back to Philosophy

Ch'ing scholarship had both public purposes and political consequences. To reconstruct the authentic *Mo-tzu* or the historical Confucius, to rescue the *Poetry, Documents,* and *Rites* Classics from the contamination of Buddhist and Taoist interpretations, was to gain firm philosophic ground from which to criticize, reject, and overcome imperially sponsored Neo-Confucian systems of thought—a political act. Tai Chen's (1724-1777) formidable role as a social critic, for instance, has been overlooked for too long in Western scholarship. His use of the *Mencius* as a foil for the articulation of a philosophy antithetical to the Chu Hsi (1130-1200) orthodoxy had important political implications. It was in the *Mencius* after all that the right to revolt was justified and the power of the people lauded. Ming emperors had had such passages expurgated from the official text of the *Mencius* used in the examination system.

Although he had to be cautious, Tai Chen was free to publish his denunciations of the Ch'ing orthodoxy in his *Meng-tzu tzu-i shu-cheng* (Evidential analysis of the meanings of terms in the *Mencius*). The latter was completed while Tai, an eminent evidential scholar, was working on the *Ssu-k'u ch'üan-shu* project and in the midst of the Ch'ien-lung inquisition. Manchu rulers did not find Tai's use of the *Mencius* particularly objectionable. Their Ming predecessors would have. Tai wrote:

> The high and mighty use *li* [underlying moral principles] to blame the lowly. The old use *li* to blame the young. The exalted use *li* to blame the downtrodden. Even if they are mistaken, [the ruling groups] call [what they have done] proper. If the lowly, the young, and the downtrodden use *li* to struggle, even if they are right they are labelled rebellious. As a result, the people on the bottom cannot make their shared emotions and desires [in all persons] in the world understood by those on top. Those on top use *li* to blame them for their lowly position. For these uncountable throngs of people, their only crime is their lowly position. When a person dies under the law, there are those who pity him. Who pities those who die under [the aegis] of *li*?
>
> . . .

Tai's philosophic writings demonstrate the impact philology had on theoretical issues. *K'ao-cheng* methods, as Paul Demiéville has noted, were now used to analyze key concepts in Confucian philosophy. The *Meng-tzu tzu-i shu-cheng*, as Tai's leading disciple Tuan Yü-ts'ai (1735–1815) indicated at the time, was intended to be Tai's final philosophic statement to his contemporaries. In a note to Tuan dated May 30, 1777, a month before his death, Tai wrote:

> Of all the works I have completed in my lifetime, the most significant is my *Evidential Analysis of the Meanings of Terms in the Mencius*. This book [contains] the essentials for rectifying the human mind. Today, peo-

ple by disregarding [the issue] of orthodoxy or heterodoxy wrongly call [their views in accord] with moral principle (*li*)—all on the basis of personal opinion. They thereby bring disaster down upon the people. Therefore, I had to write the *Evidential Analysis*.[16]

. . .

Both the title of his work and the approach used in it were clear signs of the impact of *k'ao-cheng* research on philosophic issues. The technical term *shu-cheng* (evidential analysis, lit., "verifications on the form of a subcommentary") in the title indicated that Tai saw his efforts as part of the evidential research movement. The same term had been used earlier in Yen Jo-chü's title to his definitive critique of the Old Text chapters of the *Documents Classic*. In addition, the methodology Tai applied to his study of the *Mencius* was essentially a linguistic approach, that is, *hsun-ku* (etymology, lit., "glossing"), in order to determine the precise meaning of terms in the text. He began with careful glosses of *li* (principle, reason, inherent pattern, and so forth), *ch'i* (material force, stuff, and so forth), *hsing* (nature, especially but not exclusively, human nature), and *ch'ing* (quality, especially human qualities, that is, emotions). This appeal to etymology Tai thought would enable him to refute the later meanings Chu Hsi and other Neo-Confucians had attached to these concepts. In a larger sense, Tai Chen's analysis of the *Mencius* reveals that new strategies for conceptualization and organization could advance a systematic position, in this case a philosophy of *ch'i* (see chapter 2).

The historian Chang Hsueh-ch'eng (1738–1801) and others of Tai's contemporaries were outraged by his attack. Chang thought that it was permissible "to correct the flagrant errors of Sung Confucians," but Tai was going too far in his outright dismissal of Sung moral teachings. Chang accused Tai of "forgetting where his ideas ultimately came from." Tai's criticisms also provoked responses from nineteenth-century defenders of the Chu Hsi orthodoxy. Fang Tung-shu (1772–1851), a staunch advocate of the Neo-Confucian orthodoxy from T'ung-ch'eng, Anhwei, wrote:

[To say] that the principles of heaven are not dependable and that one should rely on the emotions and desires of the people, that they should have an outlet and be allowed to follow their desires, implies that *li* [read "moral ideals"] is attained at the expense of *ch'i* [read "human desires"] and brings disorder to the Tao. However, [Tai Chen] is merely trying to make it difficult for the Ch'eng I [1033–1107] and Chu Hsi [school] without realizing that [his path] is the way of great disorder.[17]

. . .

The emergence of *k'ao-cheng* philosophy was not well received in the eighteenth century, however. Attacked for their views by orthodox Neo-Confucian scholars on the one hand, evidential scholars like Tai Chen who took an interest in philosophic problems were criticized by their colleagues for dealing with unverifiable issues usually associated with Neo-Confucian discourse. Chu Yun (1729–1781), an advocate of exact scholarship, took Tai Chen to task for his excursion into philosophy: "[Tai] need not have written this sort of thing. What he will be remembered for has nothing to do with such writing." Chu turned out to be wrong. T'ang Chien (1778–1861), an orthodox follower of the Ch'eng-Chu school wrote: "Mr. [Tai] was a student of philology, but he tried to conceal the fact that he didn't understand philosophy by writing his *Evidential Analysis of the Meanings of Terms in the Mencius.*"

In his philosophic works, Tai Chen was writing for a limited audience in the late eighteenth century. The same was true of Chang Hsueh-ch'eng and his theories of history. In a preface to one of Tai Chen's more conventional *k'ao-cheng* works, the evidential research scholar Lu Wen-ch'ao (1717–1796) betrayed the usual perspective contemporary scholars had of Tai:

My friend, Mr. Tai Tung-yuan [Chen] from Hsin-an, was born after Ku T'ing-lin [Yen-wu, 1613–1682], Yen Pai-shih [Jo-chü, 1636–1704], Wan Chi-yeh [Ssu-t'ung, 1638–1702], and other [seventeenth-century] venerables. Yet, Tai's research deserves comparison with theirs. Through meticulous achievements and penetrating constructions, [Tai] follows the path to the perfect truth.

. . .

The influential historian and classical scholar Ch'ien Ta-hsin (1728–1804), in his biography of Tai Chen, barely mentioned Tai's philosophic writings, focusing instead on his contributions to *k'ao-cheng*.

In the nineteenth century, however, the academic climate changed somewhat. Confucian literati were increasingly receptive to philosophic issues, and once again they stressed the moral aspects of Confucian discourse (see chapter 6). The distinguished evidential scholar and patron Juan Yuan (1764–1849) composed three major essays on Confucian philosophy between 1801 and 1823. Modeled after Tai's linguistic approach to philosophic terms, Juan's best-known treatise, entitled *Hsing-ming ku-hsun* (Ancient glosses on "nature" and "external necessity"), made use of etymological and phonological procedures to reconstruct the meanings of key Confucian concepts.

Juan's friend and fellow townsman from Yangchow, Chiao Hsun (1763–1820), also continued Tai Chen's philosophic interests by writing an 1820 sequel to Tai's work called *Meng-tzu cheng-i* (Orthodox meaning of the *Mencius*). In this manner, *k'ao-cheng* inquiry provided the spark for a new approach to traditional philosophic questions. Dismayed that this aspect of Tai's contributions had been overlooked, Chiao Hsun concluded:

> The "meanings and principles" [*i-li*] that [Tai] Tung-yuan has personally grasped are not the "meanings and principles," such as the Western Inscription or the Supreme Ultimate, of [Sung-Ming] discursive [*chiang-hsueh*] scholars.

. . .

Important Confucian concepts and ideals, as a result of Tai Chen's influence, were subjected to philological study. It was hoped that a methodology that had proved fruitful in textual matters would prove equally productive in moral philosophy.[18]

In the twentieth century, the impact of Tai Chen's philosophy was acknowledged by erstwhile radicals such as Chang Ping-lin (1868–1936) and Liu Shih-p'ei (1884–1919). Before his infatuation with anarchism in 1907, Liu admired Tai's critique of the oppressive aspects of the Ch'eng-Chu orthodoxy. Comparing Tai to Rousseau, Liu contended that Tai had liberated himself from the autocratic ideals of Neo-Confucianism. Chang Ping-lin and Liu Shih-p'ei, in addition to their early radical political activities, later became two of the most distinguished textual scholars of the twentieth century. Through their efforts, the harvest of Ch'ing dynasty *k'ao-cheng* studies continued into our own time.[19]

The Politics of New Text Confucianism: Philology and Philosophy

Looking at it from a synchronic framework, evidential research represented a multifaceted academic discourse during the Ch'ing dynasty. Diachronically, however, the discourse also spilled over into other areas that were less firmly grounded in empirical research. Although the exact course is still unclear and filled with many loose ends, it appears that the philosophic rebellion spawned by the *k'ao-cheng* movement played some role in setting the stage for the social and political conclusions that late Ch'ing dynasty New Text (*chin-wen*, lit., "contemporary script") scholars drew from their research and scholarship. In the process, the political and philosophic impact of Ch'ing classicism became more and more pronounced.

Much more research will be required before we can be confident about the precise role philology played in the rise of New Text Confucianism in the eighteenth century. Here we can only suggest that the philological appeal to and historical recovery of the past was tied to an emerging position enunciated by eighteenth- and nineteenth-century New Text scholars. These scholars began to argue that much of what had once been considered orthodox was in fact an Old Text (*ku-wen*, lit., "ancient script") fabrication created by Confucian scholars during the reign of the Han usurper Wang Mang (r. A.D. 9–23).[20]

Reconstruction—and it had to be philologically and historically reconstructed—of the Han dynasty (206 B.C.–A.D. 220) Old Text-New Text debate led some Ch'ing scholars to a new perspective on the Confucian tradition. Scholars in eighteenth-century Ch'ang-chou, Kiangsu, were the first Ch'ing literati to stress the *Kung-yang Commentary* (to Confucius' *Spring and Autumn Annals*), which had been out of favor among Confucians for over a millennium. This commentary provided textual support for the Former Han (206 B.C.–A.D. 8) New Text school's portrayal of Confucius as a charismatic visionary rather than a distinguished teacher. For much of the late eighteenth and early nineteenth centuries, most evidential research scholars ignored or did not know very much about the reemerging New Text position. Chuang Ts'un-yü (1719–1788) and other Ch'ang-chou scholars who turned to the *Kung-yang Commentary* seem to have recognized, however, that they were not dealing with a textual problem so much as with the recovery of a political movement that had been from their point of view stamped out by Later Han (A.D. 25–220) Old Text ideologues and subsequently forgotten.[21]

This eighteenth-century undercurrent in Ch'ing classical scholarship demands more scholarly attention. The ideological implications of this reconstruction were not fully articulated until the nineteenth century. By then, the Old Text view of Confucius as a simple teacher, who had transmitted the wisdom of high antiquity to his disciples, clashed openly with New Text protrayals of him as a messianic sage in his own right, an "uncrowned king" (*su-wang*) who had enunciated sacred social and moral principles in his *Spring and Autumn Annals.*

Because most New Text sources were from the Former Han dynasty, and therefore were unaffected by Taoist and Buddhist accretions in Later Han and post-Han writings, the New Text version of Confucius' role vis-à-vis the Classics slowly received new respect and attention. What is clear is that New Text Confucianism did not arise in the Ch'ing period as a rationalization for Westernization. Rather, New Text studies arose as respectable Han-Learning (*Han-hsueh*) scholarship, a slogan synonymous with evidential research, in mainstream centers of learning before being linked to problems of reform in the nineteenth century. Moreover, New Text scholars promoted traditional forms of Confucian reform before they initiated a radical call for Westernization.

In the late nineteenth century, first Liao P'ing (1852–1932) and then K'ang Yu-wei (1858–1927) drew on the New Text scholarship of the Ch'ang-chou school and its various followers. A Cantonese scholar, K'ang developed his ingenious and politically perilous interpretation of Confucius as a social reformer in his influential *K'ung-tzu kai-chih k'ao* (Confucius as reformer), which was published in 1897 but banned for political reasons in 1898 and again in 1900. Confucius, according to K'ang a visionary of institutional change, had enunciated a concept of progress that Old Text scholars had covered up. This provocative re-interpretation invested K'ang's ideal of "institutional reform" (*kai-chih*) with all the modern trappings of institutional reform. K'ang wrote:

> After the theories of the spurious Old Text [school] appeared, they blocked and covered up [the views of the New Text school]. No one understood the meaning of "Confucian" [*Ju*]. [The Old Text school] regarded Confucius simply as someone who had compiled and transmitted the Six Classics. Confucius was treated merely as a learned and accomplished man of exemplary conduct like Cheng Hsuan [127–200] or Chu Hsi of later generations. How could [such a man] be a great sage? Chang Hsueh-ch'eng even went so far as to claim that the great synthesizer of Confucianism was the Duke of Chou [ca. 1100 B.C.], not Confucius.[22]

. . .

As Hsiao Kung-chuan has shown, the roots of K'ang's New Text position were complicated and varied. K'ang drew heavily on Buddhist and Neo-Confucian sources for the visions of the utopia he described in his famous *Ta-t'ung shu* (The book of the great community). It is interesting, however, that in his earlier work, particularly in the *Hsin-hsueh wei-ching k'ao* (A study of the forged Classics of Hsin dynasty learning [of Wang Mang]) published in 1891, K'ang relied on earlier philological reconstructions of the Former Han New Text school. In particular, K'ang tried to add his own philological conclusions to those of Liu Feng-lu (1776–1829) and Wei Yuan (1794–1856), both followers of the Ch'ang-chou New Text tradition.

What resulted was in many ways a parody of evidential research. We should note that mainstream *k'ao-cheng* scholars such as Yen Jo-chü and Hui Tung (1697–1758) had begun to demolish the orthodox position of the Old Text Classics in the seventeenth and eighteenth centuries (see chapter 5). Their writings on the Old Text *Documents Classic* opened the way for criticism of other Old Text Classics, facilitating the emergence of a philologically tenable New Text position. Philology now determined doctrine. The heterodox implications contained in Yen's attack on the authenticity of the Old Text *Documents* reappeared in an unexpected apocalyptic vision, however. This outcome was a turn that Yen and others had neither anticipated nor intended; their philological conclusions, nevertheless, added unforeseen fuel to K'ang's notions of a redemptive history.[23]

K'ang Yu-wei's radical Confucian response to the influx of Western ideas in the late nineteenth century would not have taken the form that it did had not the Old Text versions of the Classics been partially discredited. Writing in 1904, Chang Hsieh-chih contended:

> In recent years, K'ang Yu-wei has emerged and has claimed that the Six Classics were all works forged by Liu Hsin [45 B.C.–A.D. 23]. As a result, the calamity precipitated by Yen Pai-shih's [Jo-chü] delusions and deceptions [concerning the Old Text *Documents*] has reached its most extreme expression.
>
> . . .

Mainstream *k'ao-cheng* scholars were infuriated by K'ang's preposterous position. Those who still held that the Old Text Classics were by and large authentic accused K'ang of willful misrepresentation of the Han dynasty classical tradition. Chang Ping-lin, one of the last generation of Han-Learning specialists, systematically exposed what he considered New Text historical and philological errors. Chang and others reaffirmed the more rationalistic Old Text tradition in the face of what they regarded as the absurd doctrines and fantastic visions of K'ang and his followers. Remarkably, the debate has lasted into the twentieth century.[24]

The New Text political challenge to the Old Text orthodoxy, we suggest, followed a social and intellectual logic that demonstrates the impact of philology—however bizarre the results—on political issues. We should not be surprised at this intriguing example of the impact of textual scholarship on political discourse in the late nineteenth century. To examine and reconstruct the Classics, after all, was to relearn the social and political implications of Confucian doctrine. Nor should we be puzzled that the historical reexamination and philological reconstruction of the pre-Han Confucian Classics precipitated a step-by-step unraveling of the imperial Confucian orthodoxy. Pious Christians, after all, had performed a similar feat in their recovery of first Latin and then Greek antiquity during the Renaissance, a recovery that culminated in the heady anti-Christian iconoclasm of the eighteenth-century Enlightenment. By the late eighteenth century in China, the Han Learning of antiquity evoked more interest than more recent Neo-Confucianism.[25]

. . .

The Unraveling of Neo-Confucianism

During the Ch'ing period, new vocabulary was generated in a self-conscious manner to articulate and discuss the new academic discourse. We will demonstrate in chapter 2 that the k'ao-cheng discourse popular in this period was a sum of linguistic practices that revealed rules for the formation of concepts and their modes of connection and coexistence. This approach allows us to understand the systematic manner in which Confucian scholars in the eighteenth century produced and managed a set of epistemologically unified techniques for empirical research.[26]

Evidential research represented a mode of empirical scholarship that sanctioned new, precise methods by which to understand the past and conceptualize the present. As a style of scholarly method and representation, evidential studies marked the beginning of an unprecedented strategy for research. The texts and authors who contributed to the formation of this empirical strategy became captives of the forms of discourse they employed for analysis. Their philological presuppositions predetermined the subjects chosen for analysis by sanctioning what acceptable knowledge was and how it was to be verified. What did not fit in with the new strategies was excluded.

The set of linguistic and philological practices that defined and delimited the boundaries of evidential scholarship included a system of references to books and texts that shared the same boundaries. Hence, we will focus on the individual texts and authors who contributed to the formation and maintenance of k'ao-cheng discourse. We will, accordingly, stress the determining imprint of individual writers on the collection of texts that constituted the discourse.[27] Our goal is to mark out the areas of human knowledge in which Confucian scholars were interested, identify their fields of expertise, and finally discern the relationships that developed among specialized disciplines. Before our goals can be reached, however, we should begin by asking ourselves about the aims and intentions of the Ch'ing scholars we will be studying. Why did they stress philology and initially denigrate philosophy in their research? What objectives did they hope to achieve in their precise scholarship?

The Aims of Evidential Research

For the Ch'ing scholar, what was at stake in his commitment to a philological analysis of classical texts was both the validity of received opinion concerning the nature of the Confucian past and the relevance of the past for the present. Could textual scholars reconstruct the unadulterated truths of the sages before original Confucianism had been sullied with Taoist and Buddhist doctrines by over six centuries of Neo-Confucian scholarship? Could one throw a bridge across the Neo-Confucian era and resume the interrupted conversation with antiquity? Evidential scholars answered "yes!"[28]

Ch'ing scholars were determined to pierce the thick veil of Sung and Ming metaphysical and cosmological systems of thought known popularly as "Studies of the Tao" (*Tao-hsueh*). They hoped thereby to recapture the pristine meanings formulated by the sage-kings of antiquity in the Confucian Classics. They were in effect calling into question the dominant Confucian ideology, that is, the Chu Hsi school, which the Manchu rulers had enshrined as the moral and theoretical norm in imperial examinations and official rhetoric.

The millennial connection between the Confucian Classics and Chinese political discourse, whether reactionary, moderate, or radical, suggests the power these texts had over political behavior in traditional China. The Classics provided officials, scholars, and students with a set of general assumptions about good and evil in government and society. Chi Yun (1724–1805), a patron of *k'ao-cheng* scholarship when he directed the *Ssu-k'u ch'üan-shu* project, noted in 1784, while serving as a supervisor for the highest level state examinations in Peking:

The system for selecting successful examination candidates has been established so that the latter can be divided up and sent out to handle the
affairs of the empire. If one wants to handle the affairs of the empire,
then one must weigh opinions based on moral principles [*li*]. If one wants
to clarify the principles of the empire, one must weigh opinions based on
the Classics.

. . .

The past had to be studied and cherished if the ideals of the sage-kings
were to be realized. Students gained a rich fund of human experience
from the Classics. There they found descriptions of mistakes that
should be avoided and successes that should be emulated. The Classics
contained paradigms for social order and had an absolute claim to trans-
historical truth.[29]

For the Ch'ing scholar, philology was therefore more than an auxiliary tool. It was a required discipline to recover and relearn past structures of Confucian culture. It was used to make the past live again. In
calligraphy, for instance, the impact of evidential scholarship on the
"return to antiquity" (*fu-ku*) was tangible. Reemphasis on ancient inscriptions from bronze and stone relics discovered in the eighteenth
century stimulated the revival of calligraphic forms used by the ancients
(see chapter 5). Through the power of the scholar's exegetic labors, the
original forms of texts could likewise be restored. The distinguished
eighteenth-century historian and classicist Wang Ming-sheng (1722–
1798) explained:

The Classics are employed to understand the Tao. But those who seek the
Tao should not cling vacuously to "meanings and principles" [*i-li*, that is,
moral principles] in order to find it. If only they will correct primary and
derived characters, discern their pronunciation, read the explanations and
glosses, and master the commentaries and notes, the "meanings and principles" will appear on their own, and the Tao within them.

. . .

The polymath Tai Chen described philology as follows:

> The Classics provide the route to the Tao. What illuminates the Tao is their words. How words are formed can be grasped only through [a knowledge of] philology and paleography. From [the study of] primary and derived characters we can master the language. Through the language we can penetrate the mind and will of the ancient sages and worthies.
>
> · · ·

Philology, not philosophy, became the methodology to restore the past.[30]

· ·

Criticism and Skepticism

Because it made possible the retrieval of the past, philology was not a peripheral or frivolous enterprise. This process of rediscovery, when it was coupled with an increasingly rigorous and critical approach to the Classics, awakened a critical consciousness that jeopardized the classical claim to unquestionable authority. The appeal to empirical criteria as the final arbiter of doctrine reveals the social and political implications inherent in philology.

Sung Neo-Confucians had been concerned with building symbolic structures of meaning in which all human experience would be related. This approach was perfectly respectable and gave little importance to philology. As John Henderson has shown, Neo-Confucian symbols of correspondence and political allegories, like their Han dynasty predecessors, did not require, and thus did not encourage, the development of critical thought. This is not to say that Neo-Confucianism as a whole did not favor critical analysis—of course it did—but only to indicate that significant components of the discourse did not. The charts of such symbolic correspondences, which Henderson has called "cosmograms," had to be questioned before the historical foundations of the Neo-Confucian orthodoxy could be reevaluated.

In Neo-Confucian discourse, theoretical issues usually were first reduced to their rationalistic principles (for example, yin and yang or the five phases) before conclusions based on deductive norms could be drawn. Ch'ing philologists reversed this habit by stressing concrete verifiable facts instead of abstract conceptual categories of correspondence. Writing in the late seventeenth century, Yen Jo-chü dramatically demonstrated that the questionable Old Text chapters of the *Documents Classic* were indeed a later forgery and not the original chapters discovered in Confucius' residence in the second century B.C. Hu Wei (1633–1714), Yen's friend and colleague, exposed the Taoist origins of certain Neo-Confucian cosmograms. Their studies contained corrosive implications that would not end in the seventeenth and eighteenth centuries.[31]

A form of criticism had emerged that would one day exceed the boundaries that early Ch'ing philologists attempted to impose. This alarming tendency was noted by Kuei Chuang (1613–1673) in a revealing letter written in 1668 to his hometown friend and pioneer of *k'ao-cheng* scholarship, Ku Yen-wu:

> In your previous letter you wrote that you were concentrating on phonology. You have already completed books [on this subject], but I have not yet seen them. However, a friend told me in some detail that in your discussion of rhymes you necessarily emphasize the most ancient, saying that Confucius could not avoid making mistakes [in pronunciation]. These words are startling for people to hear. Because of such statements, it seems to me that as your scholarship broadens your eccentricities will deepen. In the future it will not be limited to rhymes. If your other discussions are anything like the discussion of phonology, won't they also [be regarded] as the [expression of] unrealistic and odd opinions?[32]

. . .

Yen Jo-chü's shocking *Shang-shu ku-wen shu-cheng* (Evidential analysis of the Old Text *Documents*—henceforth *Shu-cheng*) caused a major sensation, both when it was distributed privately in the late seventeenth century and when it was finally published posthumously in 1745. Yen stipulated how his philological principles related to the Classics:

> Someone might ask: "Concerning your study of the *Documents,* you accept Han [authorities] and suspect Chin [317–420] and T'ang [authorities]. That is all right. But then you proceed to give credence to the

Histories and the Commentaries and suspect the Classics. Is that permissible?" I reply: "What Classics? What Histories? What Commentaries? My concern is only with what is true. If the Classic is true and the History and Commentary false, then it is permissible to use the Classic to correct the History and the Commentary. If the History and the Commentary are true and the Classic false, then can it be impermissible to use the History and the Commentary to correct the Classic?" Someone might still ask: "[Granted that] the *Documents* appeared later, its words and grammar truly do not compare with Fu Sheng's [fl. second century B.C.] [New Text] version, and there are many omissions that arouse suspicion. Yet its principles are pure and everything [in it] has its origins in what is orthodox. You should not criticize it as an impure text anymore. Why don't you just pass on and leave it alone?" I say: "What is not what it appears to be is what Confucius despised. What comes close to being true but in fact throws the true principles into disarray is what Chu Hsi despised. My detestation for the forged Old Text [chapters] is just as Confucius and Chu Hsi would have wanted it."[33]

· · ·

Neither Yen Jo-chü nor Ku Yen-wu intended any impiety. On the contrary, Yen made it clear that the goal of textual research should be to recapture "the true intentions of the sages" through study of ancient glosses and phonological changes. Ku Yen-wu, when he contended that Confucius in transmitting the Classics could not help but pronounce the words in the dialect of his time and locality, was attempting to reconstruct the way the sages themselves had spoken the words in the Classics. His goal was the clarity and purity of the Chinese language, which would, he thought, restore the classical ordering to the world. Little remained, however, of the strenuous self-cultivation earlier Confucians had deemed necessary toward this end.

Chiang Yung (1681–1762), sympathetic to the Ch'eng-Chu tradition of broad scholarship (*po-hsueh*), went further in the eighteenth century than Ku Yen-wu and Yen Jo-chü had in the seventeenth. He rejected outright the idealized vision of study that Ku and Yen still shared with their predecessors. Chiang approached his research on rhymes and ancient pronunciation as an interesting technical project and not as a means to an ideal sociopolitical end. A crucial transition point had been reached in *k'ao-cheng* scholarship. In the process, phonology emerged as a precise discipline to which most eighteenth-century evidential scholars devoted considerable attention (see chapter 5). The epistemological premises of evidential research proved inseparable from what Charles Gillispie has described in the history of Western science as the cutting "edge of objectivity."[34]

Nevertheless, the movement to retrieve the past during the Ch'ing period was not a conscious current of skepticism. In the long run, however, the *k'ao-cheng* identity that developed won breathing space for both skeptical and pious Confucians. In this way, evidential scholars advanced the front of objectivity and the cause of unbelief. Unbelief, in a preliminary form, was the unspoken position lurking in their meticulous excavation of ancient strata of names and their referents (*ming-wu*). Ts'ui Shu's (1740–1816) commitment to uncovering the beliefs of the past, for instance, was clearly indicated in the title of his tour de force: *K'ao-hsin lu* (Record of the examination of beliefs). This orientation led him to criticize the Neo-Confucian position as untrue to classical Confucianism.

Articulate and self-critical, seventeenth- and eighteenth-century literati sensed that their devotion to research and their love of classical antiquity had led them in new and dangerous directions. Some remained hesitant to follow, as if unsure where such research would lead. Neither Weng Fang-kang (1733–1818), a specialist in epigraphy, nor the Ch'eng-Chu scholar Fang Tung-shu, for example, felt comfortable with what the evidential scholars were writing. The fundamentalist thrust behind the return to the ancients threatened to demolish the Neo-Confucian orthodoxy without satisfying the need for some moral order and certainty. The assault on the Neo-Confucian orthodoxy, they correctly perceived, was the first step toward a rejection of the entire Confucian legacy. In due time, the ancients themselves would also be under attack.[35]

Ancients and Moderns

Ancient Confucian culture did not present itself to evidential scholars as a finished product. It had to be rediscovered and reconstructed. Ch'ing scholars thought, rightly or wrongly, that through their efforts the veil of orthodox Neo-Confucian interpretation had finally been lifted and the adulteration of antiquity in the Sung-Ming period effectively reversed. This appeal to the ancients made possible eighteenth-century denunications of the Chu Hsi orthodoxy.

Debates over the very nature of antiquity between Han-Learning (*Han-hsueh*) and Sung-Learning (*Sung-hsueh*) scholars, and those between Old Text and New Text advocates, created divisions and alliances among Ch'ing literati. *K'ao-cheng* scholars focused on the distant past to overcome limitations they found in the more recent Neo-Confucian tradition. Much of the rhetoric spilled over into the political arena as well (see chapter 6). Han-Learning scholars, for example, turned to a study of Later Han dynasty classical interpretations, because the latter were closer in time to the composition of the Classics and thereby more likely to reveal the authentic meaning they conveyed. They rejected Sung dynasty sources, which Sung-learning scholars relied on, because of their questionable authority and much later date.

Ch'ing Han-Learning scholars were able to demonstrate that T'ang and Sung scholarship was drawn from Later Han Confucianism. Turning instead to Former Han dynasty scources, scholars, especially those from Ch'ang-chou, were able to reconstruct the New Text orthodoxy that had supposedly been suppressed in the Later Han by textual scholars such as Cheng Hsuan (127–200) and others. As we have seen, the ideological implications of this across-the-board requestioning of the Old Text tradition, whose texts had been accepted since the Later Han dynasty by most Confucian literati, were immense. Because it was a movement with roots in the Former Han dynasty and thus closer to the time of Confucius, the New Text tradition was accorded considerable interest by Han-Learning scholars.

In fact, the tensions that eventually cost the Han-Learning movement its unanimity in the early nineteenth century grew out of the rediscovery of Former Han New Text Confucianism. When New Text scholars such as Wei Yuan and Kung Tzu-chen (1792–1841) finally recognized that the slogan of "Han Learning," which had been equated with *k'ao-cheng* in the eighteenth century, favored the Old Text orthodoxy of the Later Han and covered up the New Text orthodoxy of the Former Han, they went on to challenge their contemporaries to realize that Han Learning, that is, "Later Han Learning," was itself a questionable version of antiquity.[36]

The quest for the historical Confucius during the Ch'ing period laid the ground for a reevaluation of the viability and appropriateness of political institutions established in the aftermath of the fall of the Former Han dynasty and the demise of New Text Confucianism. The tense interplay of an admired Confucian antiquity with a discredited Neo-Confucian orthodoxy suggests that classicism in late imperial China was not a cult but an adaption of classical antiquity. Evidential scholars thought they had resumed the interrupted conversation with antiquity. They were firm in their belief that this rediscovery would serve them in any effort to deal with contemporary problems.[37]

In the relation between the ancients and the moderns, the ancients were not always undisputed paradigms, however. The early Ch'ing astronomer and mathematician Mei Wen-ting (1633–1721) contended that even the sages could not change the immutable truths of spherical geometry and trigonometry, which later Western and Chinese scholars had discovered. Evidential research was significantly buoyed, for example, by the Jesuit introduction of limited aspects of the Western exact sciences during the Ming and Ch'ing dynasties. Emphasis on the exact fields of scholarship that the Europeans introduced and the subsequent rediscovery of the sophistication of indigenous astronomy and mathematics during the Yuan dynasty enabled Ch'ing literati to see how far they had in fact progressed beyond the ancients (see chapters 2 and 5).

Furthermore, the idea that reconstructed texts from antiquity would lead to a revival of an authentic society modeled on the time of Confucius was not accepted by all seventeenth- and eighteenth-century scholars. Wang Fu-chih (1619–1692), Chiang Yung, and others were committed to an evolutionary perspective. Their aim was to reconstruct ancient models that would be viable in the present as a mode of renewal and not of literal reconstruction. Wang Fu-chih wrote:

When it comes to setting up regulations and plans [for government] and establishing directives, neither the *Documents Classic* nor Confucius offers any formula. Can it be that they overlooked real affairs and therefore did not try to deal with details? [No,] ancient institutions were used to govern the ancient world, but they cannot be applied across the board to the present day. Hence, these exemplary authors did not attempt to base policy on them. One applies what is appropriate today to govern the present world, but this approach in no way implies that [what is required today] must be appropriate for a later day. Hence, these exemplars did not attempt to hand down models for all ages [based on experience of their own time].

. . .

Chiang Yung and others openly acknowledged that a path that traversed the past did not exist.[38]

The search for the ancients in turn often led to an affirmation of the moderns. Chang Hsueh-ch'eng, Wei Yuan, and Kung Tzu-chen all regarded the sages as cultural geniuses who had created the appropriate conditions for human culture in antiquity. From their perspective as "moderns," however, the social and political conditions of antiquity had long since been left behind. New initiatives based on contemporary conditions were required. Wei Yuan explained:

The ancients had what pertained to the ancients. To force the ancients upon the moderns is to misrepresent the moderns. To use the moderns as the standard for the ancients is to misrepresent the ancients. If one misrepresents the present, then there can be no way [for the moderns] to order [the world]. If one misrepresents antiquity, there can be no way [for the moderns] to discuss the teachings [of the ancients].[39]

. . .

By 1800, evidential scholarship had dramatically proven itself to be a developing and cumulative field of discourse. The victory of the moderns, although not yet fully articulated, was becoming evident. The Ch'ing revolution in discourse initiated among evidential scholars a conscious recognition that scholarship was a cumulative enterprise and

and that progress in specific disciplines depended on the use of empirical *k'ao-cheng* techniques.

Impartiality and precise scholarship did not emerge as a sudden growth in China, planted by nineteenth-century imperialists and opium traffickers. Without wishing to play down the influence of the "Western impact," we would suggest that, as our understanding of the social, economic, and intellectual conditions internal to Ch'ing China before the Opium War deepens, we will achieve a more balanced appraisal of the scope and limits of nineteenth-century Western pressures as the catalyst in modern Chinese history. An overemphasis on external political factors has until now prevented us from recognizing the magnitude of the internal changes in scholarly discourse in pre-Opium War China and the scope of the academic community within which those changes were shaped. We will contend here that many of the broad undercurrents of textual, historical, and archaeological research carried out in modern China derive their sources of nourishment from the pioneering work of Ch'ing scholars in the seventeenth and eighteenth centuries.

The pillars of modern thought and scholarship in contemporary China are certainly complicated and diverse. It is clear, however, that two of those pillars are the humanistic Neo-Confucian studies begun in the Sung period and the critical philology initiated by *k'ao-cheng* scholars during the Ch'ing dynasty. We will explore in more historical depth the seventeenth-century turn from Neo-Confucian moral discourse to evidential research in the next chapter.[40]

Two

K'ao-cheng Scholarship and the Formation of a Shared Epistemological Perspective

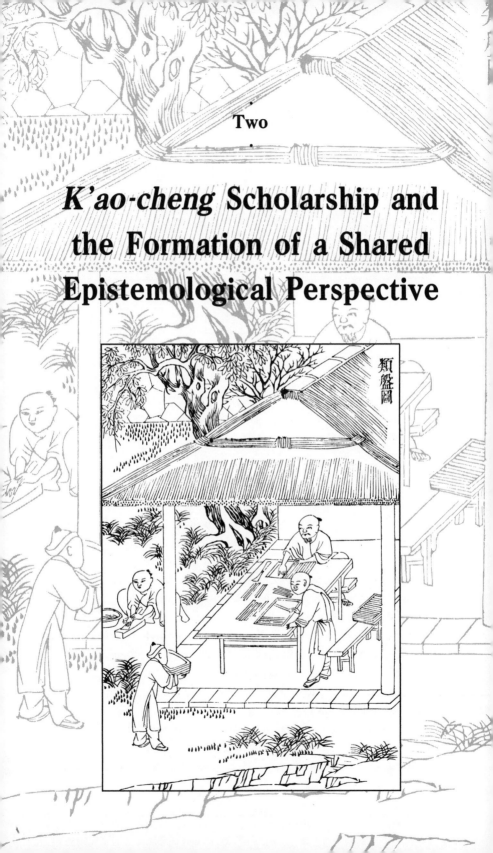

Displacement of one dominant style of scholarly discourse by another depends on many interacting social and intellectual factors. The transition from Neo-Confucian philosophy to Ch'ing philology, for example, demonstrates that changes in social norms are frequently responsible for new approaches to knowledge. Fresh intellectual impulses in turn transformed Confucian inquiry from a quest for moral perfection to a programmatic search for empirically verifiable knowledge. In this revolutionary development, a turn that in the Western intellectual tradition became tightly bound up with conditions that produced the Enlightenment, we discern how the quest for certainty surpassed the quest for sagehood among Kiangnan literati.

The rise of *k'ao-cheng* scholarship as the dominant form of academic discourse during the Ch'ing dynasty will be discussed in later chapters by examining the external factors that encouraged the use and trans-

Figure 2 Making Sorting Trays
Source: *Ch'in-ting Wu-ying-tien chü-chen-pan ch'eng-shih* (Peking, 1776).

mission of evidential methods. Discussion of external history there will help us to understand precisely how the transition from philosophy to philology followed the pattern it did. This transformation in discourse and the resulting formation of a shared epistemological perspective depended on the initial, conscious choice of Chinese literati to undertake such efforts, however.[1]

Although occupational considerations may have been a sufficient motivation in the eighteenth century (see chapter 3), the motivation for evidential scholarship during the seventeenth century is not so easily explained. This chapter presents the historical origins of evidential scholarship before the emergence of *k'ao-cheng* as the dominant form of Confucian discourse in the eighteenth century. We will then analyze the impact this change in discourse had on the specialization of academics in the Lower Yangtze Region. In the process, we will evaluate the epistemological characteristics of evidential scholarship and the role the introduction of Western science in the seventeenth and eighteenth centuries played in the transition from Neo-Confucian philosophy to Ch'ing philology. We will find that a key element in the quest for certainty among evidential scholars was their interest in the Western exact sciences. The introduction of the latter helped promote the reconstruction of the native tradition in mathematics and astronomy.

· · ·

The Emergence of
K'ao-cheng Scholarship

The lingering traces of Neo-Confucian language and habits of thought in the writings of eighteenth-century evidential scholars such as Chiang Yung (1681–1762) and Tai Chen (1724–1777) indicate that evidential scholarship resulted in part from the historical development of Neo-Confucianism itself. Movement from philosophy to philology during the Ming-Ch'ing transition period, that is, the seventeenth century, therefore, was a much more complicated process than usually has been assumed. In the seventeenth century, evidential research was undertaken by scholars who were still closely tied to the Neo-Confucian schools established by Chu Hsi (1130–1200) and Wang Yang-ming (1472–1529).[2]

Pioneers in the new empirical approach to knowledge writing in the seventeenth century were all conscious of their debt to Neo-Confucian scholarship. Ku Yen-wu (1613–1682), for example, attempted to redress what he considered the misinterpretations of Chu Hsi's school of *li-hsueh* (studies of principle) by grounding moral principles in a firm understanding of classical texts. Yen Jo-chü's respect for Chu Hsi's scholarship was a major feature in Yen's research on the *Documents Classic,* for example. Discussing the relation of Chu Hsi's findings to his own, Yen explained: "In writing this book [the *Shu-cheng*], I have followed Master Chu. Where I cite [his research], I expand on it. Where I find similarities, I enlarge on them, and that's all." In many ways, Yen Jo-chü and the others marked the last major attempt to integrate a broad range of exact scholarship into the Neo-Confucian framework.[3]

By the eighteenth century, however, many of these associations were conveniently overlooked. Seventeenth-century scholars had acknowledged their links to the Neo-Confucian tradition. Eighteenth-century *k'ao-cheng* scholars often ignored or denied their debt to Sung and Ming scholarship. The editors of the *Ssu-k'u ch'üan-shu,* for example, analyzed Wang Fu-chih's research on the Classics by employing the *k'ao-cheng* criteria of verification, organization, and use of sources. Similarly, many Ming scholars such as Fang I-chih (1611–1671) were described as forerunners of *k'ao-cheng* scholarship, and the editors all but disregarded their Neo-Confucian speculations.[4]

· ·
Roots of K'ao-cheng Discourse

Changes in the aims and criteria of explanation were already evident in the Confucian scholarship of the T'ang and Sung dynasties. Edwin Pulleyblank has described the eighth-century exegesis of the *Spring and Autumn Annals,* which he has contended represented a new trend in the criticism of the Confucian Classics. The scholars associated with this movement were reacting against the orthodox commentaries established by the T'ang court. Many of them rejected the authority of the three accepted commentaries to the *Spring and Autumn Annals* established since the Han dynasty in favor of a return to the Classic itself as the

Emergence of *K'ao-cheng* Scholarship

basis for understanding the rules of praise and blame that Confucius had employed.[5]

Although Sung philology had an amateurish look when compared with the rigorous methodology of Ch'ing philologists, Sung research did break new ground. In the philological writings of Sung *Tao-hsueh* scholars, we can begin to notice important changes in traditional modes of cognition. The Sung transformation of earlier classical exegesis began as a rejection of the Han-T'ang "notes and commentaries" (*chu-shu*) line-by-line glossing to the Classics. Instead, Sung Neo-Confucians favored expositions of "meanings and principles, that is, philosophy" (*i-li*). They stressed the theoretical and moral issues that the Classics presented, not the lexical problems that Han and T'ang commentators had dealt with.

P'i Hsi-jui (1850–1908) described one important change in Confucian discourse during the Northern Sung: the emergence of a wave of skepticism and of attacks on the authenticity of classical texts in the eleventh century. Scholars such as Ou-yang Hsiu (1007–1072), Su Shih (1036–1101), and Ssu-ma Kuang (1019–1086) also employed disciplined approaches in their analytical study of the Classics. Many of these arguments were later taken up by Chu Hsi and Yeh Shih (1150–1223) in the twelfth century.[6]

The genre of "critical essays" (*pien*) was prominent during this period. It was widely employed by Yang Shih (1053–1135), Wang Po (1197–1274), and others in their textual studies. Wang Po attacked the authenticity of portions of a number of Classics, including the *Poetry Classic* and the Old Text *Documents*. Citing Ou-yang Hsiu, Su Shih, and Chu Hsi, Wang noted:

> How can one dare to doubt the Classics of the former kings? Unfortunately, the burning of the books during the Ch'in dynasty [221–207 B.C.] had already done its damage. Later generations were not able to see intact the Classics of the former kings. Because of their incompleteness, the Classics must be called into doubt. One does not doubt [the inherent authenticity of] the Classics of the former kings. One only doubts Fu Sheng's [fl. second century B.C.] oral transmission of the Classics.[7]

· · ·

Undercurrents of skepticism and textual analysis continued in the Yuan and Ming periods. We can perceive in some works from this time gradual and sometimes dramatic changes in the uses and meanings of language that represent vicissitudes in the nature of cognition itself.[8]

Late Ming Changes in Confucian Discourse

As Shimada Kenji has demonstrated, the Ming dynasty did not lack critical and radical Confucian scholars. Within the Wang Yang-ming tradition an iconoclastic, critical spirit was most evident in the position taken by Li Chih (1527–1602) and other members of the sixteenth-century "left-wing" T'ai-chou school in Yangchow prefecture. They reacted against the Neo-Confucian orthodoxy in Kiangnan. In his attack on Neo-Confucianism, Li Chih accused members of the Ch'eng-Chu school of hypocrisy. He regarded the Classics as questionable texts, not the repository of absolute truths. Affirming the legitimacy of human desires and their fulfillment, Li Chih arrived at an uncompromising stance of intellectual independence.

There is no question that the Ch'ing scholars associated with emerging evidential scholarship were unanimous in rejecting what they considered the speculative and radical conclusions reached by members of the T'ai-chou school. Speaking for many seventeenth-century literati, Ku Yen-wu felt that these views had helped bring about the decadence that precipitated the fall of the Ming dynasty. Huang Tsung-hsi (1610–1695) maintained that the T'ai-chou scholars had lapsed into Ch'an Buddhism and thereby had thrown Wang Yang-ming's Confucian principles into total disarray.

The independent spirit that pervaded T'ai-chou scholarship, however, did not disappear under the barrage of attacks against the heterodox social and political writings associated with it. A similar stress on the autonomy of criticism remained an important element in *k'ao-cheng* discourse. Although evidential scholarship became an apolitical field of inquiry in the eighteenth century, its emphasis on scholarship as criticism assumed a degree of intellectual independence that should be understood in light of the contributions made by the T'ai-chou scholars.[9]

The T'ai-chou critique had been so powerful and profound that even when rejected it laid the ground for future directions of thought in Kiangnan. Criticism survived as a major element of Ch'ing scholarship. Critical methods triumphed over a more general critical spirit, but in an important sense the Ming-Ch'ing development of evidential methods owed a great deal to the independent spirit that enervated Ming academics. That the philological methods developed by evidential scholars were employed to defend their view of Confucian orthodoxy against the anti-intellectualist stance of the T'ai-chou radicals should not blind us to the fact that the *k'ao-cheng* scholars, in attempting to reconstruct that ancient orthodoxy, turned away from the domination of five centuries of *Tao-hsueh*.[10]

An inquiry into the manner in which evidential scholarship arose as a self-conscious field of academic discourse reveals a vaguely apprehended current of *k'ao-cheng* scholarship awakening to itself during the last century of the Ming. The research and writing of many Ming dynasty scholars was a private, sometimes heroic, endeavor to explore the possibilities of what remained an unrecognized and unorganized area of knowledge. A common field of inquiry and shared discourse emerged gradually among those Ming scholars who insisted on the centrality of "lesser learning, that is, philology" (*hsiao-hsueh*), an area of research that others found at best marginal. This concern was a necessary condition for the formation of evidential scholarship. As pioneers of a new field of discourse, these Ming philologists achieved for *k'ao-cheng* scholarship a degree of independence from other intellectual concerns. Later scholars were able to build on their pioneering studies.[11]

As strongly wedded to Neo-Confucian themes as these formative *k'ao-cheng* scholars were, they were convinced nonetheless of the need for an exact philological understanding of Confucian texts in place of the old-fashioned preoccupation with scholia to the Classics and Histories. In effect, the early evidential scholars rebuilt the Confucian tradition after the T'ai-chou attack on the Neo-Confucian orthodoxy. In this manner, criticism achieved a creative role in scholarship. The early evidential scholars favored precise research over public lectures on morality and the Tao (see chapter 5).[12]

Although the early evidential scholars continued to discuss Neo-Confucian issues, the Ming-Ch'ing transformation of exegesis signaled a change in academic discourse. Evidential scholars rejected a philosophical, that is, *i-li*, orientation to the Classics in favor of a critical analysis of the scholia prepared by Han through T'ang dynasty Confucians. The evidential scholars felt that a careful and systematic analysis of earlier exegeses, that is, *k'ao-cheng* (or *shu-cheng* [verifications of annotations]), would provide a firm basis for elucidating the Classics themselves.

A precise, technical vocabulary reflected different linguistic strategies and protocols in the *k'ao-cheng* analysis of the past. In works such as Mei Tsu's (fl. ca. 1513) *Ku-wen Shang-shu k'ao-i* (Examination of variances in the Old Text *Documents*), Ch'en Ti's (1541–1617) *Mao-shih ku-yin k'ao* (Examination of ancient pronunciation in the Mao recension of the *Poetry Classic*), and Fang I-chih's *Wu-li hsiao-chih* (Preliminary record of phenomena and their patterns of occurrence), arguments and analysis replaced glosses and annotations. Most of these scholars shared a keen respect for Han dynasty scholarship. The Han had been a period when specialized scholars in the Imperial Academy had been able to focus on a particular Classic and guide the progress of their students accordingly. Mei Tsu and others thus foreshadowed the turn to what would be called "Han Learning" (*Han-hsueh*) during the Ch'ing dynasty. Reconstruction of Han dynasty scholarship would yield it was thought more accurate sources for the reconstruction of the wisdom of antiquity.[13]

During the Ming-Ch'ing transition, new modes of thought reflected the use of different concepts and linguistic conventions. Ch'ing philologists reversed the Neo-Confucian habit of first reducing all questions to their universal principle (*li*) and then drawing conclusions on the basis of deductive norms. Yamanoi Yū has demonstrated that the Ming-Ch'ing transition was a period when a philosophy of *ch'i* (variously rendered as "material force," "ether," "stuff"; to encompass all these meanings we will use the Chinese term) replaced the Chu Hsi philosophy of principle (*li*) as the dominant framework for analysis in Confucian scholarship.

Yamanoi traced the development of this line of thought from the Ming scholar Lo Ch'in-shun (1465–1547) to Tai Chen and Juan Yuan (1764–1849) in the eighteenth century. He adduced twenty-four Ming-Ch'ing scholars, including members of the T'ai-chou school, who can be connected to the emergence of a philosophy of *ch'i*. This turn away from Chu Hsi's philosophy represents for Yamanoi a turn from abstract, conceptual thought (*i-li*) toward emphasis on concrete verifiable ideas (*k'ao-cheng*). This shift included a turn away from subjective to impartial criteria for thinking and a return to mundane human considerations instead of the transcendental philosophy of *li*.[14]

Irene Bloom in her discussion of the role of *ch'i* in Lo Ch'in-shun's thought writes: "Not only does the philosophy of *ch'i* represent an intellectual trend of the Ch'ing period, it represents one of the dominant trends and one without which Ch'ing empiricism might conceivably not have developed at all." The *Ssu-k'u ch'üan-shu* editors noted that Fang I-chih, for example, had been in the forefront of the Ming evidential scholars who had recognized that the empty speculation associated with *Tao-hsueh* (a discourse based on *li*) had to be replaced by a methodology informed by empirical verification procedures (a discourse based on *ch'i*).[15]

The attempt to break through the veil of Neo-Confucian interpretation began with an effort to explicate "names and their referents" (*ming-wu*) in classical and historical texts. Interest in "names" had a long history in China. The Confucian doctrine of "rectification of names" (*cheng-ming*) pointed to a social order in which human behavior must correspond to clearly defined names of social functions. Hence, the evidential scholar's fixation on names was not petty or peripheral. Social order demanded orderly language, and the most orderly language was thought to be that of the Classics, the repository of ancient names, terms, and institutions. For *k'ao-cheng* scholars, names were concrete evidence. The historicity of the recorded past could be corroborated or refuted by chronological and geographical evidence.[16]

The emergence of evidential discourse involved the placing of proof and verification at the center of the organization and analysis of the classical tradition. Althought the term "*k'ao-cheng*" had been employed by Wang Ying-lin (1223–1296) during the Southern Sung (1127–1279), it did not become a slogan until the seventeenth century. In their "search for truth in actual facts" (*shih-shih ch'iu-shih*) scholars during the Ming-Ch'ing transition, following their Sung and Yuan predecessors, stressed the genre of "critical essays" (*pien*) as the key to a form of scholarship based on detachment and impartiality. Verification became a central problem in the emerging *k'ao-cheng* theory of knowledge.[17]

Revivalism and fundamentalism (that is, reaffirmation of the original texts and doctrines of classical Confucianism) pervaded the late Ming and early Ch'ing "return to antiquity" (*fu-ku*) movement. This orientation to knowledge represented not merely new knowledge of and appreciation for antiquity, but a major reorientation in thought as well. Rejecting the philosophical speculations of Neo-Confucianism, the early evidential scholars favored a return to the most ancient sources available in order to reconstruct the classical tradition.

A new theory of knowledge was developed among members of the Fu She (Return [to Antiquity] Society). Many of the literati associated with the Fu She were directly or indirectly influenced by Hsu Kuang-ch'i (1562–1633), the powerful scholar-official who collaborated with Matteo Ricci (1552–1610) in translating European works on mathematics, hydraulics, astronomy, and geography into Chinese. According to Ono Kazuko, Fu She literati emphasized "concrete studies" (*shih-hsueh*), in contrast to what they considered the "empty words" (*k'ung-yen*) in Neo-Confucian discourse (see chapter 3).[18]

Rapid strides in research were made in the seventeenth century, and the Confucian past became more and more retrievable. The key was a *k'ao-cheng* methodology, whether it was applied in research on ancient rhymes or to the *Documents* debate. Once methodology became an important concern, the tension between scholars moving toward the new scholarship based on empirical criteria for verification and scholars still holding fast to the old moral and discursive concerns of *Tao-hsueh* began to emerge.

· ·

Revival of Interest in the Five Classics

An important clue to this tension was the beginning in the late Ming of a movement away from study of the Four Books to a reemphasis on the Five Classics. During the Sung dynasty, Chu Hsi and his followers had edited the Four Books, consisting of the *Analects*, the *Mencius*, and the *Great Learning* and *Doctrine of the Mean* (the latter two taken from the *Li-chi* [Record of rites]), advocating them as an alternative to the Five Classics for moral training in Confucianism.

Less abstruse and thus requiring less erudition, the Four Books served as ideal instructional guides to the moral and educational doctrines associated with Sung *Tao-hsueh*. In addition, these texts were relatively untouched by the textual controversies that had enervated Sung de-

bates on the Classics in the eleventh and twelfth centuries. The Four
Books became a formal part of the Confucian Canon when they were
included as official texts in the imperial examinations under the Yuan
dynasty. The *Ssu-shu ta-ch'üan* (Great compendium of the Four
Books), an authoritative edition compiled by Hanlin academicians during the Yung-lo Emperor's reign (1403–1425), became the standard
text for the Ming eight-legged (*pa-ku*) examination essays. John Meskill
has noted that, by the fifteenth century, an examination candidate was
permitted to present himself as prepared in only one Classic. The subordination of the Classics indicated that the examinations required less
classical training.[19]

By the late Ming, however, a growing emphasis on Confucian fundamentalism occasioned a revival of the Five Classics as the cornerstone of
Confucian scholarship. Miyazaki Ichisada has pointed to the *k'ao-cheng*
character of this movement, particularly as reflected in the writings of
Hsueh Ying-ch'i (1500–1573?). A native of Ch'ang-chou prefecture,
Hsueh's *Ssu-shu jen-wu k'ao* (A study of persons in the Four Books),
published in 1557, touched off a series of revisions of the text of the
Four Books. These revisions reflected, according to Miyazaki, a lack
of confidence in Chu Hsi and the orthodox texts in the *Ssu-shu ta-
ch'üan*. Following Hsueh, late Ming scholars called for study of the
Great Learning and the *Doctrine of the Mean* only as parts of the
Record of Rites, thereby effectively challenging the legitimacy of the
Four Books as an independent group of texts. The Four Books as a
single compilation was attacked as a Sung concoction that did not accurately portray the orthodox Confucianism of the Five Classics.

Miyazaki has noted that the scholars connected with this debunking
movement had contact with the Jesuits and their circle of literati and
took great interest in Western astronomy and mathematics. Matteo
Ricci and the Jesuits did have strong ties to the fundamentalist position
in Confucianism. Ricci attempted to distinguish what he considered
"original" Confucianism from the "materialism" he associated with
Tao-hsueh. Ricci clearly favored the earlier interpretations of the
Classics over those given by Chu Hsi and his school of *li-hsueh*. He
also tried to convince Chinese scholars (perhaps after having been convinced by other Chinese) that Chu Hsi's metaphysics were not an integral part of original Confucian doctrine. No minor concern was this.
Ricci and his successors contended that Confucianism was ultimately

assimilable to Catholicism, but only when purged of Buddhist and Taoist corruption. Ricci wrote:

> The doctrine most commonly held among the Literati at present seems to me to have been taken from the sect of idols, as promulgated about five centuries ago [that is, the Sung period] ... This philosophy we endeavor to refute, not only from reason but also from the testimony of their own ancient philosophers to whom they are indebted for all the philosophy they have.[20]

. . .

Classical studies became the center of inquiry for the return to antiquity.[21]

In contrast to a Neo-Confucian discourse that stressed discursive moral philosophy, the affirmation of a new kind of classical studies during the Ming-Ch'ing transition represented a decisive intellectualist turn in Confucian research and teaching. A change in the intellectual content and scope of knowledge was occasioned by this change in methodology and approach. The early *k'ao-cheng* scholars exhibited in their work an almost complete rejection of the "lecturing" (*chiang-hsueh*) and "questions and answers" (*wen-ta*) styles of teaching and writing that pervaded Neo-Confucian discourse. Writings based on "solid learning" (*p'u-hsueh*), which required the dedication of a specialist rather than a moralist, replaced the "record of spoken words" (*yü-lu*) genre. Notation books became the *sine qua non* of "solid learning" (see chapter 5).

Records of oral scholarly discussions were rejected by Kiangnan evidential scholars in favor of written findings that relied on precise scholarship. Seventeenth-century literati attacked the Ming emphasis on *chiang-hsueh*, particularly as it was practiced by the T'ai-chou literati, because such an approach did not take the Classics as the framework for discussion. What was needed, they thought, was a return to book-learning and precise scholarship. This approach would enable one to recover the exact meanings of texts themselves, rather than spending time on moral speculation alone. The ancient content of the Confucian tradition could be revived through exacting research and analysis.

Others linked the Sung-Ming penchant for a dialogue style to the impact Ch'an Buddhism had on *Tao-hsueh*. Ku Yen-wu contended:

"Classical studies [*ching-hsueh*] are what the study of *li* [*li-hsueh*] was called in antiquity." Only through extensive study of the Classics themselves could principles be discovered and delineated. Ku equated emphasis on oral discourse of the type associated with the fourth-century A.D. Neo-Taoists and Buddhists with speculative discussion that would lead nowhere. Traditionally, such discussions were referred to as "pure discussions" (*ch'ing-t'an*). Ku Yen-wu argued that the Confucian adoption of this approach was not only evidence of the connection to empty Ch'an speculation but was also phony *li-hsueh*.

In the eighteenth century, Ch'ien Ta-hsin (1728–1804) and other evidential scholars accepted Ku Yen-wu's assessment. Ch'ien wrote: "What the people of the Wei [220–264] and Chin [265–316] called [the teachings of] Lao-tzu and Chuang-tzu is 'pure discussion.' What the people of the Sung and Ming called [the teachings of] the mind and human nature [*hsin-hsing*] is also 'pure discussion.'" The attack on *Tao-hsueh*, whether historically just or not, is an important indication of changes that were occurring in the seventeenth-century Kiangnan academic world. These changes bore fruit in the eighteenth century. Classical studies reemerged at the center of an intellectualist turn in Confucian discourse among an increasing number of Kiangnan scholars living during the Ming-Ch'ing transition period.[22]

· · ·

The Impact of the
Fall of the Ming Dynasty

The cumulative effects of the Manchu triumph as an external factor were decisive for the internal form and direction of evidential research during the Ch'ing dynasty. Ming forerunners of evidential research in the Lower Yangtze, however important they may seem through hindsight, were not dominant during their own time. Although the roots of the shift from Neo-Confucian philosophy to *k'ao-cheng* research can be discerned in the late Ming, the acceleration of the shift depended on the dramatic rupture in the history of Confucian discourse caused by the fall of the Ming dyansty. The change of pace occurred among Chinese intellectuals who grew to maturity during the middle of the seventeenth century.[23]

In 1644 the Manchus, a partially sinicized and still tribal people, defeated rebel armies in North China and captured Peking. Manchu forces then fought with Ming armies for the lucrative Lower Yangtze Region. Yangchow, Chia-ting, and Chiang-yin were scenes of the most determined stands against the invading Manchu armies. These cities were sacked, and thousands perished after refusing to capitulate. The question "Why did the Ming fall?" became the dominating point of departure for Chinese intellectuals. All had survived the fall of a Chinese dynasty to a foreign army, which had taken advantage of the bitter and debilitating factionalism that had torn the Ming dynasty apart.[24]

The Intellectual Response

Shock among Confucian loyalists in Kiangnan and elsewhere led to a cognitive reorganization on a scale that far exceeded the changes of the late Ming. This formative political and cultural crisis, as it was manifested in thought, education, art, and behavior, shook Chinese society— Kiangnan especially—during this period.

Many blamed what they called the "pure discussion" style of learning popular during the Ming for the collapse of the dynasty and its fall to the Manchus. Contemporaries, rightly or wrongly, interpreted the debacle as the result of the moral decline and intellectual disorder brought on by what they considered airy and superficial *Tao-hsueh* speculation. They immediately recognized conditions during the Ming that were similar to the decadence that had preceded the fall of the Han dynasty in A.D. 220. The Ming loyalists, as Nathan Sivin has pointed out, "were convinced that to plumb the failure of their intellectual predecessors would be to uncover the conditions for philosophical and spiritual reinvigoration, and for responsible engagement in the world of affairs."[25]

Ku Yen-wu singled out Li Chih for his pernicious effect on other

Ming literati. Ku described Li as the most outrageous and unabashed anti-Confucian to have ever appeared in Chinese history. Li had deluded his age and helped to bring on the decadent intellectual trends that dominated the late Ming. Later scholars agreed with comments on Li Chih's popularity made by a Ming contemporary of Li, Tsou Shan (fl. 1556): "Who does not want to be a sage or be called virtuous, but it was always so inconvenient to become one. Now [according to Li Chih] nothing seems to obstruct the path to enlightenment—not even wine, women, wealth, and lack of self-control. This is quite a bargain, and who does not like a bargain?"[26]

Yen Yuan (1635–1704) in the late seventeenth century went further and placed the blame for the Ming collapse squarely on the shoulders of Chu Hsi and his school of *li-hsueh*. Yen was convinced that the *Tao-hsueh* orthodoxy, sullied as it was with Buddhist notions, was misleading and heterodox. The emphasis on moral cultivation at the expense of physical and mental training had clearly been proven stultifying. A class of literati incapable of decisive pragmatic action and thought had emerged.[27]

In the eighteenth century, the *Ssu-k'u ch'üan-shu* editors, sympathetic with Yen Yuan's rejection of Sung-Ming speculative philosophy, nevertheless criticized him for overreacting and in effect denying the basis for Confucian discourse as well.

> It appears that [Yen] Yuan, born at the beginning of the present dynasty, had witnessed the failings of Ming Confucians: their worship of "studies of the mind" [*hsin-hsueh*] and their lack of restraint in words and behavior. He therefore energetically challenged their errors by making practical application the foundation [of his teachings]. Nevertheless, his arguments were so immoderate that he struck out against our [true] Confucian predecessors . . . He denied that nature [*hsing*] and external forces that act on individuals [*ming*] could be discussed. His view of nature and external forces was such that he put them more or less in the same class as Ch'an Buddhist abstractions. This [point of view] is a major flaw in his arguments. He resembles someone who, having been burned by hot soup, must blow on cold vegetables before he eats them; he is unaware that in straightening the bent part he has gone too far in the other direction.[28]

· · ·

Many early Ch'ing literati felt that it was above all in the divisive factional disputes and school rivalries, which had dominated the late Ming, that the political futility of the age had been revealed. A revulsion against politics was not unusual. This distaste for cliques and factions had begun during the late Ming, when political infighting precipitated the demise of the Tung-lin partisans. Some Kiangnan scholars refused to join any group or party after the Manchu conquest, believing that factional rivalry had contributed to the internal dissolution of Ming society. Others, shaken by the fall of the Ming, recognized their duty to document recent events in light of the past.[29]

Huang Tsung-hsi, in search of the reasons for the Ming defeat, presented an outline of ideal government for posterity. Singling out the role factionalism and the meddling of the schools in politics had played in bringing about the fall of the Ming, Huang, nevertheless, argued that in the final analysis the fundamental problem lay within the very structure of the Confucian state and what he saw as an autocratic monarchy that dominated Chinese political culture. What was required, he thought, was a new system of government based on classical principles:

> In antiquity, the people of the realm were considered the hosts and regarded the ruler the guest. Everything that a ruler managed to accomplish in his lifetime reverted to the realm. Today the ruler is host and those in the realm his guests. . . . In antiquity, the people of the realm loved and supported their ruler. They compared him to their father. They emulated him as they do heaven and could not go far enough to demonstrate their sincerity. Today, the people of the realm harbor nothing but hatred for their ruler. They view him as an enemy. . . . Can it be that the greatness of the realm, with all its millions of people and myriads of clans, is to be enjoyed privately by one man, by one clan?[30]

. . .

Witnesses to the deficiencies of the Ming state and the failure of the elite to prevent the Ming collapse, seventeenth-century scholars doubted that self-cultivation alone could inspire effective statesmanship and vigorous government. The views seventeenth-century scholars had of the recent past in turn structured and delimited the intellectual interests of their successors. On the one hand, seventeenth-century evidential scholars broke through the limitations they perceived in the Neo-Confucian discourse of their immediate predecessors. On the other hand, however, by limiting academic discourse to certain verifiable topics they placed powerful constraints on their eighteenth-century followers not to go very far afield.

Different strategies for constituting reality gave promise of yielding new grounds for certainty. With *Tao-hsueh* scholars on the defensive, the very fact that the Manchu rulers employed Chu Hsi's school of *li-hsueh* as the dominant Confucian ideology widened the rift between imperial Confucianism and what was being taught and discussed in *k'ao-cheng* circles.[31] The Chekiang scholar Mao Ch'i-ling (1623–1716), for example, charged that *Tao-hsueh* was a form of heterodoxy. By bringing Buddhist and Taoist notions into their analysis of the Classics, the Sung *Tao-hsueh* scholars, according to Mao, had precipitated a lamentable change in Confucian studies. Mao concluded: "Confucius and Mencius did not create *Tao-hsueh*. [Instead], they were intent on putting into practice the sacred Tao and the sagely teachings. For over seven centuries there has been confusion on this matter in the world."[32]

Looking ahead, we discover that by 1750 orthodox views on the Classics (still necessary for success on official examinations) were no longer taken seriously by many scholarly Confucians and survived mainly as an acceptable—even for evidential scholars—instrument of indoctrination. Cultural discontinuity occasioned a rupture in the history of Confucian discourse. The hegemony of Neo-Confucianism was broken. Politically enshrined in Peking, *Tao-hsueh* was philologically dismantled in Kiangnan.[33]

· ·

Statecraft and the Decline
of Moral Cultivation

An indication of the dismantling of Neo-Confucianism was the sudden decline in emphasis on moral cultivation after 1644. Instead, Ming loyalists and their followers stressed practical statecraft as the key element of the Confucian legacy. By statecraft, they meant something more than just political concerns. Statecraft in their view was closely tied to a variety of fields of expertise. These included astronomy for calendrical reform, hydraulics for flood control, cartography for military purposes, and the like.

Nakamura Kyūshirō and Yamanoi Yū have shown how various forms of *k'ao-cheng* scholarship began to crystallize into distinctive fields of inquiry during the late seventeenth century. The emphasis on what was commonly referred to as practical statecraft during the Ming-Ch'ing transition provided evidential scholarship with the spark for the broad learning and inductive research methods that became popular in the eighteenth century.[34] According to Yamanoi, what grew out of the attack on late Ming "left-wing" thought in the seventeenth century was not evidential research per se, but, rather, a commitment to a broader range of scholarship within which *k'ao-cheng* methods were promoted and refined. The crystallization of a full-blown, conscious evidential research movement had to wait for a generation less concerned with the political and social issues that dominated the mid-seventeenth century.[35]

Men such as Huang Tsung-hsi and Ku Yen-wu, according to Yamanoi, were resolved above all to explain and ameliorate the chaos of their turbulent times. What united them in their rejection of Sung-Ming intuitional studies was their sense of the urgent need to resolve the political, social, and economic decay that accompanied the fall of the Ming. Huang studied astronomy and mathematics; Ku was proficient in military geography. Although their aims were dominated by statecraft issues, Ming loyalist scholars tended to employ evidential methods in their scholarship. Yü Ying-shih has aptly described their stress on erudition as the "rise of Ch'ing Confucian intellectualism." Revival of practical statecraft, with its emphasis on practical affairs and the welfare of society, stimulated the need to organize a new field of knowledge around epistemological issues. The aim was to reconstruct ancient Confucianism and reevaluate the world-ordering techniques in the Classics. This revival thus made room for an evidential methodology not yet accepted on a large scale for its own sake.[36]

With the gradual crystallization of a distinct *k'ao-cheng* identity in the late seventeenth century, the accepted forms of Confucian discourse were redirected. For example, as a result of the attack on Sung-Ming methodology and preoccupations, moral cultivation, once central, was no longer stressed. A primary commitment to empirical research and scholarship, within which moral cultivation could have a secondary place, was the result. Cultivation was no longer the primary road to knowledge. It had become epistemologically suspect. The decline in emphasis on moral cultivation was balanced by a resurgence of interest in philology, astronomy, geography, and mathematics. John Henderson has described how Ch'ing scholars "were more interested in the sage-kings as initiators of technical traditions in astronomy, divination, hydraulics, and mensuration than as paragons of virtue." Henderson sees this as evidence of a shift from "inner cultivation or sagehood studies" to "world-ordering or kingship studies."[37]

Accompanying this shift was a reevaluation of the traditional Confucian correlative order by which correspondences between the moral and natural orders were regarded as crucial in textual exegesis. The anti-metaphysical tone of Ch'ing thought was reflected in a heightened awareness of the irregularities and incongruities of the natural world. Attacks on the ideal order and symmetry of the cosmograms and traditional systems of correspondences signaled a disenchantment with theory and a decline in the speculative side of knowledge. Cosmology was replaced by mathematical astronomy.[38]

An emphasis on experiential knowledge (*wen-chien chih chih*) was closely linked during the Ming-Ch'ing transition period to the important role of doubt as the starting point for scholarly inquiry. Suspension of judgment and detached scrutiny of beliefs based on empirical criteria were required of *k'ao-cheng* scholars. The most important element in Yen Jo-chü's methodology, for instance, was his ability to question and doubt the facts and issues that earlier scholars of the *Documents* had taken for granted. In his *Shu-cheng* Yen quoted Ma Su (1621–1673) as having said:

> If the superlative knowledge and expressed doubts of previous Confucians had not reached this extent, how could our generation [of scholars] have dreamed of attaining as much? It is indeed fortunate that earlier Confucians expressed their doubts [on certain issues]. Because of [those doubts] our generation has been able to accept their important [findings]. No doubt there are still many unbelievable things that our age has not yet recognized.

· · ·

Seeing *k'ao-cheng* techniques as a tool (*kung*), Yen contended that this research aid enabled him "to employ the speculative to verify the concrete and the concrete to verify the speculative." He decried the self-serving ends toward which T'ang scholars had used the Classics and wrote that a scholar must "set his mind at rest" (*p'ing ch'i hsin*) and "compose his temperament" (*i ch'i ch'i*), if classical texts were to be properly understood. Yen Jo-chü noted that since the T'ang dynasty there had not been any impartial scholars who had employed evidential methods to analyze the Old Text chapters of the *Documents*. Had there been such scholars, they would have found that

> A forger for the most part relies on what his age thinks highly of, and his words and style are also limited to [those current] in his age. Although he may exert great effort to cover his tracks and escape detection, in the end he cannot escape the predetermined constraints [of language and grammar used in his forgery]. These elements can serve as the basis of inductive reasoning [in detecting forgeries].[39]

. . .

Yao Chi-heng (1647–1715?), Yen's friend and contemporary in Kiang-nan, in his research on the *Poetry Classic* also had made it clear that an "even mind" was a prerequisite for scholarship. In a similar way, Tai Chen later admonished his disciple Tuan Yü-ts'ai (1735–1815) concerning certain problems in phonology: "I consider it beneficial to have an even mind [*hsing p'ing*] when examining into antiquity [*k'ao ku*]. In whatever I say about a matter, I do not allow the opinions of others to mislead me, nor do I permit my own opinions to betray me." Tuan later wrote: "In order to evaluate the disagreements of the ancients, we moderns should all set our minds at rest and compose our temperaments. We should analyze who is right and who is wrong and avoid vituperation"[40]

· · ·

The Impact of
Precise Scholarship

By the eighteenth century, the *k'ao-cheng* methodology became linked to the growth in numbers of practitioners of relatively mature academic disciplines. These were men trained in a sophisticated body of philological, historical, and astronomical methods. They constituted a special community in Kiangnan, one whose informal members were the exclusive audience for, and judges of, each other's work. The problems on which they worked were no longer posed by the society at large but, rather, by an internal challenge to verify and increase the scope of knowledge in the Confucian tradition. The statecraft problems peculiar to the seventeenth century had been left behind.[41]

Nathan Sivin has noted that by 1750 a "narrowly defined scholarly methodology had become an end in itself, narrow in interpretation and intolerant of the urge to generalize." An intellectualist temper of extreme nominalism came into vogue. Although never systematically enunciated, this nominalist temper expressed itself through a disdain for Neo-Confucian discourse. Preferred instead was "solid learning," whereby historical and philological facts were isolated and compared with a minimum of interpretive integration. As new discoveries made new lines of research possible, evidential scholars, as they realized, were caught up in fields of scholarship that were changing too quickly to encourage synthesis.[42]

· ·

Han Learning and Sung Learning

In the eighteenth century, scholars routinely associated *k'ao-cheng* with the ascendency of Han Learning. Han Learning certainly was the most heralded and at the same time most opposed school of learning during the Ch'ing period. However, *k'ao-cheng* methods were not a monopoly of Han-Learning scholars. Ch'ing scholars, nevertheless, made the link between evidential studies and Han Learning a part of their definition of schools. Evidential scholars frequently saw Han Learning and *k'ao-cheng* as two sides of the same coin. Han Learning was their window on antiquity. Ch'ing philologists thought they saw in Han classical scholarship the beginnings of their own research techniques. Juan Yuan, a patron of Han Learning, noted:

> The way of the sages is preserved in the Classics. If the Classics are not glossed, then they are impenetrable. The glosses of Han scholars are very close to the time of the sages and worthies. . . .
>
> When I was young and beginning my studies, I started with the Sung Confucians. From the Sung, I sought out T'ang [Confucians]. [From the T'ang,] I sought out [first] the Chin, Wei, and [then] Han [Confucians]. In this way, I got closer and closer to the real state of affairs [in antiquity].

· · ·

Tuan Yü-ts'ai, Tai Chen's devoted disciple, similarly rejected the Sung version of classical Confucianism:

> Since I was a child, I have read the Four Books and the commentaries to them. I believed in them [at first], but I always feared that they were not very profound. As I grew up, I began to be suspicious. When I was mature, I had [already] read the Six Classics and the words of Confucius and of Mencius. I compared the latter to the words in the commentaries to the Four Books. I discovered that when [the commentaries to the Four Books] spoke of the mind [*hsin*], principle [*li*], nature [*hsing*], and Tao that [the commentators'] notions [of these terms] were very different from the Six Classics and the words of Confucius and Mencius.
>
> The Six Classics say that principles reside in things. Yet, the Sung Confucians claim principles are complete in the mind. They also say that "nature equals principle" [*hsing chi li*]. The Six Classics only say that the Tao equals yin and yang . . . Such [misrepresentations] are why Mr. Tai Tung-yuan [Chen] had to write his *Inquiry Into Goodness* and *Evidential Analysis of the Meanings of Terms in the Mencius*. In my opinion, learning should be sought in the Classics, and that should suffice.

· · ·

The turn from the Four Books to the Classics, begun during the previous century, was by the late eighteenth century almost unanimously accepted by *k'ao-cheng* scholars.

Although it is accurate to describe seventeenth-century scholars as precursors of Han learning because they rejected Neo-Confucian sources in favor of earlier Han dynasty materials, the label "Han Learning" tends to obfuscate as much as it reveals. Strictly speaking, Han Learning denotes a school of scholarship that came into fashion in Soochow with Hui Tung (1697–1758) in the eighteenth century. Although such scholarship played a significant role in the rise of evidential studies in Kiangnan, Han Learning did not monopolize *k'ao-cheng* techniques. New Text scholars in Ch'ang-chou, for example, were certainly part of the movement that stressed evidential research. Chuang Shu-tsu (1751–1816), a member of the Ch'ang-chou school, wrote an influential work entitled the *Mao-shih k'ao-cheng* (Evidential analysis of the Mao recension of the *Poetry*). Liu Feng-lu, of the same school and intimate with Han-Learning scholars, gave the title *Tso-shih ch'un-ch'iu k'ao-cheng* (Evidential analysis of *Master Tso's Spring and Autumn Annals*) to his attack on the Old Text school of Confucianism.[43]

Tai Chen and members of the Wan school in Anhwei offered a major critique of the Soochow Han-Learning school. Tai's followers pointed out that Hui Tung preserved Han Learning intact rather than focusing on the question of what was true. Tai and his followers inherited the *k'ao-cheng* techniques of Han Learning and applied them with rigorous exactness to the study of phonological changes, etymology, textual criticism, mathematics, and astronomy. Tai, according to his students, taught that all sources, even Han sources, were subject to criticism. The goal of Tai's scholarship was verifiable truth and not the preservation of Han Learning. Chiao Hsun (1763–1820), a Yangchow follower of Tai's, wrote:

> If I say I study Confucius, then how shall I say I do it? "By means of Han Learning" is the [usual] response. Alas, the Han [period] is separated from [the time of] Confucius by many many years. The Han is separated from today by even more years. Scholars claim to be ones who study Confucius. Those who study the Han scholars use them to speak of Confucius. They then proceed to shunt Confucius aside and speak [only] of the Han

Confucians. Is the learning of Han Confucians equivalent after all to [the teachings] of Confucius?

. . .

For Chiao Hsun, it was dangerous to take for granted that Han Learning was an accurate reflection of Confucius' teachings, even if Han scholars were closer in time to the master. In the end, they were not close enough.[44]

Moreover, the turn toward a *k'ao-cheng* methodology was evident not only in Han Learning but also in the Sung-Learning scholarship produced during the Ch'ing dynasty in Kiangnan. Fumoto Yasutaka has described in detail the achievements in Sung studies that resulted from the application of evidential techniques to Sung sources (see chapter 5). Some members of the orthodox Ch'eng-Chu school remained aloof from evidential research during the Ch'ing, but there was also a group of scholars who can be described as evidential Sung-Learning scholars. They provided the impetus for a syncretic movement in the nineteenth century, centering on Canton, which attempted to synthesize Han-Learning philology with Sung-Learning philosophy (see chapter 6).[45]

Fang Tung-shu's *Han-hsueh shang-tui* (An assessment of Han Learning), an important defense of the Ch'eng-Chu school of *li-hsueh*, was organized into precise textual arguments that were intended to directly refute claims made by evidential scholars. In addition, Fang included grudging praise for the phonological and etymological studies of evidential scholars in his account. Fang's vehement attack was an example of the impact that the transformation of the accepted form of scholarly discourse had on Sung-Learning scholars in Kiangnan. *K'ao-cheng* was no one's monopoly. This aspect of evidential studies should not surprise us when we remember that Sung dynasty scholars such as Wang Ying-lin had been important precursors to Ch'ing exact scholarship. The roots of a *k'ao-cheng* methodology could easily be traced to the Sung dynasty. For this reason, the *Ssu-k'u ch'üan-shu* editors did not hesitate to describe Wang Ying-lin as a *k'ao-cheng* scholar of major importance.[46]

· ·

Recovery of Native Traditions in Classical
Studies and Science

Higher criticism and a "back to the origins" orientation toward scholarship were part of an attempt to revive classical thought. Initially, the aim was to restore the spirit of the ancient world and thereby rehabilitate society. This orientation recalls the impact that the rediscovery of the Roman and Greek classical world exerted on post-Renaissance Europe. Based on the discovery of new data and sources of information, the fundamentalist critique in China reflected a desire for purification and reorientation as well as a dissatisfaction with past scholarship.[47]

In the seventeenth century, Ku Yen-wu studied ancient rhymes as a means to restore the classical ordering in phonology (see chapter 5). The purification of language would, he contended, lead to clarity of thought.

> To summarize the ten divisions of ancient pronunciation, I prepared the *Table of Ancient Pronunciation* in two chapters. As a result, the Six Classics are now readable. The books by the various pre-Han masters all contain [phonetic] variations, but the variants are not extreme. Heaven by preserving these writings has demonstrated that the sages will one day return and restore the pronunciation of today to the clarity and purity of ancient times.

· · ·

This attempt at purification also lay behind efforts to restore the extant texts of the Classics to their original form. By the eighteenth century, however, the problem of gaining access to and reconstructing the past superseded the problem of making use of the past. Tai Chen, for example, remained committed to the purification of texts in his philosophical writings, but even in his most iconoclastic discussions he never described what one was to do with the knowledge obtained. Philology was an aid to the elucidation of the Tao in Tai's study of classical philosophy, not a program for action. Critical of his *Tao-hsueh* predecessors, Tai noted:

> Confucians of later ages [that is, Sung-Ming Neo-Confucians] have discarded etymology [*hsun-ku*] and only discussed meanings and principles [*i-li*]. In this way, they maneuvered to seek meanings and principles outside of the ancient Classics.

. . .

Ch'ien Ta-hsin, who shared Tai Chen's stress on etymology as a key to understanding ancient writings, wrote in two prefaces to works on philology:

> Meanings and principles must accord with etymology. They do not emerge separately from etymology. . . .

> To say that meanings and principles exist separately from etymology is not our Confucian [path of] study.

. . .

Strongly influenced by Tai Chen (as most Yangchow scholars were), Juan Yuan analyzed ancient glosses (*ku-hsun*) to recover the original meanings (*pen-i*) of terms in the Classics. These "original meanings" had been lost, according to Juan, because of the heterodox strata of Buddhist and Taoist interpretations imposed by Sung-Ming *Tao-hsueh* scholars. In his consideration of the structure and change of written graphs over time, Juan compared the Classics with inscriptions on ancient relics. This approach was combined with an inductive analysis of Han dynasty glosses upon which Juan based his etymological reconstructions in works such as his *Hsing-ming ku-hsun* (Ancient glosses on "nature" and "external necessity"). Classical grammar and historical linguistics were thereby informed by the etymological research upon which *k'ao-cheng* linguistic theory was based.[48]

Such efforts at reconstruction carried over into the study of the native scientific and technical tradition. Nathan Sivin has explained:

> Probably the most important immediate consequence of the Jesuit educational effort was to enable the Chinese to rediscover and revive their own tradition, which had been neglected for three centuries. By 1700 the best mathematical talents in China were getting their basic training in the more immediately accessible Western methods, and going on to devote their

mature careers to the reconstuction and enrichment of the indigenous exact sciences. It was not until well into the nineteenth century that this order of study was reversed.

. . .

Spurred on by the challenge of European science, Tai Chen had been committed to a recovery of ancient mathematical and astronomical texts that would demonstrate the depth and sophistication of native expertise in calendrical studies. Tai was ecstatic when he rediscovered five ancient mathematical texts from the *Yung-lo ta-tien* (Great compendium of the Yung-lo era, 1403-1425) while he was serving on the *Ssu-k'u ch'üan-shu* commission. His accounts of these works in the astronomy and mathematics section of the *Ssu-k'u ch'üan-shu* catalog indicated the importance that recovery of the earliest mathematical texts had for *k'ao-cheng* scholarship.[49]

Jesuit impact on the study of the native scientific tradition can also be discerned later in Juan Yuan's scholarship. Juan's efforts in astronomy culminated with the publication of the *Ch'ou-jen chuan* (Biographies of mathematical astronomers) in 1799, described by Sivin as "a programmatic synthesis of traditional and Western astronomy designed to encourage the study of the latter in order to improve the former. Juan emphasized the old idea that the roots of modern astronomy are to be found in ancient China." Such an approach was indispensable in a society that habitually employed the past to sanction innovation.

Juan's scientific interests were extremely influential because of his status as a patron of Kiangnan scholarship. In addition, Juan served in 1799 as director of the mathematics section of the Kuo-tzu chien (National University) in Peking. His efforts marked the culmination of an ongoing process whereby the value of mathematics and astronomy was reaffirmed as part of a Confucian education. In essay questions Juan Yuan prepared for students at the Hsueh-hai T'ang Academy, which he founded in Canton in the 1820s (see chapter 3), he asked them to examine and critically discuss (*k'ao-cheng*), among other questions, the following:

(1) When did the mathematical astronomy of the lesser western regions [*hsiao hsi-yang*, that is, India and the Middle East] and the greater western regions [*ta hsi-yang*, that is, Europe] come to China? What route did they follow? . . .

(2) Is it true that the methods of the western regions were bound, like those of China, to develop greater precision? Whose discoveries came first, and whose methods are more exact? . . .

(3) If the Muslim techniques used in the Yuan dynasty and the European ones used in the Ming dynasty are really more ancient than ours, then why didn't their techniques appear before the Chiu-chih [Nine Upholders] calendar established in China in A.D. 718? What was the origin of the Chiu-chih calendar? Why do Westerners admit they borrowed their methods from the East?

· · ·

Emphasis on mathematics, astronomy, and geography were part of a commitment among scholars at the Hsueh-hai T'ang and academies in Kiangnan to train competent men for responsible positions. Juan's Cantonese friend Wu Lan-hsiu (Hsueh-hai T'ang director in 1826), was an accomplished mathematician. His treatise entitled *Fang-ch'eng k'ao* (On equations, lit., "square table method"; an allusion to the matrix calculation performed on the counting board to solve simultaneous linear equations) was included in the *Hsueh-hai T'ang chi* (Collected writings from the Hsueh-hai T'ang). Also included were student essays on anything from sundials to the use of mathematics to study the movement of stars. To reconstruct antiquity was to recreate the wide range of intellectual and practical domains of knowledge that had existed in the Chinese tradition.

Philology (*hsiao-hsueh*) became the route to the past. Evidential research thus provided a methodology that carried over into a wide range of disparate precise disciplines. Phonology, etymology, and paleography became the keys to unlocking the secrets of antiquity. With the publication of Hsieh Ch'i-k'un's (1737–1802) *Hsiao-hsueh k'ao* (Critique of classical philology) in 1802, it was no longer possible to dismiss philology as "lesser studies," as the term *hsiao-hsueh* literally implied. Even Sung-Learning scholars such as Yao Nai (1732–1815) had to admit that *hsiao-hsueh* was by now a formidably specialized and absolutely essential tool to reconstruct the classical heritage.[50]

. .

The Ssu-k'u ch'üan-shu Project

With the compiling of the *Ssu-k'u ch'üan-shu* in the 1770s and 1780s, *k'ao-cheng* scholarship was for all intents and purposes established as the standard for the evaluation of all available writings produced before that time. The linguistic self-consciousness of *k'ao-cheng* evaluation reflected itself in tacit standards that were employed by the *Ssu-k'u ch'üan-shu* editors to discuss, evaluate, and criticize works handed in to the commission. They saw their task as a chance to supersede irrevocably the scholarship that had preceded the Ch'ing dynasty and thus bring honor to the scholars of the seventeenth and eighteenth centuries.

· Table 1 ·

Criteria for Evaluation in the *Ssu-k'u Ch'üan-shu Tsung-mu*
(Based on 137 Articles in the *Documents* section)

Criteria	Citations
1. Proper use of sources & verification or not	21
2. Critical of arbitrary judgment	13
3. Worthy of consideration as *k'ao-cheng* or not	11
4. Use of Sung *i-li* methods or not	9
5. Link to concrete studies or not	7
6. Use of proper *hsun-ku* methods or not	6
7. Discovery & originality	4

From Table 1,[51] we can see that the overriding concern of the editors was the proper use of sources and principles of verification. To be worthy of consideration as a *k'ao-cheng* work (*k'ao-cheng chih tzu*, 12:21b) and hence receive the editors' praise, a book was expected to make use of a broad variety of sources, employ evidential techniques to analyze those sources, and emphasize studies of institutions, names, and rituals in ancient texts. If it failed to do this, the work was criticized for "being deficient in evidential research" (*shih yü k'ao-cheng*, 11:9a) or for "not constituting a contribution to evidential research" (*wu tsu-i tzu k'ao-cheng*, 14:8a).

In the process, new discoveries (*fa-ming,* 12:17b) were praised and pointed out, whereas phrases such as "made no discoveries" (*wu so fa-ming,* 14:4b) were used to describe Ming dynasty works that contributed little to the accumulation of knowledge. Concrete studies (*shih-hsueh,* 11:28a) were viewed as an attempt to get at the bottom of and illuminate phenomena and affairs. Such research entailed the study of "names and their referents" (*ming-wu*) and "statutes and institutions" (*tien-chih*). The latter were reconstructed in a firm commitment to the legacy of concrete scholarship (*tu-shih chih i,* 12:4b). Such efforts at precise scholarship were contrasted with the "empty discussions" (*hsu-t'an,* 12:4b) that dominated the Sung explications of the Classics, according to the *Ssu-k'u ch'üan-shu* editors.

Similar climates of opinion were also reflected in the criticism that Tai Chen (then on the staff of the *Ssu-k'u ch'üan-shu* project) received when he completed his philosophical texts entitled *Yuan shan* (Inquiry into goodness) and *Meng-tzu tzu-i shu-cheng.* Although Tai was admired by Ch'ien Ta-hsin and Chu Yun (1729–1781) for his talents in astronomy and mathematics, they did not hesitate to dismiss Tai's writings on *li* and *ch'i* as empty speculation on meanings and principles that need not have been written.

Chang Hsueh-ch'eng saw himself in direct opposition to the academic climate created by *k'ao-cheng* scholars. It is for this reason that Chang's theoretical writings on history and the nature of historiography were not highly regarded until the twentieth century, when interest in him was revived by Naitō Torajirō and Hu Shih. Hence, the *k'ao-cheng* specialist Ch'ien Ta-hsin, not Chang Hsueh-ch'eng, was the most acclaimed historian of the eighteenth century. Chang had comparatively little impact in his own day precisely because he was not truly representative of contemporary intellectual currents. Writing on his arrival in Peking in 1775, Chang noted: "Those who submitted writings to high officials [in hopes of patronage] usually no longer claimed skill in poetry and examination-essay writing, but claimed instead to be expert in philology, text-criticism, phonology, or paleography, trotting along with changing popular fashion." However much he disagreed, Chang Hsueh-ch'eng understood the basic commitments of his age.[52]

· · ·

Specialization and
Precise Scholarship

Reemphasis on classical studies was inseparable from the growth of auxiliary disciplines such as epigraphy, bibliography, and collation. The techniques employed in these fields became essential tools in the more formal disciplines of textual criticism, historical geography, historical linguistics, classical studies, historical research, and mathematical astronomy.

Juan Yuan described the eighteenth-century academic career of Ch'ien Ta-hsin, for example, in the following terms:

> Since the beginning of the dynasty, various Confucians have expounded on ethics, statecraft, history, astronomy, geography, paleography, phonology, epigraphy, and poetics. The number of well-trained specialists [in these fields] has in the process increased. Only Ch'ien Ta-hsin from Chiating [Kiangsu] has mastered all of these [separate areas].

· · ·

While at first sight a straightforward statement of awe at the comprehensiveness of one of the giants of the *k'ao-cheng* movement, Juan's discussion indicates the degree to which scholarly research had been divided into discrete disciplines. *K'ao-cheng* scholars saw such formal disciplines as fields where evidential methods could be applied to discrete bodies of knowledge, for example, geography as opposed to astronomy (see the discussion of the classification of knowledge in chapter 4). The clustering of these fields reveals the organizational strategy in *k'ao-cheng* studies.

In the move from the Ming "amateur ideal" to the Ch'ing specialist (see chapter 3), we discern a major change in the definition and role of a Confucian scholar. In fact, some, like the Yangchow Han-Learning scholar Chiao Hsun, feared that such specialization might go too far: "Scholars [nowadays] master one speciality and distance themselves from others. I worry that their views will as a result not be comprehensive enough."[53]

. .

Authenticity and Text Reconstruction

Studies in the authenticity and dating of texts became an important first step in the use of sources for other purposes. The emergence of "forgery detection" (*pien-wei*) as a precise discipline employing an impressive array of literary techniques was important in the accumulation of findings resulting from collation projects (*chiao-k'an-hsueh*) and careful examination of text editions (*pan-pen-hsueh*). In a letter addressed to his colleagues, Tuan Yü-ts'ai explained:

> There are two difficulties in determining the accuracy of a text. One is to determine the authenticity of the [reconstructed] basic text. The other is to evaluate the validity of its meaning. One must first determine the authenticity of the basic text before one can decide on the validity of the work's meaning . . . By basic text we mean the original version drafted by the author himself; by meaning of the text we refer to the meanings and principles [*i-li*] that the author expounds . . . Once we reconstruct each basic text, we can decide on the validity of their respective meanings and principles. Then we can proceed to reconstruct a basic text of the Classic [on which they were commenting] and gradually verify its meanings and principles.[54]

. . .

To make the past accessible to contemporary scholars, *k'ao-cheng* researchers developed impartial principles and definitive proofs for discerning forgeries. Yen Jo-chü's *Shu-cheng* became the exemplar for this form of research. Chiang Fan, for example, went further than most when he asserted that the acceptance of Yen's proofs and conclusions concerning the Old Text *Documents* was one of the requirements for consideration as Han-Learning scholarship. Epigraphical evidence was brought to bear on paleographical studies. The "forms of written characters" (*t'i-chih*) were analyzed and changes in form over time were noted and described. Paleography (*wen-tzu-hsueh*) became closely linked to changes in calligraphy styles. The study of ancient seal styles in the Han dynasty *Shuo-wen chieh-tzu* (Analysis of characters as an explanation of writing) became an important element in the New Text-Old Text debate, because the New Text versions of the Former Han dynasty had been recorded in the Han official or clerical script (*li-shu*), whereas the Old Text chapters were argued to have been written in pre-Han seal script (*chuan-shu*). Any elucidation of the issue depended on an intimate knowledge of the history of calligraphy (see chapter 5).[55]

Collection and reconstruction of texts represented an attempt to recreate a lost past. Ma Su's monumental *I-shih* (A continuous history), printed in 1670, incorporated all surviving literary material, including lost texts reconstructed from later quotations in encyclopedias, and the like, concerning Chinese history from its origins to the Warring States period (403-221 B.C.). Although uncritical and indiscriminate in his use of sources, Ma Su arranged the texts to make up a topically ordered compilation in the *chi-shih pen-mo* (recording events from their beginning to end) form. Chinese textual materials of every bibliographical category were employed as historical materials.

Textual recovery in Kiangnan played an important part in rekindling interest in the native scientific tradition. In the seventeenth and eighteenth centuries, scholars successively made important contributions to the reconstruction of ancient astronomical and mathematical traditions through their studies (see below). The *Ssu-k'u ch'üan-shu* project gave scholars access to the largest amount of rediscovered textual material since the *Yung-lo ta-tien* project in the early Ming (the products of which had not been widely available). In addition to the ancient mathematical texts that Tai Chen recovered from the *Yung-lo ta-tien*, Shao Chin-han (1743-1796) was able to retrieve the *Chiu wu-tai shih* (Older history of the five dynasties [907-960]) in the *Yung-lo ta-tien* and other early sources, thereby restoring it as an official *Dynastic History*.[56]

Reconstruction and collation were interdependent disciplines for scholars in the eighteenth century. In their search for best editions, scholars employed either the technique of "mechanical" or "elastic" collation. When they reprinted ancient texts, some scholars prepared a text to be published on the basis of the most reliable version available. This kind of collation entailed transcribing without alteration, that is, "mechanical" (ssu-chiao, lit., "dead collation"), whatever—including mistaken characters—was preserved in the accepted text. This approach was a very preliminary form of collation, which relied on ascertaining the most reliable text. Others corrected mistaken characters and filled lacunae in the text on the basis of quotations from all available texts, that is, "elastic" (huo-chiao, lit., "live collation"). Sun Hsing-yen (1753–1818) occupied a central position in the Ch'ing reconstruction of lost pre-Han philosophical texts. His reconstructions were collected from fragments of lost books quoted in earlier literary and philosophical collections as well as in later commentaries, encyclopedias, and collectanea.

A native of Hangchow, Lu Wen-ch'ao (1717–1796) was noted for his meticulous collations of ancient texts. His specialty entailed comparing texts and editions, taking note of their differences, and on the basis of the evidence printing an emended version. Collation scholarship remained one of the pillars of the exact scholarship upon which Han Learning specifically and evidential research generally were based.[57] Such tasks were so complicated that specialization was recognized as the solution to the scholar's inability to keep pace with the growth of knowledge. In the late eighteenth century, Chang Hsueh-ch'eng, for example, admitted that the modern scholar could master only a small part of the accumulated knowledge that his predecessors, living at a time when knowledge was less complicated, could have acquired easily. Yet Chang thought that the parts of the Confucian tradition that had been lost could be recovered and preserved through concentrated scholarship.[58]

. .
Historical Studies in Kiangnan

In the growing importance attached to epigraphical evidence by evidential scholars, we can discern a reform of historical method in the eighteenth century. Erudition and searching criticism were expected by the Kiangnan academic community of those who pieced together chronology, topography, institutions, rituals, and astronomy in their textual research. A pioneer in applying Han-Learning techniques to historical research, Wang Ming-sheng (1722–1798) contended that the historian should take into account all possible sources available to him. For Wang's research on the *Dynastic Histories,* such sources included the pre-Han masters (*chu-tzu*), fiction, poetry, random jottings, literary collections, gazetteers, and writings of the Buddhists and Taoists.

Epigraphy received much attention from *k'ao-cheng* historians because they were committed to the use of bronze and stone inscriptional evidence to verify the *Dynastic Histories.* Yü Ying-shih has indicated that Chang Hsueh-ch'eng, despite his dissatisfaction with the lack of synthesis in *k'ao-cheng* historiography, was also committed to a critical evaluation and use of sources, which he then employed to give a more comprehensive picture of the past.[59]

Tu Wei-yun has described in considerable detail the emergence of specialized *k'ao-cheng* historiography in the latter half of the eighteenth century. The efforts of Wang Ming-sheng, Ch'ien Ta-hsin, and Chao I (1727–1814) placed the historical disciplines in China on a firm base of impartial inquiry. They succeeded in restoring historical studies to a position of prestige and thereby attracted other evidential scholars to historical research. The credo of Ch'ing historiographic scholarship was enunciated by Wang Ming-sheng in the 1787 introduction to his study of the *Dynastic Histories:*

> Historical facts and clues reveal what [should be] praised and what [should be] deplored. Readers of the Histories ideally should not force the words and arbitrarily draw out [notions of] praise and blame. They must consider the reality to which all facts and clues point . . . Then they can proceed to record all the variations [of the facts that they can find]. When the discrepancies are analyzed one by one, and there is no [remaining] doubt, then after proceeding in this manner they can praise or blame and [still] remain sensitive in such judgments to fair discussions of the empire . . . Generally the way of scholarship should be sought in facts and not in empty [speculation]. Discussions of praise and blame are merely empty words. The writing of history is the recording of the facts. Overall the goal is simply to ascertain the truth. Besides the facts, what more can one ask for?[60]

· · ·

Critical of fruitless speculation and arbitrary "praise and blame" historiography, *k'ao-cheng* historians favored the application of epigraphy, geography, and linguistic research to portray the real face of history. Their criticism reveals the impartial bent of their scholarly positions. In complete agreement with Wang Ming-sheng's assessment, Ch'ien Ta-hsin maintained that historical facts themselves should reveal whom to praise and whom to blame. According to Ch'ien, the process of laying blame should be analogous to the deliberations involved in deciding court cases. There must be no forced or self-serving use of the historical evidence to support political and dynastic prejudices. In his use of sources, Ch'ien emphasized the most ancient account of an event in order to correct the accounts that appeared later.[61]

As we shall see in chapter 5, the use of notation books and inductive methods by evidential scholars indicated that they had discovered a rigorous methodology to apply to historiography. Their analysis of historical sources, correction of anachronisms, revision of texts, and addition of commentary and supplements represented a direct application of methods that had first been used in classical and literary research. Wang Ming-sheng and Ch'ien Ta-hsin made significant contributions to both classical studies and history. Historians focused on resolving textual puzzles or on elucidating ritual and institutional terminology. Chao I, for example, extended his historical inquiry to include topical discussions of such subjects as epigraphical discoveries during the Sung, Ming academics, and Ming institutional weaknesses. He seems to have recognized the problems inherent in a *k'ao-cheng* methodology that promoted piecemeal research.[62]

Questions concerning the relation of the Classics to the Histories had been prominent in the seventeenth century. Yen Jo-chü, for example, made use of information in the Histories to correct errors and detect forgeries in the Classics. In the eighteenth century, the relationship between the Classics and the Histories continued to be an important consideration in historical scholarship. With the rise in the status of historical studies in Kiangnan almost to parity with classical studies, the demarcation between the universality of the Classics and the particularity of the Histories was called into question. Lu Wen-ch'ao, as an examination official in Hunan in 1767, pointedly asked his examinees to reconsider the relationship between the Classics and Histories:

The Histories have different uses from the Classics, but they derive from the same sources. The *Documents Classic* and *Spring and Autumn Annals* are the historical records of the sages, which have become Classics. Later ages honored the latter and [thereby] divided [the Histories and Classics] into two genres. Can you grasp [how this happened] and then explain it?

. . .

On the other hand, Wang Ming-sheng argued that there remained a difference between the Classics and the Histories: "In ordering the Classics, one absolutely never dares to deny the Classics, whereas in history . . . if there are errors, there should be nothing to stop you from criticizing those errors. Herein lies the difference." Yet Wang relegated this difference to only minor status: "The important consideration, however, is that, although there exists a small difference between them, in general they both reveal a commitment to deal with concrete matters. This [goal] unites them."

Ch'ien Ta-hsin went even further in his claim that there was no difference between the Classics and the Histories. This artificial division had not existed in antiquity, according to Ch'ien, and it had been first used in the four divisions (*ssu-pu*, that is, Classics, History, Philosophy, Literature) system of classification after the fall of the Han dynasty. Seeing the Histories "not as books [limited to discussion] of particular imperial families but in reality books [that revealed] thousands of years [of history]," Ch'ien Ta-hsin rejected the priority given to the Classics vis-à-vis the Histories as the means to reconstruct the classical tradition. According to Ch'ien, the Histories were extremely important sources for the retrieval of the past. Both Wang and Ch'ien were indirectly criticizing scholars such as Hui Tung and Tai Chen, who had focused their research solely on the Classics, thereby overlooking the value of the Histories.[63]

Chang Hsueh-ch'eng's well-known slogan "the Six Classics are all Histories" in the late eighteenth century should be understood in light of contributions made by seventeenth- and eighteenth-century *k'ao-cheng* scholars in Kiangnan. Wang Ming-sheng and Ch'ien Ta-hsin set the stage for Chang Hsueh-ch'eng's conclusion. What Chang did was to historicize classical studies by placing the Classics unequivocally under the purview of historical inquiry.[64]

Intellectual and cultural history also became important areas of historical scholarship. Huang Tsung-hsi's *Ming-Ju hsueh-an* (Studies of Ming Confucians), completed in 1676, marked the emergence of the "studies in scholarship" (*hsueh-an*) genre as an important form of comprehensive analysis and incisive synthesis, according to schools, of the Confucian scholarship associated with a particular period of time. Huang's account included discussions and citations of two hundred Ming Confucians. Most were from Kiangnan.

The *Sung-Yuan hsueh-an* (Studies of Sung and Yuan [Confucians]), begun by Huang Tsung-hsi but completed by his son Huang Po-chia (b. 1643) and Ch'üan Tsu-wang (1705–1755), was another important contribution to China's intellectual history and to the analysis of the proliferation of Confucian schools before the Ming dynasty. As a result of these two pioneering works, the *hsueh-an* became established as the superior form for dealing with Confucian intellectual history and tracing the development of lines of thought in that tradition. This form of intellectual history stressed lines of discipleship (that is, transmission) within schools of thought.[65]

In writing intellectual history, Ch'üan Tsu-wang was committed to a recovery and preservation of materials concerning scholars who had lived during the Ming-Ch'ing transition period. Ch'üan was following in the tradition of the seventeenth-century Che-tung scholar Wan Ssu-t'ung (1638–1702). Reflecting a continued interest in the traumatic effects of the Ming collapse, Ch'üan attempted to record for posterity the tragic lives of the Ming loyalists whose heroic deeds he thought were being forgotten in the eighteenth century. Ch'üan's efforts to revive the scholarship of the seventeenth century were closely connected to his perception of late Ming history as an important record of martyrdom.

Chang Hsueh-ch'eng's interest in the nature and requirements of historical writing led him to favor the comprehensive history (*t'ung-shih*) genre as the most acceptable form for adequate coverage of the intellectual and cultural history of China. Relying on Cheng Ch'iao's (1104–1160) historiographic principles, Chang's notions of cultural history drew on an evolutionary view of political and cultural institutions.[66]

In an effort to explain texts by relating them to their historical background, Chang Hsueh-ch'eng was committed to an interpretation rooted in exhaustive bibliography and precise scholarship. He went further than other *k'ao-cheng* scholars in his effort to mold historical materials into a synthetic and well-rounded whole. Chang's *Wen-shih t'ung-i* (General meaning of literature and history) was an attempt to reconstruct the successive stages of the Confucian tradition, before there had been any efforts at conventional, that is, orthodox, explanation of the tradition. History he felt had become imprisoned by the artificial rules used in the official histories, which were the product of the collaboration of scholar-officials who owed their positions to the dynasty sponsoring the project. Chang's ideal of impartiality forced him to reject the stereotyped judgments that pervaded the official histories after the T'ang dynasty. The historian, according to Chang, should make a personal contribution to historical knowledge.[67]

Anthologies of biographies were another important form of intellectual history in the eighteenth century. Ch'ien Ta-hsin's biographies of eleven major figures in Ch'ing scholarship, which included biographies of Yen Jo-chü, Hu Wei, Hui Tung, and Tai Chen, represented this form of Ch'ing intellectual history. Chiang Fan (1761–1831) later made use of Ch'ien's biographies in his controversial account of the Han-Learning school during the Ch'ing dynasty entitled *Kuo-ch'ao Han-hsueh shih-ch'eng chi* (Record of Han-Learning masters in the Ch'ing dynasty). Chiang also compiled a work entitled *Kuo-ch'ao Sung-hsueh yuan-yuan chi* (Record of the origins of Sung Learning during the Ch'ing dynasty), in which he divided the history of Ch'ing Sung Learning into northern and southern schools.[68]

These developments demonstrate that the so-called "failure of Chinese traditional historiography to evolve scientific premises for questioning research" is largely the result of our ignorance of the contributions that evidential scholarship brought to bear on Confucian historiography during the eighteenth century (although David Nivison revealed many of these contributions over fifteen years ago). In fact, this movement in historical research was transmitted to Korea and Tokugawa Japan (1600–1867). In Japan, *k'ao-cheng* (*kōshō* in Japanese) historiography also developed into a rigorous methodology. Through the efforts of Shigeno Yasutsugu (1827–1910), Japanese historians in the nineteenth century learned to apply the methods of German Rankean history by relying on their earlier experience with evidential research.[69]

Tu Wei-yun has contended that the *k'ao-cheng* stream of impartial historiography developed independently of the Jesuit impact in China.

He has argued that Jesuit influence was limited to astronomy and calendrical studies and did not carry over into historiography. European historiography, according to Tu, was not transmitted to China during this period. Tu's argument overlooks, however, the interdisciplinary nature of evidential methods and the role of astronomy and mathematics in those disciplines, which Nathan Sivin has discussed in detail. Ch'ien Ta-hsin, for example, was one of the best informed men of his time in Western astronomy and mathematics. To assume that his training in these fields had no impact on his evidential historiography is eccentric.[70]

Chu-tzu-hsueh: Revival of Pre-Han Currents of Thought

Textual recovery, collation, and reconstruction occasioned the revival of unorthodox and non-Confucian texts overlooked for centuries. The reasoning that led Ch'ing scholars back to the Later and Former Han dynasties as sources for the beginnings of the Confucian tradition also led eighteenth-century scholars in Kiangnan back to the pre-Han masters' (*chu-tzu*) texts from the earlier Warring States period (403–221 B.C.). Seventeenth-century scholars had emphasized use of pre-Han philosophical texts to explicate the Classics, but the full implications of this approach were not worked out until the eighteenth century when Later Han dynasty sources were left behind in favor of Former Han and pre-Han texts. The revival of the *Mo-tzu, Hsun-tzu,* and *Kung-yang* texts in particular presented serious threats to the Confucianism in Later Han sources.

Wang Chung (1745–1794) and Chang Hsueh-ch'eng, although antagonists, played key roles in dethroning Confucius from his supreme position at the heart of Confucian culture. A native of Yangchow, Wang Chung was an admirer of Ku Yen-wu, Yen Jo-chü, Hu Wei, Mei Wenting (1633–1721), Hui Tung, and Tai Chen, whom he regarded as the six greatest scholars of the Ch'ing dynasty. Initially, Wang was interested in the *Hsun-tzu* text, and he reconstructed Hsun-tzu's forgotten but important role in classical scholarship during the Warring States period.[71]

In addition, Wang Chung initiated a revival of the *Mo-tzu* text at a time when the practical aspects of Mohist thought and its relation to early Confucianism already had begun to attract the attention of several *k'ao-cheng* scholars. In 1780 and 1783 prefaces for Pi Yuan's (1730–1797) edition of the *Mo-tzu*, collated by Sun Hsing-yen, Lu Wen-ch'ao, and others, Wang Chung defended Mohism from charges of heterodoxy by linking Mohism and Confucianism as related movements during the Warring States period. He also placed Mo-tzu on the same footing with Confucius:

> From the Mohist's words we know that Confucius was a grandee of Lu and Mo-tzu was a grandee of Sung. Their positions were equivalent, and they were about the same age. Their techniques for governing were not the same however. In making their arguments, each was intent on gaining victory [over the other]. These debates occurred at a time when the pre-Han masters were all doing the same thing. Hence, Mo-tzu's attack on Confucius resembled Lao-tzu's dismissal of Confucian studies.

. . .

Wang blamed Mencius for attacking the Mohist tradition and thus leading to its long neglect. What attracted Wang Chung's interest was the statecraft and technical expertise included in Mohist writings. Weng Fang-kang (1733–1818), on the other hand, found Wang's perspective infuriating: "Moreover, [Wang Chung] dares to say that Mencius libeled Mo-tzu in Mencius' accusation that [the Mohist doctrine of] 'universal love knows no [respect for] the father.' Without question this makes him [Wang] a criminal who [goes against] the orthodox teachings."

It is intriguing that revival of the *Hsun-tzu* and *Mo-tzu* texts would arouse such an emotional response. Clearly, there was more than met the eye here. Later, Fang Tung-shu, defender of the Ch'eng-Chu orthodoxy, took dead aim at those Han-Learning scholars who were returning to the pre-Han masters. He rejected, for example, Ch'ien Ta-hsin's insinuation that Hsun-tzu had been closer to Confucius' actual teachings than Mencius had been. It was clear that *k'ao-cheng* scholars were daring to reconsider the Hsun-tzu versus Mencius debate, which had been dormant for so long. To attack Mencius after all was to attack Sung Learning as well.

Fang Tung-shu also attacked Wang Chung for his use of the *Mo-tzu*.

According to Fang, Wang had been in collusion with other Yangchow scholars in reopening the Mo-tzu versus Confucius question. Such pernicious scholars were guilty of betraying the true moral teachings (*ming-chiao*) of Confucius in their haste to overturn the teachings of Chu Hsi. Defenders of orthodoxy, Weng Fang-kang and Fang Tung-shu perceived the revived interest in Hsun-tzu and Mo-tzu as a threat to the Neo-Confucian tradition. The *Ssu-k'u ch'üan-shu* editors confirmed many of Wang Chung's views on the *Mo-tzu*. They also attributed the neglect of the Mohist canon to Mencius' attacks on Mo-tzu's heterodox ideas. In their view, the *Mo-tzu* had been an influential text in the Warring States period. For this reason Mo-tzu deserved eminence of place among early Chinese philosophers, alongside Confucius (see chapter 4).[72]

For his part, Chang Hsueh-ch'eng also located in pre-Han and Former Han sources evidence to show that Confucius was simply the most important of many Warring States philosophers. Confucianism had been only one school among others, and Confucius' role had been limited to transmitting the teachings enunciated by the Duke of Chou centuries before. Chang's research on the pre-Han masters paralleled Wang Chung's efforts to reconstruct currents of thought in the Warring States period. Chang's historical research was part of the retrospective progression of research in evidential scholarship. His discussion of the different roles played by Confucius and the Duke of Chou revived debates concerning the priority of the *Rituals of Chou* (associated with the Duke of Chou) over the *Spring and Autumn Annals* (associated with Confucius). Such debates had taken place in connection with earlier Confucian reform efforts, for example, during Wang Mang's brief reign (A.D. 9–23) and during Wang An-shih's (1021–1086) reform program initiated in 1069.

The question of who was the major figure in the origin of Confucianism reflected the growing rejection in eighteenth-century Kiangnan of the Neo-Confucian "orthodox transmission of the Tao" (*Tao-t'ung*) doctrine, which since the Sung dynasty stressed Confucius and Mencius. According to Chang Hsueh-ch'eng, the Duke of Chou, not Confucius, had been the last of the world-ordering sages. This point of view also opened for reexamination the preeminent position of the Sung and Ming Neo-Confucians as the orthodox continuators of the Confucian orthodoxy. Ch'ien Ta-hsin argued, for example, that the use of the term *Tao-t'ung* occurred for the first time during the Sung not the T'ang dynasty.[73]

Revival of the unorthodox *Kung-yang Commentary* to Confucius' *Spring and Autumn Annals* by the Ch'ang-chou scholars indicates that opposing views concerning the nature of the historical Confucius and the Confucian tradition were taking shape during the eighteenth century. The revival of interest in the pre-Han masters among Ch'ing Old Text scholars was accompanied by a revival in the *Kung-yang* emphasis on Confucius' central role in the formation of the Confucian orthodoxy. According to the New Text tradition, Confucius and not the Duke of Chou had been the central figure. From this point of view, Confucius had brought together earlier strands of the tradition and forged the Confucian vision in a time of war and decline.

For the Ch'ang-chou scholars, the *Kung-yang Commentary* was the central text that elucidated Confucius' intentions in writing the *Ch'un-ch'iu* and compiling the Five Classics. Liu Feng-lu contended: "Therefore, I have noted for some time that all scholars seek to know the [wisdom] of the sages. The Tao of the sages is complete in the Five Classics, and the *Spring and Autumn Annals* is the key to the lock." Without an understanding of the "subtle principles" (*wei-li*) of the *Spring and Autumn Annals*, the Five Classics, Liu argued, would remain inexplicable, no matter how much philological research was carried out. With Confucius as their paradigm, that is, following Confucius in his attempts "to find in antiquity the sanction for institutional reform" (*t'o-ku kai-chih*) New Text scholars in the nineteenth century were then able to legitimate their critique of current politics and proposals for institutional reform.[74]

Science in Eighteenth-Century Kiangnan

Links between natural studies and textual criticism developed in seventeenth- and eighteenth-century Kiangnan as responses to the Jesuit introduction of European science. Evidential research in traditional astronomy and mathematics demonstrated the depth and complexity of early Confucian contributions to the exact sciences. Ulrich Libbrecht has noted: "After a long period in which the mathematics

of the Sung and Yuan were entirely forgotten, the study of the culminating points in Chinese algebra started again. Mei Wen-ting . . . and
his grandson Mei Ku-ch'eng (d. 1763) are the forerunners of the 'mathematical renaissance' in China."

Jesuit impact on the revival of native Chinese science has been documented in great detail. Hashimoto Keizō has described the European
role in calendrical reform during the Ming-Ch'ing transition. Efforts
at reform culminated in the 1724 promulgation of the *Li-hsiang k'ao-
ch'eng* (Compendium of observational and computational astronomy)
and a sequel. Nathan Sivin has pointed out that the Western astronomy
in the *Compendium* was mostly a century old, but that the sequel of
1742 adapted more recent European discoveries to the ends of traditional calendar reform.[75]

Attempts to resolve the differences between Western methods (*hsi-
fa*) and Chinese methods (*Chung-fa*) occupied *k'ao-cheng* scholars interested in astronomy and mathematics throughout the Ch'ing dynasty.
Writing in the seventeenth century, Mei Wen-ting carefully delineated
the differences between the two scientific traditions and pointed out
areas where Western approaches were worth considering and applying.
However, because the missionaries were not permitted by their church
to describe fully the changes taking place in the exact sciences (namely,
the discoveries of Copernicus, 1473–1543, and Galileo, 1564–1642),
many inconsistencies occurred. The Copernican system was not por-
trayed comprehensively and accurately in China until the sketchy account prepared by Michel Benoist (1715–1774) in the eighteenth
century. These inconsistencies were immediately detected by Chinese
scholars familiar with the translated Western literature. Such discrepancies eventually cast doubt on the power of *hsi-fa* as a rigorous
explanatory device, and as a result *hsi-fa* as a holistic system was
rejected.

Pointing to these contradictions, Tai Chen and Juan Yuan, nonetheless, revived Mei Wen-ting's influential rationale for studying European
astronomy and mathematics. They claimed that the mathematical
astronomy of Europe was originally developed in China and had been
carried on in the West after dying out before the Han dynasty. Tai and
Juan argued, like their predecessors (including the K'ang-hsi Emperor),
that foreign knowledge could be used together with Chinese writings of
the Han to restore the native tradition to its original, unsullied form.[76]

Tai Chen, for example, insisted on deferring to the native tradition when using foreign knowledge. In addition to his claim that the syllabic notation system (*fan-ch'ieh*) used to indicate pronunciation was an indigenous development (it was not; see chapter 5), Tai maintained that the essential elements of astronomy and mathematics could be located in Chinese classical texts. If studied properly, according to Tai, the Classics would prove themselves repositories of scientific knowledge that had been lost over the years because of neglect and lack of understanding.

Tai set out, for instance, to show that a cryptic passage in the *Documents* revealed that the ancients had been aware of the complicated path of the sun on the celestial sphere. It was "carried through a revolution about the celestial north pole in a day and night" (see Figure 1), along with all the other luminaries. At the same time, it "passed through one degree" in its yearly circuit along the ecliptic. In the process, Tai concluded that this and other examples "are clear proof that Western methods were derived from the *Chou-pei* [*suan-ching*] (Arithmetic classic of the gnomon and the circular paths of the heavens)," which he had recovered from the *Yung-lo ta-tien*.[77]

Animated by a restorationist concern, Tai Chen, Ch'ien Ta-hsin, and Juan Yuan successfully incorporated technical aspects of Western astronomy and mathematics into the Confucian framework. At the same time they criticized the Western sciences. Sivin has contended:

> Juan [Yuan] was not trying, as some writers who have not found the leisure to read him attentively suppose, to denigrate European astronomy. Exactly to the contrary, he was providing a myth which would legitimize its study—not as an exotic novelty, but as knowledge affiliated with the classical tradition despite the unfamiliarity of its expression and not withstanding the infinitely less acceptable non-scientific ideas with which it was associated by the foreigners who brought it.

. . .

The Jesuit challenge in astronomy and mathematics was taken seriously by Ch'ing scholars in Kiangnan and spilled over into other *k'ao-cheng* disciplines as well. Ch'ien Ta-hsin acknowledged this broadening of the Confucian tradition, which he saw as the reversal of centuries of focus on moral and philosophical problems:

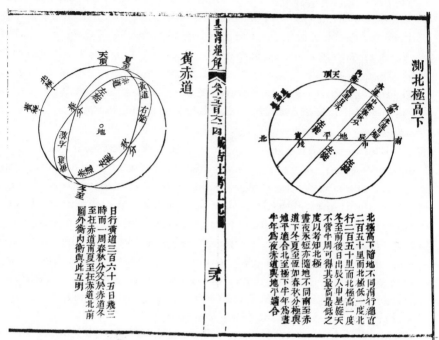

Figure 3   Tai Chen's Drawing of the Celestial Sphere
Source: Reprinted from the *Huang-Ch'ing ching-chieh,* eds., Juan Yuan et al. (Taipei, 1961).
Note: In the drawing on the right entitled "Altitude of the North Pole" from the *K'ao-kung chi t'u,* his study of archaic technology, Tai explains that the sun's daily rotation passes through the celestial north pole only at the equinoxes, when the sun follows the central of 3 slanting paths; the other 2 represent the sun's path at the summer solstice (left) and winter solstice (right). The horizontal line represents the observer's horizon. The less interesting drawing on the left shows the ecliptic and the equatorial. Their intersections represent the vernal and autumnal equinoxes. Also shown are the ecliptic and equatorial poles.

Comparing lands of the Eastern seas with those of the Western, we note that their spoken languages are mutually unintelligible and that their written forms are each different. Nonetheless, once a computation has been completed, [no matter where,] there will not be the most minute discrepancy when it is checked. This result can be for no other reason than the identity of human minds, the identity of patterns of phenomena, and the identity of numbers [everywhere]. It is not possible that the ingenuity of Europeans surpasses that of China. It is only that Europeans have transmitted [their findings] systematically from father to son and from master to disciple for generations. Hence, after a long period [of progress] their knowledge has become increasingly precise. Confucian scholars have, on the other hand, usually denigrated those who were good mathematicians as petty technicians . . . In ancient times, no one could be a Confucian who did not know mathematics . . . Chinese methods [now] lag behind Europe's because Confucians do not know mathematics.

. . .

According to Ch'ien, earlier Confucians had been guilty of metaphysical (*hsien-t'ien*) speculation.[78]

. .

Science and Its Subordination to K'ao-cheng

Hu Shih and Yabuuchi Kiyoshi have called attention to what they describe as the literary focus of *k'ao-cheng* interests in mathematics and astronomy. Yabuuchi argued that the triumph of *k'ao-cheng* discourse during the eighteenth century prevented scholars such as Tai Chen and Ch'ien Ta-hsin from concentrating on mathematics and astronomy for their own sake. Instead Tai and Ch'ien connected such studies to what they considered their more central objective: the reconstruction of antiquity. Their concern for the scientific significance of the new findings and discoveries did not enable them to recognize the potential for the growth of science as an independent field of inquiry.[79]

Hu Shih similarly has contended that the exclusive concern with documents that pervaded the *k'ao-cheng* movement restricted scholars such as Ku Yen-wu and Yen Jo-chü to a literary focus, even if they occasionally did make use of archaeological findings or carry out some astronomical investigation. Research on ancient astronomy was valued mainly for its application to classical studies. The exact sciences were never perceived as anything more than fields ancillary to more important classical and historical concerns. Inquiries into natural phenomena, for the most part, were dependent on textual evidence and not experimentation, according to Hu Shih.[80]

Although such a state of affairs did not doom evidential scholars to a lack of curiosity about the natural world, the general thrust of Yabuuchi's and Hu Shih's overstated accounts does reflect the philological biases that dominated *k'ao-cheng* scholarship during the Ch'ing dynasty. Not everyone linked to the *k'ao-cheng* movement had scientific interests. Ku Yen-wu was a contemporary of Mei Wen-ting. He was interested in astronomy, as his correspondence shows, but did not actively pursue it. Ku was a classicist. So was Yen Jo-chü, although the latter was forced to work in chronography by his own standards of rigor.

There is no justification for assuming that because a scientific revolution did not take place in China it could not have taken place, especially in light of the important place mathematics and astronomy occupied in evidential research. The triumph of modern science in China, as in Europe, required an intellectual transformation that would have exceeded the boundaries of textual scholarship, one that would support the nascent research and experimentation required in the step-by-step quantification of the natural world. Nevertheless, important scientific research did take place, and the institutions required for precise scholarship were already in place (see chapter 5).

European science in eighteenth-century China was not built upon and developed past the limits we have just sketched partly because of faulty Jesuit transmission that failed to challenge native classicism or provide an academic alternative. The preeminent position of classical studies in *k'ao-cheng* scholarship, along with its historical focus, remained intact. Interest in the exact sciences was confined within this perspective on the accumulation of knowledge.[81]

The developments described in this chapter have, for the most part, been internal to the intellectual evolution of *k'ao-cheng* as a viable discourse in the seventeenth and eighteenth centuries. These events also required appropriate institutions and social forms of status and patronage conducive to research and writing. In the chapters that follow, we will explore the external social and institutional factors that stimulated and promoted the growth of evidential scholarship in Kiangnan.

Three

The Professionalization of Lower Yangtze Academics

Since the Sung dynasty, the division between literati and merchant in China was a fluid one. A merchant subculture comparable to that of early modern Europe and Tokugawa Japan (1600–1867) failed to emerge because of the absence of absolute barriers (such as the nobility) to the translation of commercial wealth into literati (or gentry) status. This fluid situation was especially evident during the Ch'ing dynasty. Hence, it is not surprising to find that the institutional framework within which academicians learned and transmitted empirical techniques of scholarship included schools, academies, and literary staffs that all cut across the cleavage between literati and merchant in late imperial China.

A major thesis of our study is that the professionalization of Lower Yangtze academics during the eighteenth century was centered on a

Figure 4 Preparing Type Blanks
    Source: *Ch'ing-ting Wu-ying-tien chü-chen-pan ch'eng-shih* (Peking, 1776).

specific community of scholars. Their academic work, whether as collators, editors, researchers, or compilers, required occupationally defined skills that depended on an expertise in textual research. In addition, they considered themselves members of this academic community, a community that was composed of practitioners of *k'ao-cheng* scholarship bound together by common elements in education and responsible for pursuing shared goals, which included the training of their successors.[1]

In the previous chapter, we looked at the intellectual factors that occasioned the rise of *k'ao-cheng* scholarship in Kiangnan and its acceptance by a broad range of Ch'ing scholars. Here, we will use the tools of sociology to analyze the same developments from an institutional standpoint. We will first analyze what kinds of people carried out evidential research in the eighteenth century. Then, we will deal successively with the issues of where *k'ao-cheng* research was done, how scholars became trained members of the Kiangnan academic community, and, finally, who paid for their research and writing.

· · ·

Social Origins of K'ao-cheng Scholars

Important advances in intellectual history often are linked to changes in social structure and to the emergence of new groups that support new directions of inquiry. Robert Merton, for example, has described the interdependence of "socially patterned interests, motivations, and behavior" in European science and religion. He has pointed out that Puritanism, although not the only set of religious convictions that could have ushered in seventeenth-century English science, fulfilled the "functional requirement" of a socially and culturally patterned locus of support for nascent scientific inquiry. An emerging middle class was closely connected to the rise of scientific inquiry as an important intellectual endeavor in early modern Europe.[2]

With this perspective in mind, we will examine the social origins of textual scholars who participated in the Ch'ing *k'ao-cheng* wave of impartial empirical inquiry to see whether there was a change in social origins from the Ming to Ch'ing dynasties. This question will be approached by identifying the authors included in the *Huang-Ch'ing ching-chieh* (Ch'ing exegesis of the Classics), a massive scholarly collection published in Canton by the Hsueh-hai T'ang (Sea of Learning Hall) in the early nineteenth century and devoted exclusively to evidential scholarship.

Because it was the first comprehensive collection of Ch'ing contributions to classical scholarship, the 1829 publication of the *Huang-Ch'ing ching-chieh*, after four years of compiling and editing by Cantonese scholars, was greeted with great acclaim in China and elsewhere. An impressive collection of some 180 different works by 75 seventeenth- and eighteenth-century authors in more than 360 volumes totaling 1400-odd *chüan*, the *Huang-Ch'ing ching-chieh* represented a major tribute to the research carried out by *k'ao-cheng* scholars. It served as a collection of exemplary works from what evidential scholars considered their academic community in the seventeenth and eighteenth centuries. In 1818, just before he initiated the *Huang-Ch'ing ching-chieh* project, Juan Yuan (1764–1849), then Governor-General in Canton, had already sponsored the publication of Chiang Fan's *Kuo-ch'ao Han-hsueh shih-ch'eng chi* (Record of Han-Learning masters of the Ch'ing dynasty). The latter provided a detailed, although controversial, biographical pedigree for Han Learning, that is, evidential research, during the Ch'ing period.[3]

The Hsueh-hai T'ang's collection was a continuation (although in a new form) of the long-admired Sung dynasty collection known as the *Shih-san-ching chu-shu* (Commentaries and annotations to the *Thirteen Classics*), which covered Sung and pre-Sung scholarship. The latter was also reprinted by the Hsueh-hai T'ang. The *Huang-Ch'ing ching-chieh* was in one sense a response to the equally massive early Ch'ing collectanea (*ts'ung-shu*) entitled *T'ung-chih T'ang ching-chieh* (The T'ung-chih Hall's exegesis of the Classics) compiled by Hsu Ch'ien-hsueh (1631–1694). The latter was considered by Juan Yuan and the editorial staff of the *Huang-Ch'ing ching-chieh* to be biased in favor of Sung-Ming Neo-Confucian classicism. We should note, however, that Hsu Ch'ien-hsueh was an important patron of evidential research in the seventeenth century.[4]

· Table 2 ·

Geographical Origins of Authors Included in the
Huang-Ch'ing ching-chieh

Native area	Total		% of
	No.	%	Ln. 6
1. Ch'ang-chou fu	7	9	11
2. Hangchow fu	13	17	20
3. Soochow fu	9	12	14
4. Yangchow fu	15	20	23
5. Total 1–4	44	59	68
6. Total Kiangnan	65	87	100
7. Outside Kiangnan	10	13	–
8. Total	75	100	–

Beginning with works by such *k'ao-cheng* patriarchs as Ku Yen-wu and Yen Jo-chü (1636–1704), the *Huang-Ch'ing ching-chieh* collection included writings by many of the distinguished scholars associated with the eighteenth-century Han-Learning movement. Most were linked to intellectual currents in Kiangnan that emphasized study of Cheng Hsuan (127–200), Hsu Shen (58–147), and other Later Han Confucian scholars.[5] Compilers of the collection also reprinted, however, a number of works by men connected to the Ch'ang-chou New Text school, which emphasized Ho Hsiu (129–182) and Former Han scholarship. The criterion for inclusion was the use of evidential research methods. Thus, Juan Yuan and his associates considered the Ch'ang-chou scholars to be part of the *k'ao-cheng* movement (a view we would do well to accept). Juan Yuan's selection of evidential scholarship for inclusion in the *Huang-Ch'ing ching-chieh* mirrored standards of evaluation that the *Ssu-k'u ch'üan-shu* editors earlier had favored (see chapter 2).[6]

The *Huang-Ch'ing ching-chieh* was succeeded by a supplement (*hsu-pien*) compiled by Wang Hsien-ch'ien (1842–1918) and published at the Nan-ch'ing Academy in Chiang-yin, Kiangsu, between 1886–1888. The latter included works by over 100 different Ch'ing dynasty textual scholars. Because it emphasized nineteenth-century scholarship in China, it will not be included in the analysis that follows.[7] We can begin with the geographical distribution of the authors included in the *Huang-Ch'ing ching-chieh*. Table 2 summarizes the relevant biographical data collected for all 75 authors in the collection. Lines 1–6 demonstrate that almost 90 percent of the authors came from Kiangnan and that, moreover, the majority of the latter (68 percent) came from four of the most urbanized prefectures in the region. This unequal distribution confirms the centrality of the Lower Yangtze Region and the importance of its schools of scholarship.

Some reservations about Juan Yuan's selection should be noted. Juan's inclusion of works by fifteen Yangchow scholars (including his own) was somewhat self-serving, as was the overwhelming preference for works by Kiangnan scholars. An important scholar whose textual works were left out was the Chihli scholar Weng Fang-kang (1733–1818). Such apparent oversights aside, the *Huang-Ch'ing ching-chieh* maintains its value as a repository of the outstanding philological works written in the Ch'ing period. It was not entitled "Kiangnan Exegesis of the Classics." Moreover, it was compiled in Canton, not Yangchow or Hangchow, for Cantonese students. Hence, the collection was also called "The Hsueh-hai T'ang's Exegesis of the Classics."

What were the social origins of and degrees held by the scholars in the *Huang-Ch'ing ching-chieh*? We see in Table 3 that the majority were born in the eighteenth century and that, out of the total of 75 authors, 52 percent were from literati families.[8] Because the number of men for whom biographies were available but whose backgrounds were unclassifiable was so high (30, that is, 40 percent), the figure of 52 percent is not very informative. Of the 45 names for whom biographical data do give social origins, 87 percent were from literati backgrounds.

The number of scholars whose origins could be verified as merchant was low (only 8 percent of the total of 75 or 13 percent of the total of 45), yet they included three of the most important scholars associated with the *k'ao-cheng* movement (see the notes to Table 3). Furthermore, the interesting case of Tsang Yung (noted) points out that not only could merchant sons become literati, but literati families at times declined into merchant status. The biographical data available revealed no one from a peasant background, although a number did come from poor families. Traditional biographies of course would tend to conceal such information.

The vast majority of scholars (92 percent) were degree-holders, and 53 percent were holders of the highest degree (see Table 4). However, a sizable proportion (27 percent) held low degrees, which means that

· Table 3 ·
Social Origins of Authors in the *Huang-Ching ching-chih*
by Age Groups

	Total		Literati		Merchant		Lack
				Family Origins			
Born	No.	%	No.	%	No.	%	Data
1600–1645	8	11	6	75	1[a]	13	1
1646–1665	3	4	1	25	–	–	2
1666–1685	4	5	1	20	–	–	3
1686–1705	5	7	3	43	–	–	2
1706–1725	7	9	4	57	1[b]	14	2
1726–1745	16	21	11	69	–	–	5
1746–1765	19	25	5	26	3[c]	16	11
1766–1785	12	16	7	58	1[d]	8	4
1786–1805	1	1	1	100	–	–	–
Total	75	100	39	52	6	8	30

Notes:
a Includes Yen Jo-chü who came from a family of salt merchants, although his grandfather was a 1604 *chin-shih*.
b Includes Tai Chen whose father was a cloth merchant.
c Includes Juan Yuan, whose grandfather was a 1715 military *chin-shih* but whose mother came from a Yangchow salt merchant's family; Ling T'ing-k'an (1757–1809), the son of a merchant; and Chiao Hsun (1763–1820) who attended an academy reserved for children of merchant families in Yangchow.
d Tsang Yung's (1767–1811) father was a garment dealer, but his great-great-grandfather, Tsang Lin (1650–1713), had been a scholar of some note.

about one-third of the scholars achieved fame for their literary endeavors despite low or no standing in the degree hierarchy. This phenomenon is truer for the seventeenth century than the eighteenth. Part of the explanation lies in the fact that many Chinese scholars immediately after the Manchu triumph did not participate in the imperial examinations. On the basis of the data given above it would appear impossible to argue that the men who practiced *k'ao-cheng* scholarship represented a new social group. They seem to have been very much a part of the traditional elite.

Such an argument, however, is based on traditional social distinctions in standard biographies. Many biographers of Yen Jo-chü, for example, did not mention that he came from a salt merchant's family. Nor do standard biographies mention that Juan Yuan's mother was the daughter

· Table 4 ·

Highest Degrees Held by Authors in the
Huang-Ch'ing ching-chieh by Age Groups

	Highest Degrees Held					
	None	Low	*Chü-jen*	*Chin-shih*	Degree	No
Born	No. %	No. %	No. %	No. %	No. %	Inf
1600–1645	1 13	4 50	— —	3 38	7 88	—
1646–1665	1 33	1 33	— —	1 33	2 67	—
1666–1685	— —	1 25	1 25	2 50	4 100	—
1686–1705	— —	2 40	— —	3 60	5 100	—
1706–1725	1 14	— —	2 29	4 57	6 86	—
1726–1745	— —	4 25	2 13	10 63	16 100	—
1746–1765	— —	5 26	3 16	10 53	18 95	1
1766–1785	1 8	3 25	1 8	7 58	11 92	—
1786–1805	— —	— —	— —	— —	— —	1
Total	4 5	20 27	9 12	40 53	69 92	2

of a Yangchow salt merchant. Such facts were considered inappropriate for inclusion in biographies of respected literati. Thus, the data compiled cannot be accepted at face value as proof of the literati background of most participants in the *k'ao-cheng* movement. For this reason, traditional social distinctions are of limited use in pinpointing social change in the seventeenth and eighteenth centuries. Hence, the data I have compiled do not prove conclusively that evidential scholars were or were not increasingly from merchant families.

Silas Wu has contended that an economic class emerged in the seventeenth and eighteenth centuries that gave Yangchow, for example, added economic and cultural importance. The imperial court granted salt monopolies to wealthy Kiangnan merchants in exchange for their services as salt-tax collectors. These "merchant aristocrats," according to Wu, functioned as an economic arm of the imperial bureaucracy throughout the Ch'ing. They were also in the forefront of Kiangnan cultural and academic life. It is nearly impossible to distinguish literati from merchants in the academic world of eighteenth-century Yangchow, for example. Ping-ti Ho has noted the academic and bureaucratic success of salt merchant families during the Ming and Ch'ing dynasties. Such success points to the correlation between wealth and academic accomplishment in Kiangnan.

Merchants wanted official status and the prerogatives that went with such status. For this reason, they frequently sought official degrees either through education for themselves or their children or through the purchase of degrees. In addition, merchants favored marrying their sons and daughters into gentry families. An important motive for these social strategies was to put the family's present wealth under the protection of official status, which covered the entire family and, informally, the lineage. Many schools were often reserved for sons of salt merchants, such as the An-ting and Mei-hua academies in Yangchow. During the eighteenth century, scholarship flourished due to merchant patronage, and books were printed and collected in larger numbers than ever before.[9]

The fact that Yen Jo-chü and Tai Chen became important figures in evidential research certainly indicates that a merchant background was no major impediment to a life of scholarship and research. On the contrary, merchant wealth often contributed to making scholarship viable as a career. Ono Kazuko has pointed to the close connections the Ming dynasty T'ai-chou scholars in Yangchow prefecture had with the salt merchants who were at the center of cultural life there. Salt merchants (for example, Yen Jo-chü's family) made major contributions to the academic world. It is worth considering whether or not in other circumstances Tai Chen, the son of a cloth merchant, would have been received with acclaim in Peking society.

Thus, we may see a new social group that includes sons of merchants and literati carrying out evidential scholarship, and we clearly find important changes in literati career patterns. Ch'ing literati tended to be specialists in scholarship, as Yamanoi Yū has noted, in sharp contrast to Sung-Ming scholar-officials, whose official functions on the national and local levels were more important than their academic contributions. Yamanoi has attributed this Ch'ing phenomenon to the large-scale academic enterprises that were organized by the imperial court and the "national" elite after the Manchu triumph. Literati were employed in academic work in schools, on secretarial staffs, and in local and national literary projects. For many Ch'ing literati, scholarship became a way of life.[10]

Koyasu Shichishirō has described the careers of Chao I (1727–1814), Wang Ming-sheng (1722–1798), and Ch'ien Ta-hsin (1728–1804) as representative of the turn toward professional scholarship among eighteenth-century intellectuals. All were prominent members of the Han-Learning movement during the Ch'ien-lung Emperor's reign (1736–1795). Koyasu describes how in each case (all held the *chin-shih* degree) official position was principally a means to maintain high social status. Although they all accepted official positions, their main interests were in academic research, and all retired from office as soon as it was practical for them to do so. Chao, Wang, and Ch'ien spent their productive middle years engaged in specialized historical and classical research. They became known as the premier *k'ao-cheng* historians of their age.[11]

The above accounts suggest that the rise of *k'ao-cheng* studies was not only an intellectual event (as a matter of scholarly and professional choices) but also an institutional event (for institutions supported and promoted scholars who chose to carry out such research). To use Thomas Kuhn's terminology, both internal factors (motives) and external factors (institutions) must be taken into account to explain satisfactorily why Sung-Ming intuitionism was displaced by Ch'ing evidential studies among the traditional elite. Institutions in fact were not the only external factor involved. Frederic Wakeman has described the phenomenal increase in number of degree-holders during the Ch'ing dynasty. Such a development meant that holding a degree seldom guaranteed an official career. Scholarship, in many cases, filled a career vacuum that had not existed to this extent earlier.[12]

· · ·

Professionalization in
Late Imperial China

In order to describe the process whereby scholarship moves in the direction of academic professionalization, we need to understand how scholars in China developed the expertise necessary to accomplish their tasks. Responsibility on the part of scholars for the maintenance, transmission, and extension of a specialized and cumulative body of knowledge that is codified and recorded for scholarly use is a sign of professionalization in the strict sense of the word. What institutional mechanisms were essential for training men interested in evidential research and for transmitting common elements in such research? How did it happen that a specific group of people, not an occasional odd individual, regarded the rigorous, empirical investigation of texts as the best source of knowledge about the past and was rewarded for that work?[13]

The problem of what constitutes a profession is a highly contentious matter in contemporary sociology. Concepts such as "profession," "professionalization," or "professionalism" are not employed uniformly in the literature on the sociology of work and professions. Two of the major issues that have dominated the literature are the characteristics of a true or ideal profession and the process whereby an occupation develops into and achieves the status of a profession.[14]

Formal criteria for a true profession have been elusive, and the range of definitions has been bewildering. Howard Vollmer and Donald Mills have used the concept "profession" to represent an ideal occupation, that is, an abstract model that does not exist in reality. They define professionalization as a "dynamic *process* whereby many occupations can be observed to change in the direction of a 'profession,' even though some of these may not move very far in this direction." From their perspective, "many, if not all, occupations may be placed somewhere on a continuum between ideal-type 'profession' at one end and occupational categories or 'non-professions,' at the other end."[15]

Eliot Freidson, in his *Profession of Medicine,* has maintained that a profession is a special kind of occupation in which its members have gained exclusive authority to determine the proper content of and effective methods for performing some task, as well as determining criteria for admission, evaluation, and income. Freidson has stressed the autonomy of a profession, as distinct from an occupation that is subject to control by others in fundamental respects. Definitions are a distraction from the more fundamental issue of claims by groups to professional status. Training and licensing may serve, according to Freidson, as mere credentials by which members of groups that do not require long formal training, for example, social workers, seek to impress on the public their qualifications for exemption from lay control.[16]

John Jackson has argued that the significant question about occupations is not whether or not they are professions but, rather, to what extent they exhibit characteristics of professionalization. Jackson has contended that the range of criteria by which a profession may be designated varies considerably at different times and under different circumstances. He has suggested that the more important question is "what are the means by which an occupational status becomes reified and expanded into wider social significance?" According to Jackson, the emphasis should be placed on the developing professionalization of all occupations.[17]

We will employ John Jackson's concept of professionalization in this volume to refer to academic occupations that emerged in the Lower Yangtze academic community. We will be concerned with the common interests, activities, and goals of evidential scholars and the development of intricate, informal social networks and feelings of solidarity among those literati carrying out essentially similar tasks. Until we are better informed concerning occupational divisions and more confident concerning what definition of profession is useful in cross-cultural historical discussion, we can draw no conclusions about occupations and professions in eighteenth-century China. I suspect, however, a wide variety of social phenomena will bear on professions and the criteria for their existence in Confucian society. The function of academies and imperial universities as possible sources for professional authentication of teaching scholars, for example, may help us determine whether or not teaching can be fruitfully described as a profession in the Ch'ing period, if not before.[18]

Movement toward more formal scholarly occupations and roles was by no means completed during the Ch'ing dynasty. To be sure, Ch'ing literati did not become professional engineers, scientists, metallurgists, and so forth. Their roles as scholars, however, were professionalized. The textual scholars living in Kiangnan should be seen as operating somewhere on the continuum between what Vollmer and Mills consider ideal professions at one end and occupational divisions at the other. They were experts in their fields because they possessed special knowledge unavailable to laymen. Their technical activities as researchers and teachers had social implications. Their occupations were embodied in social relationships and institutions.[19]

"Professionalization" can be applied to k'ao-cheng scholarship for the following reasons:

(1) Evidential scholars were participants in a specialized occupation

based on prolonged study and intellectual training that supplied skilled service or advice to others for monetary support or patronage. Their academic roles and social responsibilities had thus been professionalized.

(2) The transformation of occupational criteria from possession of a broadly based range of intellectual and political concerns to possession of expertise in precise fields of evidential scholarship signals a movement toward professions.

(3) The possession of expertise in *k'ao-cheng* methods that could be employed only on a cumulative body of knowledge was required for the emergence, maintenance, and transmission of specialized fields of scholarship. Possession of this kind of expertise distinguished evidential scholars from officials, ordinary gentry, and laymen.

(4) Because the apolitical technical content and methods of *k'ao-cheng* research were not evaluated by outsiders, the ultimate lack of autonomy of evidential scholars from the state and their limited control over the socioeconomic terms of such work did not change the essential character of their labor as a specialized occupation heading in the direction of what we would call a profession. Freidson explains: "A profession need not be entrepreneur in a free market to be free." Autonomy, whether in evidential scholarship or European science, was always limited by the political power that made it possible and protected it. The limits varied over time and space.[20]

Before such scholarly occupations became specialities in seventeenth-century China (a process brought closer to completion in the eighteenth century), expertise in *k'ao-cheng* scholarship required the protective environment provided by the imperial court, important and powerful patrons, and in many cases the independent wealth of the members of the emerging specialities themselves. Evidential scholars were not, so far as I have been able to discern, conscious of their membership in a structurally defined scholarly profession. Loyalty to schools did not encourage an explicit broader identification.[21]

They were, however, aware of their place in an evolving academic community within which occupational specialization and precise scholarship were transforming their academic fields (see chapters 2 and 5). Evidential scholars attained and maintained their positions within this community by virtue of the protection and patronage of broader elite segments of Confucian society that had been persuaded that there was some special value in their work. The society at large in Kiangnan secured the viability of its prestigious academic community.[22]

. . .

Official and Semiofficial Patronage

During the last half of the seventeenth and the first quarter of the eighteenth centuries, while Manchu prohibitions against the founding of new academies remained in force, Confucian textual scholarship flourished within a sophisticated institutional network of national and local patronage. The K'ang-hsi Emperor's reign (1661–1722) brought an easing of tensions between Manchus and Chinese that in the early years of the dynasty had caused many Chinese literati to stand on the sidelines and refuse to participate in government functions. A change arose, however, that encouraged many literati to forgo an official career and turn instead to a life of scholarship.

The 1679 "broad scholarship and extensive words" (*po-hsueh hung-tz'u*, that is, qualifications of distinguished scholars to serve the dynasty) examination and the subsequent employment of those who passed it on the *Ming-shih* (Ming history) project ended the social withdrawal of many Kiangnan literati and, in Lawrence Kessler's words, "restored their confidence in the court's commitment to respect their traditional values and prerogatives."[23] Although the K'ang-hsi Emperor's attempts to recruit Chinese scholars for the bureaucracy were partially successful, the split between scholars and officials remained unresolved, signaling a major change in the social function of literati in traditional society.[24]

Scholarship in the period 1675–1725 was supported chiefly by forms of patronage that remained prominent through much of the eighteenth and nineteenth centuries. Protected by the K'ang-hsi Emperor's more lenient policies (when compared to those of his predecessors), directors of large-scale imperial compilation projects employed many well-known

literati in forms of official and semiofficial patronage that were crucial
to the maintenance and advancement of scholarship.

Sung Lao (1634–1713), for instance, gathered around him noted
scholars in Kiangsu when he was governor of the province for a remarkable span of fourteen years after 1692. He rebuilt the summer
retreat of a Sung dynasty poet in Soochow and used it for literary
gatherings to encourage younger scholars. In addition, he amassed a
large library of nearly 100,000 *chüan,* part of which was acquired
from the famous Chi-ku ko (Pavilion Reaching to the Ancients) collection in Ch'ang-shu (see chapter 4). Ts'ao Yin (1658–1712), appointed
by the K'ang-hsi Emperor as textile commissioner in Nanking in 1693,
was a connoisseur of rare books and antiques. In addition, he had a
reputation as a patron of scholars. His taste and influence were reflected in the books artistically printed under his supervision. The imperial printing shop Ts'ao established in Yangchow produced works
that are considered among the best examples of xylography in the early
Ch'ing period.[25]

Patronage Under Hsu Ch'ien-hsueh

Most famous among these director-patrons were the Hsu brothers,
Hsu Ch'ien-hsueh and Hsu Yuan-wen (1634–1691). They provided the
official auspices for scholarly associations of literati at a time when
academies and literary societies (*she*) were illegal. Their patronage
temporarily replaced the role of academies (*shu-yuan*) and literary
societies in providing an institutional framework for research and collaboration. Privately employed literati could gather in Peking and
elsewhere without fear of harrassment from Manchus, who after taking
power in 1644, had banned gatherings of scholars.

Natives of K'un-shan county in Soochow prefecture, the Hsu brothers
were nephews of the Ming loyalist Ku Yen-wu, who himself had refused
to participate in Manchu-run projects or examinations. The Hsu brothers, however, gladly accepted such roles. Hsu Yuan-wen was placed in
charge of the compilation of the *Ming History* from 1679–1684, and
Hsu Ch'ien-hsueh became director from 1684–1690. The project was
staffed by numerous Kiangnan literati who had passed the 1679 special
examination and was financed by imperial funds. Many on the staff

were participants in the seventeenth-century turn toward Han sources of classical scholarship. Also selected to work on the project were private scholars who as Ming loyalists could thereby justify their private responsibility to record and document their tragic era.[26]

Hsu Ch'ien-hsueh had a great deal of influence on the tenor of scholarship during these years. An opponent of the excessive tendencies in the Wang Yang-ming (1472–1529) school, especially what he considered the "left-wing's" militant stand against book learning, Hsu came out in favor of Chu Hsi's (1130–1200) school of principle (li-hsueh) because of its more intellectualist orientation. To promote the Sung school of Tao-hsueh, Hsu employed a large number of scholars to compile the massive T'ung-chih T'ang ching-chieh, which was a large collection of philosophic (li-hsueh) studies of the Classics.[27]

However, Hsu Ch'ien-hsueh had high regard for the emerging k'ao-cheng scholarship of his times, which we can see in his choice of scholars to work on the Ta-Ch'ing i-t'ung-chih (Comprehensive geography of the great Ch'ing realm) project of which he was appointed director in 1687. Hsu, for example, met Yen Jo-chü in Peking after the latter had failed the 1679 special examination and engaged Yen as his personal secretary. He then appointed Yen as an editor of topographical material for the geography project. Hsu also selected Hu Wei (1633–1714), Ku Tsu-yü (1631–1692), and Liu Hsien-t'ing (1648–1695), among others, for the project.[28]

Hu Wei and Yen Jo-chü began a lifelong friendship as a result of this association, and their mutual respect for each other's abilities allowed them to criticize and offer suggestions to each other in their efforts to promote exact scholarship. The appointment to the project of Ku Tsu-yü, perhaps the most qualified student of historical geography in his time, indicates the high degree of professionalism with which the Ta-Ch'ing i-t'ung chih project was carried out. Liu Hsien-t'ing, although he did not accompany the project when it moved to Soochow in 1690, became one of the most outstanding linguistic and geographical experts in Peking as a result of his collaboration on the Ta-Ch'ing i-t'ung-chih.[29]

When Hsu Ch'ien-hsueh, because of political infighting, was forced to leave Peking in 1690, personal links of patronage to his staff enabled Hsu to move the entire geography project, with imperial permission, to his estate near Lake T'ai southwest of Soochow. Presumably, imperial funds were also still available to Hsu. Lynn Struve has indicated that many Kiangnan scholars who might never have participated if the project had remained in Peking were now able to add their efforts to the compilation.[30] In addition, the project staff was able to take advantage of the Hsu collection of books previously brought together in a library known as Ch'uan-shih lou (Pavilion for the Transmission of the Truth).

Hsu Ch'ien-hsueh's financial support and patronage were a boon for scholars on his staff. Yen Jo-chü completed his *Ssu-shu shih-ti* (Explanation of place-names in the Four Books) during his decade of service under Hsu. A biography of Yen included in a T'ai-yuan gazetteer claimed Hsu required Yen's verification before anything could be included in the drafts of the *Ta-Ch'ing i-t'ung-chih*. Such exact scholarship involved critical collection and comparison of geographical materials. The methods used by scholars who participated in the geography project became the hallmark of evidential research during the Ch'ing. Yen and Hu Wei went on to apply their geographical expertise to dismantling geographical concepts that permeated Sung and Ming cosmological speculation.[31]

Hsu's use of his staff for his own scholarly and official advancement and prestige was an accepted part of patron-client relations (as in Europe) and was repeated frequently by others in the eighteenth century.[32] As Struve has pointed out, by providing imperially sanctioned scholarly organizations that would not be harassed by Manchu intervention and by promoting the transmission of scholarship in the late seventeenth century, "major director-patrons helped to create an atmosphere that was academically productive and intellectually stimulating as well." Ch'üan Tsu-wang (1705–1755) described the close interaction between Wan Ssu-t'ung (1638–1702) and Liu Hsien-t'ing on the *Ming History* project in Peking in the following terms:

> Mr. Wan [always] spent the whole morning sitting in a dignified manner looking over his books, or else sitting quietly with his eyes closed. But [Liu Hsien-t'ing] Chi-chuang liked to travel around and had to venture out each day, sometimes not returning for the better part of a month. When he did return, [Liu] would tell Mr. Wan all about his experiences, and Mr. Wan, for his part, would use books to verify [what Liu said]. When they finished talking, [Liu] would be off again.[33]

. . .

. .

Patronage in the Eighteenth Century

Writing in the eighteenth century, the historian Chang Hsueh-ch'eng recognized the important role that imperial patronage of scholarship played in the development of evidential studies. Chang noted that because of numerous imperial compilations, "many literary officials were rapidly promoted as compilers, and poor scholars, offering proposals through others, could quite easily get excellent secretarial jobs if they were good at bibliographical research; in this way they might even start careers of their own. Indeed there was a harvest of real talent."[34]

Imperial backing of *k'ao-cheng* scholarship came in the form of literary projects, which the K'ang-hsi and Ch'ien-lung (r. 1736–1795) emperors, in particular, actively promoted. Rejecting the link between Manchu repressive policies and the rise of evidential research, Tu Wei-yun has recently compared the official promotion of scholarship during the Ch'ing to the important role patronage played in European Renaissance scholarship. His account includes a comprehensive list of over 150 projects sponsored and published by the Imperial Household (Nei-wu-fu) during the seventeenth and eighteenth centuries that cut across all genres of Confucian scholarship.[35]

Many of these works were published in the Wu-ying-tien (Wu-ying Throne Hall, that is, the Imperial Printing Office) in Peking where, for example, numerous scholars worked as collators for the imperial editions of the *Notes and Annotations to the Thirteen Classics* and the *Dynastic Histories.* Established in 1673, the Wu-ying-tien employed both movable type and color printing techniques for publishing. One of its most notable works was the *Ku-chin t'u-shu chi-ch'eng* (Synthesis of books and illustrations past and present), which, despite the political clouds that surrounded its publication in 1728, was printed using movable type in ten thousand *chüan.* A font of some one and a half million copper type was cut for the project. Other works, such as the *P'ei-wen yun-fu* (Thesaurus arranged by rhymes) and the *Ch'üan T'ang-shih* (Complete T'ang poems), were published at the imperially sponsored printing office established by Ts'ao Yin in Yangchow.

Large groups of scholars were also employed at the start of each reign to compile the voluminous *Shih-lu* (Veritable records) of the preceding

Ch'ing emperors. Upwards of nine hundred scholars worked on the *Veritable Records* of the Ch'ien-lung Emperor's reign alone. In fact, the Ming and Ch'ing *Veritable Records* constitute the single most important source for the history of the period. A distillation of original records printed in seven thousand *chüan*, the Ming and Ch'ing *Veritable Records* exposed their compilers to government archives that no doubt often aided them in their own research.[36]

The most far-reaching compilation in terms of scope and content was the *Ssu-k'u ch'üan-shu* project. As we have indicated earlier, it was one of the most important vehicles for the transmission of Kiangnan evidential scholarship to Peking. Heavily biased in favor of Han-Learning and *k'ao-cheng* research, the editors who carried out this ambitious project initiated a well-publicized nationwide search for every written work in the empire. They then engaged in a critical review of every work available to them, selected books worthy of inclusion in the collection, and carefully collated from the best extant editions final versions of those works chosen for inclusion.[37]

Outstanding scholars in various fields were appointed to evaluate and collate books in their respective specialities. A frequent beneficiary of the director Chi Yun's (1724–1805) patronage, Tai Chen worked on the mathematical, astronomical, and calendrical texts included in the "Astronomy and Mathematics" (*T'ien-wen suan-fa*) section, for example, and Shao Chin-han (1749–1796), who had much in common with his friend Chang Hsueh-ch'eng, had special charge of books in the category of history. No less than ten thousand titles were reviewed, of which about one-third finally were copied into the imperial manuscript collection. More than 360 scholars officially worked at the apex of a staff of several thousand.[38]

Patronage of scholars continued on a large scale when the number of academies expanded after 1733. Because of their increased importance in local affairs, education officials were now held responsible for supervising charity schools and academies in their areas of jurisdiction, in addition to their earlier duties in county and prefectural schools. Directors of education (*hsueh-cheng*), the third highest ranking official in a province after the governor-general and governor, became an important source of academic patronage in provincial and educational activity. Members of secretarial staffs (*mu-yu*) and teachers were hired at all levels of the administrative and educational hierarchy on the basis of personal relationships that developed between provincial and local officials.[39]

During his term as director of education in Anhwei from 1771–1773, the Peking patron Chu Yun (1728–1781), for example, gathered around him one of the most distinguished groups of scholars to have served any scholar-official during the Ch'ing dynasty. Because a director of education had no official staff of his own, the normal practice was for him to hire personal secretaries and pay them out of his own income. Chu was interested primarily in the collection and preservation of rare books and manuscripts. Hence, he employed a number of Han-Learning scholars on his secretarial staff for projects such as editing and reprinting the *Shuo-wen chieh-tzu* (Analysis of characters as an explanation of writing) dictionary. Among those he employed were Sun Hsing-yen (1753–1818), Hung Liang-chi (1746–1809), Wang Chung (1744–1794), and Huang Ching-jen (1749–1783). All became major figures in late eighteenth-century academies.[40]

Chu Yun was also a close friend of established scholars such as Tai Chen, Wang Nien-sun (1744–1832), and Shao Chin-han, all of whom were frequent visitors to Chu's office in T'ai-p'ing prefecture. It was there that Chang Hsueh-ch'eng, Chu Yun's former pupil and a frequent recipient of Chu's patronage, met with Shao Chin-han, and the two began discussing their common interests in history. Wang Hui-tsu (1731–1807), best known as a legal secretary, was also a part of this group, sharing Chang's and Shao's concern for indexes and bibliographic tools to facilitate historical research. Discussing the Anhwei group, Kawata Teiichi has aptly written:

> Scholars who bequeathed works that with hindsight are highly valued, men who each had highly individualistic personalities . . . competed sharply with each other over scholarship at the same time that they interacted under the auspices of patrons. This Ch'ien-lung and Chia-ch'ing [r. 1796–1820] phenomenon, in addition to being interesting from the point of view of intellectual history, represents a fascinating example of human relationships.

. . .

Chu Kuei (1731–1807), Chu Yun's younger brother, succeeded Yun in 1780 as director of education in Fukien. During his two years there,

Chu Kuei did a great deal to improve scholarship and patronize promising scholars. Hung Liang-chi, after serving on various staffs, took advantage of his appointment in 1792 as director of education in Kweichow to patronize classical scholarship there.[41]

Pi Yuan (1730–1797) was one of the most important patrons of Han Learning and evidential research in the eighteenth century. A follower of Hui Tung (1697–1758), the founder of Han Learning, Pi Yuan employed noted *k'ao-cheng* scholars on his secretarial staffs to promote scholarship wherever he held office. Such patronage was a source of his prestige as a scholar-official.[42] During his appointments as governor in Shensi and Honan in the 1780s, he had as members of his staff many young scholars. Chang Hsueh-ch'eng visited Pi in 1787 when Pi was still governor of Honan. Chang tried to gain Pi's backing for an ambitious bibliographical project. The latter, which Chang knew would require the labors of many scholars, was the *Shih-chi k'ao* (Critique of historical writing), a massive study of historical bibliography modeled after Chu I-tsun's (1629–1709) 1701 *Ching-i k'ao* (Critique of classical studies). Along with his proposal, Chang Hsueh-ch'eng submitted copies of some of his earlier historiographical writings. This procedure seems to have been the normal way for scholars to seek patronage for their works.[43]

Pi Yuan accepted Chang's proposal and was able to obtain for Chang the directorship of an academy in Honan in 1788. Pi also established an office for the project, where Chang supervised and directed research by several scholars. These included Wu I (1745–1799), a noted epigraphist, Ling T'ing-k'an (1757–1809), a specialist in the *Record of Rites,* and once again Hung Liang-chi. As a governor, Pi chould channel official funds to this sort of enterprise. Ling T'ing-k'an, for example, had been serving the epigraphist Weng Fang-kang, then director of education in Kiangsi, before joining Pi Yuan's staff.

The chief drawback with such forms of patronage was that they were often unreliable. When officials were transferred (three years was the usual limit for most posts), scholars frequently had to travel to new sites with their patrons or find new patrons. Shortly after Pi Yuan was promoted to Governor-General of Hu-Kuang (Hunan and Hupei) late in 1788, Chang Hsueh-ch'eng soon lost his teaching position in Honan. He served the director of education in Anhwei before regaining Pi Yuan's patronage. In 1790 Chang was again working on the *Shih-chi k'ao* with a small staff that Pi had provided him. The project was never brought to completion, however, and Chang's manuscripts were lost during the Taiping Rebellion (see chapter 6).[44]

When Chang rejoined Pi Yuan in 1790, Pi's staff of scholars at Wu-ch'ang, Hupei, was working on a follow-up to Hsu Ch'ien-hsueh's continuation of Ssu-ma Kuang's (1019–1086) *Tzu-chih t'ung-chien* (Comprehensive mirror of history). Chang, along with others, participated in this chronological survey of Sung and Yuan dynasty history. In 1792, the completed drafts were sent to the more senior Shao Chinhan and Ch'ien Ta-hsin for editing, revision, and correction.

Many other scholars served Pi Yuan. Liang Yü-sheng (1745–1819), who gave up hope for an official career after failing the provincial examinations eight times, and Lu Wen-ch'ao (1717–1796), a respected scholar and teacher, edited the *Lü-shih ch'un-ch'iu* (Master Lü [Pu-wei's] Spring and Autumn Annals) for Pi Yuan in 1788. Chiang Sheng (1721–1799), a follower of Hui Tung's Han-Learning movement, assisted Pi in collating the *Shih-ming* (Explanation of names) dictionary. Ch'ien Tien (1744–1806), a relative of Ch'ien Ta-hsin, worked on the continuation to Ssu-ma Kuang's chronological history. Lu Wench'ao, Wang Chung, and Sun Hsing-yen all helped Pi Yuan collate the long neglected text of the *Mo-tzu* (see chapter 2 for the controversy this aroused).[45]

· ·

Patronage Under Juan Yuan

While serving as director of education from 1793–1795 in Shantung (Pi Yuan was then governor), Juan Yuan began a pattern of aiding, recommending, and promoting men of learning that was to continue throughout his official career. Chiao Hsun (1763–1820), a Yangchow relative and distinguished scholar in his own right, went to Shantung to serve on Juan's staff and later accompanied Juan to Chekiang. Sun Hsing-yen was appointed circuit intendant in Shantung when Juan was serving there and had, as a result, frequent contact with Juan's secretarial staff. These included Wu I and Kuei Fu (1736–1805), the latter having served earlier as copyist for the Shangtung bibliophile Chou Yung-nien (1730–1791, see chapter 4) before coming to Juan's staff.

It is interesting that during his stay in Shantung, Sun Hsing-yen used his official position as an opportunity to carry out archaeological research, attempting to identify the tombs of Confucius' disciples and of several emperors. In a similar way, Juan Yuan, during his tenure in Shantung, used his position as director of education to compile, under Pi Yuan's direction, a catalog of inscriptions on stone and bronze in that province. Juan also saw to it that a shrine commemorating the Later Han classicist Cheng Hsuan, to whom most Ch'ing dynasty Han-Learning scholars traced themselves, was rebuilt. Also serving as an official in Shantung during this period was Chuang Shu-tsu (1751–1816), a nephew of the Ch'ang-chou New Text scholar Chuang Ts'un-yü (1719–1788). Juan Yuan had close ties with several scholars from Ch'ang-chou; moreover, he had studied in Yangchow under Li Tao-nan (1712–1787), an examination disciple of Chuang Ts'un-yü.

In 1795, when Juan was transferred to Chekiang as director of education, he employed more than forty Chekiang scholars in Hangchow to compile under his direction a dictionary of the Classics entitled the *Ching-chi tsuan-ku* (Collected glosses on the Classics), which revived pre-T'ang annotations of the Confucian Canon. It was the most complete collection of synonyms and ancient glosses to follow in the tradition of the *Erh-ya* (Progress toward correctness) dictionary. Juan invited Tsang Yung, whose great-great-grandfather had been a pioneer in Han Learning, to assist in the project. In 1798, Tsang became the chief compiler. Many of those who worked on the project were students at the Ch'ung-wen Academy in Hangchow.[46]

In addition, Juan invited noted evidential scholars such as Chiao Hsun, Ch'ien Ta-hsin, and Ling T'ing-k'an to Hangchow to help him compile the *Ch'ou-jen chuan* (Biographies of mathematical astronomers —see chapter 2). Juan also took an interest in maintaining libraries for collections of rare books. In 1797 Juan visited the famous Ningpo library known as the T'ien-i ko (Pavilion of Everything United Under Heaven) and ordered its owners to compile a catalog of their collection (see chapter 4).

Returning from Peking to Chekiang in 1799 as acting governor (he became full governor in 1800), Juan picked up where he had left off as director of education. Using the rooms in which the *Ching-chi tsuan-ku* had been compiled, he established the Ku-ching ching-she (Refined Study for the Explication of the Classics) Academy. During this period, Juan selected the Ling-yin and Chiao-shan monasteries to house provincial collections of rare books. Juan engaged Tsang Yung once again in 1800, this time to help collate the *Shih-san-ching chiao-k'an chi* (Collation notes to the *Thirteen Classics*), a work that when completed in 1805 firmly established Juan Yuan's reputation as a scholar-official.[47]

After promoting scholarship during his official appointments in Kiangsi (1814–1816) and Hupei (1816–1817), Juan was appointed governor-general first in Liang-Kuang (Kwangtung and Kwangsi), where he served from 1817–1826, and then in Yun-Kuei (Yunnan and Kwei-chow), a post he held until 1835. During his tenure in Canton, in addition to founding the Hsueh-hai T'ang and compiling the *Huang-Ch'ing ching-chieh,* Juan brought outstanding scholars from Kiangnan to supervise the compilation of the *Kuang-tung t'ung-chih* (Comprehensive gazetteer of Kwangtung) in 1819. He invited the Yangchow Han-Learning scholar Chiang Fan to act as editor of this important undertaking and the T'ung-ch'eng Sung-Learning scholar Fang Tung-shu (1772–1851) to serve as assistant compiler. The impact on Cantonese academic life of several Kiangnan scholars, whom Juan patronized during this time, was felt even before the Hsueh-hai T'ang was established.[48]

At times it must have been difficult to keep contending views from clashing. Patronage was not always partisan, and secretarial staffs often included scholars of different persuasions. Juan Yuan presided over a number of intense clashes among his staff. In 1812, Chiang Fan, a follower of Hui Tung, had completed his *Record of Han-Learning Masters of the Ch'ing Dynasty,* one of the first attempts to set forth the history of Ch'ing scholarship from the viewpoint of its current dispensation, and thus legitimate Han Learning. Even before Juan Yuan had this work published in Canton in 1818, however, scholars were already voicing their complaints over Chiang's biased selection of scholars.

In a letter to Chiang Fan dated September 23, 1817, the peripatetic Kung Tzu-chen (1792–1841) listed ten misgivings he had concerning Chiang's book. Kung contended that the Han Learning-Sung Learning distinction was inappropriate and suggested that Chiang change the title to *Kuo-ch'ao ching-hsueh shih-ch'eng chi* (Record of classical-learning masters of the Ch'ing dynasty), and thereby avoid partisan issues (see chapter 6). Chiang Fan did not follow Kung's recommendations, but apparently as a concession Chiang did compile a work entitled *Record of the Origins of Sung Learning During the Ch'ing Dynasty.*

The controversy continued unabated after Chiang's collection of biographies was published. Fang Tung-shu, now under Chiang Fan's supervision in the *Kuang-tung t'ung-chih* project, took issue with Chiang's slighting of Sung Learning. In defense of the more orthodox T'ung-ch'eng school, with which he was associated, Fang began writing what was to become a major polemic against all aspects of what he considered Han-Learning pettiness and shortsightedness. Entitled *Han-hsueh shang-tui* (An assessment of Han Learning), the work was completed during the years Fang lived in Canton (1822–1826) and was presented to Juan Yuan in 1824. By then, Fang Tung-shu was teaching in Juan Yuan's yamen.[49]

Juan Yuan had written an introduction to Chiang Fan's collection of biographies in which he praised Han Learning because it was based on sources close to the time of the sages, before Taoism and Buddhism had been incorporated into Confucianism by *Tao-hsueh* scholars. The same introduction pointed out, however, that the aim of Ch'ing classical scholarship was to restore the purity of the "subtle words of great principles" (*ta-i wei-yen*) contained in the Classics and at the same time rid Confucianism of Buddhist and Taoist ideas. Using what in effect amounted to a New Text and Sung-Learning emphasis on "great principles," Juan was trying to have it both ways. His position in the Chiang-Fang debate is intriguing. It suggests that, while he was in Canton, Juan attempted to bring Han-Learning methods of scholarship to bear on Sung-Learning moral and theoretical concerns (see chapter 6).[50]

In the eighteenth century, evidential scholars accepted patronage and official staff employment whenever and wherever they could find them. They eagerly took commissions to compile classical works, historical texts, or local gazetteers; in addition they taught at academies. These patterns continued into the nineteenth century, until the Taiping Rebellion put an abrupt end to such academic enterprises. Moreover, because scholarly publishing during the Ch'ing was for the most part not a commercial venture, the technical works that scholars produced had to be published at their own expense, if not at the expense of a patron who could engage the copyists and xylographers to complete the task. David Nivison has explained: "A writer, then, had to find a patron whose fortunes were steady and whose loyalty was unshakable."

In return, scholars had to supply the textual expertise necessary to carry out their tasks as they moved about the country following or looking for patrons. They had to be prepared to collate classical texts, gather materials for local histories, or reconstruct flawed classical and historical documents. This institutional framework gave evidential scholars an opportunity to make scholarly contacts, see rare books, and work on important projects. In addition, the competition and desire for prestige was felt by patron and scholar alike. Officials vied for scholarly recognition, which only a talented staff of scholars could provide. Emperors competed with earlier emperors (for example, the Ch'ien-lung Emperor vis-à-vis the K'ang-hsi Emperor) to demonstrate the superior scholarly achievements of their own reigns.[51]

· · ·

Academies in the Kiangnan Academic Community

One major factor that distinguished Ch'ing scholars from their predecessors was the function of academies in the development of a relatively autonomous intellectual community committed to evidential research during the seventeenth and eighteenth centuries. Before this time, literati usually had been political figures whose official roles frequently precluded their earning their living solely by an established intellectual occupation.[52]

Since the Sung dynasty a tension had existed between academies devoted to Neo-Confucian moral and philosophic training and government schools oriented toward "official studies" (kuan-hsueh). The latter were necessary to provide training for scholars who wanted to rise in the examination hierarchy. Private academies that flourished as Confucian centers of learning during the Sung and Ming periods, with some exceptions, were chiefly concerned with preparing students to become effective political and moral leaders. This goal presupposed an education that stressed moral cultivation and the study of the Four Books, the Classics, and the Histories.[53]

By the late Ming the growth of academies had been phenomenal; they became centers for Neo-Confucian discourse on the one hand and dissent and political protest on the other. The appearance of the Tung-lin Academy and the Fu She (Return [to Antiquity] Society) at the apex of a loose association of groups, clubs, and parties during the early seventeenth century brought out into the open the covert political orientation of academy education. A formidable organization dedicated to supporting its members in the factional struggles that dominated late Ming politics, the Fu She in William Atwell's words "formed probably the largest and most sophisticated political organization in the history of traditional China."[54]

· ·
Seventeenth-Century Literati Societies

There was, however, another side to the political groups, clubs, and associations that flourished in the final years of the Ming dynasty, a scholarly trend that was transmitted through the intellectuals who survived the Manchu invasion. In addition to their function as political organizations, "literary societies" (she) also served as forums for the revival of ancient learning. This stress on antiquity also carried with it a commitment to evidential and empirical scholarship. Ōkubo Eiko has suggested: "The fact that Ku Yen-wu and Huang Tsung-hsi [1610–1695] were connected to the Fu She indicates that evidential scholarship arose from the midst of the Fu She." Atwell has noted that Ku's and Huang's statecraft interests "represent the culmination of the kind of scholarship so important in Fu She circles during the 1630's and 1640's."

Men like Ku Yen-wu, Huang Tsung-hsi, and Wan Ssu-t'ung are best understood as transitional figures in the Ming-Ch'ing transformation of Confucian discourse. Recognizing the need for scholarly and educational reform, members of the associations turned toward precise, evidential methods of research in order to reconstruct classical texts. Stressing Han dynasty sources, members showed glimmerings of the epistemological changes in the Han-Learning wave to come. There was a distinct attack on the imprecise scholarship and anti-ritual stance taken by the "left-wing" T'ai-chou school (see chapter 2).

The "return to antiquity" (fu-ku) movement nourished a reappraisal of recent scholarship and encouraged a return to the Classics and the Histories as the pillars of Confucian discourse. Seventeenth-century groups such as the Tu-shu She (Society of Book-Readers) in Hangchow took as their goal "broad learning" (po-hsueh), which reaffirmed the centrality of book learning for Confucian education. Huang Tsung-hsi, a participant in the activities of the Tu-shu She, praised the leader of the group, Chang Ch'i-jan (1600–1664), for the philological and geographical expertise he applied to classical scholarship.[55]

In the tense years after the Manchu conquest, some of the she and other such groups survived. Most, however, shut down. Legally prevented from overt political dissent, members of these groups favored informal discussions under private auspices. Men of learning hoped thereby to avoid publicity and the interference with scholarly matters that public display made inevitable. At the same time that Manchu policies toward Chinese intellectuals hardened to prevent the recurrence of late Ming factional strife, she more and more became strictly scholarly associations and poetry societies. Manchu policies included the 1652 ban on the founding of private academies, a ban on the gathering of intellectuals for political purposes, and bans on student demonstrations. In 1660–1661, more stringent measures were taken through the prosecution of Kiangnan literati for back taxes due the government.[56]

Numerous groups of scholars and Ming loyalists in Kiangnan continued to meet under the guise of poetry societies that sprang up during the Ming-Ch'ing transition period. Ku Yen-wu and his close friend Kuei Chuang (1613–1673) participated in the Ching-yin shih-she (Ching-yin Poetry Society), which was one of the largest such groups in the early years of Manchu rule. Founded in 1650, the Ching-yin Society met regularly until one of its members was executed for his involvement in compiling a banned work on the fallen Ming dynasty. Ku Yen-wu and others narrowly escaped involvement in the case. Particularly during the Shun-chih Emperor's reign (1644–1661), Chinese scholars had to be careful of their association with anything having to do with delicate aspects of the fallen Ming dynasty.[57]

Yen Jo-chü, for example, was closely connected to the Wang She

(Society of Expectations), which his father Yen Hsiu-ling (1617–
1687), had helped to found in Huai-an, Kiangsu. Although it was devoted mainly to poetry, for which Yen Jo-chü showed no talent, the
Wang She provided Yen with his intellectual training. Through its
auspices Yen was recognized by other scholars. A frequent visitor to
the Yen home during those years was the "eccentric" painter and
Ming loyalist Fu Shan (1607–1684). Remembered for his moving re-
sistance to the invitation forced upon him by the K'ang-hsi Emperor
(r. 1661–1722) to participate in the 1679 special examination (see
above), Fu Shan had numerous scholarly discussions with the much
younger Yen Jo-chü (who did participate, albeit unsuccessfully, in the
1679 examination). Their discussions ranged from the uses of bronze
and stone inscriptions for correcting mistakes in the Classics and Histories to the nature of scholarship itself.[58]

Perhaps the most representative scholarship undertaken by literati
during the early years of Manchu rule can be discerned among the
group of scholars who, led by Huang Tsung-hsi, Wan Ssu-ta (1633–
1683), and Wan Ssu-t'ung, called themselves the Chiang-ching hui
(Society for the Discussion of the Classics). Established in 1658, the
Chiang-ching hui proved to be an important turning point in Kiangnan
scholarship. Devoted to the elucidation of the Classics and the Histories, the more than twenty scholars who gathered together until 1679
affirmed the need for evidential research methods to reconstruct the
Confucian tradition.

The Chiang-ching hui was closely connected in time to Huang Tsung-
hsi's reopening of Liu Tsung-chou's (1578–1645) Cheng-jen Academy
in Shao-hsing, Chekiang, in 1667. Because Liu was Huang's revered
teacher, Liu Tsung-chou's views were the basis for discussions at the
regular meetings of the Chiang-ching hui. Although ostensibly followers
of Wang Yang-ming, both Liu Tsung-chou and Huang Tsung-hsi had
reacted against the excesses to which members of the "left-wing" T'ai-
chou school had gone into their propagation of Wang Yang-ming's
philosophy during the sixteenth century.[59]

The format of the Chiang-ching hui meetings allowed for discussion
of the Five Classics, with Huang the chief lecturer. Of particular interest to the scholars who gathered together was research on the Confucian rites (li) that had been scorned by the "left-wing" school. Both
Wan Ssu-ta's and Wan Ssu-t'ung's expertise on Confucian ritual grew

out of these discussions. In addition to mastering the accumulated scholarship on the *Li-chi* (Record of rites), *I-li* (Decorum ritual), and the *Chou-li* (Rituals of Chou), scholars attending the Chiang-ching hui carefully studied the texts character by character, comparing them with earlier glosses, in order to determine as precisely as possible the correct readings and proper exegesis. Agreement on the centrality of rituals became the cardinal point that united Han-Learning scholars throughout the Ch'ing dynasty. Their emphasis on decorum and institutions was a direct reaction against what they considered the Neo-Confucian misuse of principle (*li*) for abstract and speculative studies.

Showing no interest in an official career, Wan Ssu-ta took as his task the lifelong study of Confucian ritual. Describing Ssu-ta's research, Huang Tsung-hsi wrote:

Reflecting deeply on the Classics, [Ssu-ta] believed that unless we master all the Classics, we will not be able to master even one. Unless we grasp the errors [contained in] the commentaries and notes [to the Classics], we will not be able to master all the Classics. Unless we can use one Classic to elucidate another, then we will have no way to grasp the errors in the commentaries and the notes. What does it mean to master all the Classics in order to master one? Discrepancies between classical texts are [characterized] by lack of detail here and [plenty of] detail there, agreement here and variation there. We must use the detailed [version] to supplement [the meaning of] the cursory and make use of the variations to seek out the agreements. This [approach] is what scholars should apply their thoughts to, [according to Ssu-ta].[60]

. . .

Wan Ssu-ta attacked the authenticity of the *Rituals of Chou* in a work entitled *Chou-kuan pien-fei* (Demonstrations that the *Rituals of Chou* are inauthentic). Building on suspicions that had accumulated since the Southern Sung, Wan carefully compared the text with the other Classics and concluded that the *Rituals of Chou* was not the work of the Duke of Chou. It was, he contended, clearly a forgery done by a later hand. Wan was critical of the fact that the *Rituals of Chou* text had been used to support Wang Mang's (r. 9–23) brief usurpation. He regretted that later Confucians had lost the ability to distinguish the true from the false.

Wan Ssu-t'ung, Ssu-ta's younger brother, became famous for his tire-less efforts to make the *Ming History* project a success. Moved by an obligation to the fallen dynasty and the men and women who had per-ished with it (and not intimidated by the sensitivity of the topic), Wan immersed himself in Ming historical documents, refusing to accept stipends or official status. Ssu-t'ung's interests, however, included classi-cal scholarship, for which his *Ch'ün-shu i-pien* (Doubts and criticism of various books) was most representative. Wan Ssu-t'ung chose to cir-cumvent *Tao-hsueh* interpretations and return to an emphasis on the Classics themselves.[61]

Wan Yen (1637–1705), Ssu-ta's and Ssu-t'ung's nephew, for over ten years assisted in the compilation of the Ming History. Among Wan Yen's writings was "a letter concerning the significance of doubts about the *Documents* discussed with several of my colleagues," in which Wan revealed that one of the items for discussion at the Chiang-ching hui had been the vexing problem of the authenticity of the Old Text por-tion of the *Documents.* Throughout the Ch'ing period, one of the key debates among *k'ao-cheng* scholars was the furor over the Old Text chapters (see chapter 5). About this time, Wan Ssu-ta's son, Wan Ching (1659–1741), studied geography under Yen Jo-chü, one of the chief figures in this debate. In addition, Wan Ssu-t'ung had debated the *Shang-shu* question with Yen when they met. Although Ssu-t'ung re-fused to accept the arguments Yen Jo-chü put forward in his *Shu-cheng,* Wan Yen, perhaps as a result of Yen's influence, gave four rea-sons why the Old Text chapters should be regarded with suspicion. All were arguments that Yen employed in his demonstration that the Old Text chapters were forgeries.[62]

Members of the Chiang-ching hui associated the subjective nature of Neo-Confucian discourse with empty and futile speculation. Huang Tsung-hsi's critique of the Neo-Confucian cosmograms in his *I-hsueh hsiang-shu lun* (On the images and numbers in the studies of the *Changes*) was an attack on the Neo-Confucian cosmological ordering of the uni-verse. It set the stage for Hu Wei's definitive *I-t'u ming-pien* (Discerning clearly the diagrams in the *Changes*). On another front, Huang thought that the ancient content of the classical tradition could be revived through exacting research and analysis. This perspective caused Huang some problems, however, when it came to the *jen-hsin Tao-hsin* (mind of man and mind of Tao) passage in the Old Text chapter of the *Documents* entitled "Ta Yü mo" (Counsels of Yü the Great). At first Huang contended:

> The sayings of the sages do not rest simply on graphs and phrases but rather on meanings and principles [*i-li*]. If there are no flaws in the latter, then the graphs and phrases do no harm by being different. For example, the saying concerning the mind of man and the mind of Tao in the "Counsels of Yü the Great" could not have been forged by someone coming after the three dynasties [Hsia, Shang, and Chou].
>
> . . .

Later, Huang changed his mind. In his preface to Yen Jo-chü's *Shu-cheng,* Huang related how Chu Ch'ao-ying (1605–1670), a colleague and friend, had once voiced his fears concerning attacks on the Old Text chapters: "If not for the 'Counsels of Yü the Great,' studies of principle [*li-hsueh*, the Chu Hsi school] would never have survived. How can it be a forgery?" Huang then summarized how Yen had demonstrated to his satisfaction that the *jen-hsin Tao-hsin* passage represented a forged composite taken from the *Hsun-tzu* and Confucius' *Analects.* Huang concluded:

> Therefore, these sixteen characters [in the passage] represent a serious swindling of *li-hsueh*. [Chu] K'ang-liu [that is, Ch'ao-ying] may not agree, but as for me, [Yen's demonstrations] deserve my words of support for posterity. All of [Yen] Pai-shih's [Jo-chü] proofs are correct.
>
> . . .

Yen's demonstration that the "mind of Tao and the mind of man" passage in the "Ta Yü mo" was lifted from the *Hsun-tzu* was a cause célèbre in the attack on Sung-Ming *Tao-hsueh* during the Ch'ing.[63]

A small-scale research group, the scholars associated with the Chiang-ching hui represented an important transition from Ming intuitional studies to Ch'ing evidential scholarship.

The Development of Official Academies

The Manchu policy toward private academies was at first very strict. Existing academies were watched very carefully, and after 1652 no new private, that is, independent, academies were allowed to be established. Government schools oriented to the examination system, on the other hand were permitted to open as early as 1645, under the control of local education officials and examination supervisors. This policy was not new, however. Since imperial suppression of private academies began in the late sixteenth century, official control was an important government aim.

To avoid the divisive factionalism that had permeated Ming academies, the K'ang-hsi Emperor issued proclamations in 1713 and 1715 sanctioning the establishment of carefully supervised "charity schools" (*i-hsueh*) by local communities to complement the existing prefectural and county schools in each province. The remarkable growth in numbers of charity schools during the eighteenth century signaled an attempt by the imperial court to make officially controlled charity schools into replacements for private academies in the education system. Local merchants and gentry responded favorably to the proclamations because of the need for education facilities for growing numbers of students.

Recognition that academies were necessary in order to provide an education to a burgeoning pool of students began late in the K'ang-hsi Emperor's reign. Local initiative was needed to alleviate the shortage of schools, and there clearly was a ready pool of private capital for such enterprises. In order to prevent private academies from reasserting their traditional dominance as the highest centers of Confucian learning, the Yung-cheng Emperor in 1733, after a hiatus that had lasted approximately ninety years, initiated a new policy for establishing officially controlled academies in the provinces. They were modeled after the officially controlled charity schools that already had proven successful.[64]

By relying on a combination of local support and official supervision, the Manchu authorities hoped to prevent the recurrence of the activist academies that had troubled late Ming rulers. Provincial officials were held responsible for what went on in the areas where they served. The imperial court could expect quick news of any local disturbances that were related to local schools and academies. Public funds were set aside both for helping to construct new academies and for stipends for scholars and students in residence. Initially only twenty-one such academies were established in eighteen provinces, but this policy touched off an increase in the number of academies throughout the eighteenth century.

Although distinctions between private, public, and official schools were not clearly demarcated during the Ch'ing period, three fairly distinctive types of academies emerged after 1733. In the first place, there remained a small number of private academies that had survived since the fall of the Ming and were primarily devoted to Sung and Ming Neo-Confucian teachings. The latter schools were private in the sense that they were not controlled by official sources. These traditional academies were soon surpassed in number by newly established government schools founded in county, prefectural, and provincial capitals. This second type of academy was therefore more official than private and was from the start devoted mainly to instruction that would serve students preparing for the examination system. These official academies drew students from "community schools" (she-hsueh), charity schools, and county and prefectural schools. They were in effect equivalents of earlier Sung and Ming schools oriented exclusively toward official studies. Here students mastered the technique of writing acceptable eight-legged essays (popularly known as shih-wen, lit., "contemporary-style essays"). Success on the latter could lead to success on the examinations and an official career. Student recruitment reflected the administrative jurisdiction of the capitals where academies were located. Provincial schools in the Lower Yangtze Region in particular enjoyed clear-cut academic advantages.

As had been the case in Ming academies oriented toward the examination system, however, students at government schools were encouraged to read and memorize collections of eight-legged essays issued by bookstores. There were those who feared that a system of plagiarism might become entrenched. Many felt that students no longer read the Classics or the Histories; instead they learned how to adapt model essays into what they hoped would become passing examination papers.[65]

In response to this felt crisis in education, a third hybrid-type of academy emerged after 1750, one devoted to the reading and exegesis of the Classics and the Histories rather than preparation for the examinations alone. It was at such semi-official schools, founded at the initiative of provincial officials who were committed to an education that stressed content over mimicry, that *k'ao-cheng* scholarship penetrated the existing educational system. These schools were thus semi-private and independent but still officially patronized. In the process, the *k'ao-cheng* challenge to the Chu Hsi formalism dominating schools and academies oriented to the examination system came out into the open. Han Learning, which began in mid-eighteenth-century Soochow, soon swept through the academies there and often replaced Sung Learning as the vogue of instruction in many other Kiangnan schools.[66]

Official Academies and Evidential Scholarship

In Ch'ang-chou prefecture, the most prestigious eighteenth-century academies associated with evidential scholarship were the Lung-ch'eng Academy in Wu-chin county and the Chi-yang Academy in Chiang-yin county. Founded in the late Ming, the Lung-ch'eng Academy had Shao Ch'i-tao (1717–1768) as its head when students studied *k'ao-cheng* techniques there. Two of the most prominent scholars who studied there at this time were Huang Ching-jen and Hung Liang-chi. Both applied their academic training to the special research projects described earlier in the discussion of scholarly patronage. One of the most famous eighteenth-century evidential scholars to teach at Lung-ch'eng was Lu Wen-ch'ao, who taught there from 1788 and was made head of the academy in 1790. Lu continued to serve in this capacity until his death in 1796.

The Chi-yang Academy in Chiang-yin had existed since the early Ch'ing period, but it was not until Lu Wen-ch'ao was appointed director there in 1756 that it became famous for *k'ao-cheng* scholarship. Later, in 1823, Li Chao-lo was appointed director, a position he held until 1840. Li, a native of Yang-hu county, began his studies at Lung-ch'eng in 1789 under Lu Wen-ch'ao's tutelage. There he acquired an interest in mathematics, mathematical astronomy, and geography, in addition to the standard fields of philology and phonology. Li became well known for his wide-ranging studies, which included major contributions in geography and local history. The New Text scholar Wei Yuan (1794–1856) praised him for his efforts to synthesize Han- and

Sung-Learning fields of inquiry, efforts which Wei attributed to the influence of the Ch'ang-chou New Text school.[67]

The Chi-yang Academy remained the most prominent school in Chiang-yin until the appearance of the Nan-ch'ing Academy that the nineteenth-century "self-strengthener" Tso Tsung-t'ang (1812–1885) helped to establish in 1884. It is interesting that one of the major projects completed at the Nan-ch'ing Academy was an authoritative continuation to the *Huang-Ch'ing ching-chieh,* which was published in 1886–1888. This undertaking carried the pedigree of evidential research into the late nineteenth century.

At the pinnacle of the hierarchy of schools in Soochow was the Tzu-yang Academy (named after Chu Hsi's home area and academy) established by Chang Po-hsing (1652–1725), an adherent of the Ch'eng-Chu orthodoxy that the imperial court promoted. This focus changed, however, with the appointment of Shen Te-ch'ien (1673–1769) as head of Tzu-yang in 1751. Although more famous for his poetry and literary criticism than his textual scholarship, Shen during his stay at Tzu-yang brought together at one time students who became three of the most influential Han-Learning scholars of the eighteenth century: Ch'ien Ta-hsin, Wang Ming-sheng, and Wang Ch'ang (1725–1807).

All three were strongly influenced by the Han-Learning movement that Hui Tung and his followers popularized in Soochow at this time. In addition, one of their teachers at Tzu-yang impressed on them the importance of historical studies in classical research. This was Wang Chün (1694–1751), who previously had taught at the An-ting Academy in Yangchow. Wang stressed "ancient learning" (*ku-hsueh*) in his role as a teacher at both An-ting and Tzu-yang. Ch'ien Ta-hsin subsequently admitted that his own interests in historical studies developed as a result of Wang Chün's influence on him. Later Ch'ien Ta-hsin was appointed director of his alma mater in 1789, teaching there for the final sixteen years of his life. During his tenure at Tzu-yang, over two thousand students matriculated there. By all accounts, they mastered "ancient learning" and "sought the truth in actual facts" (*shih-shih ch'iu-shih*). Graduates of Tzu-yang during this time went on to distinguish themselves as specialists in mathematics, geography, paleography, technical statecraft, and historical studies.[68]

Yangchow's most prestigious academies were the An-ting and Mei-hua Academies. Ping-ti Ho has indicated that An-ting and Mei-hua were established during the Ch'ing dynasty exclusively for children of salt merchants, demonstrating that salt merchant families "probably received the best schooling in the empire." A number of scholars associated with Han Learning and evidential research taught at both academies. These included Tai Chen's protégé, Tuan Yü-ts'ai (1735–1815), as well as Wang Nien-sun, Sun Hsing-yen, and Hung Liang-chi.

K'ao-cheng studies had become important in Yangchow through the efforts of Wang Mao-hung (1668–1741), who applied evidential research techniques to the study of the Chu Hsi tradition. Another important figure in Yangchow academics was Ch'en Tsu-fan (1675–1753), who took over the directorship at An-ting after leaving Tzu-yang in Soochow. The more formative influences in Yangchow, however, were Hui Tung and Tai Chen. Chiang Fan (1761–1831), for instance, studied for a time in Soochow under Hui Tung's Han-Learning followers. Chiang later compiled a controversial genealogy of Han Learning (see chapter 6). Although from Anhwei, Tai Chen lived and taught in Yangchow from 1756–1762, initially at the home of Wang An-kuo (1694–1757), father of Wang Nien-sun. The latter acquired his training in phonology and etymology from Tai, which he then transmitted to his son, Wang Yin-chih (1766–1834).

An influential Han-Learning advocate in his own right, Wang Chung came to Hang Shih-chün's (1696–1773) notice around 1770, when Hang, a leading historian, was head of An-ting Academy. He quickly took Wang on as his student, and, as a result, Wang made rapid progress in his classical studies. Describing the academic environment in Yangchow at this time, Wang Chung wrote:

> At this time, ancient learning [ku-hsueh] was popular. Hui Tung of Yuan-ho [in Soochow] and Tai Chen of Hsiu-ning [in Anhwei] were admired by everyone. In the area north of the Yangtze River [that is, Yangchow], Wang Nien-sun promoted ancient learning and [Li Ch'un (1734–1784)] did the same. Liu T'ai-kung [1751–1805] and I came along and continued [their efforts]. We worked hard together to realize our potential, and each of us formed his own [speciality of] learning.
>
> . . .

Likewise, Chiao Hsun, a relative of Juan Yuan, studied at the An-ting Academy in 1779, and the k'ao-cheng historian Chao I was director there from 1784–1786. Both An-ting and Mei-hua remained centers of learning in the nineteenth century.

In Nanking, the Chung-shan Academy, founded at the beginning of the Yung-cheng Emperor's reign, attracted many of the premier scholars of the eighteenth century. Lu Wen-ch'ao taught there between 1772–1778 and again in 1785–1788. Sun Hsing-yen, destined to become a celebrated textual scholar, entered the academy as a student in 1774. He studied Han Learning first under Lu Wen-ch'ao and then under Ch'ien Ta-hsin, when the latter became a director in 1778. Later Sun was honored by being named head of his former school in 1811. Yao Nai (1732–1815), a Sung-Learning follower of the T'ung-ch'eng school, developed a large student following in Nanking when he taught at Chung-shan in the late eighteenth and early nineteenth centuries. Despite his orthodox beliefs, Yao recognized the importance of evidential research. The Chung-shan Academy maintained its prominence into the nineteenth century under Yao's and Ch'eng En-tse's (1785–1837) guidance.[69]

Ch'i Shao-nan (1706–1768), who was employed as an editor and collator for numerous literary projects in Peking, studied at the Fu-wen Academy in Hangchow in 1720–1721. Later in 1750 he was appointed director of Fu-wen, a position he held for ten years. Wang Ch'ang, completing a distinguished career of textual scholarship, took charge of Fu-wen in his last years, before retiring to Soochow. Another famous academy in Hangchow that was oriented toward evidential scholarship was the Ch'ung-wen Academy. Lu Wen-ch'ao taught at Ch'ung-wen in 1779, transferring to Hangchow's Tzu-yang Academy in 1780. From 1795–1798, Juan Yuan (then Chekiang director of education) employed students from Ch'ung-wen on a Han-Learning project to compile the *Ching-chi tsuan-ku* dictionary. Evidential research remained dominant at both Ch'ung-wen and Tzu-yang in the nineteenth century.[70]

As we have seen, when Juan Yuan was governor of Chekiang in 1801, he established with the help of local salt merchants the Ku-ching ching-she in Hangchow. Juan noted that he had founded the academy to honor Cheng Hsuan and Hsu Shen, both Later Han classicists. In an effort to link a classical education with a commitment to "concrete studies" (*shih-hsueh*), Juan, who was also an amateur patron of science, saw to it that students at the Ku-ching ching-she would be examined in astronomy, mathematics, and geography, in addition to their literary and textual studies. This belief that an education oriented solely to the examination system was ill-suited to dealing with the practical problems then facing Chinese officials was felt among literati several decades before the Opium War. Juan Yuan, T'ao Chu (1779–1839), Ho Ch'ang-ling (1785–1848), and other leading provincial officials became aware of the need for educational and bureaucratic reform simply out of their concern for problems internal to the Ch'ing administrative system (see chapter 6).[71]

Juan Yuan invited two outstanding *k'ao-cheng* scholars, Sun Hsing-yen and Wang Ch'ang, to share the directorship of the Ku-ching ching-she. Sun took charge of classical studies and Wang was responsible for literature. Han-Learning and Sung-Learning topics filled the pages of the *Ku-ching ching-she wen-chi* (Prose collection of the Ku-ching ching-she), which included essays by teachers and students. Also included were essays on astronomy and calendrical studies.

Sun Hsing-yen was very much involved in the complex philological problems related to the Old Text and New Text chapters of the *Documents*. Frequently in charge of collation projects, Sun had employed the Soochow textual scholar Ku Kuang-ch'i (1776–1835) around 1798 to reconstruct and collate Mei Tsu's (fl. 1513) *Ku-wen Shang-shu k'ao-i* (Investigation of variances in the Old Text *Documents*), an important Ming dynasty work that held a pivotal position in the growing criticism of the Old Text chapters.[72]

Sun himself produced a highly regarded work on the topic entitled *Shang-shu chin-ku-wen chu-shu* (Notes and annotations to the New and Old Text *Documents*), which remains one of the most reliable sources for reference. Yen Jo-chü's seventeenth-century demonstration that the Old Text chapters were a forgery dating from the late third or early fourth century A.D. had been widely heralded in the eighteenth century. Scholars such as Sun Hsing-yen were proceeding to investigate problems that Yen had not dealt with. Sun Hsing-yen's preoccupation with this question was imparted to his students at the Ku-ching ching-she.[73]

The Hsueh-hai T'ang was established by Governor-General Juan Yuan in Canton in 1820 on the model of the Ku-ching ching-she and other Kiangnan academies. To counteract the popularity of Sung-Ming Neo-Confucian themes then still popular in Canton, Juan stipulated that classical and historical topics taught at the Hsueh-hai T'ang should be supplemented by concrete studies. With the Ku-ching ching-she and the Hsueh-hai T'ang as precedents, academies devoted to classical and practical education began to spring up elsewhere during the nineteenth century. Breaking with the usual organization of academies, Juan Yuan established eight directors (*hsueh-chang*) for the Hsueh-hai T'ang, instead of the accepted practice of a single principal (*shan-chang*). For future vacancies, all directors were to be appointed by the governor-general after nomination by the rest of the directors. This policy was initiated in Juan's words because "this academy is devoted intensively to the mastery of concrete studies. It is necessary to have eight directors, each employing his own strengths, all working together to enlighten and guide, so that we can expect men of talent to arise daily."[74]

Students were carefully selected from all over Kwangtung, but they were drawn predominantly from other academies in Canton. As a minimum requirement students were expected to have attained "imperial student" (*kung-sheng*) status before beginning their studies at the Hsueh-hai T'ang as "regular students" (*chuan-k'e sheng*) or "adjunct students" (*fu-k'e sheng*). "Junior students" (*t'ung-sheng*) were not accepted. This admission procedure meant that the Hsueh-hai T'ang would only accept students who already had mastered the eight-legged essay or attained gentry status through purchase of a *kung-sheng* degree. Although training for the examinations was not given at the Hsueh-hai T'ang, students were expected to continue their careers by taking the appropriate examinations required for official appointment.

Financed by a combination of official subsidies (much of which came from Juan Yuan's personal income), merchant investments (for example, from hong merchants), and rent from a generous endowment of land (Juan arranged for the land to be given to the school), students at the Hsueh-hai T'ang were given monthly stipends in addition to monetary prizes for superlative studies and examination papers. Outstanding examination essays were printed in the *Hsueh-hai T'ang chi* (Collected writings from the Hsueh-hai T'ang), along with prose and poems by the eight directors. In addition, students were required to keep diaries concerning their readings, and once a month students and teachers would dine together and discuss their progress.[75]

Four sessions of classes were scheduled each year with two of the eight directors in charge of each session on a rotating basis. The two directors presented lectures twice a month and set topics for examinations and essays. They were responsible for grading and evaluating students. Examinations were held at the end of each session. After 1834, students were expected to study in depth a single work, which could be drawn from the Classics, the Histories, poetic collections, or the writings of Chu Hsi. Library books were donated by Juan Yuan, other high officials in the province, and teachers in the academy. In addition, the Hsueh-hai T'ang did its own publishing and rented out its woodblocks to other publishing companies.

A written take-home examination given to the students at the Hsueh-hai T'ang provides us with an interesting glimpse into a Confucian academy oriented toward *k'ao-cheng*. To answer the essay questions on the Classics and Histories required precise and explicit use of evidential research methods. Administered in December 1868, the examination was divided into a series of eight questions summarized as follows:

(1) In the *Li-chi Cheng tu k'ao* (Examination of Cheng Hsuan's readings for the *Record of Rites*), it is shown how Cheng Hsuan emended characters in the *Li-chi*.[76] You are to examine in detail and verify Cheng's phonological and etymological evidence for his emendations.

(2) The *Kung-yang chuan-chu yin Han-lü k'ao* (Examination of citations of Han law in the notes to the *Kung-yang Commentary*) indicates that Ho Hsiu made use of the Han dynasty laws of his time to verify his annotation of the *Kung-yang* text. Examine his claims on the basis of the laws of today and extend his conclusions.

(3) In the "*Sung-shih* Sun Shih chuan shu-hou" (Afterword to Sun Shih's biography in the *History of the Sung*), it is explained that Sun Shih was regarded as a great Northern Sung Confucian. Yet [Huang Tsung-hsi's] *Sung-Yuan hsueh-an* (Studies of Sung and Yuan Confucians) does not mention him. Read Sun's biography and explain the omission.

(4) Imitate an inscriptional record written in parallel prose style titled "Inscriptional Record on the Reopening of Wen-lan Hall on Yueh-hsiu Hill."

(5) Compose a prose-poem (*fu*) in ancient style (*ku-t'i*) on the theme of plum blossom fields.

(6) Compose a poem to the title "Wandering Immortals Beyond the Five Ridges (that is, in Kwangtung)," adhering to the rhyme scheme in Kuo P'u's (276–324) "The Wandering Immortal."

(7) Compose a seven-character-to-a-line ancient-style poem (*hsing*) on steamboats.

(8) Compose a seven-character-to-a-line poem on travels in regulated verse in the form of a miscellaneous chant poem (*yung*) in eight parts.

"Deadline for the examination to be handed in is January 2, 1869. If there are any smudge marks, changes, or cut-and-paste additions, the examination paper will not be accepted. Please return to the Hsueh-hai T'ang all examination papers that have accumulated since the time [1859] when earlier papers were printed in the third series [of the *Hsueh-hai T'ang chi*]. They will be used to complete the printing of the fourth series [1886]."[77]

. . .

Intended to be major steps forward in Confucian education in the late eighteenth and early nineteenth centuries, the Ku-ching ching-she in Hangchow and the Hsueh-hai T'ang in Canton were nonetheless outgrowths—and thus representative of—the Han-Learning educations received in academies founded in Kiangnan during the Ch'ien-lung Emperor's reign.

Academies during the Ch'ing dynasty served communities of scholars, many of whom engaged in secular, intellectual pursuits, not preparation for imperial examinations. The academic debates described in chapter 5 were articulated within the framework of academies. Such debates and discussions transmitted to students the key issues of scholarship. In this manner, academies helped to promote the research environment that made possible the advancement in Chinese textual scholarship during the eighteenth century.

Teacher-pupil relationships in traditional Chinese society had previously allowed knowledge transmitted by the teacher only to be accepted dutifully, not improved upon, by the student. This phenomenon had been especially true of the schools of learning during the Han dynasty. Among the latter, the special theories or techniques of a master had been passed down unchanged through generations of disciples by personal teaching. *K'ao-cheng* scholars reacted against this passive absorption of knowledge, which demanded humble attentiveness, in favor of independent inquiry.

Despite some attempts by eighteenth-century Han-Learning scholars in Soochow to revive more traditional master-disciple relationships, most scholars in Kiangnan recognized the cumulative nature of scholarship and emphasized preparing students to make contributions to the accumulated literature. Such relationships were characteristic of the changes wrought by evidential scholars in many academies. The scholars who associated with Tai Chen went beyond the traditional confines of the master-disciple relationship. They emphasized making new discoveries, in addition to the restoration, preservation, and transmission of knowledge.[78]

The low academic prestige of the imperial schools and the growing criticism of Sung-Ming *Tao-hsueh,* which included in many cases the public rejection of the Chu Hsi orthodoxy entrenched in the examination system, enabled "independent," officially controlled academies to become centers of Confucian *k'ao-cheng* scholarship. They provided the institutional context in which empirical methods were learned and transmitted. Lu Wen-ch'ao, for instance, kept notebooks recording his findings when he taught at Chung-shan Academy in Nanking and Lung-ch'eng Academy in Ch'ang-chou (see chapter 5). In a similar manner, Ch'ien Ta-hsin's reading notes were produced during his years of teaching and research, after retiring from official life. The diary he kept while teaching at Tzu-yang in Soochow indicates that Ch'ien was constantly taking notes on the rare editions and epigraphical specimens that came to his attention.

Teaching and classical research became attractive alternatives, as we shall see more clearly, to an official career. The institutionalization of evidential scholarship was possible only under conditions in which intellectual activity in general had been previously accepted and embodied in public institutions enjoying far-reaching autonomy. Academies in Kiangnan became the centers for continuity and consensus in *k'ao-cheng* scholarship. Within this expanding intellectual community in Kiangnan, the rise of evidential scholarship as the dominant form of Confucian discourse became intellectually and institutionally possible.

Academy appointments in the Lower Yangtze cities were symbols of prestige and high scholarly position. Scholars such as Ch'ien Ta-hsin and Sun Hsing-yen were honored by being named head of the academies where they had once been students. Tuition support, prizes, and recognition served to reinforce the prestige of education in the official academies and to reward academic promise and achievement.[79]

. . .

The Transformation of
Literati Roles

In the early Ch'ing, it became considerably more difficult than in Ming times for scholars in the Lower Yangtze to obtain higher degrees, because of restricted regional quotas designed to control the phenomenal success of Kiangnan literati on the examinations. Without a degree, advancement in the official hierarchy was generally precluded. Ping-ti Ho has noted that the late Ming state did not restrict the numbers of those who achieved licentiate status (*sheng-yuan*, that is, students who qualify for the examination system). In the early years of Manchu rule, however, imperial quotas for degree candidates were reinstated and strictly enforced. In 1661, the minimal quotas of 1575 became the maximum. As the population rapidly expanded, quotas for officials did not keep pace. Chung-li Chang and Ho both have estimated that the total number of licentiates remained roughly half a million in the seventeenth and eighteenth centuries. Substantial increases occurred only after the Taiping Rebellion, when the government began to pad quotas in return for financial contributions to state coffers.

Moreover, a substantial number of official positions were taken by Manchus and descendants of Chinese bannermen who had served the Manchus before 1644. These limitations were later exacerbated by long overdue increases in quotas for graduates in the late eighteenth and nineteenth centuries. An official career thus was effectively ruled out for most of those who succeeded in the examinations. While the number of gentry was expanding, not enough new positions in the bureaucracy were created to take care of the surplus of qualified candidates. Literati who passed the lower examinations were forced into a host of new occupations. By 1800 only *chin-shih* degree-holders could be reasonably sure of eventually receiving official posts, and even they frequently had to wait several years for an appointment.[80]

Scholars began to seek employment as secretaries to officials, tutors in wealthy families, academy teachers, and the like in order to make a living. Frederic Wakeman has pointed out that, by the early nineteenth century, local gentry had moved into other fields as well. These included mediation of legal disputes, supervision of waterworks, recruiting and training local militia, and collection and remittance of local taxes to yamen clerks. Although this perspective explains the pressure to create new career patterns for the intelligent and ambitious, it does not account for the internal factors that drove seventeenth-century literati toward *k'ao-cheng* scholarship in the first place. It is doubtful whether institutional factors alone would have occasioned the transformation of academic discourse that occurred during the Ch'ing dynasty. This institutional account does illuminate, however, why so many literati were attracted to scholarly careers. Although scholarship usually reflects social institutions, it is also the case that social institutions are changed in order to bring them into line with emerging norms of academic discourse. In the following pages, we will focus on the social consequences that resulted from the institutionalization of evidential research during the eighteenth century.[81]

Teaching as a Career

The emergence of a specialized intellectual community in Kiangnan can be discerned first in the numerous examples of scholars who during the eighteenth century spent major portions of their lives, despite high degree status, teaching in academies and lower-level schools in the educational hierarchy. Ch'ien Ta-hsin, perhaps the most respected scholar-teacher of his day, was in many ways typical of the scholars of his age. Although on occasion he held official appointments (he retired to private life in 1776), for most of his career he was employed as a teacher in prestigious Kiangnan academies. This occupation complemented his prodigious research on epigraphy, history, phonetics, calendrical science, and geography. Like Ch'ien, the distinguished textual scholar Lu Wen-ch'ao spent much of his career in education, serving at one time or another at many of the most acclaimed academies in the Lower Yangtze.

After beginning his teaching career in 1777 at an academy in Chihli, Chang Hsueh-ch'eng went on to hold five academic posts by the time he was forty-nine in 1787. During these years, waiting for an official appointment (he received the *chin-shih* degree in 1778), Chang was able to combine teaching with research and writing. He was interested in the theory and practice of teaching and prepared a textbook for his students containing literary selections depicting good style and solid learning. When Chang was finally on the verge of receiving an official appointment in 1787, he turned it down, realizing that his talents were academic and not administrative.

Hang Shih-chün and Ch'üan Tsu-wang (1705–1755) both accepted teaching posts at academies in Kwangtung in 1752. Hang remained there until 1755, when he returned to his home in Hangchow. Hang finished his academic career teaching at the An-ting Academy in Yang-chow until 1770. Ch'üan Tsu-wang had taught at an academy in Shao-hsing, the heartland of the Eastern Chekiang school founded by Huang Tsung-hsi, before moving to Kwangtung. Sheng Pai-erh (fl. ca. 1756), whose study of the astronomy in the *Documents* was included by Juan Yuan in the *Huang-Ch'ing ching-chieh,* taught in academies for over a decade. Sheng's expertise in astronomy and trigonometry influenced many of his students. Li Fu-sun (1764–1843), a friend of Lu Wen-ch'ao, Ch'ien Ta-hsin, Wang Ch'ang, and Sun Hsing-yen, spent a major portion of his career teaching in academies and writing on the Classics and Histories.[82]

The New Text philologist Ch'en Shou-ch'i (1771–1834), after taking his *chin-shih* degree in 1799, began his distinguished career teaching in academies in Hangchow (including the Ku-ching ching-she), before returning to Fukien, his native province. Retiring from official life in 1810, Ch'en taught at academies in Fukien over the next two decades. For a final example we can include Yao Nai, who during a career spanning four decades as head of various academies in Kiangnan gathered many followers around him. Although Yao was a Sung-Learning advocate, his students were taught to recognize the advantages evidential research offered in textual scholarship.

Teaching was not only a source of income during the eighteenth century but also a source of prestige and a basis for research and writing. In contrast to Sung-Ming scholars, whose exact scholarship, if any, was strictly a personal matter and was not transmitted in schools, *k'ao-cheng* scholars used academies to further their own research and in the process transmitted their methods and conclusions to their colleagues and students. Chung-li Chang has indicated that the upper gentry (all gentry above licentiates and purchased degree-holders) monopolized teaching positions in official and private academies. Through most of the nineteenth century, according to Chang, "a sizable proportion of gentry were deriving an income from their work in the teaching profession." What Chang is describing is the continuation of an earlier phenomenon. In Chang's calculations, about one-third of the gentry studied (whose biographies contained relevant data) were teachers. Although Chang's sources are somewhat biased, his count does have some value as an indication of the changing activities of upper gentry.

The literati who achieved the highest income and enjoyed the highest prestige and influence in their teaching careers were the lecturers in urban academies in Kiangnan. After 1733, teachers in these academies were formally appointed to their positions by the joint decision of the governor-general, governor, and provincial director of education. The hierarchical organization of the Ch'ing education system, with academies at the apex, suggests very strongly that the prestige and competitiveness of appointments to academies were significant factors in the Kiangnan educational milieu of the eighteenth century.[83]

· ·

Private Research and Secretarial Staffs

Closely linked to academies established after 1733 was the rise of professional scholars who rarely held official positions. This phenomenon had begun in the seventeenth century, as we have seen, with the careers of men such as Yen Jo-chü and Hu Wei, who were primarily research scholars employed on secretarial staffs. The mathematician Mei Wen-ting (1633–1721) and the scholar-bibliophile Yao Chi-heng (1647–1715?) are other examples of seventeenth-century literati who devoted their careers to research and writing. Mei stressed mastering mathematics and astronomy to resolve difficulties in calendrical science and spent a large portion of his time studying the scientific methods and discoveries introduced by the Jesuits. Devoting himself exclusively to scientific research and writing after his father's death in 1662, Mei never held office, although he was actively patronized in Peking by Li Kuang-ti (1642–1718) and drafted the astronomical section of the *Ming History* project. Disinclined toward an official career, Yao Chi-heng also retired to private life, spending his most productive years in philological research and book collecting.

In the eighteenth century, we find that many participants in the

Han-Learning movement devoted major portions of their careers to research and writing. Hui Tung, the creator of the slogan "Han Learning," remained a private scholar throughout his life, working in his studio, which was famous for its library. Chiang Sheng (1721–1799) and Chiang Fan, both followers of Han Learning, also did not hold official positions, preferring instead to rely on the patronage of officials and influential scholars in order to carry on classical research. Many scholars like Liang Yü-sheng, after repeated failures, abandoned the "examination life" and began work privately on critical studies of the Classics and *Dynastic Histories*. Likewise other scholars such as Wang Chung and Chiao Hsun, after initial failures, turned away from the examination system, securing employment as secretaries on the staffs of various officials.[84]

As we have seen from the careers of Wang Ming-sheng, Chao I, and Ch'ien Ta-hsin, early retirement from official position in order to carry out research and teaching was frequent. Hsu Tsung-yen (1768–1819), a member of a distinguished and wealthy family, resigned from office after brief service and lived out his life in retirement in Hangchow; his studies focused on literature, the Classics, astronomy, and mathematics. Tai Chen's disciple Tuan Yü-ts'ai retired from official life in 1780, pleading poor health at the age of forty-five. During the rest of his life (he died in 1815) he wrote extensively. His chief contributions to classical philology were his analysis of the characters in the *Shuo-wen chieh-tzu* and a study of the *Documents,* entitled *Ku-wen Shang-shu chuan-i* (Textual variances in the Old Text *Documents*), each the fruit of years of research. Sun Chih-tsu (1737–1801), a noted Hangchow bibliophile (see chapter 4), retired from office in 1775. He spent the remainder of his life in research and book collecting.[85]

In addition to positions on secretarial staffs, many Ch'ing scholars who were not independently wealthy were employed on local history projects, such as compiling county, prefectural, and provincial gazetteers financed by local gentry. Chang Hsueh-ch'eng and Tai Chen were among the busiest compilers of local gazetteers (*fang-chih*) during the eighteenth century. Tai worked on several gazetteers before taking a position on the staff of the *Ssu-k'u ch'üan-shu* project. Chang Hsueh-ch'eng was in many ways responsible for raising local history to a level of academic esteem. Pi Yuan recognized the informational value of local gazetteers. While he was governor of Shensi alone he ordered the compilation of some thirty-three local histories; he was also quick to make use of Chang's experience with this form of historical writing when Chang came to him in 1787 seeking patronage. Sun Hsing-yen also participated in the compilation of several Shensi local histories when he served on Pi Yuan's staff in Sian from 1781–1785. The passion local officials had to compile or revise local gazetteers for their assigned areas of responsibility continued into the nineteenth century.[86]

Non-Bureaucratic Sources of Income

Except for those scholars whose families were independently wealthy, teaching and secretarial services were important sources of income for literati during the Ch'ing dynasty. Chung-li Chang estimates that a yearly income of some 350 taels of silver (486 silver dollars) represented the average income one could expect from teaching in the nineteenth century. For those who chose a bureaucratic career, a civil servant of the first rank in the nineteenth century received a salary (actually the smallest part of his income) of 189 taels (250 silver dollars) plus 90 piculs of rice (12,000 pounds). An ordinary county magistrate, as a seventh-rank civil official, received an annual salary of 45 taels (62.5 silver dollars) and 22.5 piculs (3,000 pounds). These salaries were supplemented by a "nourish incorruptibility allowance" (yang-lien) that started at 600 taels (833 silver dollars) annually for magistrates and advanced by the nineteenth century to 20,000 taels (27,778 silver dollars) a year for a governor-general in more backward areas such as Yunnan or Kansu. Provincial education officials received lower overall incomes than other provincial civil servants. Chang estimates their salary to be roughly 1,500 taels (2,083 silver dollars) annually, which includes income from customary contributions and gifts for educational services. Some provincial directors of education received as much as 4,000 taels (5,555 silver dollars) of yang-lien.

Clan and merchant backing for local schools and academies also helped defray teacher salaries and student stipends and prizes. Such finances took four basic forms: school-land endowment, capital investment, urban real estate, and regular government payments. Part of the funding for the Hsueh-hai T'ang in Canton, for example, came from local merchants, including a sizable investment of over 1,607 taels of silver (2,232 silver dollars) at fixed rates of interest by the senior hong merchant (Howqua) Wu Ping-chien (1769–1843). In addition, Juan Yuan saw to it that funds and land were donated to the academy.[87]

We have seen that during the eighteenth century it was usually regional and local officials in such key positions as governor and director of education who enlisted the help of secretarial assistants. Secretarial positions were at times monopolized by close-knit groups of scholars from Kiangnan, particularly in the cases of Pi Yuan's and Chu Yun's overlapping staffs. Appointed for their literary expertise, such assistants were not burdened with the administrative duties of the officials they served. It was important to the reputations of officials as scholars in their own right to have literary men on their staffs. In this way they could sponsor scholarship and research and receive much of the credit.

Provided with shelter, food, and often with concomitant appointment at a nearby academy, literati who served on such staffs had a yearly income averaging roughly 560 taels of silver (778 silver dollars) in the nineteenth century. Secretarial assistants of high provincial officials received much more. Governors-general and governors could channel official funds directly to their staffs. Provincial education officials, on the other hand, were forced to dig into their own salaries or seek financial contributions from local merchants and gentry.

When the imperial government's support for literary projects and schools is included in our picture of the emergence of an academic community during the Ch'ing dynasty, we can detect a sophisticated and far-reaching institutional network for the promotion of scholarship. To encourage government students, the Ch'ing government in 1733 set up a quota of stipends to be distributed to students in each county. Stipends were granted by the provincial director of education on the basis of academic merit. Students and teachers were eligible for stipends, and in some academies there were monetary rewards for students who wrote the best essays. This support was separate from the travel subsidies supplied to participants in higher examinations. In addition, the Ch'ien-lung Emperor presented sets of the Classics and Histories to the Chung-shan, Tzu-yang, and Fu-wen Academies in 1751. He was adhering to a 1685 precedent initiated by his grandfather, the K'ang-hsi Emperor. The cumulative result was the promotion of scholarly careers that existed independent of the bureaucratic world of official position and examination status.[88]

Research Institutions in Kiangnan

One of the conditions for the relative autonomy in the academic in-quiry promoted by academies, literary projects, and literary secretarial staffs was that scholarship be apolitical. Manchu policy deliberately aimed at creating an apolitical orientation on the part of the Chinese gentry, especially the Kiangnan literati, through overt educational pres-sure and the limiting of political discussion. This policy created the necessary institutional preconditions for the emergence of evidential research as an independent field of inquiry and discourse. Provided by powerful patrons with a degree of economic security and a modicum of social insulation from political reprisals, *kao-cheng* scholars during the eighteenth century competed for the fame and priority in discovery that exact scholarship could bring (see chapter 5).

A failure to recognize the professionalized academic roles of Ch'ing literati has prevented an accurate appraisal of the ties between Confu-cian precise scholarship and research institutions in late imperial China. For example, Joseph Ben-David, in his discussion of the lack of contin-uous scientific growth in Europe before the seventeenth century, has stressed supporting institutions and organizational forms as the keys to the formation of the scientist's role in contemporary society. Ben-David dismissed the Confucian tradition because of what he called its "moral-social" emphasis, which did not provide the appropriate institutional support for the emergence of the scientific role in China. Our account should demonstrate that in late imperial China academic institutions ex-isted and functioned as research sites, which incorporated many ele-ments of precise scholarship. These could have been adapted (indeed they were in the twentieth century) to the needs of modern science with less effort than we have supposed.[89]

Our analysis leaves still open the question of why science in China did not play the central role it did in early modern Europe (see chapter 2). Had the natural sciences been recognized and developed as important individual disciplines in eighteenth-century China, the organizational mechanisms required for their growth and development were readily available. These communication patterns will be further explored in chapter 4.[90]

Four

Scholarship, Libraries, and Book Production

Public discourse in an academic community requires that the accumulated literature of a discipline be widely available. The organization of knowledge must allow it to accumulate accessibly and thereby increase the speed with which further work is carried out and recorded. In addition to the academies and forms of patronage discussed in chapter 3, *k'ao-cheng* scholars required a communications network of bibliophiles, printers, and booksellers that would serve their expanding fields of research. Libraries and printing were pivotal in the emergence of evidential scholarship within the Kiangnan academic community.[1]

The effects of print on the development and growing sophistication of scholarship is a relatively well-known phenomenon in European history. Printing has been recognized as the most obvious connection between science and the general movement of Renaissance humanism. Elizabeth Eisenstein has described the advent of printing in Europe

Figure 5 Cutting Type
Source: *Ch'in-ting Wu-ying-tien chü-chen-pan ch'eng-shih* (Peking, 1776).

as an epochal event that marked the end of scribal culture and the beginning of typographical culture. Pointing out that in theory historians agree that the invention of movable type was revolutionary but in practice overlook its importance, Eisenstein has contended that our notions of "medieval" and "modern" can best be understood in terms of the differences between scribal and typographical cultures. The preservative power of print hastened the recovery of antiquity and the development of techniques for investigating past events. As a result, classical scholarship and historical research became subject to "continuous cognitive advance."[2]

Although Denys Hay has warned against the tendency to exaggerate the impact of printing and credit it with causing a rapid change in human consciousness in Europe, he has admitted that printing encouraged textual accuracy and was instrumental in the growth of private libraries in the sixteenth century. The pace of intellectual change was thereby quickened, and traditional notions of authority were challenged by new discoveries. Scholars and teachers found it easier to extend knowledge of their subjects independently of large book-owning institutions.[3]

Printing was more than just a technical phenomenon in Western civilization. It became an effective technique for bringing together scattered writings of representative thinkers. For research, it enabled scholars to transmit their results quickly to others interested in similar problems. In neither China nor the West, however, did printing replace professional correspondence as the fastest means of communication (see chapter 5). The difference was in the number of people reached. Printed books were one of the first uniform and repeatable commodities based on mass production.[4]

Printing in China has been studied as a technological phenomenon, but its cultural impact remains poorly understood. Invented during the T'ang dynasty, printing developed during the Sung and Ming periods into a sophisticated art that by the late Ming included multicolor printing, woodblock illustration, the use of copper movable type, and woodcut facsimiles of earlier editions. In the process, scholarship, book production, and libraries, according to K.T. Wu, "formed a triad in the cultural fabric of the nation."[5]

Classical learning revived during the Sung dynasty in part due to the increased circulation of books and diffusion of classical texts brought on by the spread of printing. One of the principal functions of acade-mies (*shu-yuan*) during the T'ang and Sung dynasties was as repositories for books used by scholars and students. These collections were made possible by the widespread use of woodblock printing for classical texts. Such publishing enterprises in turn brought an increased interest in scholarship and education. Editions were, however, still too small and prices still too high to make book collecting a possibility for most scholars.[6]

Woodblock printing reached its peak in technical sophistication in the mid-sixteenth century with the rise of scholar-printers in Soochow, Nanking, Hangchow, Hui-chou, and Yangchow in Kiangnan and some-what more commercially oriented printers in Chien-yang, Fukien. Hu Ying-lin (1551–1602), one of the most famous scholar-collectors during the Ming, noted that, during the late Ming period, Soochow was the cen-ter for quality printing and that printing shops there were staffed by outstanding xylographers. Fukien, the center for commercial publish-ing, produced a larger quantity of novels, dramas, and popular manuals (including medical handbooks) than elsewhere.[7]

In his description of the proliferation of books and manuals during the late Ming, Sakai Tadao has linked the spread of knowledge on every social level in the sixteenth and seventeenth centuries to the printing of numerous encyclopedias (*lei-shu*) during this period. Encyclopedias, according to Sakai, functioned as repositories and manuals of popular knowledge during the late Ming, in addition to serving as scholarly com-pendiums for students preparing for the imperial examinations. In this environment of readily available reference books, practical manuals, and popular compendiums of knowledge, Sakai has seen the roots of a book-oriented atmosphere conducive to the development of evidential scholarship and interest in the practical arts.[8]

. . .

Libraries in Kiangnan

Of first importance in the growing access to knowledge were bibliophiles. By locating sources and having them reprinted, they provided
the reference works necessary for coherent scholarly disciplines. The
close connections between bibliophiles and evidential research are evident in the library collections built up in the seventeenth and eighteenth centuries. Without such collections, textual scholars could not
have located the materials necessary for their research. The growth of
large libraries in Kiangnan and the concomitant printing and reprinting
of rare items made possible open communication of findings and provided new sources for critical inquiry.[9]

Hu Ying-lin, for example, took advantage of his father's official positions to satisfy his passion for books. The Hu family collection was
acquired mainly from bookstalls in Peking, Nanking, Soochow, and
Hangchow. Hu Ying-lin mastered the art of distinguishing rare items
from ordinary or forged editions, and this know-how served him well
in the late Ming book trade. In addition, Hu used his library for textual
research. While going through his books, Hu made numerous notes and
in the process became an expert in textual matters.[10] The legacy of the
Ming dynasty, when book collecting became a passion among literati, in
many ways set the stage for the Ch'ing wave of evidential research.
Cheuk-woon Taam has written:

> The period of the Ch'ing dynasty is undoubtedly the one in which the
> library achieved its greatest importance. The amazing development of
> libraries during these two hundred and sixty-seven years had overshadowed
> the library achievement of all the previous dynasties combined. Not only
> was the literary heritage of the past carefully preserved, but it was also
> augmented. The library activities thus became an invisible force behind
> the intellectual movement, and thus rendered to the literary world an in-
> valuable service.

. . .

Despite advances in printing, however, manuscript copying remained
the principal means that scholars employed to gather together materials
previously unpublished or for which woodblocks no longer survived.

Manuscripts formed a substantial portion of many libraries. In the Ch'ing period, manuscripts of earlier works were prized as collector's items, as were original and copies of rubbings of stone and bronze inscriptions. With regard to the latter, connoisseurs still favored exact copies of originals over printed versions. Scholars often received permission to visit a particular library and copy items that were not available elsewhere. Such copying was an important factor in the dissemination of information. Interesting aspects of scribal culture survived alongside printing in Kiangnan during the Ch'ing dynasty.[11]

Libraries in Kiangsu and Chekiang

Among Ming dynasty private libraries, the T'ien-i ko (Pavilion of Everything United Under Heaven) collection founded by Fan Ch'in (1506–1585) in Ningpo was the best known. Rich in items from the Sung and Yuan periods, such as early printed books, manuscripts, and epigraphic inscriptions made in the Northern Sung, the T'ien-i ko grew until it reached its zenith at the end of the eighteenth century. In 1774, Fan Mou-chu (1721–1780) sent 638 rare items from the T'ien-i ko to the *Ssu-k'u ch'üan-shu* commission, of which 473 were valuable enough to receive descriptive notice in the annotated catalog. Ninety-six rare items were actually copied into the imperial collection. Only the Ma brothers, salt merchants from Yangchow, presented more items. In recognition of the Fan family's contribution to scholarship, the Ch'ien-lung Emperor presented Fan Mou-chu with a set of the *Ku-chin t'u-shu chich'eng* (Synthesis of books and illustrations past and present) encyclopedia, an honor shared by only three other contemporary bibliophiles (see Table 5).[12]

Catalogs of the T'ien-i ko were compiled by some of the most prominent evidential scholars. Huang Tsung-hsi (1610–1695), founder of the Ch'ing Che-tung (Eastern Chekiang) school of scholarship, visited the T'ien-i ko in 1673 and wrote a discursive account of his findings there, in addition to preparing a catalog of its holdings. In 1738 Ch'üan Tsu-wang (1705–1755), a follower of Huang Tsung-hsi, visited the library and compiled a list of its rubbings of bronze and stone inscriptions. Ch'üan's efforts were followed up by the Han-Learning scholar Ch'ien Ta-hsin (1728–1804). In 1787, Ch'ien examined the library and, in collaboration with others, prepared a more comprehensive list of the rubbings in the collection. A catalog of the T'ien-i ko completed under Juan Yuan's (1764-1849) official orders listed over four thousand works in some 53,000 *chüan*, not including the ten thousand *chüan* of the *Ku-chin t'u-shu chi-ch'eng.* This catalog was printed, together with the list of 764 epigraphical items recorded by Ch'ien Ta-hsin, in 1808.[13]

During the Ming and Ch'ing dynasties Ch'ang-shu, near Soochow, was a center for book collecting. Among the collector-printers there, Mao Chin (1599-1659) was the most prolific. Esteemed for its high-quality printing and its precious Sung editions, Mao Chin's Chi-ku ko (Pavilion Reaching to the Ancients) was the source for the largest noncommercial production of books before the eighteenth and nineteenth centuries.[14] Mao Chin was willing to pay high prices for rare books, and as a result he accumulated a library of some 84,000 *chüan.* He began reprinting rarities in his well-ordered collection in 1628; his youngest son, Mao I (b. 1640), continued the work. In all, about six hundred titles were published by the Chi-ku ko. These editions included complete sets of the *Thirteen Classics,* the *Seventeen Dynastic Histories,* and a collectanea known as the *Chin-tai pi-shu* (Rare books of Ch'ien Ch'ien-i) containing 140 titles and printed in fifteen installments.[15]

Although criticized for their numerous errors due to some slipshod xylography, the Chi-ku ko versions of the Classics and the *Dynastic Histories* were highly prized editions. Among Mao's specialties was a process for making facsimiles of Sung editions by tracing every feature of the rare books he borrowed from other collectors. This process, known as "tracing Sung manuscripts" (*ying-Sung-ch'ao*), preserved the exact features of the many Yuan and Sung dynasty works that have since been lost. Because they were based on Sung recensions and readily available, Chi-ku ko editions were widely employed in textual research and collation. Tuan Yü-ts'ai (1735-1815) collated Mao I's reprint of a Sung edition of the *Shuo-wen chieh-tzu,* which in turn became the basis for Tuan's *Shuo-wen chieh-tzu chu* (Notes to the *Analysis of Characters as an Explanation of Writing*), the most important Ch'ing study of the *Shuo-wen* (see chapter 5). The historian Wang Ming-sheng relied on the Chi-ku ko edition of the *Seventeen Dynastic Histories* for his 1787 *Shih-ch'i-shih shang-ch'üeh* (Critical study of the *Seventeen Dynastic Histories*) because it had been a standard reference for over a century.[16]

Other noted seventeenth-century Ch'ang-shu bibliophiles included

Ch'ien Tseng (1629–1699?) and Chi Chen-i (b. 1630). A great-great-nephew of the scholar and poet Ch'ien Ch'ien-i (1582–1664), whose famous library of rare books had been engulfed by flames in 1650, Ch'ien Tseng took over what was left of Ch'ien-i's collection. He compiled a catalog of the collection and also wrote a detailed bibliographic study entitled *Tu-shu min-ch'iu chi* (Record of an earnest search in the interest of study) that listed 601 Sung and Yuan works in his collection. The study included precise, comparative annotations concerning editions. Such studies were considered an important part of the technical field known as the "study of editions" (*pan-pen-hsueh*). The latter provided the bibliographic basis for the textual work known as "collation scholarship" (*chiao-k'an-hsueh*). Chi Chen-i accumulated one of the largest libraries in Kiangnan. Much of his collection was purchased from duplicates in Ch'ien Tseng's library. Mao Chin and Mao I also exchanged duplicate copies of rare books with Chi Chen-i, and later Chi purchased a large portion of the Chi-ku ko collection.[17]

Chu I-tsun (1629–1709), and Huang Tsung-hsi were famous examples of Kiangnan scholar-bibliophiles during the early years of Manchu rule in Kiangnan. Chu I-tsun had built up a sizable private collection in Chia-hsing, Chekiang, by 1658. Fearing Chu might be implicated in the 1660 inquisition that resulted after the publishing of a banned account of the Ming dynasty, his family burned the collection. After his appointment to the *Ming History* project and the Hanlin Academy in 1679, Chu had access to the imperial library in Peking and was able to hire a copyist to reproduce important material. By 1699, Chu I-tsun's Chekiang collection had reached 80,000 *chüan*, and it was the major source for Chu's massive descriptive bibliography of lost and extant works on classical studies entitled the *Critique of Classical Studies*. Chu also had a large collection of stone rubbings and inscriptions for which he prepared a preliminary catalog.[18]

Huang Tsung-hsi collected a library of some 30,000 *chüan*, built up by visiting other collections and copying the rare books that his library lacked. Included were visits to Huang Chu-chung's (fl. ca. 1585) Nanking collection of 60,000 *chüan* between 1630–1641 and the T'ien-i ko in Ningpo in 1673. According to Ch'üan Tsu-wang, Huang Tsung-hsi was able to obtain, through funds provided by Wu Chih-chen (1640–1717), the rare editions in Chao Yü's (1689–1747) family library in Hangchow in about 1666. In addition, Huang had access to the Hsu family collection in Soochow, and he praised Hsu Ch'ien-hsueh (1631–1694), a major patron of scholarship during this period, for making his library available to scholars for research and copying. Similarly, Chang Shih-chün had access to a Sung edition of the *Kuang-yun* (Expansion of rhymes) in the Hsu family library, which he compared with another Sung edition he found in the Chi-ku ko. Chang's edition became the most widely used version of this important rhyming dictionary in the eighteenth century (see chapter 5).[19]

Lu Wen-ch'ao (1717–1796), for example, noted the centrality of Soochow scholar-bibliophiles since the Ming dynasty. In Lu's view, the Soochow collections added immeasurably to the stature of the prefecture as a cultural center. Sun Ts'ung-t'ien's (ca. 1680–1749) library in Soochow, known as the Shang-shan T'ang (Summum Bonum Hall), was a center for literati groups there. Besides his book collecting, Sun prepared a manual for book collectors entitled *Ts'ang-shu chi-yao* (Bookman's manual) in which he dealt with problems concerning acquisitions of books, copying, collation, binding, cataloging, and preservation.[20]

Yao Chi-heng (1647–1715?) was a seventeenth-century Hangchow bibliophile who also used his collection of rare books for a variety of textual projects. Yao's extensive holdings included a painting and antique collection. In addition, Yao maintained a collection of rare books that enabled him to determine to his own satisfaction that a number of works, including portions of such Classics as the *Documents,* were forgeries. Other noted Hangchow bibliophiles during the eighteenth century included the collation scholar and teacher Lu Wen-ch'ao, the textual critic Sun Chih-tsu (1737–1801), and the historian Hang Shih-chün (1696–1773), each of whom accumulated large libraries through years of effort.[21]

. .

The Eighteenth-Century Hangchow
Interlibrary Group

In the eighteenth century, Hangchow in particular was a mecca for book collectors and scholar-printers. The bibliophiles there serve as an excellent sample of the kinds of literary groups that were formed and

· Table 5 ·

Major Contributors to the *Ssu-k'u ch'üan-shu* Commission
(300 items or more)

Library and Rank	Location	No. of Items
1. Ma brothers	Yangchow	700 (approx.)
2. T'ien-i ko	Ningpo	638
3. Pao T'ing-po	Hangchow	626
4. Wang Ch'i-shu	Hangchow	542
5. Wu Ch'o (and son)	Hangchow	305

Note: Contributors of 500 items or more received a copy of the 1728 edition of the *Ku-chin t'u-shu chi-ch'eng* printed using copper movable type. Those who presented 100 to 500 items were awarded a copy of the K'ang-hsi edition of the *P'ei-wen yun-fu.*

the close friendships that promoted the exchange of information. Nancy Lee Swann has described in detail the emergence in Hangchow of what she has called an "interlibrary loan group" of seven libraries. This group served the owners and their friends. Six of the seven were located in the southeast portion of the walled section of metropolitan Hangchow, making them mutually accessible and for all practical purposes a library association. Without any apparent formal organization, bibliophiles there were building up their libraries by lending their books to each other for copying.[22]

The activities of the libraries in the Hangchow area were at their height in the period between 1740–1790. Swann points out that of the nine private donors whose presentations to the *Ssu-k'u ch'üan-shu* commission were accepted and numbered more than one hundred items, five came from the Hangchow library group. Three presented over three hundred items (see Table 5). Wang Hsien (1721–1770) seems to have been the central figure for this group of bibliophiles, but Sun Tsung-lien's (fl. ca. 1744) collection was also important as a gathering center. In a retrospective account that praised Wang Hsien's collection, the New Text scholar Kung Tzu-chen (1792–1841), also a Hangchow native, described the intimacy among those who frequented the literary group. All of the group exchanged visits, made loans of books, borrowed manuscripts, and shared collated texts. They also exchanged views on textual criticism as well as granting copying privileges for rare texts.[23]

Wu Ch'o (1676–1733) and Chao Yü made extensive use of each other's materials for scholarly research. In addition to exchanging books, they prepared introductory and bibliographical notes and accounts for each other's editions. Wu's library, known as the P'ing-hua-chai (Vase of Flowers Study), eventually was sold en masse to the Yangchow salt merchant Ma Yueh-kuan (1688–1755). Wu's son, Wu Ch'eng (ca. 1703–1773), spent years rebuilding his father's collection, punctuating the texts he found, correcting errors, and collating various editions.[24] Chao Yü spent three decades reviving his family's collection, major portions of which had been divided among scholar-bibliophiles such as Huang Tsung-hsi, Lü Liu-liang (1629–1683), and Wu Chih-chen. Chao Yü's son, Chao I-ch'ing (1710?–1764?), was also a noted book collector, and I-ch'ing used the family collection as the source for his annotations of the *Shui-ching chu* (Notes to the *Classic of Waterways*) and the *San-kuo chih* (History of the Three Kingdoms), both of which became embroiled in famous priority debates that will be discussed in chapter 5.

Before the nineteenth century, many of the greatest Kiangnan collections were made possible by capital earned in the salt trade (for instance, the Ma brothers in Yangchow). Pao T'ing-po (1728–1814), for example, came from an Anhwei family that had been salt merchants in Chekiang and established a home in Hangchow. It was through Pao T'ing-po's introduction that Wang Ch'i-shu (1728–1799?), whose family had amassed a fortune as Anhwei salt merchants, was initiated in 1745 into the Hangchow poetry club known as the Hsi-hu yin-she (Poetry Society of West Lake). Pao and Hang Shih-chün were senior members of this literary group, which overlapped to a considerable degree with the interlibrary association.

Both Pao T'ing-po and Wang Ch'i-shu were prodigious book collectors and were among the four men in the empire who presented over five hundred items to the *Ssu-k'u ch'üan-shu* commission (see Table 5). An outsider from Anhwei, Wang Ch'i-shu often elicited criticism from the other members of the Hangchow library group. Pao T'ing-po, for example, became upset with Wang for not permitting Yü Li, then working on a research problem, to see an otherwise inaccessible text in Wang's library. Pao had referred Yü Li to Wang. To allow a friend to see one's collection, or a friend of a friend, was an expected courtesy and a prerequisite for scholarly communication.

From the early nineteenth century on, profits from the opium trade in Canton enabled hong merchants such as Wu Ping-chien (1769–1843, known as Howqua) and P'an Shih-ch'eng (fl. 1832) to acquire sizable collections. The cultural flowering of nineteenth-century Canton rested in part on such large collections, from which several important collectanea were published and disseminated.[25]

Figure 6   Making Type Cases
                            Source: *Ch'in-ting Wu-ying-tien chü-chen-pan
                            ch'eng-shih* (Peking, 1776).

· · ·

Printing in Kiangnan

In addition to their book collecting efforts, bibliophiles in Kiangnan undertook major printing projects. Publishing had been an important part of library activity in larger private collections since Mao Chin's efforts in the late Ming. Pao T'ing-po, for example, used his Hangchow collection to publish rare editions and manuscripts in his possession under the collective title *Chih-pu-tsu-chai ts'ung-shu* (Collectanea of the Can't Know Enough Studio). The latter first appeared in 1776. As works were added to the collection, the collectanea went through twenty-eight series during Pao's lifetime and a total of thirty in all. Printing was also an important activity of Wang Hsien's Hangchow library, as well as those of many other scholar-bibliophiles such as Huang P'ei-lieh (1763–1825), Wang Ch'i-shu, and Lu Wen-ch'ao. Scholar-printers became invaluable members of the Kiangnan academic community.

Although movable type was experimented with in China, woodblock xylography was generally more economical, when many copies of a particular work were published. Woodblocks could be easily stored and, with reasonable care, could be preserved for frequent reuse. In fact, prints of the same woodblocks were often used for collectanea of different titles and compilers. Books set with movable type accommodated misprints and errors more easily, whereas a woodblock, once proofread, was permanently correct. Moreover, breaking down type matrices after a printing rendered later editions very expensive. A used woodblock, on the other hand, had no other use except for cheap later editions. When relatively few copies were needed (for projects such as the *Ku-chin t'u-shu chi-ch'eng*), then it was feasible to employ movable type.[26]

· ·

The Role of Collectanea (Ts'ung-shu)

Ts'ung-shu provided a medium by which Chinese scholar-printers could publish or reprint their rare books, as well as short works of scholarship and newly collated versions of previously published texts. In this way, such works were made accessible to other scholars and collectors. Generally, a "collectanea" was a collection of independent works of many periods published together in a single edition. They were an answer to the loss of literature, especially monographs too small to circulate independently, because of warfare and social upheaval. Pao T'ing-po's *Chih-pu-tsu-chai ts'ung-shu,* which contained 148 works, and Juan Yuan's famous *Wen-hsuan-lou ts'ung-shu* (Collectanea from the Hall of Literary Selections), which contained fifty-three rare works, led the way in preserving ancient writings in their respective collections.[27]

Such collectanea originated in the Sung dynasty and were particularly popular during the late Ming period. Mao Chin initiated the practice of private libraries publishing *ts'ung-shu* with his *Chin-tai pi-shu* mentioned above. By the eighteenth century, a collectanea resembled a miniature library. According to Arthur Hummel, *ts'ung-shu* were usually constituted according to five criteria: (1) common authorship, for example, the *Yen-Li ts'ung-shu* (Collectanea of Yen Yuan [1635–1704] and Li Kung [1659–1733]); (2) similar subjects such as geography, history, *Tao-hsueh,* philology, Buddhism, Taoism, for example, the *Tao-tsang* (Taoist patrology); (3) same locality, for example, the *Chi-fu ts'ung-shu* (Collectanea of works by Chihli natives); (4) same period of time, for example, the *T'ang-Sung ts'ung-shu* (Collectanea of the T'ang and Sung dynasties); (5) special collections issued by schools and societies, for example, the *Huang-Ch'ing ching-chieh* issued by the Hsueh-hai T'ang in Canton.

Hummel has pointed out that such collectanea were the principal medium used in traditional China to preserve anything corresponding to modern periodical literature. In them authors could print short articles, papers, or monographs that today find their way into journals and magazines before they are finally deposited in book form. Collectanea that focused on one class of subjects were also very popular. In the absence of systematic library facilities, collectanea (for example, the *Fo-tsang* [Buddhist patrology]) also served as subject bibliographies that complemented existing library catalogs.[28]

· ·

The Book Trade in Kiangnan and Peking

Private libraries, as we have seen, flourished in the social and academic environment of the Ch'ien-lung Emperor's reign. Because of the avid interest in book collecting, rare books were already expensive during the K'ang-hsi era (1662–1722), and by the Ch'ien-lung period their value increased tenfold. During the early Ch'ing, the bookstalls in Peking, where new, old, and rare books and manuscripts were sold, were located outside the city at Tz'u-jen Monastery. Ku Yen-wu, a pioneer of evidential research, had lived in the area in 1668 and frequented the stalls there looking for rare items. Literati such as Wang Hui (1632–1717), who was famous as a painter and a connoisseur of ancient paintings and artifacts, were frequently consulted on the purchase of rubbings and the like.

The Liu-li-ch'ang (Glazed Tile and Glass Factory Street), located in an area known as the "southern city" inside Peking that originally had been a factory site, by the eighteenth century was the major book emporium and center for antiques in China. A note by Lu Lung-ch'i (1630–1693) dated 1675 indicates that the Liu-li-ch'ang was already a market for books in the early Ch'ing period. The bibliophile and textual scholar Chu I-tsun, for example, lived in a famous studio near the Liu-li-ch'ang after being dismissed from office in 1684. In 1686, Chu printed a collection of prose and poetry, in addition to starting work on his well-known history of Peking. Many of the sources for the latter probably were found at the Liu-li-ch'ang.

The Liu-li-ch'ang reached its height as a book market during the Ch'ien-lung era, when Li Wen-tsao (1730–1778) wrote his famous account entitled *Liu-li-ch'ang shu-ssu chi* (Record of bookstalls in the Glazed Tile and Glass Factory Street), which was published in 1769. The Liu-li-ch'ang emporium, because it was located near the Hanlin Academy, became a gathering spot for intellectuals, scholars, and degree candidates who came to Peking. A cultural atmosphere emerged that stressed the value of rare works and ancient artifacts, promoted the exchange of books, and stimulated scholarship during the eighteenth century. Books and manuscripts of all kinds moved freely between Peking and the main book markets in Kiangnan. Families whose fortunes were waning (for example, Wang Hsien in Hangchow) were forced to liquidate their rare book collections to pay off mounting debts. Much of the Chi-ku ko was sold off in this manner.[29]

Li Wen-tsao, like countless others, would walk through the Liu-li-ch'ang during his free time looking for rare books. During this period, Li's friend Chou Yung-nien (1730–1791), the famous Shantung bibliophile, was a compiler for the *Ssu-k'u ch'üan-shu* project. Chou accumulated in Peking a private library of about 100,000 *chüan*, which he named the Chi-shu Yuan (Garden of Lending Books) in order to stress that book collections should be put to their widest possible use.[30] The catalog to Chou's library contained an introductory essay entitled "Ju-tsang shuo" (A plea for a Confucian patrology) in which Chou contended that scholars should contribute to a single comprehensive collection of Confucian works in order to preserve the tradition intact. Such a collection would serve as source materials for students and would be the most effective way to counter the large Taoist and Buddhist temple collections. According to Leung Man-kam, Juan Yuan's *Huang-Ch'ing ching-chieh* project was inspired in part by Chou's proposal. In addition, Chou advocated the establishment of public libraries and the exchange of catalogs among scholars.[31]

Ch'ien Ta-hsin, like most Han-Learning scholars, also frequented the bookshops at the Liu-li-ch'ang while a member of the Hanlin Academy in 1757. There he acquired over three hundred rubbings of stone inscriptions from the Han and T'ang dynasties. Recognizing the importance of such materials for historical research, Ch'ien spent three decades buying, borrowing, and making rubbings himself. Ch'ien's *Nien-erh-shih k'ao-i* (Examination of variances in the *Twenty-two Dynastic Histories*), a project that he completed in 1782 after fifteen years of work, grew out of his research on stone inscriptions and again demonstrates the important impact that epigraphic findings had on eighteenth-century Chinese historians. As a result of his efforts, Ch'ien was able to produce four collections of interpretive notes for his holdings that by around 1800 came to more than two thousand items.[32]

The famous Soochow bibliophile Huang P'ei-lieh pursued a career as a printer and bookseller. Residing in Soochow, a major center of the book trade, Huang was able to amass a large collection of rare editions by purchase, exchange, or copying from libraries of friends. Unsuccessful in official life, Huang visited Peking and frequented the Liu-li-ch'ang from an early age in search of rare books and manuscripts. From about

1794, Huang employed the evidential scholar Ku Kuang-ch'i (1776–1835) to assist him in collating and discriminating rare editions. Friendly with evidential scholars and bibliophiles such as Ch'ien Ta-hsin, Tuan Yü-ts'ai, and Pao T'ing-po, who frequented his Soochow bookstore, Huang was known for his Sung editions and for his detailed bibliographic notes on the history of over three hundred rare works he had gathered together.[33]

The book trade in China also attracted the interest of scholars from Korea, who accompanied their country's tribute missions to Peking. Hong Tae-yong (1731–1783) noted that many of the merchants in the Liu-li-ch'ang were from the south, a remark that suggests the important role played by Kiangnan proprietors such as Huang P'ei-lieh in the book trade. Huang, for instance, was intimate with the Korean scholar Pak Che-ga (1750–1805?), with whom he would discuss rare books and editions available in China and Korea. A leader in the eighteenth-century "northern learning" (pukhak, that is, pei-hsueh) school of Korean Confucianism, which favored study of Ch'ing institutions, technology, administration, and evidential research, that is, "concrete studies" (sirhak or shih-hsueh), Pak Che-ga visited Peking four times beginning in 1776 and associated with leading Confucian scholars and men of letters.[34]

Korean scholars had been visiting the Liu-li-ch'ang in Peking since at least the K'ang-hsi era, looking for books to send back to Korea. In the seventeenth century, when Manchu restrictions made it impossible for Korean envoys to leave their compound, Korean scholars purchased books from merchants with licenses to trade with diplomatic missions in Peking. Gari Ledyard has described how the Peking merchant Cheng Shih-t'ai (fl. ca. 1765) managed to sell the Koreans the rare books and antiques they wanted. A process of cultural exchange and correspondence ensued that closely linked the eighteenth-century Korean pukhak wave of learning to the Ch'ing evidential movement. Chi Yun (1724–1805) and Weng Fang-kang (1733–1818), in particular, developed a warm relationship with a number of Korean scholars who accompanied the Korean tribute missions to Peking during the eighteenth century. In search of books to send back for the Korean royal library started in 1776, Korean scholars, with the help of their Chinese friends, collected a number of collectanea and encyclopedias.[35]

Pak Che-ga met Sun Hsing-yen (1753–1818) accidentally on one of his trips to the Liu-li-ch'ang in 1781. Sun was then living near the book market, and he struck up a friendship with the Korean scholar, presenting him with a reprint of the T'ang stone Classics. Juan Yuan's scholarship was admired by the Koreans, and he met with Pak and later with Kim Chong-hui (1786–1856). These encounters initiated an interesting exchange of information about Chinese texts still in existence in Korea and Japan that had long since been lost in China.

Kim sent Juan Yuan a Yuan dynasty mathematical text that had survived in Korea, and for his efforts Kim was sent a complete set of the *Huang-Ch'ing ching-chieh* as soon as it was published in 1829. In addition, Kim sent Juan a copy of the original edition of Yamanoi Tei's (1670–1728) influential *Shichikei Mōshi kōbun* (Textual study of the *Seven Classics* and the *Mencius*). Presented to China between 1731–1736 by the Tokugawa shogun Yoshimune (r. 1716–1745), this Japanese commentary to the Confucian Classics became very popular among *k'ao-cheng* scholars because it was based on Chinese sources that had survived in Kyoto in the Ashikaga archives. Later, the bibliophile Wang Ch'i-shu submitted Yamanoi's work to the *Ssu-k'u ch'üan-shu* commission. The editors enthusiastically accepted the book, but they apparently did not know that the author was Japanese. Kim corrected the error.

Although the presumed bibliographic riches extant in Korea did not match those later recovered in Japan (except for a few important commentaries and mathematical texts), Korea did contribute a large amount of epigraphical material to Ch'ing scholars. Kim Chong-hui in particular systematically collected rubbings of stone inscriptions extant in Korea and gave (or traded) copies of these to Chinese specialists in epigraphy, who then cited and published them. To the extent that these inscriptions represented the writings of Chinese historical figures who had been forgotten in China, the rubbings were rightly regarded in China with great interest.

To some degree, what we see in this international exchange of books and knowledge in early modern China, Korea, and Japan is the emergence, before the coming of the Western powers, of an East Asian community of evidential scholars. In the late eighteenth and early nineteenth centuries, they learned and adapted the evidential techniques pioneered by Chinese members of the Lower Yangtze academic community.[36]

· ·

Imperial Support for Libraries
and Publishing

In addition to the literary and scholarly projects that they sponsored, the K'ang-hsi and Ch'ien-lung emperors actively promoted the imperial collection housed in the Wu-ying Throne Hall. The latter also served as the Imperial Printing Office (see chapter 3). Although an invaluable collection of books from the Ming imperial library had survived the Manchu conquest, large numbers of items in the Ming collection had been lost, however, when Peking fell first to rebel and then Manchu forces. Losses included two out of the three complete sets of the *Yung-lo ta-tien,* the major repository of ancient works from antiquity to the fifteenth century.

The first significant increase in the imperial library under Manchu rule began after the K'ang-hsi Emperor ordered the Hanlin Academy in 1686 to devise a scheme for collecting and preserving books. More than 15,000 books in all genres of learning were published under the K'ang-hsi Emperor's patronage. Included were the complete works of Chu Hsi (1130–1200) and the *Hsing-li ching-i* (Essential ideas of nature and principle), choices that indicated the emperor's penchant for the Ch'eng-Chu school. Also compiled and published under imperial sponsorship during this time were such noted encyclopedias and dictionaries as the 1710 *Yuan-chien lei-han* (Classified repository of profound appraisals), the 1711 *P'ei-wen yun-fu* (Thesaurus arranged by rhymes), the 1716 *K'ang-hsi tzu-tien* (K'ang-hsi dictionary), and the 1725 *Ku-chin t'u-shu chi-ch'eng.* Casting of a million and a half font of movable type was required for the latter. According to R. C. Rudolph, some Jesuits may have supervised the manufacture of the copper type. Their supervision may not have been necessary, however, because of demonstrated Korean expertise in movable-type printing over the centuries.[37]

Designed first to preserve existing literature on all subjects and then later to ferret out prohibited books, the *Ssu-k'u ch'üan-shu* project set off a flurry of book hunting by private individuals and official scholars in the 1770s and 1780s. In the process, prices for rare books rose sharply. The first manuscript copy in over 36,000 *chüan* (it was not printed because only seven copies were ordered) was finished in 1782 and was housed in the Wen-yuan ko (Pavilion of the Profundities of Literature)

Figure 7   Making Form Trays
Source: *Ch'in-ting Wu-ying-tien chü-chen-pan ch'eng-shih* (Peking, 1776).

in the imperial palace in Peking. Built especially for this purpose, the Wen-yuan ko was modeled after the T'ien-i ko in Ningpo. Three additional sets were completed and housed in Mukden, the Old Summer Palace, and in Jehol. Essentially closed to literati and the public, these collections were largely maintained for imperial prestige. The Ch'ien-lung Emperor and his editors justifiably thought that in preparing an accurate and permanent copy of the most important writings from antiquity to the present, they were making a highly significant contribution to Chinese letters.

In 1733, for example, the Ch'ien-lung Emperor had already ordered Chin Chien (d. 1795), a typographer of Korean origin, to supervise the production of reprints of recently discovered rare books. Between 1774–1794, many of the rare works discovered by the *Ssu-k'u ch'üan-shu* staff were printed using movable wooden type in the Imperial Printing Office. Later, all the books printed in this manner were brought together to form a single collectanea consisting of 138 items.[38] To show his appreciation to the Kiangnan bibliophiles who had helped make the *Ssu-k'u ch'üan-shu* project a success, the Ch'ien-lung Emperor ordered three more sets of the collection to be completed. Finished in 1787, these sets were housed at special imperial libraries in Yangchow, Chinkiang, and Hangchow. These three libraries were the only ones open to students and scholars possessing the required literati credentials. Copying of rare materials was permitted, and scholars took advantage of the collections placed there for their use.

Sun-Hsing-yen, for example, copied some of the materials for his library from books he found at the Wen-lan ko (Pavilion of Literary Currents) in Hangchow. Wang Chung (1744–1794) was asked to check the copy of the *Ssu-k'u ch'üan-shu* deposited at Chinkiang for accuracy in 1790. This work took him the better part of two years to complete, and he seems to have done the same for the collection housed in his native Yangchow. Wang passed away shortly after an invitation in 1794 to undertake similar work at the Wen-lan ko in Hangchow. Juan Yuan acknowledged that many of the sources (including translations of Western works) for his *Ch'ou-jen chuan* (Biographies of mathematical astronomers) came from the Hangchow Wen-lan ko. Between 1795–1798, his staff (Juan was then Chekiang director of education), which included Ch'ien Ta-hsin and Ling T'ing-k'an (1757–1809), frequently made use of the public collection housed there.[39]

. . .

Reference Materials and
Evidential Research

By the eighteenth century, large-scale publishing and book collecting, made possible by the spread of printing in China, helped produce a dramatic change in the conditions of scholarly research and teaching. Commercial development in the Lower Yangtze Region during the Ming and Ch'ing dynasties and the concomitant growth of wealth there were important background factors that enabled Kiangnan scholar-printers to publish works on an unprecedented scale. Printing helped transform the conditions under which texts in Kiangnan and elsewhere were produced, distributed, and read. It made possible the forms of library collecting and book exchanges described above, in addition to encouraging systematic and extensive data collection (see chapter 5). Scholar-printers contributed to the advancement of *k'ao-cheng* scholarship by providing the Kiangnan academic community, its schools, academies, and libraries, with access to more specialized works than ever before.

Descriptive catalogs and annotated bibliographies became essential elements in the growth of evidential scholarship in Kiangnan during the eighteenth century. Such catalogs were closely linked to lists of bronze and stone inscriptions that enabled scholars to compare their texts with epigraphic relics. At the beginning of his study of the *Seventeen Dynastic Histories,* Wang Ming-sheng explained:

> Bibliography is the most important field in scholarship. Only from it can one learn the way by which to enter the gate [of scholarship]. However, this subject is not easily mastered without hard work, penetrating analysis, and inquiry of outstanding teachers. From Ch'ao Kung-wu [fl. ca. 1165] in the Sung to Chiao Jo-hou [Hung, 1541–1620] in the Ming, the scholarship and knowledge of all such men was not very high. They could not determine the genuineness of ancient books. Nor could they discern the quality of their editions or correct the mistakes [in them].[40]

. . .

Chang Hsueh-ch'eng (1738–1801), for example, found Chou Yung-nien's proposals for a Confucian patrology, mentioned above, congenial to his own archive proposals. After visiting Chou in Peking in 1775,

Chang wrote a preface for the catalog to Chou's lending library. In his *Chiao-ch'ou t'ung-i* (General principles of bibliography) completed in 1779, Chang emphasized the importance of critical bibliography for compiling local histories and discussed how to analyze, catalog, and compare texts in order to determine authenticity, authorship, and completeness. Chang saw bibliography as the basis for all textual and historical criticism and, according to David Nivison, was establishing "very general principles for the science of 'bibliography.'"

Stressing organization, Chang Hsueh-ch'eng was primarily concerned with cataloging techniques and "bibliographic studies" (*mu-lu-hsueh*) in his efforts to trace schools of scholarship back to their sources in antiquity. Chang, despite his protestations, was in this regard firmly in the mainstream of eighteenth-century *k'ao-cheng* discourse. Without careful bibliography, books would easily be lost and academic specialization would be impossible. According to Chang, the solution was to ensure that the state collected books and manuscripts on a regular basis. Teachers and local historians should be routinely held responsible for preserving writings of all genres in their communities. These materials would then be handed over for preservation and criticism (including censorship of heretical statements) by central authorities.[41]

In most collections, systematic descriptions of holdings were accompanied by colophons added to collated texts. Colophons either outlined the main points of a book's contents or gave a history of its manuscript copies or printed editions. Serving a function akin to modern reviews, the colophons added by collectors would often discuss the strong and weak points of the author. The *Ssu-k'u ch'üan-shu tsung-mu* (General catalog of works in the *Complete Collection of the Four Treasuries*), completed in 1782, was the most comprehensive collection of colophons ever compiled by Confucian scholars. The staff of the project attempted to set down the gist of a book in outline form so that readers could get a general idea of its contents without having to read it. The *Ssu-k'u ch'üan-shu chien-ming mu-lu* (Abridged catalog), also completed in 1782, included a brief criticism of each work copied. This account was usually a summary of the original description in the complete bibliography but occasionally differed from the latter. These accounts concisely gave the reader an accurate idea of the nature and importance of the work described.[42]

Bibliographies like Chu I-tsun's influential *Ching-i k'ao* and Hsieh

Figure 8   Making Strips and Blanks
                            Source: *Ch'in-ting Wu-ying-tien chü-chen-pan
                            ch'eng-shih* (Peking, 1776).

Ch'i-k'un's (1737–1802) highly praised *Hsiao-hsueh k'ao* (Critique of classical philology) served as specialized reference sources. The *Ching-i k'ao* was a descriptive bibliography of all classical commentaries and other studies of the Classics written from the beginning of the Han dynasty to 1700. Chu's collection included discussion of stone inscriptions of the Classics, studies of the bibliographic sections in the *Dynastic Histories,* and important private bibliographies.

Chu I-tsun, however, had not included any of the subsections classified under "lesser learning" (*hsiao-hsueh;* philology and ancillary disciplines), except for works on the *Erh-ya* (Progress toward correctness) dictionary. To make up for this deficiency, Hsieh Ch'i-k'un, then financial commissioner of Chekiang, employed Chang Hsueh-ch'eng's long-time friend Hu Ch'ien to compile the *Hsiao-hsueh k'ao* in Hangchow. Hsieh's work was arranged in four sections dealing with "glosses" (*hsun-ku*), "primary and derived graphs" (*wen-tzu*), "initials and finals" (*sheng-yun*), and "pronunciation and meaning" (*yin-i*), giving bibliographic information for 1,099 titles. Chang Hsueh-ch'eng's *Shih-chi k'ao*, never completed and subsequently lost, was intended to fill a similar gap for historical studies (see chapter 3).[43]

. . .

Classification of Knowledge

As a form of analysis and a clue to the emerging disciplines that made up Confucian scholarship, the classification of knowledge in the eighteenth century can reveal the manner in which types of learning were perceived and the nature and structure of the concepts used. We can deduce from the bibliographic clustering of subjects the culturally conditioned biases in Ch'ing scholarship. Moreover, the eighteenth-century conception of the structure of knowledge shaped evidential discourse and influenced how new research would be understood.

Liu Hsiang (ca. 80–8 B.C.) put together the first known Chinese bibliography, which his son Liu Hsin later completed. Liu Hsin's bibliography was composed of seven major categories with thirty-eight subdivisions. These categories were employed throughout the Han period, especially by Pan Ku (32–92) in the bibliography included in his *Han-shu* (History of the Former Han dynasty). However, when the imperial library was reestablished during the Western Chin dynasty (265–316), a new four-division system (*ssu-pu*) was used.[44]

The four-division classification of Classics, Histories, Philosophy, and Literature was adopted for official bibliographies as early as the *Sui-shu* (History of the Sui dynasty [581–618]), which was completed in 656. It gradually was elaborated and was used almost universally during the T'ang and Sung dynasties. Cheng Ch'iao, however, devised a system

· Table 6 ·

Forty-four Subdivisions of the *Ssu-k'u ch'üan-shu*

Classics	History
Changes	Dynastic Histories
Documents	Annals
Poetry	Topical Records
Rituals	Unofficial Histories
Spring & Autumn Annals	Miscellaneous Histories
Filial Piety	Official Documents
General Works	Biographies
Four Books	Historical Records
Music	Contemporary Records
Philology	Chronography
	Geography
Philosophy	Official Registers
	Institutions
Confucians	Bibliographies and Epigraphy
Military Strategists	Historical Criticism
Legalists	
Agriculturalists	**Literature**
Medicine	
Astronomy & Mathematics	Elegies of Ch'u
Calculating Arts	Individual Collections
Arts	General Anthologies ·
Repertories of Science	Literary Criticism
Miscellaneous Writers	Songs & Drama
Encyclopedias	
Novelists	
Buddhism	
Taoism	

of twelve major bibliographic categories, which he subdivided into 257 subheadings. Cheng restored some of Liu Hsiang's categories and appended new categories in pharmacology, philology, astronomy, the arts, the five phases (often translated as "five elements"), and encyclopedias. Subsequently, the Ming imperial catalog, completed in 1441, was divided into thirty-eight categories, although books were listed in approximately the same order that they would have been in a four-division classification. Many of the new categories reflected new types of books, for example, the "nature and principle" (*hsing-li*) category devised to accommodate works associated with Neo-Confucianism.[45]

Eighteenth-century evidential scholars rejected attempts to replace the four-division system. Ch'ien Ta-hsin characterized the Ming imperial catalog as little more than unsystematic notes and drafts. Chang Hsüeh-ch'eng admitted that Liu Hsiang's categories were no longer appropriate for modern cataloging. Both Ch'ien and Chang favored the four-division system. The *Ssu-k'u ch'üan-shu* editors in turn employed the system as their standard of classification. Their annotated catalog was arranged according to the four main divisions and then subdivided into forty-four classes and subclasses (see Table 6).[46]

At the beginning of each category and subdivision, brief notes compiled by the editors were printed. These notes outlined the organizational rationale and summarized the history of each division. The *Ssu-k'u ch'üan-shu* editors' account of philology gave a particularly clear discussion of their attitudes toward scholarship. Table 6 reveals that philology was included as part of the Classics division. The editors noted that the Sui and T'ang histories included works on stone and bronze inscriptions in the "lesser learning" (*hsiao-hsueh*) section of their respective bibliographies. In a decision that reflected the growing association of epigraphy with annotated descriptions of facsimiles, the editors of the *Ssu-k'u ch'üan-shu,* following the lead of the fourteenth-century compilers of the *Sung-shih* (History of the Sung dynasty), opted to place most works on epigraphy in the bibliography section under history. Furthermore, the editors rejected placing mathematics in the *hsiao-hsueh* section, which the late seventeenth-century compilers of the *Ming History* had done, in favor of what they regarded as a more logical linking of mathematics to astronomy.[47]

Within the field of textual scholarship, the *Ssu-k'u ch'üan-shu* editors indicated that philology (*hsiao-hsueh*) was itself composed of three distinct disciplines: (1) etymology with an emphasis on ancient glosses in the *Erh-ya;* (2) paleography with the *Shuo-wen chieh-tzu* as the paradigm for research; (3) phonology with the *Kuang-yun* (Expansion of rhymes) as the key classical text. Rejecting the T'ang bifurcation of *hsun-ku* (glossing) and *hsiao-hsueh* into distinct fields, the *Ssu-k'u ch'üan-shu* editors contended that because *hsun-ku* was primarily used to explain and gloss the meanings of "names and their referents" (*ming-wu*), it could not be regarded as a separate discipline. Relying on Pan Ku's Han dynasty precedent, the editors reintegrated *hsun-ku* into *hsiao-hsueh.* Han Learning was defined not only according to content but also organization of disciplines. This reintegration meant that philology had three overlapping disciplines, which textual scholars were expected to master and employ in their research.[48]

The content of *hsiao-hsueh* was shaped by Hsieh Ch'i-k'un's *Hsiao-hsueh k'ao* mentioned above. Eighteenth-century evidential scholars contended (as did the *Ssu-k'u ch'üan-shu* editors) that Hsieh's disciplines represented an independent branch of learning with its own contributions to classical studies. In his introduction to Hsieh's *Hsiao-hsueh k'ao*, Ch'ien Ta-hsin noted:

> The Six Classics are expressed through [the medium of] characters. Without phonology, [our grasp of] the classical language misses the mark; without ancient glosses, the meaning of the Classics is unclear . . . The intentions of the sages have not been transmitted, but their texts are the same in all times. By relying on primary and derived characters [that is, their phonetic derivation], we can recapture their ancient pronunciation. By depending on their ancient pronunciation, we can recapture their ancient glosses [that is, meanings].[49]

.   .   .

Limiting philology to the disciplines of paleography, phonology, and glossing endorsed their importance in classical studies and reversed earlier practices.

The *Ssu-k'u ch'üan-shu* editors also made important innovations in the philosophy category. Works on the Han and pre-Han masters were placed together under the heading "miscellaneous writers" (*tsa-chia*). Huang Yü-chi (1629–1691) had been the first Ch'ing scholar to develop this category for his own library, and the editors followed his example. Texts that filled up the first subsection of this category had been objects of increasing scholarly attention since the 1770s. Included were the *Mo-tzu*, the *Huai-nan-tzu* (Master of Huai-nan), the *Kuei-ku-tzu* (Master of Demon Gorge), the *Lü-shih ch'un-ch'iu* (Master Lü [Pu-wei's] Spring and Autumn Annals), and many others. As we have seen in chapter 2, the revival of interest in these previously neglected heterodox texts occasioned a new understanding in the eighteenth century of Chou and Han dynasty history and of the development of the orthodox Confucian tradition.[50]

Sun Hsing-yen specified a new scheme of twelve major divisions of knowledge in 1800. This system reflected the emergence of specialized

· Table 7 ·
Sun Hsing-yen's Divisions of Scholarship

1. Classics	7. History
2. Philology	8. Epigraphy
3. Philosophy	9. Encyclopedias
4. Astronomy	10. Poetry
5. Geography	11. Arts
6. Medicine & Law	12. Fiction

fields that deserved independent consideration. Expanding and adjusting the *ssu-pu* system, Sun raised a number of previous subdivisions to the rank of major divisions. Philology (*hsiao-hsueh*) was separated from the Classics, and both geography and epigraphy were divided off from history (see Table 7). According to Sun, bronze and stone epigraphy, begun in the Sung dynasty, had developed progressively since then into a "specialized field" (*i-chia chih hsueh*) deserving separate status. T.H. Tsien has explained: "This rational approach may be credited to Sun's wide background in various branches of knowledge, which made this contribution and adjustment possible."

In discussing classical works then available, Sun Hsing-yen did not hesitate to dismiss Sung and Ming explications of the Classics as "contrived" (*i-chien*), "fragmented" (*chih-yeh*), and hence "inappropriate for etymological studies" (*pu ho hsun-ku*). In effect, Sun was clearly enunciating the fields of research in Confucian scholarship as China entered the nineteenth century.[51]

The evidential scholars' conception of the structure of knowledge led them to propose innovations and redefinitions in order to restore what they considered the proper boundaries of knowledge. Chu Hsi's subordination of "lesser learning" (*hsiao-hsueh*) to what the Neo-Confucians called "the great learning" (*Ta-hsueh;* moral philosophy) was irrevocably reversed. Far from having any connotation of elementary education or less important studies, *hsiao-hsueh* in the hands of the *k'ao-cheng* scholar became a sophisticated and precise methodology to retrieve the past and thereby controvert the overblown rhetoric of *Ta-hsueh.* Philology upstaged moral philosophy.

Classification of knowledge in the eighteenth century was closely tied to the disciplines of textual scholarship. Scholars who engaged in evidential research were provided with clear guidelines that effectively channeled their efforts in specific directions. The fields of paleography, phonology, and glossing were the accepted means by which scholars added their findings to their cumulative disciplines. Students in academies where *k'ao-cheng* studies were promoted were taught to apply these techniques to a wide variety of textual problems. Bibliophiles were instrumental in providing the sources needed to carry on evidential research, but how these materials were to be studied and evaluated depended on the manner in which scholarship was perceived and organized.

Tai Chen, as long as he operated within the accepted guidelines of *k'ao-cheng* studies (astronomy, mathematics, and so forth), was regarded as one of the best scholars of his day. When, however, he ventured beyond the boundaries of precise scholarship into the realm of philosophy, his achievements were summarily dismissed. Chu Yun (1729–1781), a patron of Han Learning, was upset enough with Tai's excursion into Neo-Confucian philosophy—even though Tai was critical of Chu Hsi—to rebuke him for his foray into abstract speculation (see chapter 1).[52] Hence, *k'ao-cheng* discourse placed important constraints on evidential scholars, constraints that most Sung-Learning advocates rejected. The classification of knowledge in the Ch'ing period encouraged the application of rigorous philological tools to cumulative disciplines.

The bookish culture of Ch'ien-lung's China brilliantly succeeded in reconstructing the Chinese past. *K'ao-cheng* scholars demonstrated their veneration for the ancients by recovering their lost writings and removing distortions and corruptions that had accumulated over millennia. Recent historians of China who have ridiculed Ch'ing philologists are apparently unaware of how great a role Renaissance bookmen played in recovering ancient Greek and Roman literature and thought for Western civilization.

Writing in 1911, Yeh Te-hui (1864–1927), a staunch Confucian when it was becoming unpopular to remain so, described how much easier it had been for a scholar during the Ch'ing dynasty than ever before to have access to large amounts of materials collected together in his own home or in academies. Even the standard texts of the Classics and Histories had seldom circulated in printed form before the Northern Sung. Not until the Ming-Ch'ing period could ordinary scholars afford to purchase books for their own use. Because of the tireless efforts of Ch'ing scholar-printers, most of the works in the four divisions were printed and widely distributed for other scholars to use. In the next chapter, we will examine the communications network that grew out of the publishing industry in seventeenth- and eighteenth-century China. We will describe how scholars shared a common experience in acquiring new means to achieve old ends. This experience added impetus to differences of opinion and to reassessments of inherited views.[53]

Five

Channels of Scholarly
Communication in Kiangnan

An unfortunate result of the historian's dismissive approach to Ch'ing textual scholarship has been the failure to recognize the startling degree to which Confucian fields of textual research represented cumulative disciplines. Evidential scholars not only engaged in rigorous textual studies, but they also were cognizant of the essays and books produced by their colleagues in the Kiangnan academic community. In their quest for originality, Ch'ing literati regarded their efforts as contributions to the progress of their research fields. Convinced that their empirical approach was the correct way to verify knowledge, *k'ao-cheng* scholars ridiculed their Neo-Confucian predecessors for their inexactitude and their fixation on unverifiable metaphysical questions.

Arnold Thackray and Robert Merton have pointed out that changes in the organization of knowledge are part of the shifts that a field of scholarship undergoes as it changes from a diffuse, unfocused area of

Figure 9 Making Page and Column Rule Forms
Source: *Ch'ing-ting Wu-ying-tien chü-chen-pan ch'eng-shih* (Peking, 1776).

research inquiry into "a conceptually discrete discipline, able to command its own tools, techniques, methodologies, intellectual orientations, and problematics." In the process of the institutionalization of a field of learning, a "cognitive identity" develops alongside the creation of a "professional identity" for new research enterprises.[1]

The institutionalization and professionalization of evidential scholarship initiated a sense of common purpose among its practitioners by defining the content and methods of textual scholarship. Common purpose was translated into shared research techniques and into the emergence of a complex communication network through which evidential research was transmitted and evaluated. The result was a sense of and commitment to progress in *k'ao-cheng* scholarship on the part of members of the Kiangnan academic community. The formation of a sense of common orientation and purpose enabled *k'ao-cheng* scholars in Kiangnan to agree on central problems facing their scholarship and on relevant concepts and methods of analysis. The emergence of this consensus was an important factor in the development of evidential research as an integral part of the Lower Yangtze academic community.[2]

Evidential methods, if they were to be applied properly, demanded a concentration of research efforts on selected textual problems. Textual puzzle-solving replaced ethical reflection. As a result, a *k'ao-cheng* "cognitive identity" insulated members of the community from and allowed them to ignore many important social and theoretical problems. Evidential scholars ignored them because many such problems could not be formulated and resolved in terms of the conceptual and analytic frameworks of discourse that the evidential orientation to knowledge supplied. Neo-Confucian discourse, on the other hand, had a theoretical importance that was lacking in *k'ao-cheng* investigation.

. . .

Shared Research Techniques:
Notation Books

The way in which evidential research techniques were transmitted in Kiangnan and the cumulative and progressive nature of the knowledge to which those research skills were applied in the eighteenth century will demonstrate the extent to which Lower Yangtze scholars considered themselves members of an academic community. Through the medium of shared examples of successful practice, scholars mastered evidential research skills and learned how to apply them to many different kinds of problems. Certain key types of works helped to establish an identity for *k'ao-cheng* discourse and served as models for students to follow.[3]

Liang Ch'i-ch'ao, in an autobiographical aside included in his *Intellectual Trends in the Ch'ing Period,* described his student days at the Hsueh-hai T'ang in Canton in the 1890s as follows: "Everyone interested in learning had his 'notation book,' in which he recorded his findings as he read." Liang's account pointed to Ku Yen-wu's (1613–1682) *Jih-chih lu* (Record of knowledge gained day by day) as the exemplary work that influenced scholars to record their findings with precision and detail. The link between "notation books" (*cha-chi ts'e-tzu*) and data collection became a major characteristic of Ch'ing scholarship and clearly distinguished it from the "dialogue records" (*yü-lu*) format (see chapter 2), which dominated Sung-Ming *Tao-hsueh* writings.[4]

Seen in their earliest form in Wang Ying-lin's *K'un-hsueh chi-wen* (Hard-earned scholarship and record of findings) and Lo Ch'in-shun's *K'un-chih chi* (Record of hard-earned knowledge), notation books became the basic tool evidential scholars employed. As the titles indicate, they were anything but offhand jottings. The editors of the *Ssu-k'u ch'üan-shu* described Wang Ying-lin's *K'un-hsueh chi-wen* as a notation book employing evidential research techniques to investigate all fields of Confucian discourse. For this reason, the *k'ao-cheng* scholars Yen Jo-chü (1636–1704) and Ho Ch'o (1661–1722) had earlier been employed to annotate Wang's text for a new Ch'ing edition. Irene Bloom sees in Lo Ch'in-shun's *K'un-chih chi* an indication of Lo's "conviction

that intellectual and spiritual growth are achieved at the cost of dili-
gence and painstaking effort." Much of the *K'un-chih chi* was composed of reading notes and revealed Lo "as a scholar of remarkable
erudition, given to meticulous accuracy in his textual research."[5]

The majority of Sung-Ming Neo-Confucian writings had been records
of spiritual quests, however. These records mainly took the form of
dialogues, aphorisms, reflections, anecdotes, and poetry. In contrast
to the transmission of perceptions and reflections recorded verbatim
by students from talks with Chu Hsi and Wang Yang-ming (1472–
1529), Ch'ing scholars from Ku Yen-wu in the seventeenth century to
students at the Hsueh-hai T'ang in the nineteenth centered their educations around notebooks used to record pertinent information they hap-
pened to read, find, or hear about. In these notebooks, Ch'ing evidential scholars collected materials for studies of particular subjects. In
fact, notation books themselves became an important genre of writing
during the Ch'ing dynasty and served in turn as source books for other
scholars to use.[6]

Ch'ing notation books represented the accumulation of years of carefully gathered and considered facts, observations, and records.[7] On his
travels, Ku Yen-wu collected source materials for his own research in
historical geography and epigraphy. Ku's writings on historical geography
were informed by his own experiences in areas he had visited. Although
much of his research was based on literary sources, Ku did gather primary evidence to supplement his reading. In particular, Ku searched
for stone inscriptions of historical relevance. When he found a stele
that had not been previously recorded, Ku was so excited he did not
sleep. Ku also used ancient inscriptions to corroborate or emend the
Classics.[8]

Ku Yen-wu was able to purchase, borrow, and copy rare books and
unpublished texts that helped to enlarge his own library. These copies
included some eighty rubbings of Han and T'ang stone inscriptions and
a large amount of manuscript material. In addition, Ku's travels enabled
him to develop friendships with scholars who influenced his own research. Ku met with many noted Confucians in North and South China,
and in the winter of 1672 he arrived in T'ai-yuan, Shansi, where he met
Yen Jo-chü. The meeting with Yen was a boon for both men. Ku allowed Yen to see his accumulated notebooks, and Yen made a number
of additions and corrections that Ku gladly incorporated. For his part,

Yen Jo-chü included some fifty amendments to items in Ku's manuscripts in his own notation book under the heading *Pu-cheng Jih-chih lu* (Making additions to and correcting the *Record of Knowledge Gained Day by Day*).[9]

Yen Jo-chü had been gathering material for his research on the *Documents,* much of which he included in his notebook known as the *Ch'ien-ch'iu cha-chi* ([Yen] Ch'ien-ch'iu's reading notes). Later fearing that his unpublished notebooks would not be preserved for posterity, he included a good deal of extraneous material from them in his *Shu-cheng,* giving the latter the appearance of a notation book in many places as well. The dignity of a step-by-step empirical approach to knowledge based on wide reading and meticulous observation was an important element that model works such as the *Jih-chih lu* conveyed to scholars during the eighteenth century.

Ch'ien Ta-hsin's (1728–1804) *Shih-chia-chai yang-hsin lu* (Record of self-renewal from the Ten Yokes Study) was emblematic of the eighteenth-century approach to gathering and verifying knowledge. Other examples of this trend include notation books such as Lu Wen-ch'ao's *Chung-shan cha-chi* (Notes from Chung-shan Academy) and *Lung-ch'eng cha-chi* (Notes from Lung-ch'eng Academy), which grew out of Lu's stint as a teacher at the most prestigious academies in Kiangnan.

Most Han-Learning scholars used notation books to accumulate raw data, which they would later refine in their published essays. Wang Ming-sheng's (1722–1798) *I-shu pien* (Chapters on the antlike [accumulation] of scholarship), Wang Chung's (1745–1794) *Chih-hsin chi* (Record of new knowledge), Wang Nien-sun's (1744–1832) *Tu-shu tsa-chih* (Miscellaneous reading notes), and Tsang Yung's (1767–1811) *Pai-ching jih-chi* (Daily record of reverence for the Classics) are a small but representative sample of such academic strategies. Wang Ming-sheng, a meticulous scholar of the Classics and Histories, chose the metaphor of the "antlike accumulation of knowledge" to describe his notebooks because they were the product of thirty years of continuous research and reading.[10]

. . .

The Use of Data in K'ao-cheng Discourse

Relying on systematic gathering of materials that they would then critically scrutinize and in certain cases even quantify, Kiangnan scholars
combined evidential research methods with data collection and organization. Liang Ch'i-ch'ao has estimated that Ch'ien Ta-hsin recorded over
one hundred items in his notebooks before he could shed new light on
the linguistic phenomenon of dental labials (*ch'ing ch'un-yin*) recorded
in ancient Chinese texts. Ch'ien presented his data within a systematic
discussion of ancient pronunciation. Likewise, rigorous collection and
analysis of facts characterized research on the Old Text *Documents* during the Ch'ing period.[11]

. .

Yen Jo-chü on the Old Text Documents

Rigorous, systematic use of data, although still rudimentary outside the
fields of calendrical science and related mathematical subjects, was
already common among textual scholars in the seventeenth century.
Yen Jo-chü, for example, in his examination of a number of questions
concerning the Old Text chapters of the *Documents* employed chronological and statistical data in his conclusions when it was appropriate
to do so. Yen was the first *k'ao-cheng* scholar to compare carefully the
chapter names of the forged twenty-five Old Text chapters with the
names of the lost sixteen Old Text chapters mentioned by Cheng Hsuan
and other Han classicists. When he had finished giving a consecutive
listing of the twenty-five and sixteen chapter names for each Old Text
version, Yen then exposed K'ung Ying-ta's (547–648) erroneous explanation for the discrepancies.[12]

Applying a keen sense of chronology, Yen analyzed K'ung An-kuo's
(156–74? B.C.) dates of birth and death and their relevance to An-kuo's
presentation of the Old Text chapters to the imperial court. K'ung An-
kuo had, according to the *Shih-chi* (Records of the grand historian),
collated the Old Text version during the later years of Han Wu-ti's reign
(140–87 B.C.).[13] Yen noted at first that King Kung of Lu (Lu Kung

wang, r. 154–127 B.C.), when he assumed the throne and decided to enlarge his palace, had discovered the Old Text chapters hidden in the wall of Confucius' old residence. Therefore, sixty years had elapsed between the discovery of the missing chapters and their presentation to the throne, according to Yen's calculations. An-kuo must have been very old by this time, yet the K'ung-tzu chia-yü (School sayings of Confucius) stated that An-kuo had died young. This statement was odd, Yen thought, but he concluded only that by the time they were presented to the throne, the Old Text chapters must have contained a number of corrupt passages. No wonder then that Wu Yü (fl. 1124), Chu Hsi, and Wu Ch'eng (1247–1331) had been uneasy about the uncanny coherence of the twenty-five chapters that had appeared later.[14]

Subsequently in the Shu-cheng, Yen Jo-chü pursued the question of An-kuo's dates still further. Yen accepted the assertion of Ssu-ma Ch'ien (145–90? B.C.), who knew An-kuo, that the latter had died young. K'ung An-kuo became an erudite in 126 B.C. The Han-shu (History of the Former Han dynasty) claimed on the basis of the "An-kuo Introduction" that he presented the Old Text chapters to the imperial court after 97 B.C. The presentation was interrupted, however, by the 92–91 B.C. witchcraft trials. Yen calculated that the difference between An-kuo's serving as an erudite and the witchcraft trials was 35–36 years. Yen assumed that at the time An-kuo became an erudite, he had to be at least twenty years of age. This assumption meant that An-kuo had presented the Old Text version when he was fifty-five. How then could the Shih-chi say that An-kuo died young? When Confucius' disciples died at age forty or fifty, they were not said to have died young. If the Shih-chi was reliable, and there was no reason to doubt Ssu-ma Ch'ien, then An-kuo could not have lived to present the Old Text chapters himself.[15]

To explain the discrepancy Yen contended that it was not An-kuo but a member of his family who had presented the texts to the imperial court. From this perspective, it was clear that the introduction to the Documents purportedly written by An-kuo must be a forgery because it claimed that he himself made the presentation. This event An-kuo could not have lived to see. An internal contradiction was thereby resolved.[16]

Among the many teachings and doctrines in the Documents, the distinction between the "mind of man" (jen-hsin) and the "mind of Tao"

(*Tao-hsin*), enunciated for the first time in the "Counsels of Yü the Great" (Ta Yü mo) attracted major attention from Sung and Ming dynasty Neo-Confucians. Both Chu Hsi and Wang Yang-ming used this passage to wed a classical sanction to their different analyses of *li* (moral principle) and the orthodox transmission of the Tao (*Tao-t'ung*). In this way, Neo-Confucians attempted to locate classical passages that would verify their philosophic positions. Increasingly, however, Confucian scholars were forced to reconsider the authenticity of the texts they were using. Many contended that because the "Ta Yü mo" was one of the Old Text chapters of the *Documents,* and therefore likely to be a later forgery, the doctrines in it were also suspect. Yen Jo-chü, picking up where his predecessors had left off, made use of what loosely might be called statistical methods to clarify this long-standing debate.

After demonstrating that this famous section in the "Ta Yü mo" chapter on the "mind of Tao and the mind of man" was taken from a passage in the *Hsun-tzu* that cited the *Tao-ching* (Classic of the Way), Yen went on to prove why "*Tao-ching*" could not be a reference to the *Documents* (see also chapter 3 and below). Citing every instance where Hsun-tzu quoted from the *Documents,* Yen showed that out of the sixteen total references he found in the *Hsun-tzu,* twelve gave the *Documents* itself as the source, three mentioned a particular chapter of the *Documents,* and one source cited the *Documents* as "the Commentary says." Yen concluded:

> Why only in the case of the "Ta Yü mo" chapter would [Hsun-tzu] change his mode of reference and cite the *Tao-ching?* In this way I know that the "mind of man is fearful and the mind of Tao is too subtle to know" passage must necessarily have come from an authentic [text entitled] the *Tao-ching.* Moreover, the forger of the Old Text [passage in the "Ta Yü mo] probably just copied the whole of it because he was unable to construct subtle words to this degree.[17]

· · ·

Another phenomenon to which Yen Jo-chü applied a numerical calculation method was the curious fact that quotations in the *Tso chuan* (Tso's commentary) taken from the chapters of the *Documents* that the Han dynasty scholar Cheng Hsuan had called "missing" were all included in the Old Text version that Mei Tse (fl. 317–323) presented to the

Chin dynasty imperial court. Using the *Tso chuan* as his criterion, Yen counted the number of quotations in it that were from extant poems in the *Poetry* and the number of quotations it contained from missing poems. He then compared these numbers to the number of quotations in the *Tso chuan* from the New Text *Documents* and the number from what Cheng Hsuan had called the "missing chapters" (*i-shu*).[18]

Yen demonstrated that the *Tso chuan* quoted the extant *Poetry* 178 times, while quoting missing poems only 11 times. It quoted the *Documents* 25 times, while quoting from the missing chapters 43 times. The number of quotations from missing chapters of the *Documents* was almost double those from the extant version and almost four times as high as quotations from the missing poems not in the extant *Poetry*. How was it possible for Mei Tse to suddenly come up with a version of the *Documents* that included all the missing chapters from which the author of *Tso chuan* had taken a large number of quotations, but which Cheng Hsuan described as lost or dispersed? According to Yen, the only possible conclusion based on the evidence was that the forger of the missing chapters had relied on the *Tso chuan* for much of his material.[19]

Yen's research and the definitive conclusions he drew had wide impact. Scholars realized that if a complicated problem such as the possible forgery of the Old Text *Documents* could be resolved using *k'ao-cheng* methods, such an approach might prove valuable for many other long-standing textual puzzles. Hui Tung (1697–1758), the founder of the Han-Learning movement, for example, reviewed the evidence on the Old Text *Documents* in the middle of the eighteenth century. With minor caveats, Hui and his followers pushed Yen Jo-chü's conclusions even further.

. .

Mathematics, Astronomy, and Archaeology

John Henderson has described the same systematic use of data in connection with a more expected topic: he has indicated that Mei Wen-ting (1633–1721), in his attempt to reconcile natural philosophy and mathematical studies, in the seventeenth century altered "the signification of *li* [principle] by reducing it to something that might be grasped through mathematical induction. It is, at least, no longer the numinous 'principle' of the Sung Neo-Confucianists." In the move from numerology to numerical data, the use of mathematics in Confucian discourse was fundamentally transformed in the Ch'ing dynasty. Mei Wen-ting saw mathematics as the inductive process of collecting numerical data that could be used to fathom patterns of *li*.[20]

Wang Hsi-shan (1628–1682) and other prominent Confucian scholars interested in astronomy shared this emphasis on the empirical induction of *li* through the collection and study of quantifiable data. Nathan Sivin has argued persuasively that by 1700 what were the key problems in Chinese astronomy and how they were to be approached had been fundamentally redefined. Chinese scholars began to approach mathematical astronomy through the use of geometric models, an approach that placed considerable emphasis on geometry and trigonometry in numerical procedures.[21] Ch'ing mathematical scholars increasingly tended to repudiate or ignore purely numerological constructions. In the eighteenth century, Chiao Hsun's (1763–1820) contribution to the study of the *Changes,* for example, was his application of mathematical principles to determine the meaning of the text. Comparing philology to mathematics, Chiao Hsun accepted Mei Wen-ting's notion of *li* as something quantifiable. He was convinced from his study of astronomy and mathematics that textual knowledge accumulated and gradually grew more precise.[22]

Well-versed in native and Western computational astronomy, Chiao was in strong agreement with his patron Juan Yuan (1764–1849) that mathematics was one of the keys to "concrete studies." Chiao prepared a detailed study of early Chinese mathematics, and he aided Li Jui (1765–1814), a disciple of Ch'ien Ta-hsin, in Li's reconstruction of Sung-Yuan algebra. Seeing a computational logic lying at the heart of the numerology in the *Changes,* Chiao Hsun was in effect attempting to demythologize studies of the *Changes* and demonstrate that it contained firm, discoverable mathematical principles. Chiao noted:

> One must comprehend the theory of proportion [*pi-li*] and the method for finding the mean proportional [*ch'i-t'ung*], which [are elements of] the nine methods of mathematical calculation, in order to recognize [the meaning] of line movements in the hexagrams. One must master the principle of phonetic borrowing [*chia-chieh*] and extension of meaning [*chuan-chu*], which [are elements of] the six formation types governing characters, in order to grasp the meaning of the decision texts [*t'uan-tz'u*], line texts [*yao-tz'u*], and the Ten Wings [Commentary] . . . [Otherwise,] one cannot

possibly understand the Way of Fu Hsi, King Wen, the Duke of Chou, and Confucius.

· · ·

Juan Yuan, following the same line of thought, discriminated between Shao Yung's (1011–1077) arbitrary numerology and legitimate mathematics. Chiao Hsun, according to Juan, had been able to master the mathematical order in the 64 hexagrams and 384 (6 x 64) lines.[23]

Coupled with his distinguished philological studies, Tai Chen's (1724–1777) interests in astronomy and mathematics led him to realize that without a keen understanding of mathematics, it was impossible to understand passages in the Classics that dealt with technical, calendrical, and astronomical phenomena. In his study of the "K'ao-kung chi" (Record of technology) chapter of the *Rituals of Chou,* Tai indicated that without mathematical training scholars could not understand the texts describing engineering techniques used by the ancients. Ch'ien Ta-hsin and other eighteenth-century scholars trained in calendrical science and mathematics followed Tai in this line of argument.[24]

Tai used mathematics to estimate the size and shape of the ceremonial bronze bells mentioned in the "Record of Technology." In his own work on the subject Tai included diagrams based on his calculations of what the bells should look like. Because they employed texts and relics as archaeological evidence, Tai's drawings proved to be highly accurate when a large bronze bell was unearthed in Kiangsi during the Ch'ien-lung era (see Figure 10). Chiang Yung also had made attempts to reconstruct the appearance of the bells. Because he relied on Cheng Hsuan's descriptions too heavily, however, his drawings were somewhat less accurate. Yet, like Tai Chen's diagrams, Chiang's drawings served as explanatory devices for the reconstruction of ancient objects, Ch'eng Yao-t'ien (1725–1814) read Tai's and Chiang's descriptions very carefully and attempted on the basis of his own findings to cast bells like those in the diagrams. Ch'eng was attempting on the basis of archaeological and technical data to reconstruct actual instruments used in ancient music. Kondo Mitsuo has described Ch'eng's attempt as the work of a technician using textual and mathematical data literally to recreate the past.

In 1788, Juan Yuan in his first published work entitled *K'ao-kung chi ch'e-chih t'u-chieh* (Explications using diagrams of the design of wheeled

Data in *K'ao-cheng* Discourse

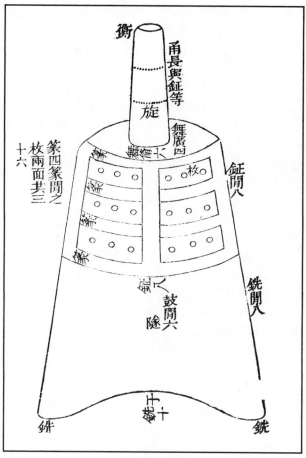

Figure 10   Tai Chen's Diagram of the Chou Dynasty Ceremonial Bronze Bells Mentioned in the "K'ao-kung chi"
Source: Reprinted from the *Huang-Ch'ing ching-chieh* collection.

carriages in the "Record of Technology"), reconstructed the ancient dimensions of vehicles. Juan improved on Tai Chen's earlier research on this problem and boasted that now anyone could build a replica of an ancient carriage if they followed his guidelines. Archaeological research was taking on a momentum of its own as an exact field of Confucian scholarship.[25]

Applying mathematics and using ancient relics to decipher ancient texts, Tai Chen and Ch'ien Ta-hsin paved the way for a cumulative field of inquiry that culminated in nineteenth- and twentieth-century breakthroughs in the application of epigraphy and archaeology to research on the oracle bones. The attempts of Tai Chen, Chiang Yung, and Ch'eng Yao-t'ien to reconstruct the ancient bronze bells demonstrate that *k'ao-cheng* scholars had begun to move from philology to a focus on artifacts and their importance as historical evidence. It was, after all, Confucian scholars who were specialists in the *k'ao-cheng* fields of epigraphy and paleography that first recognized the importance of inscriptions on oracle bones, not Western-trained specialists (see chapter 6).[26]

The account above corroborates Sivin's suggestion that there existed a much closer connection between the Jesuit impact on mathematical, calendrical, and astronomical studies in China and the long-term evolution from Neo-Confucian philosophy to Ch'ing exact scholarship than has been hitherto realized. We see the clear interaction between evidential methods of textual research and the use of native and Western astronomical and mathematical studies. As Sivin points out, "Astronomy, as it was understood and used by neo-Confucian thinkers, converged with philology, gave it added weight, and obviously played a part in tipping the scale."[27]

· ·

Use and Citation of Sources in
Evidential Research

The search for the best editions of the Classics, Histories, and other writings stimulated *k'ao-cheng* scholars to use a wide range of materials to verify their sources. Ku Yen-wu in his geographical studies was one of the first to rely on and call attention to local gazetteers. In a preface to one of his works on historical geography Ku wrote: "First I drew on the general gazetteers of the empire; next on the provincial, departmental, and county chronicles; and finally on the *Twenty-one Dynastic Histories.* In all I consulted more than one thousand works."[28]

On another tack, Ch'ien Ta-hsin in the eighteenth century continued Ku Yen-wu's novel use of poetry as a source for biographies. According to Kondo Mitsuo, a significant change in the Confucian perception of poetry had started in the Ch'ing. One of the consequences was to place composition of poetry in a subordinate position to research and scholarship. Ch'ien Ta-hsin, for instance, was more interested in making a name for himself as a Han-Learning scholar than a poet. Chang Hsueh-ch'eng (1738–1801) in his writings reveals the priority of scholarship over literary production during the eighteenth century through his use of "literary collections" (*wen-chi*) as documentary sources for bio-graphical material. Chang, according to Nivison, was using literary collections as histories of individuals.[29]

Citation and criticism of sources also were integral aspects of evidential scholarship. The recognition that it was important to corroborate research with citations was clearly evident in the writings of Kiangnan scholars. In his analysis of Yao Chi-heng's *Ku-chin wei-shu k'ao* (Analysis of forged works in ancient and modern times), Murayama Yoshihiro has pointed out that most of Yao's citations from more than forty different sources went back to important textual scholars during the preceding dynasties. Besides relying on Sung bibliographic scholarship (38 citations), Yao was also deeply indebted to the work of Hu Ying-lin (1551–1602) (10 citations) and Sung Lien (1310–1381) (6 citations) for his analysis of the authenticity of numerous works. The variety of sources Yao used presupposed a firm commitment to citation as a key element in scholarly discourse.[30]

Analysis of Yen Jo-chü's *Shu-cheng* similarly establishes the extent and direction of intellectual influence on his research and reveals his intellectual heritage. Yen's citations not only give evidence for the points being argued, they also demonstrate that evidential scholars voluntarily revealed through citations what the basis for their conclusions were. In his search for scholarly support for his position, Yen acknowledged and discussed in some detail his predecessors' studies of the Old Text *Documents*. In the last *chüan* of the *Shu-cheng*, Yen quoted extensively from preceding research, discussed its relevance for his own work, and pointed out the strengths and deficiencies of earlier writers on the *Documents* question.[31]

Yen's own analysis of his scholarly debts to his predecessors was employed by the *Ssu-k'u ch'üan-shu* editors in the late eighteenth century to demonstrate that Yen's *Shu-cheng* was the final link in a long and continuous chain of scholarly works.

> The Old Text portion of the *Documents*, when compared to the New Text portion, had sixteen more chapters. Since the Chin [265–316] and Wei dynasties [221–280], no explanation for this excess has been passed down. Tu Yü's [222–284] annotations called all the quotations in the *Tso chuan*

from the sixteen chapters of the *Documents* "lost parts." In the beginning of the Eastern Chin period [ca. 317–323], this book first appeared with twenty-five more chapters [than the New Text version]. The Old Text portion was given equal authority with the New Text chapters. Since Lu Te-ming [556–627] compiled his [*Ching-tien*] *shih-wen* [Explanation of primary graphs in the Classics] and K'ung Ying-ta compiled his [*Shang-shu*] *cheng-i* [Orthodox exegesis of the *Documents*] on the basis of this composite version, the twenty-five chapters were blended with Fu Sheng's [fl. 2nd century B.C.] twenty-nine [New Text] chapters.

Since the T'ang dynasty, although there were those who doubted the Classics and questioned ancient works such as Liu Chih-chi [661–721], the Old Text chapters were still classed with the [genuine] *Documents*. [Liu's] *Shih-t'ung* [Historiographic penetrations] never suggested the inauthenticity of the Old Text version. Beginning with Wu Yü, for the first time there were dissenting opinions. Chu Hsi also expressed some doubts. Wu Ch'eng and others, basing themselves on Chu Hsi's words, continued to pick out flaws so that the forgery [of the Old Text version] became increasingly evident. But they still were unable to make the systematic and detailed analysis that would have pinpointed its failings. The Ming dynasty's Mei Tsu [fl. ca. 1513] was the first to study a variety of books to prove its falsity, but his experience was narrow and his selection of material was not exhaustive.

Coming to [Yen] Jo-chü, it was he who adduced material from the Classics and other old works to set out one by one the reasons for the contradictions in the text. The falseness of the Old Text portion became quite clear . . . Mao Ch'i-ling [1623–1716] wrote his *Ku-wen Shang-shu yuan-tz'u* [In defense of the Old Text *Documents*], in which he used a hundred schemes to crush Yen, but in the end Mao's forced words could not overcome true principles. Arguments based on evidence finally were established in an unassailable position.[32]

. . .

What is remarkable is not so much the sources of Yen's position but the fact that he openly acknowledged them.

The choice of sources was also a reflection of the anti-*Tao-hsueh* orientation of Ch'ing *k'ao-cheng* scholars. The major research materials employed by scholars who worked on classical exegesis, for example, were derived from the Later Han dynasty. By the late eighteenth century, however, more and more scholars were turning to Former Han sources. A devotee of Han Learning, Sun Hsing-yen (1753–1818), in his choice of sources for his commentary to the *Documents* used no Sung commentaries, basing his work primarily on the *Shih-chi, Han-shu,* and works by Cheng Hsuan and other Later Han commentators. In his evidential historiography, Ch'ien Ta-hsin refused to employ T'ang or post-T'ang sources for his research on the early *Dynastic Histories.*[33]

Most eighteenth-century scholars were extremely careful to give the sources of their knowledge. Chang Hsueh-ch'eng noted that whenever he expressed a view that had already been enunciated by some past writer, he always cited the earlier man's words to show that he was not plagiarizing. This requirement was one of the marks of evidential research.[34] In the eighteenth century, it was considered poor scholarship not to cite sources, especially those from the Han dynasty. The *Ssu-k'u ch'üan-shu* editors were critical of Ming "encyclopedias" (*lei-shu*), because they rarely mentioned the sources for the material contained in them. This Ming oversight contrasted sharply with Sung encyclopedias such as the *T'ai-p'ing yü-lan* (Imperial encyclopedia of the T'ai-p'ing reign period [976–984]) where the origins of all entries were clearly given. Hsueh Ying-ch'i's (1500–1573?) *Ssu-shu jen-wu k'ao* (A study of persons in the Four Books), discussed in chapter 2, was singled out for criticism by the *Ssu-k'u ch'üan-shu* editors for failure to reveal sources:

> In the Ming period, students of Confucianism [those who prepared for the state examinations] gave great weight to [the study of] eight-legged essays. These essays emphasized in turn the Four Books. As a result, we have compilations like this one. They patch together and rip apart [authoritative sources] so as [to allow students] to impress examination officials. This approach represents an extreme in the corruption of classical studies. Not only could not the Ch'eng brothers and Chu Hsi have predicted this outcome when they edited and established the Four Books, neither could this result have been foreseen when the Four Books were used for the first time as essay topics [for the official examinations] during the Yen-yu reign [1314–1320] of the Yuan dynasty, nor when the Hung-wu Emperor [r. 1368–1399] during the Ming dynasty set up the three-stage examination system.

· · ·

Likewise, the editors berated Chiao Hung's *Kuo-shih ching-chi-chih* (Bibliography of our country's [Ming] history) for merely containing copies of old catalogs, without adding any textual research or even indicating whether the books included were still extant or not.[35]

Eighteenth-century scholars favored the precise use of diagrams (*t'u*) and tables (*piao*) to aid in discussion, explanation, and tabulation of data. One of the most prominent features of *k'ao-cheng* historiography (see chapter 2) was the use of *jen-wu piao* (tabulation of personages), supplemental tables, and factual supplements to make the *Dynastic Histories* more accessible as research tools. Ku Tung-kao's (1679–1759) *Ch'un-ch'iu ta-shih piao* (Tables of major events in the Spring and Autumn period [722–481 B.C.]), printed in 1748, served as a model for the collection of chronological, geographical, genealogical, and economic information concerning the pre-Ch'in and Han period. Arranged in tabular form under fifty topics, Ku's tables included supplementary notes by other scholars after each topic whenever there was an element of dispute or doubt. Also attached were maps that included explanations in which the ancient and present forms of place-names were given.

Hui Tung, Ch'ien Ta-hsin, Sun Hsing-yen, Hung Liang-chi (1746–1809), Hang Shih-chün (1696–1773), and Ch'üan Tsu-wang (1705–1755)—all major figures in the Han-Learning movement—completed important works in these areas in the eighteenth century. In particular, stress was placed on making the *Han-shu* (History of the Former Han) and the *Hou Han-shu* (History of the Later Han) more accessible and accurate. Similarly, Chang Hsueh-ch'eng adamantly insisted that historical writing should include documentation devices that would describe the institutional forms and workings of local government, as well as *jen-wu piao* to facilitate reference.[36]

· ·

Archaeology and Epigraphy

In addition to references to other scholars and the reworking of historical sources, the citing of bronze and stone epigraphical and archaeological evidence became, as we have seen, a major element in *k'ao-cheng* scholarship. Inscriptions on bronze and stone were the two major subjects of study in Chinese archaeology before the discovery of writings on bones and shells, pottery and clay, and bamboo and wood at the end of the nineteenth century. Epigraphy (*chin-shih-hsueh*) developed as a special field of study in the eleventh century. Ou-yang Hsiu's (1007–1072) *Chi-ku lu* (Record of collecting relics), printed in 1061, touched off a remarkable series of works during the Northern Sung that focused on the art of epigraphical copying and collecting.

R.C. Rudolph points out that Sung scholars had progressed beyond collecting curiosities and were actively engaged in research concerned with identification, etymology, dating, and interpretation of findings. Chao Ming-ch'eng and his talented wife Li Ch'ing-chao (1081–1140), for example, compiled the *Chin-shih lu* (Records of bronze and stone) that appeared in 1132. In it they cataloged some two thousand inscriptions, 702 of which received descriptive notice.[37]

During the Ming dynasty, an interest in ancient artifacts was evident, but as in so many other fields, the Northern Sung concern for exact scholarship was not continued. Ming collectors were mainly concerned with aesthetic elements of color and shape in their antique collections. No extensive archaeological fieldwork was attempted, nor was there any serious paleographical study. The Ming preference for linking archaeology with aesthetics marked a reaction against what Yü Ying-shih considers the "intellectualist" orientation adopted by Sung scholars.

An exception to this tendency, Ts'ao Chao's (fl. 1387–1399) *Ko-ku yao-lun* (Essential criteria of antiquities) was one of the earliest comprehensive and systematic treatises on Chinese art and archaeology. Apart from the traditional subjects of calligraphy, painting, zithers, stones, jades, bronzes, and ink-slabs, Ts'ao Chao included discussions of ceramics and lacquer, as well as foreign items. Wang Tso (ca. 1427) made additions to Ts'ao's collection by including findings from the Cheng Ho (1371–1433) expeditions, but he also broke new ground by adding subjects such as imperial seals, iron tallies, official costumes, and palace architecture.[38]

Ch'ing scholars, rejecting the preponderantly aesthetic criteria employed by most Ming collectors, kept records of their journeys and findings. As in the Sung, such accounts generally included complete descriptions of important temples, tombs, monuments, and other objects studied. These recordings gave specific locations of discoveries, and frequently transcriptions of epigraphical findings were appended. The scale of collecting also increased dramatically. More than three thousand ancient bronze items were recorded during the Ch'ing compared with 643 during the Sung. In comparison with some twenty known Sung catalogs, there were upwards of five hundred such compilations during the Ch'ing.[39]

Ku Yen-wu was one of the pioneers in the use of bronze and stone relics for research purposes. In the preface to his *Ch'iu-ku lu* (Record of the search for antiquities), Ku wrote: "Then when I read Ou-yang Hsiu's *Chi-ku lu* I realized that many of the events recorded in these inscriptions are verified by works of history so that, far from being merely bits of high-flown rhetoric, they are of actual use in supplementing and correcting the histories." While in Shansi, Ku acquired a set of 124 ink rubbings from 126 engravings of the *Avataṁsaka Sūtra* (*Hua-yen ching*) carved in 551 in a grotto located in the mountains. Yen Jo-chü also used the extensive relics in his ancestral place in T'ai-yuan to correct errors he discovered in the Classics and the Histories. Seventeenth-century scholars such as Yao Chi-heng and Chu I-tsun (1629–1709) maintained large collections of relics and rubbings in their libraries. In addition, Chu I-tsun in 1687 completed a well-known history of Peking and its environs in which he described its archaeological and historical sites of interest.[40]

Interest in epigraphy peaked during the late eighteenth and early nineteenth centuries. Pi Yuan (1730–1797) was credited with epigraphical collections compiled in Shensi in 1781 and Honan in 1787 under his direction. Both works dealt with ancient inscriptions discovered in Central and Northwest China. Pi Yuan also was one of the first to study inscribed roof tiles that he found in Shensi. In this effort he was followed by Feng Teng-fu (1783–1841) whose *Che-chiang chuan-lu* (Brick inscriptions of Chekiang) contained findings bearing dates as early as 140 B.C.

Weng Fang-kang (1733–1818) also was an authority on bronze and stone inscriptions. His well-known *Liang-Han chin-shih chi* (Record of bronze and stone epigraphy in the Former and Later Han) was printed in 1789. While serving as director of education in Kwangtung from 1764–1771, Weng had already described many ancient and contemporary inscriptions from that province in a work entitled *Yüeh-tung chin-shih lüeh* (Treatise on bronze and stone epigraphy in eastern Kwangtung). Ch'ien Ta-hsin, who applied epigraphy to historical research, noted:

> For the most part, writings on bamboo and silk deteriorated rapidly over time. In the process of recopying [these writings] by hand over and over again, their original appearance was lost. Only bronze and stone inscriptions survive from hundreds and thousands of years ago. In them, we see the real appearance of the ancients. Both the writings [of this type] and

the affairs [described in them] are reliable and verifiable. Therefore, they are prized.

. . .

Juan Yuan's extensive collation of the Classics relied in large part on remnants of the Classics engraved on stone during the Han, T'ang, and Sung dynasties. In more than fifty years of travel and study, Wang Ch'ang (1725–1807), like Ch'ien Ta-hsin, put together a collection drawn from antiquity to the end of the Sung of more than 1,500 bronze and stone inscriptions. Later, pre-T'ang inscriptions in Wang's collection were reproduced in facsimile with every item described in full, including quotations from various authorities. Tuan Yü-ts'ai (1735–1815) and others completed enlarged and annotated editions of Hsu Shen's (58–147) *Shuo-wen chieh-tzu*. Under each of Hsu's items scholars like Tuan placed a chronological series of ancient forms of writing copied from stone and bronze relics or books from tombs.[41]

Bringing to a close a tradition that had seen six major attempts to record the Confucian Canon on stone tablets since the Later Han, the Ch'ien-lung Emperor, at Chu Yun's (1729–1781) urging, ordered in 1791 that a complete version of the Classics be engraved in stone and erected in the Imperial Academy in Peking. Completed in 1794, the tablets (like predecessors since the Han) were meant to serve as a permanent, standard text for the preservation and diffusion of classical literature.[42]

. .

The Impact of Epigraphy on Ch'ing Calligraphy

Interest in bronze and stone inscriptions during the seventeenth and eighteenth centuries rekindled interest in ancient writing forms. As a result, there was a great deal of enthusiasm for the art of seal engraving in artistic circles throughout Kiangnan. Stimulated by epigraphical studies, calligraphers began to recreate the ancient seal (*chuan-shu*) and official or clerical (*li-shu*) styles of writing inscribed on stone and bronze objects. Known as the "stele school" (*pei-hsueh p'ai*), the artists associated with this movement revived the seal and clerical styles of calligraphy that had been out of vogue since the T'ang dynasty.[43]

The great works of Han dynasty calligraphers had all been monumental inscriptions engraved on stone stelae. Seal and clerical style scripts on such stelae tended to be public and commemorative in intent during that period. Cursive forms were used mainly for casual and unofficial functions and were not yet written with aesthetic intent. In the Six Dynasties (221–589) period, artistic attention began to shift away from stone inscriptions and focused instead on small pieces of writing on paper and silk, such as personal letters. These were called "writings on small sheets" (*t'ieh*). *T'ieh* calligraphy, as opposed to "monumental" (*pei*) calligraphy, became the representative form for master works until the eighteenth century.

Evolution of the Chinese script from seal through clerical to regular (*k'ai-shu*) styles was completed by the third century A.D. During this period, Wang Hsi-chih (307–365) achieved an archaistic synthesis of calligraphic styles. His eclectic mixing of styles became the basis for the classical tradition of Chinese calligraphy. Most works in this tradition were written in cursive (*ts'ao*), running (*hsing*), or regular script styles.[44] According to Lothar Ledderhose and Shen Fu, it was not until the eighteenth century that the classical tradition in calligraphy was further modified. Although archaic forms of writing continued to be practiced by calligraphers before the Ch'ing period, it is nonetheless clear that seal and clerical scripts gave way to cursive, running, and standard scripts for most artistic writing after the Han dynasty. Ch'ing calligraphers, however, went directly back to Ch'in dynasty inscriptions and expanded their sources to include Han and Six Dynasty stone inscriptions as well. Shen Fu has noted that it was the breadth, variety, and historicity of the latest archaeological finds in the eighteenth century that enabled calligraphers to break away from post-Han conventions for seal and clerical script styles.[45]

Followers of the "stele school" based their authority on the *k'ao-cheng* claim that their models were closer and therefore more faithful to the original script used by the ancients. T'ang, Sung, and Ming dynasty models for seal and clerical styles seemed overly precise and symmetrical. Such models had been molded and limited by rigid aesthetic considerations after the balanced and symmetrical standard script (*k'ai-shu*) formally established during the T'ang became the prevailing calligraphic type. The turning point was exemplified by Fu Shan (1607–1684) and Wang Shu (1668–1739), who both returned directly to the monument tradition. It was not until the eighteenth century that, in retrospect, orthodox calligraphy modeled after Wang Hsi-chih's writing was called the "school based on writings on small sheets" (*t'ieh-hsueh*). This identification reflected the first serious questioning of the aesthetic values of *t'ieh* calligraphy by members of the emerging stele school.[46]

The "seal craze" was felt strongly among members of the Yangchow "eccentric" school of painting as well. Tao-chi (1641–ca. 1720) occasionally employed seal script for titles of his paintings and more frequently for the stone seals he carved himself. Chin Nung (1687–1763), for example, was one of the first to revive these ancient art forms. A student of ancient artifacts, Chin attempted to simulate on paper the characters engraved on bronze and stone. Calligraphy gained a fresh input of models and inspiration from contemporary trends in epigraphical research. Seal designing and engraving at the same time became a skill expected of accomplished scholars.[47]

Teng Shih-ju (1743?–1805) and Pao Shih-ch'en (1775–1855) were among the eighteenth-century leaders of this turn to archaic calligraphy. Modeling their calligraphy on bronze and stone inscriptions, both Teng and Pao were avid students of ancient relics. After Fu Shan's and Wang Shu's innovations, others continued conservative and conventional styles in their seal and clerical calligraphy. Teng Shih-ju, however, led a second group of calligraphers who advocated calligraphy types inscribed on Ch'in, Han, and Three Kingdoms (221–280) relics. By seeking out the earliest sources of seal and clerical scripts, Teng, according to Shen Fu, literally made the earlier conventional forms obsolete.

Stylistically, Teng rejected the mechanical precision of earlier seal script styles in favor of an imposing degree of irregularity in his seal and clerical calligraphy (see Figure 13). Pao Shih-ch'en's studies of ancient stone inscriptions were brought together in an extensive collection later enlarged upon by K'ang Yu-wei (1858–1927). K'ang said of Teng that his contribution to seal writing was comparable to that of Mencius in Confucian philosophy. Teng's style remains a major influence in seal engraving in China and Japan today.[48]

Followers of the stele school cast serious doubts on the authenticity and validity of the classical tradition modeled after Wang Hsi-chih's calligraphy and aesthetic standards. A discovery in 1778 of a stele dated A.D. 405 prompted scholars such as Juan Yuan to dismiss the authenticity of Wang Hsi-chih's models and the *t'ieh* tradition altogether. The stele, as well as bricks from tombs of the fourth and fifth centuries

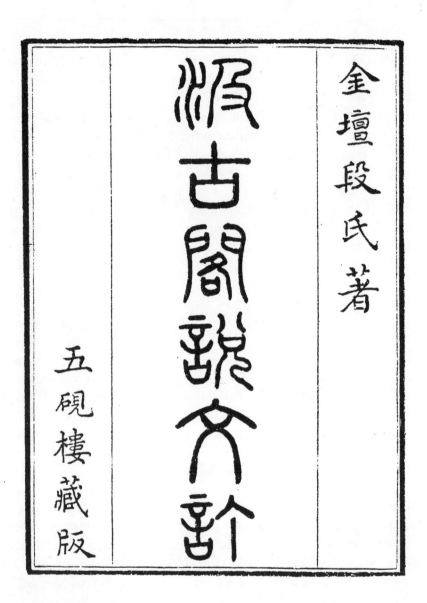

Figure 11

1771–1772 Title Page of Tuan Yü-ts'ai's
Chi-ku-ko Shuo-wen ting (Emendation of the
Chi-ku-ko's *Shuo-wen*)
Source: Reprinted from *Tuan Yü-ts'ai i-shu*
(Taipei, Ta-hua shu-chü Reprint, 1977).
Note: The title, written in seal script, is flanked
by *k'ai-shu* (regular script).

Figure 12

1825 Title Page of Tuan Yü-ts'ai's *Shih-ching hsiao-hsueh* (Philological Analysis of the *Poetry Classic*)

Source: Reprinted from *Tuan Yü-ts'ai i-shu.*

Note: The title, written in Han dynasty official script, is flanked by regular script.

Figure 13   A Sample of Teng Shih-ju's Seal Calligraphy
Source: Reproduced from *Teng Shih-ju chuan-shu* (Peking, 1982).

A.D., were inscribed in stern and angular clerical script forms and revealed no stylistic relation to Wang Hsi-chih's allegedly contemporary cursive and running script styles.

In two pioneering essays on the history of calligraphy in China written in 1823, Juan Yuan maintained that the inscriptions on stone stelae and bricks, not the styles employed by Wang Hsi-chih and his son Wang Hsien-chih (344–388), typified the styles of the post-Han era. Juan dismissed the two Wangs' *t'ieh* calligraphy because he believed their calligraphy styles had been falsified in the process of constant copying and forging. Juan Yuan in effect was making use of archaeological pieces as evidence for the historical development of calligraphy in China and as proof that the classical tradition transmitted since the T'ang dynasty had been misguided.[49]

The accomplishments of calligraphers who studied archaeological relics grew out of the inseparability of their technical and artistic interests. The stele school calligraphers possessed a thorough knowledge of archaic conventions and the appropriate configurations for their archaic calligraphy. This knowledge in turn depended on study of etymology and philology, the key elements of evidential research.

. .

Genealogies and Chronological Biographies

Another indication of the eighteenth-century turn to the precise and the determinable was the practice of compiling chronologies, genealogies, and chronological biographies (*nien-p'u*) for earlier scholars. Ch'ien Ta-hsin took special interest in recording the dates of historical figures in Chinese history, and his work entitled *I-nien lu* (Record of uncertain dates) became the starting point for most of the important dictionaries of dates that followed. Johanna Meskill has noted that the overwhelming majority of printed genealogies were produced during the Ch'ing dynasty and in Kiangnan, especially its urban centers. Of the total of 1,197 datable extant genealogies, only 14 originated prior to the Ch'ing dynasty.

In an effort to cut through the legends that surrounded men who lived in the past and avoid the didactic biographies compiled for the *Dynastic Histories,* Ch'ing scholars emphasized the chronological biography genre to recreate the lives of important figures. Sung scholars were especially singled out for this treatment. Ch'ien Ta-hsin, for instance, compiled five chronological biographies, four for Sung Confucian scholars, including Wang Ying-lin. Wang Mao-hung (1668–1741) earlier had compiled a detailed chronological biography for Chu Hsi. This development suggests that compilers of chronological biographies were using biography to legitimate their own collective activities. The large number of chronologies prepared for Sung literati made an important contribution to Sung Learning during the Ch'ing dynasty. They are emblematic of the impact of evidential research as a broad intellectual enterprise on both Sung Learning and Han Learning. When looked at as one aspect of the *k'ao-cheng* reaction against Sung-Ming moral discourse, it becomes clear how a chronological list of events with little interpretation became widely accepted as biography.[50]

. . .

Collaboration, Correspondence, and Meetings

Living in an academic environment where much depended on patronage, eighteenth-century scholars frequently were involved in projects that required on joint effort and communication. These elementary types of cooperative practice began with projects such as the *Ming History* and *Ta-Ch'ing i-t'ung-chih* in the seventeenth century and continued in the eighteenth century with academic projects carried out under imperial and semiofficial patronage (see chapter 3).[51] The *Ssu-k'u ch'üan-shu* project (1772–1788) was the most far-reaching academic enterprise to require the collaboration in a unified and systematic manner of experts in a wide variety of disciplines. In many ways the project exemplified the academic and social ties conducive to the exchange of information and its subsequent publication. Bibliophiles and scholars were drawn into a book collecting system that produced one of the most sophisticated premodern libraries and catalogs anywhere in the world.

In addition to imperial compilations and provincial secretarial staff (*mu-yu*) projects, which required the collaboration of numerous textual scholars, private scholars often enlisted expert help on works they were writing. Ch'in Hui-t'ien (1702–1764), in a typical colleague network, was aided by Ch'ien Ta-hsin and Wang Ming-sheng on certain parts of a massive work entitled the *Wu-li t'ung-k'ao* (Comprehensive examination of the five Classics of Rites) that he was compiling. When Tai Chen arrived in Peking for the first time in 1754, Ch'ien Ta-hsin, recognizing Tai's talents in mathematics and astronomy, recommended Tai to Ch'in for consultation on the difficult parts of the texts on ritual that included mathematical and astronomical references. Ch'in quickly called in Tai and asked his opinions on numerous passages. In fact, Ch'in included almost verbatim the complete text of one of Tai's earlier writings on mathematics.[52]

Frequently employed as a collator, Sun Hsing-yen profited from the assistance of such friends and colleagues as Ku Kuang-ch'i (1776–1835) and Yen K'o-chün (1762–1843). Both Ku and Yen were experts in epigraphy. The Soochow bibliophile Sun Ts'ung-t'ien (ca. 1680–1749) explained the importance of collaboration in the field of collation as follows:

> Should there be something amiss in the collation of the ancients and should your own research fail to improve upon their work, you will have to confer far and wide with men of extensive knowledge and scholars well versed in the study of ancient scripts; further, you will have to compare your text with the scripts of old steles and check it with a copy held by some other collector; then you will be able to make your correction. On the other hand, this may be said of collating a book: only if you can assemble a number of scholars with whom you stand on friendly terms in the villa where your study is located, to discuss and disentangle ancient texts, will your understanding turn out to be fruitful; otherwise there will be always some imperfection.[53]

. . .

Apart from official and semiofficial academic projects, private meetings and correspondence played an important role in the transmission of information between individuals during the seventeenth and eighteenth centuries. Yuan Mei (1716–1798), for example, was particularly gratified when Lu Wen-ch'ao (1717–1796), then director of the Chung-shan

Academy in Nanking, would come to him to borrow a book. Yuan
wrote in a poem:

> When other people borrow books, they borrow them and that is all;
> But when you come to borrow a book my heart leaps for joy.
> Every book you take away comes back in ten days
> With every gap filled in, every confusion in order.
> You tell me that collating texts is the great passion of your life—
> To sort them out with as fine precision as a sieve sifts rice;
> That to get a single right meaning is better than a ship-load of pearls,
> To resolve a single doubt is like the bottom falling off the bucket.[54]

. . .

The Debate Over the Old Text Documents

The polemic over the Old Text chapters of the *Documents* presents a
concrete example of scholarly communication among Ch'ing evidential
scholars. Meetings and correspondence played an important role in this
seventeenth-century debate, which then carried over into the eighteenth
century. Yen Jo-chü and Mao Ch'i-ling were the two chief antagonists.
Through a net of correspondence and personal connections, they attracted the attention of many of the leading scholars of their time. Yen
and Mao exchanged views over the matter, and two of Mao's letters to
Yen Jo-chü have survived.

In a letter written after receiving a copy of Yen's *Shu-cheng* in 1693,
Mao countered with a direct attack on Yen's position: "Yesterday I
received a copy of your book called the *Evidential Analysis Into the
Documents Classic*. It is a complete perversion of the words of earlier
men. It mistakenly makes the *Documents* no more than a forged book."
On the key point of the "mind of man and the mind of *Tao*" passage
in the "Ta Yü mo" chapter, Mao challenged Yen's demonstration that
this passage was lifted from the *Hsun-tzu* by writing: "Moreover, although the *Hsun-tzu* contains the *jen-hsin Tao-hsin* [passage], Hsun-tzu
is in fact citing the text of the Classic [of *Documents*]. It is not a case
of the Classic citing the *Hsun-tzu*." According to Mao, the *Tao-ching*
that Hsun-tzu cited as his source for the passage was in fact a reference
to texts that had been compiled before the *Changes* and used to in-
struct the sage-kings of antiquity. Mao took Yen's attack on the Old
Text chapters as an affront to the "sacred Classics."[55]

Later in 1699, Mao Ch'i-ling sent Yen Jo-chü a letter accompanying a copy of his recently completed *Ku-wen Shang-shu yuan-tz'u* (In defense of the Old Text *Documents*). In it Mao wrote that he had given the matter careful consideration and concluded that the entire *Documents* was authentic. Furthermore, he had discussed the question with Li Kung (1659–1733), who had traveled from North China to study with him after studying with Yen Yuan (1635–1704). Mao summarized some of his key arguments and noted: "Even if Ch'ien-ch'iu's [that is, Yen Jo-chü] scholarship surpasses mine by [a factor of] ten thousand upon ten thousand, still it cannot be said that he surpasses the Six Classics!"[56]

Both Li Kung and Yao Chi-heng studied under Mao Ch'i-ling. Yao Chi-heng, although very close to Mao and his elder brother Mao Wan-ling, regarded the Old Text chapters as a forgery. He met with Yen Jo-chü in 1693 (Mao Ch'i-ling introduced them) to discuss the issue, and Yen copied down some of Yao's findings for inclusion in his *Shu-cheng*. Yen discovered that Yao had made use of the *Kuo-yü* (Discourses of the states) and the *Tso chuan* in very much the same way that he himself had, that is, to demonstrate where the forger of the Old Text chapters had gotten his material. Earlier in the *Shu-cheng*, Yen had quoted Yao Chi-heng to the effect that both the text and the commentary of the Old Text *Documents* were the work of the same hand, and "Yao had laughed at the fact that people had known only enough to question the authenticity of [K'ung An-kuo's] commentary but not the Classic itself." In effect, Yen was employing one of Mao Ch'i-ling's associates to solidify his own stand against Mao's position.[57]

Li Kung, on the other hand, wrote a preface for Mao's *Ku-wen Shang-shu yuan-tz'u*. In it Li described how Mao had answered many of the doubts he had had concerning the text of the *Documents*. Later in 1699, Li Kung stopped in Huai-an on his way home and met and talked with Yen Jo-chü about this debate. In a 1700 letter to Mao Ch'i-ling, Li wrote that he had in fact informed Yen of Mao's new research on the Old Text chapters. Li also noted that Yen had said that Mao's work was no doubt intended to refute his *Shu-cheng*.[58]

In a letter about this time to Huang Tsung-hsi, the patriarch of the Eastern Chekiang school to which Mao belonged, Mao Ch'i-ling discussed certain aspersions cast on the authenticity of the Old Text chapters and diplomatically (unusual for him) wrote: "I have heard that you

[Huang] once also pointed out that [the Old Text chapters] are forgeries. Perhaps there is some more evidence [I am not aware of]." Mao then discussed a recent attempt by an old friend to demonstrate that the "An-kuo Introduction" was a forgery. This argument was based on discrepancies in the dating of K'ung An-kuo's death and the dates for the onset of the witchcraft trials that prevented the Old Text chapters from being accepted by the Han imperial court.

This "old friend" can only be a reference to Yen Jo-chü and his efforts in the *Shu-cheng* to prove through chronological inconsistencies that An-kuo could not have lived to see the 92–91 B.C. witchcraft trials. Mao's letter to Huang was in fact an attempt to discredit Yen's demonstration. Mao attacked on two fronts. First he contended: "Even if [An-kuo's] 'Greater Introduction' was a forgery, such [a disclosure] does not prove that the *Documents* itself is a forgery." Second, Mao attacked the reliability of Yen's major textual source—Ssu-ma Ch'ien's *Shih-chi.* Yen had relied in his proof on Ssu-ma Ch'ien's assertion that An-kuo had died young; Mao attempted to show that the *Shih-chi* was filled with so many chronological mistakes that it could not be regarded as reliable evidence for the claims Yen made. In conclusion, Mao asked Huang Tsung-hsi to carefully consider the arguments contained in his letter because they were based on "solid empirical evidence" (*ch'ueh-ch'iu shih-chü*). Mao was attempting by use of *k'ao-cheng* criteria to line up Huang Tsung-hsi on his side.[59]

Yen's meeting and debate with Wan Ssu-t'ung (1638–1702), another prominent member of the Eastern Chekiang school, at about this time over the Old Text *Documents* (see chapter 3) was another element in this interesting example of proof and counterproof, rejoinder and surrejoinder. These encounters reveal the careful research and care of detail that lay at the heart of the scholarly debates of the age. Standing on opposite sides of the Old Text chapters issue, both Yen and Mao were committed to the use of empirical criteria to prove their claims. After meeting together and debating the issue, both men returned to write down their views. Beneath the difference in conclusions lay a unity of methodology and discourse. This seventeenth-century example was repeated during the eighteenth century in the priority debates discussed below.[60]

· ·

The Role of Letters in Evidential Research

David Nivison has explained that letters were written in eighteenth-century China to be passed around, copied, and eventually published. Arthur Waley noted that there existed no learned periodicals in the eighteenth century. Their place was taken by letters exchanged between learned friends. Many writers such as Yuan Mei used correspondence as a means to make known the random items of knowledge that they could not incorporate into their books or essays. Often scholarly letters were later collected together or printed, either in the collected writings (*wen-chi*) of their author or as a separate volume.[61]

Chang Hsueh-ch'eng, for example, exchanged letters with numerous contemporaries. His correspondence with Shao Chin-han (1743–1796) in particular was filled with discussion of problems in historiography and bibliography. It was not unusual for a writer to publish letters written to colleagues who were still living, even without their permission. Nevertheless, Chang Hsueh-ch'eng became indignant when Hung Liang-chi published a 1797 letter addressed to Chang critical of Chang's ideas concerning the historical value of local gazetteers. Chang wrote a letter to Sun Hsing-yen later that year containing criticism of Sun's views and submitted a copy to Yao Nai (1732–1815) for comment. Chang no doubt expected Yao to distribute the letter among Yao's coterie of friends in Nanking.

Letters and essays were often copied by friends and then sent off to still other friends to be read and discussed. Chang Hsueh-ch'eng's writings enjoyed this kind of circulation as did the letters of more famous scholars such as Ch'ien Ta-hsin. In this manner scholars could become moderately well known and carefully read by a large critical audience. Relying on correspondence for exchange of information, junior scholars, as Liang Ch'i-ch'ao has noted, frequently initiated communication with more senior men to inquire about learned problems; at times they enclosed copies of their writings. Chang Hsueh-ch'eng was again typical. He included an account of his *Wen-shih t'ung-i* (Comprehensive meaning of culture and history) in a 1772 letter to Ch'ien Ta-hsin, the most acclaimed historian of the day. Chang also corresponded frequently with Tai Chen, another key figure in eighteenth-century intellectual life, after their first meeting in 1766. Similarly, Liu T'ai-kung (1751–

1805), although he published no work during his lifetime, exchanged letters on classical research with such noted Han-Learning scholars as Juan Yuan, Tsang Yung, and Tuan Yü-ts'ai. In this way, Liu influenced many leading scholars of his time.

Ch'ien Ta-hsin, whose published writings were remarkable in both volume and extent, used letters to colleagues and friends as a tactful way to point out mistakes they had made. For example, he gently pointed to errors he felt Tai Chen had committed in calendrical mathematics, something few others would have dared to do, in a letter written after Ch'ien and Tai met in Peking in 1754. Likewise, Ch'ien pointed to problems he had with Tuan Yü-ts'ai's analysis of the New Text *Documents,* which Ch'ien articulated in a careful letter. Many others corresponded with Ch'ien in this fashion, frequently providing him with the information or materials he requested for further clarification.

For a final example, we should mention Lu Wen-ch'ao, whose reputation as a *k'ao-cheng* scholar rested on his expertise in textual collation (see chapter 2). His correspondents included Wang Chung, Wang Nien-sun, Chou Yung-nien (1730–1791), among other textual scholars. In his letters, Lu exchanged information with his colleagues, offered his own opinions on numerous textual issues, and stipulated how collation contributed to evidential research as a whole. Collation, according to Lu, was a corporate effort to provide the most reliable texts upon which to build further analysis. The technical matters discussed in letters were impressive. To understand the issues demanded a thorough mastery of the texts, their interpretation, and the *k'ao-cheng* techniques used.[62]

. . .

Cumulative Research

During the Ch'ing dynasty there was noticeable progress in *k'ao-cheng* fields of inquiry. Such progress was possible because *k'ao-cheng* scholars, unlike their Sung and Ming predecessors, stressed research topics that lent themselves to cumulative results. The frequency of works written in the "additions and corrections" (*pu-cheng*) and "analysis of evidence" (*pien-cheng*) genres during this period directs our attention to one aspect of this phenomenon—the follow-up of previous research and an attempt to carry earlier findings somewhat further. Such cumulative research was distinguishable from the traditional forms of annotating and commenting on earlier texts.

. .

Follow-up Scholarship in the Ch'ing Period

Recognizing Wang Ying-lin as a precursor to their own scholarship, many Ch'ing scholars, working independently, all examined various aspects of Wang's pioneering research. Yen Jo-chü began a detailed annotation of Wang Ying-lin's famous notation book entitled *K'un-hsueh chi-wen* that was completed by Ho Ch'o after Yen's death in 1704. The standard version now includes further eighteenth-century contributions by Ch'üan Tsu-wang. Chiao Hsun and Feng Teng-fu continued and corrected Wang\Ying-lin's research on the *Poetry Classic* and its textual variants.[63]

Eighteenth-century scholars similarly spent much of their time evaluating and continuing the work of their seventeenth-century predecessors. Weng Fang-kang completed the *Ching-i k'ao pu-cheng* (Additions and corrections to the *Ching-i k'ao*) to correct and bring up-to-date Chu I-tsun's bibliography of the Classics. Sung Hsiang-feng (1776–1860) compiled a continuation to Yen Jo-chü's geographical study of the Four Books, which Sung entitled *Ssu-shu shih-ti pien-cheng* (Analysis of evidence in the *Explanation of Place-names in the Four Books*).[64]

Chiang Yung read Mei Wen-ting's *Li-suan ch'üan-shu* (Complete works on calendrical science) in order to advance his own studies in astronomy and mathematics. On the basis of his findings, Chiang compiled a work called *I Mei* (Wings [that is, Commentary] for Mei [Wen-ting]), which represented Chiang's attempt to carry Mei's scholarship further. Mei Ku-ch'eng (d. 1763), Mei Wen-ting's grandson, continued his grandfather's work and reprinted Wen-ting's collected works, correcting posthumous textual errors that had crept into Wen-ting's astronomical and calendrical studies. Chiang Fan (1761–1831), a disciple of Hui Tung's Han-Learning students Chiang Sheng (1721–1799) and Yü Hsiao-k'o (1729–1777), authored the *Chou-i shu pu* (Continuation to to the *Discourse on the Chou Changes*) to finish Hui's incomplete work.

In the field of bronze and stone epigraphy, we have seen that Ku Yen-wu's *Record of the Search for Antiquities* was influenced by Ou-yang Hsiu's *Record of Collecting Relics*. In addition, Ku's work on epigraphy included references to epigraphical collections begun in the Northern Sung. During the eighteenth century, Hang Shih-chün, in a work entitled *Shih-ching k'ao-i* (Examination of variants in the stone Classics), followed up Ku Yen-wu's *Shih-ching k'ao* (Examination of the stone Classics), emending and correcting Ku's omissions and errors.

In the nineteenth century, Ting Yen (1794–1875) compiled his *Yü-kung chui-chih cheng-wu* (Correction of errors in [Hu Wei's] *A Modest Approach to the Tributes of Yü*) to follow up Hu Wei's (1633–1714) decisive critique of misuses of the oft-cited geography in the "Tributes of Yü" chapter of the *Documents*. Ting also completed a work entitled *Shang-shu yü-lun* (Remaining issues on the *Documents*), adducing additional reasons to confirm Hui Tung's view that Wang Su (195–256) had forged the Old Text *Documents*. Ch'en Li (1810–1882), a Cantonese textual and geographical expert trained at the Hsueh-hai T'ang, went on to prepare a remarkable further study of Hu Wei's research, which Ch'en called *Hu-shih Yü kung t'u k'ao-cheng* (Examination and correction of Master Hu [Wei's] charts of the "Tributes of Yü").[65]

Accompanying this sense of the continuity of academic progress was a quest for originality. Although new discoveries had been praised during the Sung and Ming dynasties, novelty became an explicit aim during the Ch'ing. The pressure to "discover what our predecessors had not yet discovered" (*fa ch'ien-jen so wei fa*) became felt on all levels of *k'ao-cheng* research. The importance of Tuan Yü-ts'ai's research on the *Shuo-wen*, for instance, was demonstrated by the large number of supplementary studies prepared afterwards by other scholars. These included a critique by Yen K'o-chün, a specialist in epigraphy, entitled *Shuo-wen ting ting* (Emendation of [Tuan's] definitive edition of the *Shuo-wen*), Wang Shao-lan's (1760–1835) *Shuo-wen Tuan-chu ting-pu* (Emendation of and additions to Tuan's annotation of the *Shuo-wen*), and Niu Shu-yü's (1760–1827) *Tuan-shih Shuo-wen chiao-ting* (Collation and emendation of Master Tuan's *Shuo-wen*).

Evidential criteria were, as we have seen, the standard of evaluation for books submitted to the *Ssu-k'u ch'üan-shu* editors. Among the criteria employed (such as the use of sources, use of verification procedures, and so forth) was the editors' praise for "discovery" (*fa-ming*) and "unique perception" (*hsin-te*). Scholars were encouraged to surpass past achievements and add to the fund of common knowledge.[66]

Many were ambivalent about these developments. Shao Ch'ang-heng (1636–1704), for example, bemoaned the recent trend among scholars to emphasize what he considered to be purely philological questions in their quest for novelties. Although Chang Hsueh-ch'eng showed interest in many elements of evidential scholarship, such as an emphasis on bibliography and textual criticism, his commitment to the high moral import of history prompted his numerous attacks on the narrow research carried out during the eighteenth century. Chang decried the use of notation books, for example. He saw them as obstacles that blocked the way to real scholarship based on comprehensiveness and synthesis.

In an essay entitled "Yuan Tao" (Inquiry into the *Tao*), Chang Hsueh-ch'eng discussed the conflict between different "fashions" (*feng-ch'i*) in scholarly research and concluded: "Glossing meanings and punctuating phrases and sentences, annotating and explicating meanings and principles, as well as examining the relations between names and their referents do not enable one to speak of the Tao." For Chang, only a comprehensive synthesis of these disparate orientations—philology, philosophy, and bibliography—could yield real scholarship. Hence, for Chang, both Han Learning and Sung Learning represented partisan scholarship. This perspective, a prophetic preview of nineteenth-century intellectual debate (see chapter 6), did not prevent Chang from praising Tai Chen for "discovering what earlier persons had not yet discovered." Describing his own research in a letter to Ch'ien Ta-hsin, Chang wrote: "In my labors in literary and historical criticism and in bibliography, I may perhaps have achieved something new, but in my arguments there is much that runs against popular taste. I would not want these essays too widely known." A sense of progress was pervasive.[67]

. .

Research on the Documents After 1740

As we have seen, Ch'ing scholars stressed Han scholia of the Classics, which they scrutinized in search of previously overlooked information.

The search for evidence was especially evident among scholars who labored on the Old Text *Documents*. Research on the *Documents* during the seventeenth century revealed a definite progression and development. The scholarly communications associated with the *Documents* debate occasioned a series of works in the eighteenth century that probed the issue still further. Because Yen Jo-chü's *Shu-cheng* was passed around only in manuscript form until 1745, Hui Tung wrote that he did not see it until 1743. By then Hui was already deep into his own analysis of the Old Text chapters in a work entitled *Ku-wen Shang-shu k'ao* (Analysis of the Old Text *Documents*). Hui admitted that much of Yen's work agreed with his own findings, and he cited Yen as an authority to corroborate textual questions that overlapped in their research. Appending Yen's points of agreement, Hui noted that it had taken several centuries for suspicions concerning the Old Text chapters to lead anywhere conclusive.[68]

Some of Hui Tung's followers continued research on the Old Text *Documents*. Initially, Hui's early publications on the topic had more impact than Yen's, especially in Soochow, until Yen's *Shu-cheng* was finally published in T'ai-yuan and more widely distributed in the eighteenth century. Chiang Sheng in his *Shang-shu chi-chu yin-shu* (Phonological annotations to collected notes on the *Documents*), completed in 1773, picked up where Hui Tung had left off and attempted to reconstruct the text of the authentic chapters and thereby restore the Han dynasty appearance of the *Documents*.

Wang Ming-sheng (1722–1798) produced the next major work on the question entitled *Shang-shu hou-an* (Appended cases on the *Documents*), which he completed in 1779 after years of work. Annotating only the New Text chapters, Wang placed almost complete reliance on the Later Han Confucian Cheng Hsuan as his source, unlike Chiang Sheng who was more critical of Cheng. Wang did, however, make use of Former Han sources, something that Chiang had not done. Such efforts marked the beginnings of the turn away from Later Han scholarship toward that of the Former Han, an approach that coincided with the emergence of New Text Confucianism in Ch'ang-chou and elsewhere.[69]

Tuan Yü-ts'ai with his *Ku-wen Shang-shu chuan-i* (Textual variations in the Old Text *Documents*) and Sun Hsing-yen with his *Shang-shu chin-ku-wen chu-shu* (Notes and annotations to the New and Old Text

Documents) brought to completion the attack on the spurious Old Text chapters "discovered" by Mei Tse. On the basis of research he carried out between 1788 and 1791, Tuan rejected what he considered Chiang Sheng's and Wang Ming-sheng's arbitrary and often mistaken emendations of the text of the authentic chapters. Making a careful study of the New Text and Old Text variants *for the authentic chapters* in both versions, Tuan concluded that there were in fact two families of authentic texts, one New Text and one Old Text. In his view, the Old Text recension was more reliable because it was linked to the more ancient, authentic Old Text chapters discovered in Confucius' home and then later lost.

Sun Hsing-yen read and as a result recognized the significance of Tuan Yü-ts'ai's analysis. Imitating Tuan's approach, Sun made the Old Text and New Text variants the organizational basis for gathering together pre-Sung annotations of the authentic chapters. The variants had been mixed together since the T'ang, until Tuan had demonstrated that they represented different textual traditions surviving from the Han dynasty. Sun acknowledged that his research was based on the work of Chiang Sheng, Wang Ming-sheng, and Tuan Yü-ts'ai. His family library, for instance, contained earlier studies on the authenticity of the Old Text *Documents* by Mei Tsu, Yen Jo-chü, Hui Tung, Hu Wei, Wang Mingsheng, Chiang Sheng, and Tuan Yü-ts'ai.

Begun in 1794 and completed in 1815, Sun's analysis of Later and Former Han sources marked the high point of the Old Text school's prestige in the eighteenth century. Although Sun and those who immediately preceded him acknowledged that the present twenty-five Old Text chapters were forgeries, they still maintained that the original sixteen Old Text chapters long since lost had been authentic. The latter version soon became a bone of contention as well.[70]

Scholars in the late eighteenth century began to push back the frontiers of their knowledge and focus on the scholarship of the Former Han as a better source for classical research. Ch'en Shou-ch'i (1771–1834) was among the first to recognize the superiority of the New Text version of the authentic chapters of the *Documents.* Around 1800, Ch'en produced a work entitled *Shang-shu ta-chuan ting-pen* (Definitive version of the great commentary to the *Documents*), in which he attempted to reconstruct the New Text commentary known as the *Ta-chuan* (Great commentary); the latter was associated with

Fu Sheng's Former Han recension of the *Documents.* Later, Ch'en's son, Ch'en Ch'iao-ts'ung (1809–1869), wrote the *Chin-wen Shang-shu i-shuo k'ao* (Examination of scattered comments on the New Text *Documents*). In addition to collating the New Text version of the *Documents,* Ch'iao-ts'ung brought together in one work most of the conclusions reached by critical scholars in the preceding centuries.

Liu Feng-lu (1776–1829), in his 1829 *Shang-shu chin-ku-wen chi-chieh* (Collected notes to the New and Old Text *Documents*), did very much what Tuan Yü-ts'ai and Sun Hsing-yen had done, but with an important new framework for analysis. Instead of automatically favoring the Old Text variants as Tuan and Sun had done, Liu Feng-lu, under the influence of his grandfather Chuang Ts'un-yü's (1719–1788) New Text studies, began to argue that the New Text variants were more reliable. In this way, the philological debate over the *Documents* led to political issues that earlier scholars had not envisioned (see chapter 1).

Once New Text scholars could demonstrate that their positions were based on sound philological arguments, they could begin to employ New Text philology as a preliminary step for validating the political and social assumptions that permeated New Text Confucianism. Tung Chung-shu's (179?–93 B.C.) notions of institutional reform and Ho Hsiu's (129–182) reformist interpretation of Confucius' *san-shih* (three ages) concept now had solid textual support and commanded new respect.[71]

Although Liu Feng-lu still accepted the authenticity of the original sixteen Old Text chapters, he had opened the door for other New Text scholars to pass through. Wei Yuan was the first to take advantage of the widening breach between the Old Text and New Text version of the authentic New Text chapters, a breach first perceived by Yen Jo-chü and other Old Text scholars. A student of Liu Feng-lu, Wei moved away from his teacher's emphasis on Ho Hsiu's Later Han commentary to the *Kung-yang chuan.* Instead, Wei turned to what he considered Tung Chung-shu's "more complete" work on the *Spring and Autumn Annals* entitled *Ch'un-ch'iu fan-lu* (The *Spring and Autumn Annals'* radiant dew). The latter work was not a systematic treatise devoted to New Text Confucianism. Rather, Tung's intent in this book had been to speak to urgent political and social questions and thereby provide a viable Confucian rationale for imperial authority. Wei Yuan's research led him directly into the Former Han New Text Confucianism that Tung Chung-shu had helped to install as orthodox in the second century B.C. The fragile unanimity of Han Learning was over.

Wei Yuan pushed the *Documents* debate one more important step in his *Shu-ku-wei* (Ancient subtleties of the *Documents*) completed in 1855. There he argued that not only was the Eastern Chin version of the Old Text chapters a forgery, as Yen Jo-chü and Hui Tung had already demonstrated, but so also had been the earlier version purportedly discovered in Confucius' house, which the Later Han Old Text scholars such as Cheng Hsuan had mentioned.[72] For his part in the continuing debate, Shao I-ch'en (1810–1861), in his research on the Classics, placed the blame for the forging of the sixteen Old Text chapters on Liu Hsin (45 B.C.-A.D. 23), whom he also accused of forging the thirty-nine chapters known as the *I-li* (Leftover chapters of the *Rites*). However, in a work entitled *Shang-shu t'ung-i* (General meaning of the *Documents*), completed around 1860, Shao argued for the authenticity of the later twenty-five Old Text chapters, which Yen Jo-chü and Hui Tung had demonstrated to the satisfaction of most evidential scholars were forgeries. Shao's position was weak, but his stance indicates that even upholders of the Old Text chapters were now suspicious of Liu Hsin's role in the appearance of the earlier sixteen-chapter version of the Old Text *Documents*.[73]

The forger of the Old Text chapters that emerged in the fourth century A.D. could only have been a Later Han, Chin, or Wei dynasty scholar such as Wang Su, Huang-fu Mi (215–282), or Mei Tse himself. Because of the growing accusations against the earlier sixteen Old Text chapters, Liu Hsin, due to his complicity with Wang Mang (r. A.D. 9–23) in overthrowing the New Text orthodoxy in the period between the Former and Later Han dynasties, became the logical candidate for the earlier forgery, in addition to most others dated to this period. This perspective meshed significantly with Liu Feng-lu's earlier research on the *Tso chuan,* in which Liu Feng-lu accused Liu Hsin of extracting the *Tso chuan* from the *Kuo-yü* and unscrupulously employing it as an orthodox commentary to the *Spring and Autumn Annals.* According to Liu Feng-lu, Liu Hsin had thereby managed to drive the *Kung-yang Commentary* out of the imperial academy and to replace it with a spurious Old Text version.

Similar debates raged during the eighteenth and nineteenth centuries concerning the Mao recension of the *Poetry,* and its relation to the three earlier, Former Han recensions, as well as the uproar that surrounded Wang Su's role in the Later Han reappearance of the *K'ung-tzu chia-yü* (School sayings of Confucius). Wei Yuan in his *Shih-ku-wei* (Ancient subtleties of the *Poetry*) mounted a direct attack on the Mao recension and the "Great and Small Prefaces" to the *Poetry.* Wei tried to prove that the prefaces were all later forgeries. The poems of the Mao version, Wei argued, although not forgeries, were also of a much later date and therefore were not as reliable as the Ch'i, Lu, and Han recensions of the *Poetry.*

The stage was set by 1865 for Liao P'ing (1852–1932) and K'ang Yu-wei to argue in the late nineteenth century that the entire Old Text tradition had been the result of a malicious hoax perpetrated by reactionaries, who had misrepresented the progressive teachings of Confucius. These conclusions relied in part on a coherent body of accumulating philological data. The cumulative results of seventeenth- and eighteenth-century research on the *Documents* occasioned a major assault on the Confucian orthodoxy in the nineteenth.[74]

Research on Phonology

Research on the history of Chinese phonology, like studies of the *Documents* in the Lower Yangtze, was also cumulative. Ch'ing students of phonology, upon discovering empirical evidence in Han and T'ang treatises on pronunciation, were able to place their discipline on a firm and impartial footing. In this way, they circumvented what they considered the disastrous paleographical studies prepared by Sung scholars. During the Han dynasty, Hsu Shen had completed the first systematic treatment of the Chinese written language in his *Shuo-wen chieh-tzu,* which he presented to the throne in 121 A.D. Hsu arranged 9,353 different characters according to 530 radicals (*pu-shou*), a system that with subsequent modification remained the basis of organization in most Chinese dictionaries.

Not only did Hsu Shen provide the orthography of the archaic form for each character, he also specified the phonetic element for the vast majority of characters (over 80 percent) that were formed as phonetic compounds. The *Shuo-wen* became the definitive statement of the six formation types (*liu-shu*) governing Chinese characters (see

· Table 8 ·

The Six Types of Characters

1. *Chih-shih* 指事 : simple ideographs, e.g., *shang* 上 (above) and *hsia* 下 (below).
2. *Hsiang-hsing* 象形 : pictographs, e.g., *shan* 山 (mountain), which was originally
3. *Hsieh-sheng* 諧聲: phonetic compounds, e.g., *chiang* 江 (Yangtze River) made up of the water radical 氵 for meaning and the phonetic element (*kung*) 工 for sound.
4. *Hui-i* 會意 : compound ideographs, e.g., "fields" (*t'ien* 田) and "strength" (*li* 力) to form "male" (*nan* 男 —one who puts his efforts into farming).
5. *Chuan-chu* 轉注: extant characters used for new words by extension of meaning, e.g., *pu* 布 (cloth) for "money."
6. *Chia-chieh* 假借 : borrowed characters, e.g., *wan* 萬 (scorpion) also used to mean "myriad" because of the same pronunciation.

Table 8). From the end of the Later Han dynasty until the Northern Sung, Hsu's research was accepted as the final authority in paleography and etymology.

Study of ancient phonology continued during the Han when Cheng Hsuan recognized that contemporary and ancient forms of pronunciations differed. However, many scholars of the Han through T'ang dynasties were unable to explain why certain words in the *Poetry* and other classical texts no longer rhymed in expected places. They began to force the rhyme by emending characters so that the proper rhyme sequence was reestablished. Ignoring the possibility that the text had been correct and that the pronunciation of certain words subsequently had diverged, scholars introduced arbitrary changes into the Classics solely on the basis of rhyming criteria.[75]

A by-product of Buddhist translation work from Sanskrit into Chinese after the fall of the Han dynasty was a Chinese phonetic system for the transcription of foreign proper names. In this system, every foreign word was divided into syllables, each represented by a Chinese character. In addition, Chinese syllables were subsequently transliterated by separating them into two parts, the initial sound and the remainder represented by two characters. Known as *fan-ch'ieh* (syllabic transcription), this system became the basis for precise investigation of phonetics during the T'ang dynasty.

Using this phonetic system, Lu Fa-yen (ca. A.D. 600) compiled a rhyming dictionary entitled *Ch'ieh-yun* (Rhymes indicated by syllabic transcription), which gave the pronunciation of characters in *fan-ch'ieh*. Later, Lu Te-ming, in his seventh-century etymological and phonological reference book entitled *Ching-tien shih-wen* (Explanations of primary graphs in the Classics), which was based on some fourteen classical texts, reconstituted from more than 230 different classical commentaries the pronunciation of the Han, Wei (220–264), and Six Dynasties periods, giving each syllable in *fan-ch'ieh* transcription. Lu acknowledged that ancient and modern rhymes were not equivalent.

Ch'en P'eng-nien (961–1017) revised and enlarged Lu Fa-yen's rhyming dictionary, titling the result the *Kuang-yun* (Expansion of rhymes). The latter was the best-known rhyme dictionary of the Sung period. It contained 26,194 characters arranged under four classical tonal categories. Within each tone, words were further divided into rhymes and then classified according to homophonic groups. Pronunciation in *fan-ch'ieh* and the meaning were included for all characters. Ch'en's dictionary was prized by Ch'ing phonologists because it faithfully preserved one of several phonological systems of the sixth century A.D.

Wang An-shih's (1021–1086) influential *Tzu-shuo* (Explanation of characters) represented a pivotal position in Sung philological and linguistic research because of Wang's prestige as a Confucian scholar-official. Although Wang An-shih made some effort to trace the archaic forms of characters, for the most part he attempted to reduce all graphs to words formed as compound ideographs. Wang saw the *hui-i* rule of character formation as the key to textual analysis. He contended that Hsu Shen's phonological derivations were arbitrary and unnecessary to understand the meaning of a character. Instead, Wang argued that by analyzing all the characters that made up a complex graph and by understanding the meaning of each component, one could determine the precise meaning of the whole.[76]

Wang An-shih's ahistorical structural approach depended on an imaginative observation of and inference from the makeup of the characters themselves. This orientation represented a clean break with the legacy of Hsu Shen's dictionary, which was rooted in the historical analysis of paleography, etymology, and phonetics. Not recognizing the phonetic elements of such characters, Sung scholars often juggled the structure of the graphs in order to come up with plausible etymologies (as many scholars still do). The cumulative efforts of earlier philologists to reconstruct accurate etymologies based on historical evidence were overlooked. However, limitations in Wang's approach were recognized by scholars who dealt with characters that were formed through phonetic, not ideographic, rules. Cheng Ch'iao (1104–1162), for example, in a monograph on the six rules of character formation, analyzed 24,235 graphs, of which 90 percent were phonetic compounds, 7 percent ideographs, and only 3 percent pictographs.[77]

Renewed interest in phonology grew out of the rigorous rhyming requirements in Chinese poetics. During the twelfth century, Chu Hsi and his followers emphasized the notion of "rhyming pronunciation" (*hsieh-yun*), whereby they emended the rhymes of the *Poetry* where the words no longer rhymed. Chu Hsi's approach was drawn in part from his predecessor Wu Yü's reconstruction of ancient pronunciation. Wu Yü, however, in his eleventh-century *Yun-pu* (Restoration of rhymes) had tried to reconstruct the ancient pronunciation of words on the principle that the rhyme should reappear without arbitrarily emending characters. Wu divided ancient rhymes into nine categories and thereby placed the study of ancient rhymes and pronunciation on firm ground. Wu Yü's perspective gained increasing sophistication during the Ming dynasty through the phonetic research carried out by Cheng Hsiang and Yang Shen (1488–1559). Following Wu Yü's approach, Yang Shen attempted to reconstruct the pronunciations of the pre-Ch'in period by classifying ancient rhymes and examining their changes over time. The breakthrough, however, came with the 1616 publication in Nanking of Ch'en Ti's (1541–1617) *Mao-shih ku-yin k'ao* (Examination of ancient pronunciation in the Mao recension of the *Poetry*).[78]

With the help of Chiao Hung, who encouraged him to focus on the *Poetry* in order to reestablish ancient pronunciation, Ch'en Ti, by means of a systematic arrangement of rhyming words, determined with a fair degree of accuracy the ancient pronunciation for several hundred rhyming words. In order to demonstrate what the ancient pronunciations were and how words orginally rhymed, Ch'en listed all the instances he could gather from the *Poetry* itself, and then followed this proof with all the corroborating evidence from what he considered to be contemporary or only slightly later sources. The former he called "internal" (*pen-cheng*, lit., "basic") evidence and the latter "external" (*p'ang-cheng,* lit., "subsidiary") evidence. By applying a rigorous historical methodology, Ch'en Ti brought together all known instances of a particular rhyme to show that they all pointed to a given reading.

Chiao Hung seems to have been acquainted with Matteo Ricci's (1552–1610) translated works on Latin alphabetic writing. This connection has been seen by some as evidence for Western influence on Ch'en Ti's phonological research. Other contemporaries of Ch'en Ti also recognized the advantage of the Latin alphabet for the transcription of Chinese sounds. Influenced by the scientific contributions made by the Jesuits, Liu Hsien-t'ing (1648–1695), for example, recognized the value of the Latin alphabet for the transcription of sounds and the importance of Sanskrit for phonological research. The *Ssu-k'u ch'üan-shu* editors indicated that after Ricci's alphabet system was introduced, Tai Chen contended that it was originally plagiarized from the Chinese syllabic transcription system. This critique was part of Tai's attempt to argue that various astronomical and mathematical notions were all of native origin (see chapter 2). The editors rejected Tai's argument and pointed out that Tai had failed to realize that phonology had also become an independent specialty in "the Western regions" (*Hsi-yü*).

We might note that the *fan-ch'ieh* transcription system did not give absolute pronunciation. It could only show how ancient readings were grouped homophonically and not how to reproduce what they sounded like at a given time. Absolute pronunciation, although impossible to reproduce definitively, was more closely approximated by an alphabet. An alphabet at least limited the range of possibilities. It is unclear, however, how many Ch'ing scholars had mastered an alphabetic language well enough to grasp this point.

Wu Yü's and Ch'en Ti's research proved to Ch'ing scholars such as Ku Yen-wu and Chiang Yung that what had been termed "rhyming pronunciation" during the T'ang and Sung dynasties was a poor excuse for emending characters. More importantly, Ch'en Ti showed them that the ancient rhyming system could be recovered through precise analysis and research. The inferior success of Sung scholars in literary research was seen in large part as a result of their lack of a rigorous methodology. Ch'ing scholars recognized that the remarkable achievements of recent scholarship in phonetics were a product of the conscious application of precise methods of analysis. Evidential scholars now realized how various types of evidence could be brought to bear on phonetic transformations.[79]

Ku Yen-wu sadly noted that the "rhyming pronunciation" theory not only had caused ancient rhymes to be lost but, because of arbitrary emendations, had also resulted in the loss of the original text. In his *Yun-pu cheng* (Corrections to the *Restoration of Rhymes*) and *Yin-hsueh wu-shu* (Five books on phonology), Ku consciously picked up where Wu Yü and Ch'en Ti had left off and made further discoveries in ancient pronunciation. Extending the inquiry from the *Poetry,* Ku included the pronunciation of the other Classics as external evidence for the ancient rhyming system in the *Poetry.* He divided the rhyming system into ten major divisions. Summarizing Ku's contribution, the *Ssu-k'u ch'üan-shu* editors maintained that Ku was instrumental in "discovering the guidelines" (*fa ch'i chih*) and "definitive theories" (*ting lun*) needed for the study of ancient rhymes.[80]

It had been recognized generally by the seventeenth century that the phonetic element of each character was the decisive element in establishing meaning. Ch'ing philologists rejected the speculative conclusions that Wang An-shih and other Sung scholars had introduced in their glosses of characters. The consensus of scholarly opinion was that the rules for compound ideographs had played a very limited role in the formation of Chinese characters. The overwhelming majority of graphs had been composed on the basis of phonetic rules and not ideographic combinations. A system of analysis known as "characters formed through phonetic borrowings" (*chia-chieh-tzu*) was employed not only to reconstruct ancient phonology but, more importantly, to decipher the ancient meaning of characters by means of ancient phonology.

The investigation of ancient script was shown to be a hopeless proposition unless one took into account the archaic pronunciation of the characters. Bernhard Karlgren has explained:

> It was the great phonetic similarity, sometimes homophony of large groups of monosyllabic words that gave rise to the principle of phonetic loans [*chia-chieh*], the character for one word being applied, as a loan, to a totally different word that was identical or similar in sound, a principle which in its turn, by the elucidating addition of determinatives ("radicals"), led to the creation of the great, even dominating category of

characters known as *hsieh-sheng*, phonetic compounds, consisting of one "Radical" and one "Phonetic."

. . .

Although phonetic compounds formed the majority of characters in Ch'in and Han times, borrowed characters had been very common during the Chou dynasty and phonetic compounds somewhat rarer. That is, characters were borrowed without adding radicals, or sometimes by adding radicals that did not ultimately become standard. If the ancient pronunciation of a character could be reconstructed, its ancient meaning could be restored—hence the centrality of phonetic research in Ch'ing philological studies. Phonology too became a systematic vehicle to "restore the past."

Ch'ing evidential scholars gradually developed a more sophisticated notion of how the phonetic element operated in the formation of complex characters. By introducing the notion of "the right side of a graph theory" (*yu-wen*), scholars were able to demonstrate that the right-hand side of a character, which according to the simple view of the phonetic element was supposed to supply only the sound of the character, also provided a clue to its meaning, although not in the same way that Wang An-shih had argued.[81]

In the eighteenth century, Chiang Yung took issue with some elements in Ku Yen-wu's phonological research. Chiang carefully examined the more than three hundred poems in the *Poetry* and compared his findings with the pronunciation used during the Chou and Ch'in dynasties; he then took into account more recent examples of pronunciation and rhyme. With a wider body of Chou and Ch'in dynasty data to build on, Chiang Yung was able to increase Ku Yen-wu's ten divisions of rhymes to thirteen. The *Ssu-k'u ch'üan-shu* editors pointed out that Chiang's contributions brought the "systematic organization" (*t'iao-li*) of ancient rhymes to its most precise form until later improvements.[82]

In his analysis of the relation of the four tones to ancient pronunciation, Chiang Yung carefully noted Ku Yen-wu's claim that Confucius had transmitted the *Changes* using the dialect of his own time and place. Following up this point, Chiang recognized that tonal and phonetic transformations depended on place and individual variations, in addition to undergoing the vicissitudes of time. Having historicized pronunciation, Chiang then transformed Ku Yen-wu's overly rigid notions of phonetic changes. Arguing that in antiquity the number of written characters, that is, ideographs and pictographs, was limited, whereas the number of spoken words, that is, sounds referring to things, objects, concepts, and so forth, was unlimited, Chiang theorized that all characters had had sounds attached to them but many sounds had not yet had characters devised for them. Chiang saw this situation as the fundamental linguistic, dare one say transformative, dynamic whereby, through a system of borrowed characters, oral discourse generated a phonetically derived written language. Chiang's recognition of the priority of the spoken language explained why so few characters were pictographs or ideographs. The same phenomenon can be discerned in the transliteration of Sanskrit names and words from India in medieval China and from Europe (for example *Ou-lo-pa* for "Europe") in more recent centuries.[83]

Although Chiang accepted much of Ku Yen-wu's analysis, he rejected its underlying intentions. Ku had seen language as a moral, social, and political tool. If the ancient language employed by the sage-kings could be reconstructed, then Ku thought the ideal institutions and manners of antiquity could be restored as well. Chiang, however, noted that, although both he and Ku had made considerable headway in reconstructing ancient pronunciation, it would be impossible to restore fully the ancient language. Chiang's historicist analysis thus prevented him from accepting Ku Yen-wu's ideal vision of language as a tool to revive the past. Chiang had severed the tie between fact and value from its classical moorings.[84]

Further research carried out in the eighteenth century brought phonology to the state of a rigorous discipline. Tuan Yü-ts'ai employed the *Shuo-wen* as a systematic tool for dividing rhymes into more precise categories. Adding four new divisions, Tuan increased the number of Chiang Yung's divisions from thirteen to seventeen. K'ung Kuangsen (1752–1786), a student of Tai Chen, and Liu Feng-lu divided ancient rhymes into eighteen and twenty-six divisions respectively. Analysis became more and more refined.

Although Tuan Yü-ts'ai was Tai Chen's disciple, Tuan had published a number of treatises on phonetics while Tai was still carrying out research on the subject. In a famous reply to Tuan, Tai Chen rejected Tuan's seventeen divisions and explained why he had increased the number of rhyming divisions first to twenty and then to twenty-five.

Summarizing Ku Yen-wu's and Chiang Yung's research, Tai advised Tuan Yü-ts'ai on methodology (see chapter 2). Tai saw their research as an attempt to add to the growing precision of phonological studies. He wrote: "Master Ku [Yen-wu] pioneered the study of ancient pronunciation. Mr. Chiang [Yung] and you [Tuan] merely have continued [Ku's research] and added precision to it."[85]

Similar patterns of development occurred in the study of tones and their historical changes. Both Tai Chen and Ch'ien Ta-hsin also made important contributions to this field. Kinoshita Tetsuya recently has contended that Tai Chen focused his phonetic research not on ancient pronunciation per se, to which he nonetheless made important contributions, but rather on "typologies of sounds" (sheng-lei) that were the basis of both ancient and modern pronunciation. Seeing remarkable resemblances between ancient and modern rhymes, Tai rejected Ch'en Ti's and Ku Yen-wu's absolute bifurcation between the two. Rather than just delimit ancient and modern rhymes, Tai Chen employed the classification of rhyming words to discuss language at a higher level of linguistic significance. Tai contended that, although there were changes in the pronunciation of words over time, the ranges of sounds remained remarkably constant. This phenomenon was due, Tai thought, to the "natural limitations" (tzu-jan chih chieh-hsien) of the human voice that made the production of only certain sounds possible. These limitations were shared by ancient and modern speakers.

Phonological research in the late eighteenth century was turning away from the almost completely reconstructed field of ancient rhymes toward the relation of tones to pronunciation. The nature of sound production itself became an object of inquiry, and it was in this context that Ch'ien Ta-hsin's research on dental labials was understood. Occurring in a section entitled "The Theory That the Ancients Lacked Dental Labials," Ch'ien was extending Tai's analysis into sophisticated new directions.[86]

Because the reconstruction of ancient Chinese phonology had been so closely tied to ancient rhyming criteria, most Chinese scholars had focused on reconstructing ancient finals in pronunciation. Work on archaic initials by Ch'ien Ta-hsin and others in the late eighteenth century indicates that such studies were also making considerable progress before Bernhard Karlgren initiated his pioneering work on archaic initials early this century. We overlook at our peril the development of the systematic study of language in China. As in the West, the history of linguistics in China presents an interesting analogy to the evolution of empirical methods of verification in the natural sciences. The development of language study and the emergence of historical and comparative linguistics are not uniquely Western achievements. Ch'ing evidential scholars in particular established the foundations of modern Chinese linguistics. We can still see traces of that influence in present-day Chinese linguistic studies.[87]

· · ·

Priority Debates

Eighteenth-century scholars' frequent references to and citations of each other's work reflected the vitality of the k'ao-cheng approach and the frequency with which data was passed on. One of the by-products of this cumulative and often overlapping process, for which I have given the examples of the *Documents* debate and the development of phonology, was the rise of priority questions and debates.

Within an academic environment that reinforced and rewarded originality in textual scholarship, attempts by scholars to pass off their work as that of an earlier illustrious author effectively came to an end. In contrast to literary projects that were imperially sponsored and therefore attributed to the emperor upon completion, eighteenth-century cultural activities increasingly were initiated by provincial officials such as Chu Yun and Juan Yuan. When the latter undertook a literary project, they sought out financial support and scholarly expertise from the local area and then sent a copy of the completed work to the emperor. These activities revealed, according to Leung Man-kam, the growing independence of the provinces in cultural life. Juan, for instance, took credit for the *Huang-Ch'ing ching-chieh* and helped bring to national prominence many of the authors whose works were included for publication.

Debates over priority became virtually inevitable in Kiangnan when the necessary kinds of knowledge and techniques of research began to accumulate and when the attention of a number of researchers was focused on particular questions. Priority debates were the result of the rise of the *k'ao-cheng* community of scholars in the Lower Yangtze and of the cumulative development of textual research fields that I have described above. With recognition for discoveries acting as an important motivational element in an academic environment where many scholars were carrying on evidential research, competition for recognition and priority became expectable.[88]

Multiple discoveries are an important indication that evidential scholars in Kiangnan were all responding to the same social and intellectual forces in the seventeenth and eighteenth centuries. Bound to the past by building upon accumulated knowledge, and bound to the present through social institutions and interactions that drew attention to particular problems, Ch'ing literati were also bound to the future by a social obligation to communicate their findings and discoveries. With due humility, Wang Ming-sheng described his own contributions to historical research as follows:

> How can I have had the intention to write a book? I merely offer my insights from study and collation to my successors . . . [Regarding philological studies needed to support historical research,] I have accepted the responsibility for dealing with such tiring labors in order to enable those who come later to work with ease. I have lived with these difficulties, but [my work] will enable those who follow to enjoy ease [in reading the *Dynastic Histories*]. Isn't this [goal] worthwhile?

. . .

In their preface to the *Ch'ou-jen chuan* (Biographies of mathematical astronomers) Juan Yuan and his staff praised those men who had improved upon ancient mathematics and astronomy or had uncovered new mathematical theories. They noted that the achievements of later scholars were more advanced than those of their predecessors because the former had access to a wider fund of accumulated knowledge.[89]

. .

Priority and the Old Text Documents

Research on the Old Text chapters of the *Documents* is an important example of multiple discoveries in Ch'ing scholarship. Independently of each other, Yen Jo-chü in the seventeenth, Hui Tung in the mid-eighteenth, and Ts'ui Shu (1740–1816) in the late eighteenth century came to the same conclusions concerning the Old Text chapters. Each employed evidential methods to prove his claims. These proofs were not simultaneous, but that was not important in a millennial tradition. Simultaneity became important in Europe only with the rise of modern science. Priority for the conclusive demonstration that the Old Text chapters were forgeries became even more difficult for Ch'ing scholars to ascertain when Yen Jo-chü's acknowledged debt to Ming scholars such as Mei Tsu was taken into account. Yet, the felt need to assign priority, regardless of who received it, indicates that evidential scholars had initiated a discourse in which they wanted to determine fairly and accurately who should be given priority in research.

The *Ssu-k'u ch'üan-shu* editors, who regarded themselves in this as in other matters ultimate arbiters, gave priority to Yen Jo-chü. Although they recognized that his work was the culmination of earlier research, the editors argued that Yen's *Shu-cheng* was the definitive demonstration of why the Old Text version was spurious. But Ch'ien Ta-hsin argued in his 1792 preface to his teacher Hui Tung's *Analysis of the Old Text Documents* that the priority in research went to Hui and not Yen:

> This [debate over the Old Text chapters], an unresolved issue for over four-teen hundred years, was first settled with evidence for every detail by Mr. Hui Sung-yai [Tung]. His contribution to the Classics discovered in the wall [of Confucius' house] is very great. Before this work, T'ai-yuan's Yen Pai-shih [Jo-chü] had written a book containing several hundred thousand words. His interpretation, by coincidence, largely agreed with that of Mr. Hui. However, concerning the "Great Declaration" (T'ai shih) [chapter], Yen still followed the mistakes of the T'ang author [K'ung Ying-ta]'s *Orthodox Exegesis [of the Documents]*. Yen was not as precise and to the point as was Mr. [Hui]. Today, the great respect of literati for Han Learning truly arose from Mr. [Hui's] pioneering discussion.[90]

· · ·

P'i Hsi-jui, (1850–1908), in his *Ching-hsueh li-shih* (History of classical studies), gave the priority for the proof that the Old Text chapters were forgeries to Mei Tsu, who during the Ming dynasty "opened the way for Yen Jo-chü and Hui Tung." The problem with this view, as the *Ssu-k'u ch'üan-shu* editors earlier had pointed out, was the fact that

Mei Tsu had been overlooked during his own time and his *Ku-wen Shang-shu k'ao-i* (Examination of variances in the Old Text *Documents*) almost lost.[91]

Ts'ui Shu and his brother Ts'ui Mai (1743–1781) both had been intent in the late eighteenth century on proving that the Old Text chapters of the *Documents* were forgeries. Owing to their relative isolation in Chihli (the capitol region!), they apparently did not have access to many outside writings on the *Documents* such as Yen Jo-chü's *Shu-cheng*. They did see Li Fu's (1675–1750) work on the subject in which Mei Tsu's research was mentioned. The subsequent neglect of Ts'ui Shu's writings, writings that should have placed him in the forefront of the *k'ao-cheng* scholarship of his day, indicates that there remained kinks in the transmission of knowledge during the eighteenth and nineteenth centuries. Such neglect also suggests that evidential research had begun to lose its central position in the early nineteenth century (see chapter 6). Despite the neglect, the unity of Ts'ui Shu's approach with that of his *k'ao-cheng* predecessors demonstrates how broad an impact evidential methods had during the eighteenth century.

The multiple discoveries made by Yen Jo-chü, Hui Tung, and Ts'ui Shu were not redundant. Their overlapping research renewed what had been done before. Through remarkable convergence, their writings heightened the likelihood that their discovery concerning the Old Text *Documents* would be firmly incorporated into evidential scholarship (as it eventually was). In this manner, Yen, Hui, and Ts'ui facilitated the further advancement of knowledge.[92]

During the eighteenth and nineteenth centuries, a number of scholars attempted to demonstrate (albeit unsuccessfully) that the Old Text chapters were authentic. If the focus of their counterattacks is any indication of priority, it is interesting that most of the defenders of the Old Text *Documents* blamed Yen Jo-chü as the culprit who had deluded their age. Weng Fang-kang, in an introduction to Liang Shang-kuo's (1748–1815) defense of the authenticity of the Old Text chapters entitled *Ku-wen Shang-shu t'iao-pien* (Systematic refutations concerning the Old Text *Documents*) contended:

> All of the Old Text chapters are the [true] words of the sages. Because their words are an aid to the people and the state and a boon to learning, they cannot be lightly criticized. Mister Yen [Jo-chü] employed a great

many spiteful and provocative words [in his account]. Therefore, Master Liang [Shang-kuo] also has employed spiteful and provocative words to oppose him. This [lack of moderation] is not Master Liang's fault. The blame should be placed on Mister Yen.[93]

. . .

Priority and the Classic of Waterways

Perhaps the most famous priority debate during the Ch'ing dynasty centered on Chao I-ch'ing (1710?–1764?) and the *Shui-ching chu* (Notes to the *Classic of Waterways*). Chao I-ch'ing, building on earlier geographical research, wrote an annotation to the *Classic of Waterways* that included notes by Li Tao-yuan (d. 527). Ch'üan Tsu-wang, a friend of the Chao family, also was working on collating the *Shui-ching chu;* he seems to have been the first to render the original text readable by differentiating Li Tao-yuan's comments from the actual text of the *Classic of Waterways.* The two had been confused for centuries by scribes and scholars.[94]

In 1754 Chao I-ch'ing and Ch'üan Tsu-wang met in Hangchow where they compared and made liberal use of each other's notes. Ch'üan informed Chao of his discovery that certain passages of Li Tao-yuan's commentary had been mixed with the original text. Chao and Ch'üan then proceeded to isolate the comments from the text itself. Ch'üan later wrote an introduction to Chao's study of this question, which Chao entitled *Shui-ching chu shih* (Clarification of the *Shui-ching chu*).

When Tai Chen was employed as one of the *Ssu-k'u ch'üan-shu* editors in 1774, he submitted to the throne his own edition of the *Shui-ching chu,* claiming that he had had access to an hitherto unknown edition of the text that he had found in the fifteenth-century *Yung-lo ta-tien.* Tai's work was greeted with much fanfare and was printed by imperial order. Chao I-ch'ing's manuscript on the subject was also submitted to the *Ssu-k'u ch'üan-shu* commission and was transcribed into the imperial library. Hu Shih has claimed that Tai Chen had not seen Chao's book.

Later Pi Yuan was persuaded to publish Chao I-ch'ing's *Shui-ching chu shih,* and did so in 1794. Tuan Yü-ts'ai, believing that Tai Chen's discoveries had been infringed upon, wrote a letter in 1809 to Liang Yü-sheng (1745–1819), who had helped prepare Chao's manuscript for publication. In the letter, Tuan accused Liang of having helped

Chao I-ch'ing's sons appropriate material from Tai's book to include in Chao I-ch'ing's without mentioning Tai's research at all. Tuan, nevertheless, acknowledged that, through their collaborations, Chao I-ch'ing and Ch'üan Tsu-wang had been able to come up with almost identical results as those prepared by Tai Chen.[95]

The similarity of Tai's and Chao's texts soon attracted the attention of Wei Yuan and Chang Mu (1805–1849), who both turned the tables and openly accused Tai Chen of having used Chao I-ch'ing's then still unpublished manuscript without giving Chao due credit. Wei Yuan and Chang Mu had had opportunities in 1841 to inspect the manuscript copy of the *Shui-ching chu* in the *Yung-lo ta-tien*. They contended that Tai's discoveries could not have come from this copy. Hu Shih examined this intricate question and concluded that the work of Tai, Ch'üan, and Chao on the *Classic of Waterways* "affords a very interesting instance of independent though convergent discovery in the intellectual history of China." Because scholars such as Chu Yun and Ch'ien Ta-hsin had accepted Tai's collation as soon as it appeared, Hu Shih accused both Wei Yuan and Chang Mu of coming to their unwarranted conclusions on the basis of a superficial perusal of the Yung-lo text that Tai Chen had indeed used.[96]

. .

Other Priority Debates

Chao I-ch'ing's name also became involved in a priority dispute surrounding the annotation of the *San-kuo-chih* history. In 1788, Hang Shih-chün had published a work entitled the *San-kuo-chih pu-chu* (Additional notes to the *History of the Three Kingdoms*). Because Chao I-ch'ing, Hang's fellow townsman (they were both from Hangchow) and contemporary, had written a work on the same topic entitled *San-kuo-chih chu-pu* (Additions to the annotated version of the *History of the Three Kingdoms*), the question arose in Ch'ing academic circles whether one had used the work of the other. Hang's book was copied by the *Ssu-k'u ch'üan-shu* commission and also printed several times, but Chao's remained in manuscript form until the late nineteenth century. After comparing the two works, Cheng T'ien-t'ing concluded early in this century that Hang had not seen Chao's manuscript, but that Chao had had access to Hang's book.

Ch'ing scholars at times also acknowledged the priority of other scholars when research interests clearly overlapped. We have seen that both Yen Jo-chü and Hui Tung acknowledged the research that preceded their own findings on the *Documents*. Hui admitted Yen's precedence during the final stages of his own analysis of the *Documents* debate. Similarly, Chiang Sheng stressed the origin and formation of seal characters as the key to textual criticism. For this reason he studied the *Shuo-wen*, but finding that Tuan Yü-ts'ai had been occupied with the same subject for a number of years, Chiang Sheng gave up his own research and sent his manuscripts to Tuan for his use. There was no need for duplication of efforts, and Tuan clearly had priority.[97]

Priority debates were also an important element in nineteenth-century Confucian scholarship. K'ang Yu-wei allegedly lifted the thesis and thunder in his New Text scholarship from the writings of Liao P'ing after they met in Canton. Later Liao P'ing wrote a letter to K'ang demanding that K'ang acknowledge him as the source for the New Text doctrines K'ang espoused. K'ang claimed coincidence, but even K'ang's disciple, Liang Ch'i-ch'ao, admitted that K'ang had been influenced by Liao P'ing's New Text studies. Seeing their dispute as a loss for both of them, Liao called upon K'ang to join with him in taking credit for the theories that K'ang contended were his own. Claiming precedence for his own philological discoveries, Liao P'ing admitted that K'ang had enlarged on his views by giving them social and political significance. Since the theories now belonged to both of them, Liao reasoned that K'ang and he should be known as "Liao-K'ang," just as Chu Hsi and Lu Hsiang-shan (1139–1193) were known as "Chu-Lu." K'ang, however, refused to recognize Liao's claims.[98]

In the twentieth century, the question of priority in *k'ao-cheng* scholarship has taken on international significance. The fact that Tai Chen's ideas coincided so closely with those of the Japanese scholar Itō Jinsai (1627–1705) on many points of classical scholarship gave rise to claims that Tai Chen had read Itō's works in China and had used Itō's ideas in his own writings. Not only did the title of Tai Chen's *Evidential Analysis of the Meanings of Terms in the Mencius* closely resemble Itō Jinsai's *Go-Mō jigi* (Meanings of terms in the *Analects* and the *Mencius*), but both rejected the Ch'eng-Chu school of *li-hsueh* in favor of a "philosophy of *ch'i*." In addition, Yoshikawa Kōjirō has pointed out that Itō Jinsai and Yen Jo-chü were both attacking the authenticity of the

Old Text version of the *Documents* at about the same time, although there is no evidence of anything except coincidence in this case.

Although it would take us too far afield to discuss it in the detail it deserves here, evidential research spilled over from Ch'ing China to Yi Korea and Tokugawa Japan. In the late eighteenth and early nineteenth centuries, Korean and Japanese scholars learned and adapted the *k'ao-cheng* techniques pioneered by Ch'ing literati.[99]

· · ·

Progress in Evidential
Scholarship

"Early Ch'ing scholars," according to John Henderson, "were nearly unanimous in their conception of the cumulative, even necessary progress of astronomy." This idea was most fully reiterated by Mei Wen-ting and Wang Hsi-shan, who as specialists in mathematical astronomy were aware of the contributions Western methods could offer the native tradition. Mei Wen-ting, for instance, based his notion of the progress of astronomy on advances over the years in both computational techniques and astronomical instrumentation. The *Ssu-k'u ch'üan-shu* editors, relying on Mei Wen-ting's notion of progress, noted in their introduction to books on astronomy and mathematics that, as a result of recent refinements introduced by the Jesuits, the cumulative efforts of Western and native astronomy could be combined to resolve remaining problems in calendrical science.[100]

Consciousness of progress in astronomy was not new. Increased precision was mentioned regularly in writings on the subject, for example, the calendrical treatise of the *Yuan-shih* (History of the Yuan dynasty). But the transfer to philology was unprecedented. In the eighteenth century, the notion of the cumulative development of knowledge pervaded all the disciplines associated with evidential research. Hsu Tsung-yen (1768–1818) in his introduction to the *Ku-ching ching-she wen-chi*, composed as China entered the nineteenth century, remarked that

classical scholarship had accumulated to such an extent during the
Ch'ing dynasty that modern scholars knew things Han scholars had
never known, not to mention such illustrious T'ang Confucians as
K'ung Ying-ta or Lu Te-ming.[101]

The account of cumulative scholarship and priority debates given
above makes it clear that a notion of progress was implicit in *k'ao-cheng*
scholarship. Ch'ing scholars were as conscious of this progress in philology as in astronomy. Influenced by Huang Tsung-hsi, Mei Wen-ting,
and Jesuit writings, Yen Jo-chü applied astronomy and chronography
to analyze the *Documents.* Yen also frequently cited mathematical
astronomy as an example of a progressively developing field of inquiry
in which research gradually became more and more precise. Yen, for
instance, mulled over Ma Su's (1620–1673) arguments concerning the
forged Old Text chapters of the *Documents* in his *Shu-cheng,* but what
appealed to Yen was Ma's cumulative view of scholarship (see chapter
2). Discussing the cumulative nature of knowledge, Yen also mentioned
a criticism that his friend Hu Wei had leveled against one of his arguments. Accepting Hu Wei's correction, Yen concluded that Hu's remarks were an example of "discussions that gradually push [our knowl-
edge] forward, the matters in question becoming clearer and clearer
until after a certain time they are finally settled."

The eighteenth-century compilers of the *Ch'ou-jen chuan* were also
conscious of progress in precise scholarship. Juan Yuan and his staff in
Hangchow were convinced that their collection of biographies traced
the consecutive changes in and linear development of technical knowledge in China and Europe.[102] This sense of progress did not last. As we
shall see in the final chapter, the social and economic deterioration that
began in China in the late eighteenth century took its toll at all levels
of Chinese society, including the Lower Yangtze academic community.
The intellectual foundations of evidential scholarship were not only increasingly attacked, but the institutional viability of the Kiangnan academic community was also threatened.

Six

Denouement

The Battle of Muddy Flat: April 4, 1854.

The academic community in which evidential research had flourished was no longer intact in the middle of the nineteenth century, when the impact of the Western powers penetrated the Chinese interior. Remnants of the Kiangnan academic community, which had survived the Taiping Rebellion (1850–1864), were but a pale shadow of a once vibrant field of academic discourse. In this final chapter, we will first describe the growing criticism of evidential scholarship by Chinese literati in the early nineteenth century and the effect such criticism had on the Lower Yangtze academic community. Then, in the second part, we will turn to an account of the devastation in the mid-nineteenth century of the key institutions upon which evidential scholarship depended. A rebellion, whose defeat required death and destruction on a military scale that probably has never been equaled on earth, laid waste in little more than a decade to the academic institutions of two centuries.

Figure 14 The Taiping Rebellion: the Battle of Muddy Flat, April 4, 1854
Source: H. B. Morse, *In the Days of the Taipings* (Salem, Mass., The Essex Institute, 1927).

· · ·

The Fracturing of the
K'ao-cheng Movement

Although evidential scholarship reached its zenith in the late eighteenth century, there was significant dissatisfaction even then with the non-theoretical bent in most *k'ao-cheng* writing. Although considered an authority in evidential studies, Tai Chen (1724–1777), for example, was troubled throughout his career by the contrast between the piecemeal evidential scholarship upon which his reputation rested and his unpopular writings in philosophy. Tai's personal satisfaction over the completion of his major philosophical studies during his last years, according to Yü Ying-shih, reveals his disappointment with what he perceived to be the anti-philosophical biases of his own time (see chapter 1).[1]

Chang Hsueh-ch'eng (1738–1801), despite the fact that he disagreed with Tai Chen on many points, shared with him a commitment to philosophical issues broader than those pervasive in evidential studies. Chang refused to accept the fashionable distinction between Han Learning (read "philology," that is, *k'ao-cheng*) and Sung Learning (read "moral philosophy," that is, *i-li*). In his discussion of the Eastern Chekiang (Che-tung) intellectual tradition, Chang attempted to reassert the emphasis on statecraft in the Che-tung school, in contrast to what he considered the uninvolved erudition in the Western Chekiang (Che-hsi, including southern Kiangsu as well) schools.

Although he upheld the distinction, Chi Yun (1724–1805) acknowledged that neither Han Learning nor Sung Learning could stand alone. In 1796, while supervising the imperial examinations in Peking, Chi wrote:

> Concerning [examination essays elucidating] the meaning of the Classics [*ching-i*], there are now two schools. Those who study Han Confucians trace [graphs] back to their origins in the six types of writing. They carefully examine etymological [connections] and thereby reilluminate the ancient meanings [*ku-i*] [of the Classics] for the benefit of later ages. This is one school.
>
> Those who study the Sung Confucians, discriminate subtle meanings and take into account similarities and differences. They prevent the subtle

lessons in the Six Classics from being confused with [other] contending theories. This is still another school.

. . .

Chi advocated a complementary approach. Sung Learning, he thought, should be the guide for classical "meanings and principles"; Han Learning should be used to supplement the former and to prevent the theoretical constructions of Sung Learning from getting out of hand.[2]

. .

Statecraft and New Text Confucianism

Scholars associated with the New Text movement in Ch'ang-chou and the T'ung-ch'eng "ancient prose" (*ku-wen*) literary school had since the middle of the eighteenth century felt that the Han-Learning movement was ignoring the theoretical import of the "subtle words of great principles" (*ta-i wei-yen*) contained in the Classics. The goal of these scholars remained the mastery and execution of concrete studies (*shih-hsueh*). The appeal to practice, however, was now considered an essential part of moral philosophy, not its opposite.

Ch'ang-chou scholars called for a more comprehensive vision of Confucianism, one that would go beyond the limited textual studies in typical evidential scholarship by stressing the moral principles contained in Confucius' *Spring and Autumn Annals*. In their hands, evidential research was informed by theoretical and ethical issues and was not an end in itself. A follower and relative of Chuang Ts'un-yü (1719–1788), Chuang Yu-k'e (1742?–1822) wrote:

> There are many people all over the realm who read books voraciously. The only book they do not know how to read is the *Spring and Autumn Annals*. . . .
> I have been studying the *Annals* for over thirty years, but I [still] sigh in wonder that the meanings and principles [*i-li*] in it are boundless . . . [The *Annals* contains] the Tao that encompasses a thousand changes and ten thousand transformations. It never fails to amaze and please me that in this book I can find the essentials [of the Tao].[3]

. . .

Even Juan Yuan was influenced by these currents of thought. Although his reputation was made in Han Learning, he had been influenced by several *Kung-yang* scholars more concerned with moral philosophy, including Liu Feng-lu (1776–1829), K'ung Kuang-sen (1752–1786), and Ch'eng En-tse (1785–1837). In a preface to the New Text patriarch Chuang Ts'un-yü's collected works, which he helped to publish, Juan wrote: "[Chuang] did not focus on the [distinction between] Han and Sung [dynasty] scholia. He sought only to grasp the 'great principles in subtle words' [*wei-yen ta-i*] that existed separately from the words and characters themselves. Such [insight] made him a great Confucian of our enlightened age."

Kung Tzu-chen (1792–1841), a follower of the Ch'ang-chou New Text tradition, composed a preface for Juan's chronological biography on the occasion of Juan's sixtieth birthday in 1823. There Kung praised Juan's talents in the textual fields associated with evidential scholarship, but he also pointed to Juan's considerable contributions to philosophy and literature. According to Kung, Juan's prodigious erudition had enabled him to encompass both Han and Sung Learning. In his introduction to the *Kuo-shih Ju-lin chuan* (Biographies of Ch'ing Confucians), Juan himself contended that Ch'ing scholars had been successful in paying heed to the questions of nature (human and otherwise) and the Tao, emphasized in Sung Learning, and in using the principles of Han Learning to apply these questions to practical use. Yet Juan went on to write:

> To sum up, the Tao of the sages is like the house of a teacher. The [study of] primary and derived characters and their glosses is the entrance. If one misses the path, all steps lead away from it. How can one reach the hall and enter the studio? If a student seeks the Tao too high and regards with scorn the art of punctuating a text, it is just as if he were a bird soaring into the heavens from the roof of his teacher's magnificent studio. He gets high all right, but then he doesn't get to see what lies between the door and the inner recesses of the room. Some seek only to classify names and their referents and do not consider the sacred Tao. This [failure] is just like living out one's life between the gate and the entrance, never recalling that there remain a hall and a studio [to enter].[4]

· · ·

Such syncretic tendencies remained a strong undercurrent through much of the late eighteenth and early nineteenth centuries. By 1830, however, Confucian discourse could no longer remain untouched by the political and social tremors that began to be felt in the society at large. The return to favor of *Kung-yang* studies and Sung Learning was paralleled and in part provoked by an intense moral concern for the state of the country and involvement with administrative problems growing out of the social and political pressures of the late eighteenth and early nineteenth centuries. These concerns, in turn, made themselves felt in an overt attack on the apolitical stance that *k'ao-cheng* scholars had accepted.

Population pressures, accompanied by inevitable increases in competition for land, education, and official status, had had a debilitating effect on all levels of Chinese society by 1830. Changes in the character of the elite (see chapter 3) and the increasing competition for access of the educated to power and livelihood produced serious social problems. An atmosphere of corruption had begun to pervade the bureaucracy and even the countryside.

These were also the years when internal rebellions, especially the Chin-ch'uan (1770–1776), Wang Lun (1774), White Lotus (1796–1805), and Eight Trigrams (1813) uprisings, put an end to the long period of relative peace that had lasted since the late seventeenth century. Philip Kuhn has explained that the White Lotus Rebellion "uncovered startling weaknesses in the apparently powerful Ch'ing military system." The "dazzling facade for inner decay" had been destroyed in a struggle that strained the financial and military resources of the dynasty. Foreign trade exacerbated these internal dislocations. The deflationary effects of a silver drain brought on by the British opium trade began to force the Ch'ing state into serious economic depression. Internal rebellion and external imperialism were to culminate in the destruction of the traditional Chinese tributary system and initiate an age of Western and then Japanese militarism along the China coast.[5]

In response to external and internal problems, scholar-officials from outside Kiangnan, such as Ho Ch'ang-ling (1785–1848) from Hunan, began in the early years of the nineteenth century to emphasize statecraft proposals in their attempts to shore up the sagging imperial bureaucracy. Ho Ch'ang-ling was in part inspired by the statecraft orientation of the *Huang-Ming ching-shih wen-pien* (Collected writings on statecraft during the Ming dynasty), compiled in 1638 by Ch'en Tzu-lung (1608–1647), the Ming loyalist and Fu She activist from Sung-chiang, Kiangsu. Because Ch'en's collection contained passages critical of the Manchus (it was published in 1639 before the Manchu take-over), the entire work had been banned during the Ch'ing dynasty. It did, however, continue to circulate privately, and its value as a guide to practical affairs in the nineteenth century was recognized by Ho Ch'ang-ling and others. Ho began to compile the *Huang-ch'ao ching-shih wen-pien* (Collected writings on statecraft during the Ch'ing dynasty) in 1821 as an expression of revived interest in practical administration.

Statecraft proposals were enunciated by pragmatically oriented scholar-officials who believed they were avoiding both the scholastic philology associated with Han Learning and the empty speculation of Sung-Ming *Tao-hsueh*. They took as their inspiration early Ch'ing scholars, such as Ku Yen-wu (1613–1682) and Huang Tsung-hsi (1610–1695), who they argued had remained committed to the welfare of the country in their scholarly pursuits and had not succumbed to the bookish orientation that they felt had plagued eighteenth-century evidential scholarship.[6]

It has been customary to link the movement for reform in the early nineteenth century to the rise of New Text Confucianism as the philosophic rationale for the reemergence of the statecraft movement. Most often this connection has been deduced from Wei Yuan's (1794–1856) and Kung Tzu-chen's commitment to New Text Confucianism and the role *Kung-yang* ideas played in their statecraft proposals. A straight historical line of transmission frequently is assumed, linking the eighteenth-century Ch'ang-chou school of New Text studies to K'ang Yu-wei (1858–1927) and Liang Ch'i-ch'ao (1873–1929) in Canton via Wei Yuan, Kung Tzu-chen, and the early nineteenth-century statecraft school.[7]

Others have recently argued that there was no *Kung-yang* statecraft school at all. James Polachek has noted that the members of the Kiangsu "statecraft party" in the early nineteenth century were not members of a scholarly movement but men who "operated mainly within a framework of bureaucratic and political relationships—relationships, that is to say, which were structured through hierarchical ties contracted in office, and which functioned, at least in part, to promote the personal and career interests of these literati as a discrete group." From this point of view, the common interest shared by many members of this group in New Text Confucianism has been exaggerated.[8]

One side has argued from a synchronic standpoint that novel intellectual currents, such as the revival of "muscular" New Text Confucianism, were popular in the nineteenth century because they legitimated the critique of current politics and supported proposals to reform existing institutions. The other side has denied the significance of such a synchronic structure of ideas. Both sides, however, overlook an important element in the so-called rise of New Text Confucianism during the Ch'ing dynasty.

New Text Confucianism was in fact the outgrowth of two centuries of philological evidence that had been accumulating through painstaking research by Ch'ing *k'ao-cheng* scholars. The New Text versus Old Text debate did not emerge automatically from the *Kung-yang Commentary* or from Ho Hsiu's (129–182) influential commentary. The debate was reconstructed by relying on philological and historical research. This need to reconstruct the debate explains why Chuang Ts'un-yü and other early members of the Ch'ang-chou school still included many Old Text doctrines drawn from the *Rituals of Chou* in their writings. New Text tenets were not yet clearly distinguished from Old Text precepts.[9]

New Text Confucianism during the Ch'ing dynasty was indeed reformist. The debates between the various schools of evidential research reveal the more reformist intent among the Ch'ang-chou scholars, when compared to their colleagues in Soochow and Yangchow. Liu Feng-lu's New Text writings, for instance, were decidedly more political than Ch'ien Ta-hsin's (1728–1804) influential Han-Learning studies. Moreover, New Text philology aided and abetted the reaction against what were considered sterile textual studies. Increased interest in the *Kung-yang Commentary* helped to stimulate a revival of the seventeenth-century statecraft orientation. Instead of so-called "empty" notions associated with Sung-Ming *Tao-hsueh*, *k'ao-cheng* scholarship itself, especially the Han-Learning movement, was made the chief culprit. The appeal to practice and concrete studies, which earlier had been employed against Neo-Confucian philosophy, was now turned against precise textual scholarship.

Kung Tzu-chen, for example, was critical of the pettiness that he thought pervaded textual studies in the early nineteenth century. In a famous letter to the Han-Learning advocate Chiang Fan (1761–1831), mentioned in chapter 3, Kung expressed ten misgivings concerning the Han-Learning movement during the Ch'ing dynasty. Among his complaints were:

> Those who read books "search for the truth in actual facts" [*shih-shih ch'iu-shih*]. For a thousand ages it has been this way. Although "to search for the truth in actual facts" is a Han dynasty expression, it is not the monopoly of Han [Learning]. This is my first misgiving.
>
> The present dynasty has a form of scholarship that is its own, and it is not [simply] Han Learning. There were Han figures who pioneered [such research], but today scholars have increased the exactitude in our knowledge. To call avenues of research that were not opened in the Han "Han Learning" is for me unsatisfactory. This is my second misgiving. . . .
>
> To place Han and Sung in opposition is not at all well-informed. Didn't the people of the Han discuss [issues such as] nature [*hsing*] or the Tao? This is the fifth.
>
> How can one deny that people of the Sung discussed names and their referents [*ming-wu*] and textual glosses? That is not the way to generalize about Sung scholars. This is the sixth. . . .
>
> The present dynasty has its own superlative gentlemen who patiently master their texts and make new discoveries concerning the Classics. They are neither Han [Learning] nor Sung [Learning], but search only for the truth.[10]

. . .

The letter revealed that Kung's criticism of Han Learning was not entirely negative, however. A student of his distinguished grandfather, Tuan Yü-ts'ai (1735–1815), under whom he studied the *Shuo-wen*, Kung was prepared to acknowledge the value of evidential scholarship; his position, however, did not prevent him from recognizing that Sung scholars had made important contributions to Confucian studies. Nor could his respect and nostalgia for the prestige of *k'ao-cheng* scholarship during the Ch'ien-lung era blind him to the hard realities of his time. Later he wrote:

> Those who subsequently have served as Confucian teachers no longer [serve the state]. If they emphasize their ruler, they do not know how the ruler should deal with the people. If they emphasize the people, they do not know how the people should serve the ruler. After birth such men never handle a rake or hoe. As they mature, they are unversed in the work of the civil service. For every ten ancient books and elegant records, they glance at only three or four. They gaze blindly upon the achievements and merits of the enlightened ages [that have preceded them]. Looking upward,

they do not place themselves in the position of the ruler. Looking downward, they do not place themselves in the position of the people... For this reason, the [perfection of the] Tao and its worldly manifestations do not correspond, and the customs of the people do not reflect the moral teachings [of the realm]. The ideal order of kingship does not penetrate to those below. The secret sufferings of the people do not reach those above. Our country has an obligation to nourish its literati [*shih*], yet the literati never repay that obligation. This situation is extremely dangerous! In the end, won't it be the literati themselves who will suffer the consequences?

. . .

Decline seemed apparent to Kung, and textual studies could no longer be enough. Statecraft and moral reform were more important than apolitical evidential scholarship. Kung found the rationale for this perspective in the New Text doctrines that he learned while studying under Liu Feng-lu in Peking. Confucius' role in the formation of the Confucian tradition became for him the key to reestablishing the primacy of the *Spring and Autumn Annals* and the *Kung-yang Commentary* in a time of social and political dissolution.[11]

Wei Yuan also was dissatisfied with what he considered petty philology and with the standard distinction between Sung Learning and Han Learning. Unlike Kung Tzu-chen, Wei Yuan served at one time or another on the administrative staffs of several important provincial officials interested in statecraft. He was thus able to use these influential positions to blend statecraft concerns with New Text notions of institutional reform. In 1825, Ho Ch'ang-ling, then financial commissioner of Kiangsu, invited Wei Yuan to become editor of the *Huang-ch'ao ching-shih wen-pien.* This large collection was regarded by nineteenth-century scholars as a valuable source for Ch'ing administrative history and an important starting point for the study of efforts to handle the dual problems of domestic unrest and foreign incursion.

Under Wei Yuan's editorial policy, the collection reflected criteria for inclusion that were the exact opposite of those used in Juan Yuan's 1829 *Huang-Ch'ing ching-chieh* (and hence the *Ssu-k'u ch'üan-shu* as well). Wei Yuan excluded all purely philological studies and included only those works that pertained to statecraft topics and proposals since the early Ch'ing. In the *hsueh-shu* (scholarship) section of the *Huang-ch'ao ching-shih wen-pien,* for example, Wei cited only those scholarly writings that supported his emphasis on self-cultivation and statecraft. Juan Yuan's syncretic position on Han and Sung Learning, translated in part above, was incorporated, for example. Also reprinted was Tuan Yü-ts'ai's critique of Han dynasty philology for its lack of the comprehensive concern that pervaded Chu Hsi's (1130–1200) textual scholarship. Philology was discussed but only within the context of comprehensive statecraft.[12]

In his writings, Wei Yuan attempted to reverse what he considered the fascination with textual minutiae in *k'ao-cheng* scholarship and replace it with a concern for theoretical issues that would support a moral and social revival in society. The ill-conceived Han Learning-Sung Learning debate was no longer relevant to the challenges that faced the Ch'ing state. Writing in 1841, Wei Yuan noted his misgivings about the status of China's elite class: "Since the middle of the Ch'ien-lung Emperor's reign, all literati in the empire have promoted Han Learning. This movement is especially popular north and south of the Yangtze River [that is, Kiangnan] ... Such a state of affairs has confined the bright and talented of the realm and tempted them onto a useless path."[13]

T'ao Chu (1779–1839), an important Ch'ing official from Hunan, invited Wei Yuan (also from Hunan) to Yangchow in 1831 to advise him on plans to reform the Huai-pei salt administration. Although committed to statecraft in his official career, T'ao himself was no orthodox purist when it came to scholarship. He very much admired the empirical techniques evidential scholars employed, perhaps because they were also applicable to statecraft studies. In particular, T'ao praised the Han-Learning scholar Wang Ming-sheng (1722–1798) for his contributions to Ch'ing academics. During these years, Wei began the draft of a work entitled *Sheng-wu chi* (Record of imperial military achievements). A thoroughly researched account of the major military campaigns of the dynasty up to the Tao-kuang reign period (1821–1850), the book was also a vehicle for Wei's analysis of weaknesses in the Ch'ing military system. Similarly, Wei's famous *Hai-kuo t'u-chih* (Treatise on the maritime kingdoms), based on research begun in 1841, represented a continuation of the precise geographical research carried out by evidential scholars, as well as a statecraft approach to geopolitical realities. As Jane Leonard has pointed out, Wei's geographical treatise marked a practical response to the Opium War crisis that stimulated the collection of geographical and historical information about Western maritime expansion.[14]

New Text scholarship, in its distaste for what was now considered useless scholasticism, became in the hands of Wei Yuan a weapon to attack Han Learning. At the same time, it served as a vehicle for new directions in thought, directions that were themselves based in part on the use of evidential methods. New Text scholars in the early nineteenth century still had more in common with the mainstream of evidential scholarship than with the utopian and messianic notions later associated with K'ang Yu-wei. Their intent was to initiate bureaucratic and moral reforms within the framework of the existing political structure.[15]

. .

Fang Tung-shu in Canton: The Attack on Han Learning

Statecraft issues began to dominate academy education in Hunan and and Kwangtung in the early nineteenth century. Nascent statecraft schools emerged from academies in Changsha and Canton, where the administrative problems facing the empire were more clearly evident. The role of Hunanese scholar-officials such as Ho Ch'ang-ling and T'ao Chu in promoting statecraft studies in the nineteenth century suggests that the anti-Han-Learning movement was initially led by literati whose native origins were outside the Lower Yangtze Region. In the mid-nineteenth century, the Hunanese scholar-official Tseng Kuo-fan (1811–1872), a major exponent of "self-strengthening" in the wake of the intrusion of Western military power in East Asia, patronized Sung Learning in local and national academics. Kwangtung also emerged as a center for statecraft studies. These developments indicate a general backlash against Kiangnan intellectual currents.

Published in 1831 and revised in 1838, Fang Tung-shu's (1772–1851) *Han-hsueh shang-tui* (An assessment of Han Learning) was closely associated with the growing recognition of weaknesses in the Ch'ing bureaucratic structure before the Opium War. Hamaguchi Fujio has pointed out that what was at stake in Fang's attack was not simply textual scholarship. In an 1824 letter to Juan Yuan, accompanying his presentation of a manuscript copy of *An Assessment of Han Learning*, Fang Tung-shu made it clear that his opposition to Han Learning was not simply a matter of textual issues. He was in effect blaming the chaotic situation in Canton vis-à-vis the foreigners on the moral passivity and useless erudition that the Han-Learning movement had fostered throughout China, an echo of the charges against Neo-Confucianism that had launched Han Learning less than two centuries earlier.[16]

Fang was critical of what he considered the trivialization of knowledge and antiquarian research that reflected a cult of useless facts. He saw evidential studies as mere industry, devoid of intellectual and moral content. Dismissing the very nature of the "concrete studies" in *k'ao-cheng* scholarship, Fang Tung-shu wrote:

> The Han-Learning scholars all have evidence to back up every statement and research to support every word. However, they are only debating on paper with the ancients over glosses, phonetic elements [in characters], scholia, and textual corruptions. They adduce from various books ancillary evidence by the hundreds and thousands of items. Yet, if they were to apply to themselves their attitudes and activities, or extend them to the people and the country, it is of no benefit whatsoever. It only causes people to become deluded and inconstant so that they are good for nothing. Thus, although [Han-Learning scholars] may be "searching for the truth in actual facts," in reality they are performing the most extreme form of empty activity.

· · ·

Fang Tung-shu favored the "concrete learning" that the orthodox Ch'eng-Chu school of principle (*li-hsueh*) had enunciated, whereby both theory and action were stressed. Juan Yuan and Chiang Fan, in their promotion of Han Learning at the Hsueh-hai T'ang of Canton and in the *Huang-Ch'ing ching-chieh,* were guilty of restricting Confucian scholarship to philology, according to Fang. Moral teachings that could be used to order the country and bring peace to the empire were required.[17] Moved by what Hamaguchi Fujio has called a "crisis mentality," Fang Tung-shu lashed out at the heterodox implications in Tai Chen's assault on the Ch'eng-Chu orthodoxy (see chapter 1). Although laden with ideological assumptions, as was Chiang Fan's defense of Han Learning, Fang's account charged evidential scholars with the intent to overturn the Neo-Confucian orthodoxy:

> Those Han-Learning scholars are deeply envious and abhor studies of meanings and principles [*i-li chih hsueh*]. They accuse the latter of lapsing into Ch'an [Buddhism] ... They really have no desire to seek the truth or to get at the facts. About all they are interested in is to establish theories that will overturn [the views of] Sung Confucians.

Fang believed China was faced with a moral crisis precipitated by the decline in social concern and lack of moral cultivation manifested in *k'ao-cheng* scholarship. The shared commitments in Sung Learning and New Text Confucianism in the early nineteenth century indicate that these were new movements with new content. The Sung-Learning defense of the Ch'eng-Chu orthodoxy reveals that Sung-Learning scholars such as Yao Nai (1732–1815), Fang Tung-shu, T'ang Chien (1778–1861), and others were under considerable attack by their Han-Learning contemporaries.

As the foreign threat in Canton mounted in intensity during the 1820s, Juan Yuan (then governor-general) and members of the Hsueh-hai T'ang faculty were drawn into foreign affairs and the problem of opium trafficking in Southeast China. Juan adopted what seemed at the time a strict policy toward opium in 1821, arresting sixteen opium dealers in Macao and temporarily forcing the opium trade out of the Pearl River. Although Juan's policy marked the end of the first phase of the trade, in reality the prohibitions meant very little. Opium trading continued uninterrupted and in fact increased at Lintin Island. At most the crackdown was a face-saving device for Juan Yuan, after attention had been directed to the opium problem by the Tao-kuang Emperor (r. 1821–1850). The latter had just ascended the throne in a reformist frame of mind, and the opium problem was one of his chief concerns.[18]

Having had a firsthand view of Juan Yuan's opium policies in the 1820s, Fang Tung-shu recommended in the 1830s that the policies that for a decade had been proven a dismal failure be rescinded. Han Learning had shown itself to be morally bankrupt, according to Fang. He became associated in the 1830s with the policy for the complete eradication of the opium evil. In Canton, the teachers and students at the Yueh-hua Academy were the leaders of the anti-opium movement. Hsu Nai-chi's famous 1836 memorial, recommending the legalization of opium for all except civil servants, scholars, and soldiers, was connected with the proposal by a number of directors at the Hsueh-hai T'ang that opium restrictions be relaxed. Juan Yuan himself seems to have leaned toward the legalization of the trade. These apparent capitulations angered Fang and others in Canton who took a hard line on the opium question. It was no accident then when Lin Tse-hsu (1785–1850), charged by the emperor with the task of eradicating the opium evil, took office in Canton, he established his headquarters at the Yueh-hua Academy, where hardliners were in the majority.

The Legalizers versus the Moralists in the Canton opium debate reflected in many ways the widening rift between Han Learning and Sung Learning. The political aspects of this debate certainly deserve more intense study than we can engage in here. Fang Tung-shu's main concern was for what he considered the lack of moral training and commitment on the part of Han-Learning scholars. Looking back on the Opium War, Fang wrote in the summer of 1842:

> In my considered opinion on the basis of close observation, the disaster at the hands of the English barbarians was not the result of the recent policy of total prohibition and confiscation of opium. In fact, [the disaster] resulted because of the rapacious and corrupt behavior of the foolish foreign merchants, the vacillating policies of earlier governors-general [that is, Juan Yuan] who have cultivated a festering sore, and the greed of Chinese traitors who sold out their country. Plots have been left to hatch and chaos to brew for a long time.

. . .

It is interesting that many scholars later also blamed Han Learning for the onset of the Taiping Rebellion. In more recent times, the Neo-Confucian revivalist T'ang-Chün-i has contended that the intellectual triumph of Marxism-Leninism in modern China grew out of the vacuum created by the rejection of Sung humanistic philosophy on the part of bookish and empirically oriented Ch'ing philologists.[19]

. .

Han- and Sung-Learning Syncretism

Although *k'ao-cheng* scholarship remained an important field of discourse in the first half of the nineteenth century, promoted particularly by scholars such as Wang Yin-chih (1766–1834), Juan Yuan, and Chang Mu (1805–1849), it was effectively challenged by advocates of Sung Learning and New Text studies. Their efforts did not, however, represent an attempt to return to earlier forms of thought. Rather, they were moving forward to stress moral and political issues that evidential scholars had overlooked or dismissed.

The popularity of moral philosophy and practical statecraft in the nineteenth century has usually been explained as a revival of Sung and Ming Neo-Confucianism. By opposing the earlier turn to philology, nineteenth-century Confucians are said to have initiated a reaffirmation of Neo-Confucian forms of moral cultivation. Sung-Learning advocates were not purists, however. Their methods of reasoning and manner of exposition, as we have seen, had been heavily influenced by evidential research.

Attempts to reassert the validity of Neo-Confucian ideals did not entail wholesale rejection of *k'ao-cheng* methods and techniques. One of the important outgrowths of this challenge was the formation of an overt syncretic movement that attempted to reconcile the Han- and Sung-Learning positions. *K'ao-cheng* scholarship remained popular, but it was becoming difficult to justify on its own terms. Juan Yuan's increasing emphasis on philosophical themes in the last decades of his life was indicative of the tension within Confucian discourse in the nineteenth century.

Canton became known as a center for the movement to synthesize Han-Learning methods with Sung-Learning political and moral concerns. Both Han- and Sung-Learning currents of thought filled the student essays included in the Hsueh-hai T'ang's literary collections, for example. Lin Po-t'ung (1775–1845) was a major figure in the beginnings of this effort. Lin attempted to reconcile the differences between Han and Sung Learning; he also admired *k'ao-cheng* scholars such as Ch'ien Ta-hsin for their contributions to phonology and ancient rhymes.[20] Juan Yuan's interests in Sung Learning and New Text studies indicate that the intellectual atmosphere at the Hsueh-hai T'ang was not as monotonously oriented to Han Learning as Fang Tung-shu supposed. Lin Po-t'ung's most famous student at the Hsueh-hai T'ang, Ch'en Li (1810–1882), continued his teacher's eclectic approach and became one of the most influential advocates of Han- and Sung-Learning syncretism.

In a work entitled *Han-Ju t'ung-i* (Comprehensive meaning of Han Confucianism) printed in 1858, Ch'en Li, who was by then one of the most widely respected literati in Canton, contended that the attack on Han Learning for its lack of theoretical significance was unfair. He outlined the philosophical issues Han dynasty scholars had discussed. Ch'en took the other side of the argument in his collected notebooks published late in his life. He pointed out that those who criticized Chu Hsi for not emphasizing ancient glosses and etymologies in Han commentaries were equally mistaken. According to Ch'en, Chu Hsi had been as concerned with philology as with philosophy, a line of thought more recently taken up by Ch'ien Mu in his study of Chu Hsi's scholarly contributions.[21]

By the middle of the nineteenth century when Western ideas began to pose a serious challenge to Confucianism, many defenders of the Confucian tradition, such as Tseng Kuo-fan, were followers of Sung Learning. Others like Chang Chih-tung (1837–1909) from Chihli were influenced by Juan Yuan's educational policies and took a stand midway between Han and Sung Learning. Confucian reform was upheld by Sung-Learning, New Text, as well as syncretic scholars. They all contended that reform of institutions would be successful only if it were based on a moral fervor that reintroduced self-cultivation and a concern for statecraft to Confucian discourse. Tseng Kuo-fan reacting against the apolitical roles of evidential researchers, adopted a conservative position (that is, pro-Sung Learning) in scholarship. Conservative scholarship was now tied to reformist politics. A partisan of the T'ung-ch'eng school, Tseng wrote in 1845:

> In the recent Chien-lung and Chia-ch'ing eras, Confucians have insisted on broad [scholarship]. The followers of Hui Ting-yü [Tung] and Tai Tung-yuan [Chen] deeply investigate ancient glosses. Relying on the [Former Han] dictum enunciated by King Hsien of Ho-chien [to the effect that] "one must search for the truth in actual facts," they denigrate the worthies of the Sung for empty scholarship. What they call "facts" [*shih*], are these not "phenomena" [*wu*]? Isn't [what they consider] "truth" [*shih*] "the pattern underlying phenomena" [*li*]? [The doctrine that] "one must search for the truth in actual facts"—isn't this [process] precisely what Chu Hsi called "fathoming the pattern underlying phenomena" [*chi-wu ch'iung-li*]?[22]

. . .

Evidential research continued to be an important enterprise. Despite growing dissatisfaction, particularly among Hunanese and Cantonese scholars, *k'ao-cheng* was effectively defended by Kiangnan literati until the Taiping nightmare. To be sure, the defense of *k'ao-cheng* scholarship by political reformers such as Chang Chih-tung and others in the nineteenth century was argued less and less in terms of the utility of an apolitical discourse in the "search for the truth in actual facts" and more and more in terms of statecraft goals and concerns. A change was evident. As a direct result of the Taiping Rebellion, Hunan and Kwangtung economically and intellectually replaced Kiangnan as the trend-setting region.[23]

The Impact of the Taiping Rebellion

Fragmented intellectually as a result of the early nineteenth-century reaction against evidential research, the institutions of the *k'ao-cheng* academic community in Kiangnan eventually perished in the havoc brought on by clashes between Taiping and imperial armies in the Lower Yangtze River Basin. Ho Ping-ti has contended that the total estimated loss of life during the rebellion, usually placed at between twenty or thirty million, is far too low. "The regional urban system," as G. William Skinner has explained, "was shattered in the Lower Yangtze region." Skinner has estimated that population in the Lower Yangtze fell from 67 million in 1844 only to reach 45 million in 1894.[24]

In his discussion of the impact the Taiping Rebellion had on population in southern Kiangsu, Yeh-chien Wang has described the different ways the eastern and western prefectures there were affected by the fighting. During the period after the establishment of the Heavenly Kingdom in 1853 until the fall of Nanking in 1864, the western prefectures of Chiang-ning, Chinkiang, and Ch'ang-chou, in addition to the independent department of Nanking (the Taiping capital), became the battleground for the struggle between the opposing armies. Although the situation in the eastern prefectures of Soochow, Sung-chiang, and T'ai-tsang was not as serious, the destruction there was also considerable.[25]

Refugees streamed out of Kiangsu's western prefectures to seek shelter in the eastern part of Kiangsu. There was additionally a continuous exodus of people from Chekiang, where the devastation was also total. Shanghai, protected from the Taipings by foreigners, became an asylum into which gentry, merchants, and the populace of Kiangsu and Che-kiang crowded to avoid the hostilities. While Nanking, Ch'ang-chou, Yangchow, and Soochow suffered disastrous drops in population, Shanghai grew into a flourishing urban center. After the war, new immigrants moved into the depopulated areas in western Kiangsu and elsewhere.

Yeh-chien Wang estimates the loss of life in southern Kiangsu alone to be around six or seven million people during this period. These losses were chiefly reflected in the sudden population drops in the major cities of Soochow, Nanking, Ch'ang-chou, Chinkiang, and Chiang-ning. The rise to power of Hunanese such as Tseng Kuo-fan, Tso Tsung-t'ang (1812–1885), and Hu Lin-i (1812–1861) was made possible by the devastation in Kiangnan. It was no accident that Hunan and Kwangtung gentry emerged as the leading spokesman of literati interests after the rebellion was suppressed.[26]

· ·

The Intellectual Impact

The impact of this destruction on the schools, libraries, and academies in Kiangnan, although it cannot be measured exactly, totally disrupted intellectual life in the Lower Yangtze. In addition to the destruction of the organizational infrastructure required to maintain a community of scholars, the disruption in lost lives, forced flight, and emergency military involvement on the part of literati, who otherwise would have continued their research and writing, meant that *k'ao-cheng* scholarship was brought to a virtual halt in Kiangnan in the 1860s. Also brought to a halt in the 1860s was the examination system in Kiangsu. In the territory controlled by Ch'ing forces, recommendation became the basis for recruitment.[27]

Yeh Te-hui (1864–1927), a well-known bibliophile and political conservative, noted that after the Taiping Rebellion few libraries were left intact in the Lower Yangtze. Two centuries of book collecting had been swept away. Many of the most famous private libraries had been lost or dispersed. Especially hard hit was Hangchow, where libraries had been one of the centers of cultural life. When Hangchow was sacked by Taiping forces in 1860–1861, most of the family libraries there were lost. Hangchow literati later attempted to salvage some of the volumes from the *Ssu-k'u ch'üan-shu* collection deposited at the Wen-lan ko, after the Taipings had ransacked the collection there. The library at the Ku-ching ching-she and the Ling-yin Library, both established by Juan Yuan when he was governor of Chekiang, were also destroyed. The latter, at the Ling-yin Monastery near West Lake, perished when Taiping forces took Hangchow for the second time in 1861.[28]

Kondo Mitsuo points out that after the Taiping armies pillaged Yangchow in 1853, the city never recaptured its scholarly and literary position in Chinese academics. Lo Shih-lin (d. 1853), a noted mathematician and astronomer, perished in Yangchow when the city fell to the Taipings. The city was reoccupied by Taiping forces from April to May, 1854, and was again the scene of a major confrontation in the spring of 1856. According to Frederick Mote, the Taiping sack of Soochow in 1860 may have cost half a million lives. Rebel occupation of the city lasted the better part of a year; the literati who managed to escape spent their time in exile in Shanghai. Hsu Yu-jen (1800–1860), then governor of Kiangsu and a noted mathematician, lost his life in the battle for Soochow. The well-known mathematician Li Shan-lan (1810–1882), then serving on Hsu Yu-jen's staff, escaped to Shanghai where he remained for several years, but his printed works were destroyed along with the governor's yamen.[29]

When Chin-shan, Kiangsu, was overrun in the summer of 1860, the printing blocks for three important collectanea (*ts'ung-shu*), formerly in the possession of Ch'ien Hsi-tso (d. 1844) were destroyed. In the same year, the blocks for the *Ching-hsun T'ang ts'ung-shu* (Collectanea from the Hall for Glossing the Classics) perished. Pi Yuan had included in this important collection works on restored texts such as the *Mo-tzu*, which he had collated with the help of his usual entourage of *k'ao-cheng* scholars (see chapter 3). The rebellion was also the immediate cause of the loss of much of Chang Hsueh-ch'eng's unpublished writings. A number of his local histories, along with the many drafts for the completed portions of the *Shih-chi k'ao* (Critique of historical writing) bibliography, have never been recovered. Similarly, the woodblocks for Ch'en Shou-ch'i's (1771–1834) important writings (see chapter 5) as well as those of his son, were lost when Taiping forces invaded Fukien.

The list of lost lives, lost works, destroyed schools and libraries does not end here. All we can say is that the Taiping Rebellion, for all intents and purposes, had liquidated the community of evidential scholars in nineteenth-century Kiangnan. Gone were many of its institutions of higher learning and its precious libraries. The book trade was reduced to a frantic effort to salvage what little was left of a once thriving publishing industry. The Lower Yangtze Region had lost a major part of one generation of scholars during this time.[30]

Scholarship and the T'ung-chih Restoration

Mary Wright has explained that one of the major goals during the T'ung-chih Restoration (1862–1874) was to rebuild the schools, academies, and libraries that had been lost. In 1865, Tseng Kuo-fan and Li Hung-chang (1823–1901), the leaders of the anti-Taiping armies, were ordered to restore the academies of Nanking and Ch'ang-chou, nearly all of which had been destroyed. Later in 1867, Wu T'ang (d. 1876), then governor-general of Fukien and Chekiang, presented a plan for the restoration of the academies of those provinces. Tseng Kuo-fan's main objective after the defeat of the Taipings was to restore peace and order in Kiangnan. To promote the rehabilitation of scholarship in the Lower Yangtze and elsewhere, Tseng established at his headquarters in Anking a printing office designed to reprint the Classics and the Histories. Scholars such as Mo Yu-chih (1811–1871) and Wang Shih-to (1802–1889) were invited to be chief editors. Other printing offices were established in Nanking, Soochow, Yangchow, Hangchow, and Wuchang.

The revival of scholarship depended on the rebuilding of libraries. To remedy the complete loss of over half of the more than five hundred important collections in Kiangnan, officials and literati joined together in an effort to recover and rehouse the scattered books, manuscripts, and woodblocks that remained. Publishing was encouraged, and the reprinting of the Classics and the Histories received considerable imperial and local support. Mo Yu-chih, after serving on Tseng Kuo-fan's staff, spent the years after 1865 traveling through Kiangnan in the hope of rescuing stray volumes from the three sets of the *Ssu-k'u ch'üan-shu* originally deposited in Chinkiang, Yangchow, and Hangchow, which had been dispersed during the Taiping Rebellion. The *Ssu-k'u ch'üan-shu* collections in Yangchow and Chinkiang were never restored.

While the city was still in Taiping hands, the Ting family, their library destroyed by the battles over Hangchow, had sent a bookseller there to retrieve what remnants they could of the Wen-lan ko collection. From 1866 until 1871, the Ting family searched for and bought what items they could find from the *Ssu-k'u ch'üan-shu* collection that had been housed in Hangchow. It was not until 1881 that the Wen-lan ko was rebuilt and the surviving volumes of the *Ssu-k'u ch'üan-shu* restored to the collection.

Likewise, Lu Hsin-yuan (1834–1894) and Ting Jih-ch'ang (1823–1892), who served both Tseng Kuo-fan and Li Hung-chang during the Taiping Rebellion, attempted to salvage what they could of the dispersed contents of many of the famous collections that had suffered serious losses as a result of the warfare. Lu Hsin-yuan, for example, was able to gather portions of some ten of these collections together for his own library in Kuei-an, Chekiang. The loss of books and the dispersal of the great private collections in Kiangnan during the Taiping Rebellion was an important motivation for Sun I-jang (1848–1908), a pioneer in the use of oracle bones for research, in his search for rare books, manuscripts, and inscriptions. Some of these, no longer extant in China, he obtained from Japan.

Huang P'eng-nien (1823–1891), a scholar and bibliophile, emphasized the printing of books and the promotion of libraries. He tried to revive the pre-Taiping academic world by founding academies all over Kiangnan. Perhaps the most famous product of Huang's efforts to promote scholarship was the Hsueh-ku T'ang (Hall for the Study of Antiquity), which he founded in Soochow in 1889. Through this academy, Huang hoped to restore Soochow to the cultural prominence the city had had during the heyday of Han Learning.[31]

Despite these efforts, however, the Kiangnan academic community upon which the success of evidential studies had depended was not adequately rehabilitated. After the Taiping Rebellion, education was caught up in an ideological debate over whether Western learning should be welcomed, a debate that lasted for the duration of the dynasty. The debate was accompanied by the growth in numbers of politically active literati. In addition, men from areas not affected so drastically by the Taiping Rebellion, notably Hunan and Kwangtung, had risen to power in the bureaucracy. Such new figures were influential supporters of statecraft, not old style *k'ao-cheng*. Discussion of Han Learning versus

Sung Learning was replaced by arguments concerning Chinese learning (*Chung-hsueh*) versus Western learning.

Internal threats were shunted aside for the time being, but the external threat remained and gathered momentum. The Hsueh-hai T'ang, for instance, was destroyed during the 1858 attack on Canton by French and British troops. The *Huang-Ch'ing ching-chieh* collection housed there, along with its woodblocks, was lost; evidential scholars such as Ch'en Li were forced to seek shelter elsewhere until the Hsueh-hai T'ang was rebuilt. Eventually the *Huang-Ch'ing ching-chieh* was reconstructed and reprinted. During the Boxer Rebellion in 1900, the only remaining copy of the *Yung-lo ta-tien* was dispersed and destroyed in the fighting between Chinese and Western forces in Peking.[32]

Compilation of the late nineteenth-century *Huang-Ch'ing ching-chieh* supplement (*hsu-pien*) at the Nan-ch'ing Academy between 1886–1888 in many ways represented a last commemoration of evidential scholarship. Nan-ch'ing had been founded by Wang Hsien-ch'ien (1842–1918) to restore the scholarship of the late nineteenth century to the level achieved earlier at the Hsueh-hai T'ang in Canton. However, the intellectual content of Confucian discourse (whether Han or Sung Learning) was now openly challenged in a growing tide of Confucian radicalism (for example, K'ang Yu-wei and the New Text initiative), a tide in which evidential scholarship had played a preliminary role. Canton (where the *Huang-Ch'ing ching-chieh* was printed) in the 1820s and Chiang-yin (where the *Huang-Ch'ing ching-chieh hsu-pien* was printed) in the 1880s were situated in very different historical contexts. Canton in the 1820s looked to Soochow, Yangchow, and Hangchow. By the 1880s Chiang-yin (in Ch'ang-chou prefecture) looked to Shanghai, the symbol along with Canton and Changsha of new forces overtaking China.[33]

. . .

Epilogue

In the preceding chapters, we have described Confucian academic life as it appeared to educated literati before the Taiping invasion of Kiangnan and before the prism of imperialism refracted their perception of Chinese society. In particular, we have seen how evidential scholarship was practiced in its own social and political milieu. Its institutions were promoted by a society that saw in *k'ao-cheng* a viable discourse that could verify and continue the wisdom of antiquity. Chinese scholars had outgrown the shackling forms of discourse that were entrenched as imperial Confucianism since the Yuan dynasty. The Neo-Confucian orthodoxy, with its imperial symbolism and powerful formalism, no longer dominated intellectual life. Participants in the *k'ao-cheng* movement were gripped by a profound optimism that the limits of Neo-Confucian discourse had been irrevocably left behind.

Sung and Ming Confucians had lived in the shadow of the ancients. Influenced by Taoism and Buddhism (influences that Neo-Confucians rhetorically denied), they interpreted Confucian doctrine according to what they regarded as truly classical principles: moralism, personal cultivation, and correlative metaphysics. There followed, however, an intellectualist turn in Confucian discourse during the seventeenth and eighteenth centuries. What scholars saw as the incomparable purity of ancient culture and its precision of conception and expression were reconstructed through the use of new research techniques. Cultivation of virtue was rejected as an idle pastime. Precise scholarship became the central concern.

The eighteenth century in China was indomitably Confucian at heart. Although they initiated what we have called "the unraveling of Neo-Confucianism," Ch'ing philologists could only imagine a world in which Confucian doctrines were inviolate. When evidential scholars looked forward in time, they did not perceive the imperialists, capitalists, and revolutionaries who populate our world of discourse. Yet they had made linguistic, social, political, and scientific discoveries that belie the usual picture of this period as one stuck in the quicksand of the past. Although the new discourse had its roots in traditional soil, the tone of intellectual life was transformed. Hu Shih thought he was revolutionary when he wrote in his 1917 Columbia University dissertation, "I am firmly of the opinion that the future of Chinese philosophy depends on its emancipation from the moralistic and rationalistic fetters of Confucianism." Later he discovered that the groundwork for this emancipation had been provided by his Ch'ing predecessors.[34]

In the fall of 1899, for example, a dealer in antiques sold Wang I-jung (1845–1900) some specimens of Shang dyansty (1751–1123 B.C.) inscribed oracle bones. An expert in epigraphy, Wang had earlier accumulated many bronze and stone inscriptions dating from the first millennium B.C. Upon seeing the oracle bones, he quickly recognized that the inscriptions on them were in a form of writing more ancient even than the bronze and stone inscriptions he previously had studied. "With this event," writes Herrlee Creel, "an entirely new epoch in our understanding of the history of man in the Far East was begun."[35]

Laboring in obscure, technical fields of scholarship, Wang I-jung, Liu E (1857–1909), and the celebrated specialists who followed them touched off a transformation in our understanding of ancient China. Yet this dramatic discovery depended upon the most specialized and technical minutiae of paleographical research. There are moments in precise fields of scholarship when what would otherwise be recondite discoveries spill over into the social and intellectual realms of knowledge in which we all participate.

Momentous discoveries are not unprepared for, however. Recognition of the potential importance of the oracle bones for the study of ancient China did not grow out of the introduction of a Western, scientific perspective to Chinese scholarly circles in the late nineteenth century. Rather, the importance of the oracle bones was first recognized by Confucian scholars such as Wang I-jung, who saw in them a new source of knowledge about China's past. Sun I-jang, a noted bibliophile and expert in the traditional Chinese field of research known as bronze and stone epigraphy (chin-shih-hsueh), went through Liu E's facsimile reproductions of oracle bone inscriptions that had been printed in 1903. As yet, few scholars had paid much attention to the oracle bones, but Sun I-jang's earlier training in bronze and stone inscriptions enabled him to decipher the bone inscriptions with some facility. Sun soon published his findings in a series of works that described how the study of such inscriptions might eventually shed light on Chinese etymology, history, calendrical science, geography, and paleography. In this manner, a new frontier of research grew out of the accumulating base of Ch'ing dynasty bronze and stone studies.

This direct link between pre-modern Chinese precise scholarship and the rise of oracle bone studies in the twentieth century suggests that the critical research carried out by contemporary Chinese scholars is not due to the influence of modern Western social and natural science alone. The decisive impact of Western scholarship in the seventeenth century should not be underestimated. Impressed with European achievements in astronomy, mathematics, and surveying, Confucian scholars were clearly capable of distinguishing between the Christian faith and the scientific notions that the Jesuits in China attempted to weave together in the late Ming and early Ch'ing periods. Research completed by Confucian scholars such as Wang I-jung, Liu E, and Sun I-jang points to the continuity between the exact scholarship begun during the Ch'ing dynasty and twentieth-century Chinese scholarly discourse.[36] Revival of the *k'ao-cheng* slogan "to search for the truth in actual facts" after the Cultural Revolution, accordingly, should not surprise us.

Notes

Bibliography

Glossary

Index

Abbreviations Used in Notes

ECCP   *Eminent Chinese of the Ch'ing Period.* Arthur W. Hummel, ed. (Taipei, Ch'eng Wen Reprint, 1972).

HCCC   *Huang-Ch'ing ching-chieh.* Edited by Juan Yuan et al. (Taipei, Fu-hsing Reprint, 1961).

HCCCHP   *Huang-Ch'ing ching-chieh hsu-pien.* Edited by Wang Hsien-ch'ien et al. (Taipei, Fu-hsing shu-chü Reprint, 1972).

HJAS   *Harvard Journal of Asiatic Studies.*

MB   *Dictionary of Ming Biography, 1368–1644.* Luther C. Goodrich et al. (New York, Columbia University Press, 1976).

SKCS   *Ssu-k'u ch'üan-shu.* Imperial Library Collection.

SKCSTM   *Ssu-k'u ch'üan-shu tsung-mu.* Chi Yun et al. (Taipei, I-wen yin-shu-kuan Reprint, 1974).

SPPY   *Ssu-pu pei-yao.* (Shanghai, Chung-hua shu-chü, 1927–1935).

Notes

1: A Revolution in Discourse in Late Imperial China

1. Donald Kelley, *Foundations of Modern Historical Scholarship: Language, Law, and History in the French Renaissance* (New York, 1970), pp. 19–50. See also Quentin Skinner, *Foundations of Modern Political Thought*, Vol. 1 (Cambridge, 1979), *passim*.
2. Willard Peterson, *Bitter Gourd: Fang I-chih and the Impetus for Intellectual Change* (New Haven, 1979), pp. 1–17.
3. For a socially conditioned definition of "milieu," see Robert Merton, *The Sociology of Science: Theoretical and Empirical Investigations* (Chicago, 1973), p. 373.
4. For discussion of the differences between external and internal history, see Thomas Kuhn, *The Essential Tension*, pp. 105–126, 293–319.
5. See G. William Skinner, "Regional Urbanization in Nineteenth-Century China," *The City in Late Imperial China* (Stanford, 1977), pp. 211–249, and *Marketing and Social Structure in Rural China* (Ann Arbor, *Journal of Asian Studies* Reprint, 1964–1965), *passim*. See also Fu I-ling, *Ming-tai Chiang-nan shih-min ching-chi shih-t'an,* (Shanghai, 1957), pp. 1–23. In this work, "Kiangnan" and the "Lower Yangtze Region" will be equivalent terms.
6. E. A. Kracke, Jr., "Sung Society: Change Within Tradition," *Enduring Scholarship Selected from the Far Eastern Quarterly* (Tucson, 1972), pp. 65–74, Miyazaki Ichisada, "Min-Shin jidai no Soshū to keikōgyō no hattatsu," *Ajia shi kenkyū*, vol. 4 (Kyoto, 1964), pp. 306–320, and "Mindai So-Shō chihō no shidaifu to min-shū," *Shirin* 33.3:219–251 (June 1954). Miyazaki points out that Soochow's central importance was finally superseded by Shang-

hai's growth in the nineteenth century. See Frederick Mote, "A Millennium of Chinese Urban History: Form, Time, and Space Concepts in Soochow," *Rice University Studies* 59.4:33–65 (Fall 1973), and Silas Wu, *Passage to Power: K'ang-hsi and His Heir Apparent, 1661–1722* (Cambridge, Mass., 1979), pp. 4–6, 83–105, 194n. See also Marilyn and Shen Fu, *Studies in Connoisseurship: Chinese Paintings from the Arthur M. Sackler Collection in New York and Princeton* (Princeton, 1973), pp. 4–5, James Cahill, *Parting at the Shore: Chinese Painting of the Early and Middle Ming Dynasty, 1368–1580* (New York, 1978), pp. 4, 60, and *Fantastics and Eccentrics in Chinese Painting* (New York, 1967), pp. 20, 90. On Yangchow, see Sir William H. Scott, "Yangchow and Its Eight Eccentrics," *Asiatische Studien* 1–2:1–2 (1964–1965), Ping-ti Ho, "The Salt Merchants of Yang-chou: A Study of Commercial Capitalism in Eighteenth-Century China," *HJAS* 17:130–168 (1954), and Thomas Metzger, "The Organizational Capabilities of the Ch'ing State in the Field of Commerce: The Liang-Huai Salt Monopoly, 1740–1840," in W. E. Willmot, ed., *Economic Organization in Chinese Society* (Stanford, 1972), pp. 9–45.

7. See Ping-ti Ho, "The Salt Merchants of Yang-chou," pp. 155–157, Cahill, *Fantastics and Eccentrics,* p. 92, and Colin Mackerras, *The Rise of the Peking Opera, 1770–1870: Social Aspects of the Theatre in Manchu China* (Oxford, 1972), pp. 49–80. See Wu Ching-tzu's *The Scholars* (New York, 1972), *passim,* for a description of Nanking cultural life, and Cahill, *Parting,* pp. 97–98, for Nanking's lively interaction between officials and merchants during the Ming dynasty. See also Scott, "Yangchow and Its Eight Eccentrics," pp. 1–19, Nancy Lee Swann, "Seven Intimate Library Owners," *HJAS* 1:369 (1936), and Tu Wei-yun, *Hsueh-shu yü shih-pien* (Taipei, 1971), p. 118. On merchant support of schools, see Ōkubo Eiko, *Min-Shin jidai shoin no kenkyū* (Tokyo, 1976), pp. 221–361. See also Chung-li Chang, *The Chinese Gentry: Studies on Their Role in Nineteenth-Century Chinese Society* (Seattle, 1967), pp. 102–111. On merchant literacy, see Evelyn Rawski, *Education and Popular Literacy in Ch'ing China* (Ann Arbor, 1979), pp. 9–10.

8. Ping-ti Ho, *The Ladder of Success in Imperial China* (New York, 1962), pp. 226–237, Frederic Wakeman, *The Fall of Imperial China* (New York, 1975), pp. 19–24, and Kwang Tsing Wu, "Scholarship,

Book Production, and Libraries in China, 618–1644," (PhD dissertation, University of Chicago, 1944), pp. 184, 260.

9. For detailed discussion of schools of learning during the Ch'ing dynasty, see my "Ch'ing Dynasty 'Schools' of Scholarship," *Ch'ing-shih wen-t'i*, 4.6:1–44 (December 1981). See Ping-ti Ho, *The Ladder of Success*, p. 228, and Achilles Fang, tr., "Bookman's Manual by Sun Ts'ung-t'ien," *HJAS* 14:214 (1951). See also Skinner, *The City in Late Imperial China*, p. 247. On the "national elite," see Kuhn, *Rebellion and Its Enemies*, pp. 180–188.

10. This view has been generally accepted since the publication of Luther C. Goodrich's influential *The Literary Inquisition of Ch'ien-lung* (Baltimore, 1935), pp. 30–67. For a Marxist development of this theme, see Hou Wai-lu, *Chin-tai Chung-kuo ssu-hsiang hsueh-shuo shih*, vol. 1 (Shanghai, 1947), p. 422. See also Albert Feuerwerker, *State and Society in Eighteenth-Century China: The Ch'ing Empire in Its Glory* (Ann Arbor, 1976), pp. 25–31.

11. See Winston Lo, "Philology, An Aspect of Sung Rationalism," *Chinese Culture* 17.4:5 (December 1976), Ku Chieh-kang, "A Study of Literary Persecution During the Ming," *HJAS* 3:254–311 (1938), Charles Hucker, "The Tung-lin Movement of the Late Ming Period," in John K. Fairbank, ed., *Chinese Thought and Institutions* (Chicago, 1957), pp. 153–156, and Tilemann Grimm, "Some Remarks on the Suppression of *Shu-yuan* in Ming China," *International Conference of Orientalists in Japan: Transactions* 2:8–16 (1957), for discussion of earlier persecutions.

12. See Henderson, pp. 75, 137–138, 216, and Susan Jones, "Scholasticism and Political Thought in Late Eighteenth-Century China," *Ch'ing-shih wen-t'i* 3.4:28–49 (December 1975). See also Thomas Metzger's important *The Internal Organization of Ch'ing Bureaucracy: Legal, Normative, and Communication Aspects* (Cambridge, 1973), *passim*, and also his article "The Organizational Capabilities of the Ch'ing State," p. 11.

13. Pei Huang, *Autocracy at Work: A Study of the Yung-cheng Period, 1723–1735* (Bloomington, 1974), pp. 222–224. Pei Huang notes: "Nonetheless, during the Yung-cheng period cases of literary persecution had nothing to do with heterodox ideas. These cases sprang directly from Yung-cheng's political considerations." See also

Fujitsuka Chikashi, *Shinchō bunka tōden no kenkyū* (Tokyo, 1975), pp. 10–11.

14. See Goodrich, *Literary Inquisition,* p. 67, and Cheuk-woon Taam, *The Development of Chinese Libraries Under the Ch'ing Dynasty, 1644–1911* (Taipei, 1977), pp. 40–41. See also Kent Guy, "The Scholar and the State in Late Imperial China: The Politics of the *Ssu-k'u ch'üan-shu* Project" (PhD dissertation, Harvard University, 1981), the concluding chapter.

15. Guy, "The Scholar and the State," the concluding chapter, and ECCP, pp. 805–806. See Yü Ying-shih, "Some Preliminary Observations on the Rise of Ch'ing Confucian Intellectualism," *Tsing Hua Journal of Chinese Studies* 11:128 (1975), and Yü, "Ch'ing-tai ssu-hsiang-shih te i-ko hsin chieh-shih," *Chung-kuo che-hsüeh ssu-hsiang lun-chi Ch'ing-tai p'ien* (Taipei, 1977), pp. 12–16. See also Tu Wei-yun, *Hsüeh-shu yü shih-pien,* pp. 120–131, and Hayashi Tomoharu, "Shinchō shoin no kyōiku," *Gakushūin daigaku bugaku-bu kenkyū nempō* 6:179 (1959).

16. Tai Chen, *Meng-tzu tzu-i shu-cheng,* appended to Hu Shih, *Tai Tung-yuan te che-hsüeh* (Taipei, 1967), pp. 55–56, and Tuan Yü-ts'ai, *Tai Tung-yuan (Chen) hsien-sheng nien-p'u* (Taipei, n.d.) pp. 68–69.

17. Chang Hsüeh-ch'eng, *Chang-shih i-shu* (Taipei, 1973) 8:25 (*pu-i*). For discussion of the philological basis of Tai Chen's political and philosophic formulations, see Paul Demiéville, "The First Philosophic Contacts Between Europe and China," *Diogenes* 58:81–85, 98–101 (Summer 1967). For an account of Chang's reactions to Tai's attack on Chu Hsi, see Kawata Teiichi, "Dōjidaijin no ne-muri—Shō Gakusei no Tai Shin kan," *Chūgoku tetsugaku shi no tembō no mosaku* (Tokyo, 1976), pp. 777–783. See also Fang Tung-shu, *Han-hsüeh shang-tui* (Taipei, 1963), 2A:19a.

18. Yü Ying-shih, *Lun Tai Chen yü Chang Hsüeh-ch'eng* (Hong Kong, 1976), pp. 63–75. For Chu Yun's remarks, see Chiang Fan, *Kuo-ch'ao Han-hsüeh shih-ch'eng chi* (SPPY edition), 6:6a. T'ang Chien's criticism is from his *Ch'ing hsüeh-an hsiao-chih* (Taipei, 1975), p. 454. See Ch'ien Ta-hsin, *Ch'ien-yen T'ang wen-chi* (Taipei, 1968) 5:619–624 (*chüan* 39). For Lu Wen-ch'ao's assessment, see *Pao-ching T'ang wen-chi* (Shanghai, 1937) 2:76 (*chüan* 6). On Juan Yuan, see Leung Man-kam, "Juan Yuan (1764–1849): The Life, Works, and Career of a Chinese Scholar-Bureaucrat," (PhD dissertation, University of Hawaii, 1977), pp. 80–96, and ECCP, pp. 144–

145. On Chiao Hsun, see Chiao's *Tiao-ku chi* (Shanghai, 1936), 2: 95 (*chüan* 7), and 3:184–185 (*chüan* 12).

19. See Kawata Teiichi, "Shimmatsu no Tai Shin zō–Ryū Shibai no bai," *Tōyōgaku ronshū* (Kyoto, 1979), pp. 1015–1034.

20. I am presently engaged in a broader study of the impact the *k'ao-cheng* movement had on the appearance of the New Text school during the Ch'ing dynasty.

21. Joseph Levenson and more recently Thomas Metzger have described only the nineteenth-century aspects of the revival of New Text Confucianism. See Levenson, *Confucian China and Its Modern Fate: A Trilogy,* vol. 1 (Berkeley, 1968), pp. 79–94, and Metzger, *Escape From Predicament: Neo-Confucianism and China's Evolving Political Culture* (New York, 1977), pp. 218–220.

22. Hou Wai-lu, *Chin-tai Chung-kuo* 2:599, and ECCP, p. 519. See also K'ang Yu-wei, *K'ung-tzu kai-chih k'ao* (Peking, 1958), p. 164 (*chüan* 7). See Hao Chang, *Liang Ch'i-ch'ao and Intellectual Transition in China, 1890–1907* (Cambridge, Mass., 1971), pp. 35–37.

23. Hsiao Kung-chuan, *A Modern China and a New World: K'ang Yu-wei, Reformer and Utopian* (Seattle, 1975), pp. 41–189. See also Benjamin Schwartz, "Foreword," *Intellectual Trends in the Ch'ing Period* (Cambridge, Mass., 1959), pp. xxi–xxii, Ch'i Ssu-ho, "Wei Yuan yü wan-Ch'ing hsueh-feng," *Yen-ching hsueh-pao* 39:177–226 (1950), and Levenson, *Confucian China,* vol. 1, pp. 79–94. For the role philology played in determining doctrine, see my "Philosophy Vs. Philology: The *Jen-hsin Tao-hsin* Debate," *T'oung Pao* 69.4&5: 175–222 (1983).

24. For the quotation, see Chang Hsieh-chih, "Hsu" (Introduction), in his *Shang-shu ku-wen pien-huo* (1904 edition), p. 1b. On Chang Ping-lin's position, see his *Kuo-hsueh kai-lun* (Taipei, 1974), pp. 27–38, 44–46. See also Charlotte Furth, "The Sage as Rebel: The Inner World of Chang Ping-lin," *The Limits of Change: Essays on Conservative Alternatives in Republican China* (Cambridge, Mass., 1976), pp. 115–128. For further discussion, see the recent findings of Huang Chang-chien in his article "Ching chin-ku-wen hsueh wen-t'i hsin-lun (shang)," *Ta-lu tsa-chih* 58.2:49–87 (February 1979), and Yang Hsiang-k'uei, "Ch'ing-tai te chin-wen ching-hsueh," *Ch'ing-shih lun-ts'ung* 1:177–209 (Peking, 1979).

25. A parallel can perhaps be drawn between the impact of charters and constitutions as texts on modern Western political behavior and

the role of the Confucian Classics in premodern Chinese, Korean, and Japanese politics.

26. On my use of "discourse," see Foucault, pp. 50–63. See also Edward Said, *Orientalism,* p. 23, his *Beginnings: Intention and Method* (Baltimore, 1975), pp. 281–315, and "Linguistics and the Archaeology of Mind," *International Philosophical Quarterly* 11.1:104–134 (March 1971).

27. See Peter Berger and Thomas Luckmann, *The Social Construction of Reality: A Treatise in the Sociology of Knowledge* (New York, 1966), p. 116, and Said, *Orientalism,* pp. 15–25.

28. See, for example, the confidence that the Yangchow textual scholar Chiao Hsun (1763–1820) had that his contemporaries had made major breakthroughs in research, summarized in Chiao's *Tiao-ku chi,* pp. 181–186 (*chüan* 12). Much of the account that follows is indebted interpretatively to Peter Gay's *The Enlightenment: An Introduction. The Rise of Modern Paganism* (New York, 1966), *passim.* Cf. Frank Kermode, *The Classic: Literary Images of Permanence and Change* (New York, 1975), p. 16, and T. S. Eliot, "What is a Classic," *On Poetry and Poets* (New York, 1961), pp. 52–74. The Western notion of a classic, however, is more literary and less institutionally defined than its Chinese counterpart. In traditional China, before the abolition of the examination system in 1905, the Five Classics were the backbone of the academic system. They included the *Changes, Documents, Poetry, Rites,* and the *Spring and Autumn Annals.* A *Classic of Music* had been lost in the classical period.

29. For discussion of the emergence of *Tao-hsueh* in the Sung period, see John Haeger, "The Intellectual Context of Neo-Confucian Syncretism," *Journal of Asian Studies* 31:499–513 (1972), James T.C. Liu, "How Did a Neo-Confucian School Become the State Orthodoxy?" *Philosophy East and West* 23.4:483–505 (1973), and Conrad Schirokauer, "Neo-Confucians Under Attack: The Condemnation of *Wei-hsueh,*" *Crisis and Prosperity in Sung China* (Tucson, 1975), pp. 163–198. Chi Yun's remarks are from his *Chi Hsiao-lan shih-wen-chi* (Hong Kong, n.d.), p. 34. See also Benjamin Wallacker, "Han Confucianism and Confucius in Han," *Ancient China: Studies in Early Civilization* (Hong Kong, 1978), p. 227, and Uno Seiichi, "*Shurai Ryū Kin gisaku setsu ni tsuite,*" *To A ronsō* p. 272.

30. Lothar Ledderhose, *Mi Fu and the Classical Tradition of Chinese Calligraphy* (Princeton, 1979), pp. 29–30. See Wang Mingsheng, "Hsu" (Introduction), in *Shih-ch'i-shih shang-ch'ueh* (Taipei, 1960), p. 2a, and Tai Chen, *Tai Chen wen-chi* (Hong Kong, 1974), p. 146.

31. On the Han cosmograms and magic squares, see Schuyler Cammann, "The Evolution of Magic Squares in China," *Journal of the American Oriental Society* 80:116–124 (1960), Henderson, "The Ordering of the Heavens and Earth," pp. 1–13, Winston Lo, "Philology, An Aspect of Sung Rationalism," pp. 17–26, and Joseph Needham et al., *Science and Civilization in China,* vol. 3 (Cambridge, 1954–), pp. 55–62. Cosmograms aside, the symbolic worldview of Sung Confucians may have been closer to that of the Classics as a whole than the views of Ch'ing philologists.

32. Kuei Chuang, *Kuei Chuang chi,* vol. 2 (Peking, 1962), pp. 323–324. My thanks to Willard Peterson of Princeton University for pointing this letter out to me.

33. Yen Jo-chü, *Shu-cheng* in the HCCCHP, 2:2a–2b. For discussion of the *Shu-cheng,* see P. K. Yu, comp., *Chinese Collections in the Library of Congress,* vol. 1 (Washington, D.C., 1974), pp. 317–319.

34. See Yen's 1697 "Hsu" (Introduction) to Tsang Lin's *Ching-i tsa-chi shu-lu* (Taipei, 1967), p. 2a, and the discussion of Ku's phonology in SKCSTM, 42:45a–45b and especially 44:50b for Chiang Yung's continuation of Ku's approach. Although Chiang was a follower of the Chu Hsi tradition, like Yen Jo-chü and others, he stressed the more intellectualist aspects of Chu Hsi's scholarship (see chapter two). See also Charles Gillispie, *The Edge of Objectivity: An Essay in the History of Scientific Ideas* (Princeton, 1960), *passim.* The parallel should be qualified somewhat. Gillispie describes a technical transition within the physical sciences to purely mathematical or otherwise objective descriptions with no moral implications remaining in scientific explanations. Ch'ing philology never reached that point.

35. Yü Ying-shih, "Some Preliminary Observations," pp. 105–144. See also Lawrence Schneider, *Ku Chieh-kang and China's New History* (Berkeley, 1971), pp. 195–200.

36. See Elman, "The Hsueh-hai T'ang and the Rise of New Text Scholarship in Canton," *Ch'ing-shih wen-t'i* 4.2:51–82 (December 1979).

37. Chou Yü-t'ung, *Ching chin-ku-wen hsueh* (Taipei, 1967), *passim.*
38. Wang Fu-chih, *Tu T'ung-chien lun* (Peking, 1975), p. 1112. I have modified the translation in Wm. T. de Bary et al., *Sources of Chinese Tradition*, vol. 1 (New York, 1964), p. 549. See also Ssu-yü Teng, "Wang Fu-chih's Views on History and Historical Writing," *Journal of Asian Studies* 28.1:115–116 (November 1968), and Frederick Mote, "The Arts and the 'Theorizing Mode' of the Civilization," in Christian Murck, ed., *Artists and Traditions: Uses of the Past in Chinese Culture* (Princeton, 1976), pp. 7–8. On Mei Wen-ting, see Hashimoto Keizō, "Bai Buntei no rekisangaku," *Tōhōgaku hō* 41:510 (1970).
39. Wei Yuan's words can be found in *Wei Yuan chi,* vol. 1 (Peking, 1976), p. 48. See also Takada Atsushi, "Shō Gakusei no shigaku shisō ni tsuite," *Tōhōgaku hō* 47.1:71–73 (June 1964), Sakade Yoshinobu, "Gi Gen shisō shiron," *Kaitoku* 35:45–48 (1964), and Hou Wai-lu, vol. 2, pp. 609–642.
40. Shimada Kenji, *Chūgoku ni okeru kindai shii no zasetsu* (Tokyo, 1970), pp. 4–5.

2: K'ao-cheng Scholarship and the Formation of a Shared Epistemological Perspective

1. Peterson, *Bitter Gourd,* pp. 2, 12, 79. See also Najita, pp. 8–13.
2. See Yü, "Some Preliminary Observations," pp. 126–129. See also Shimada Kenji, "Shō Gakusei no ichi," *Tōhōgaku hō* 41:519–530 (March 1970), David Nivison, *The Life and Thought of Chang Hsueh-ch'eng, 1738–1801* (Stanford, 1966), p. 286, and Foucault, p. 173.
3. Cited in the preface to the 1796 edition of the *Shu-cheng* written by Yen Jo-chü's son Yen Yung (1709 *chin-shih*), p. 1a. See also Henderson, pp. 38ff.
4. Chang Hsueh-ch'eng, *Wen-shih t'ung-i* (Taipei, 1973), pp. 52, 55. See also SKCSTM, 6:7b–8b, 14:13a–13b, 119:11b–12b, and Henderson, pp. 38–41.
5. Edwin Pulleyblank, "Neo-Confucianism and Neo-Legalism in T'ang Intellectual Life, 755–805," in Arthur Wright, ed., *The Confucian Persuasion* (Stanford, 1960), pp. 77–114.

6. See P'i Hsi-jui, *Ching-hsueh li-shih* (Hong Kong, 1961), pp. 220–221, James T.C. Liu, *Ou-yang Hsiu: An Eleventh-Century Neo-Confucianist* (Stanford, 1967), pp. 85–99. See also Schirokauer, pp. 184–187.

7. Cited in Chu I-tsun, *Ching-i k'ao* (SPPY edition), 84:3b. See also Winston Lo, pp. 1–26, but especially 6n.

8. See my "Yen Jo-chü's Debt to Sung and Ming Scholarship," *Ch'ing-shih wen-t'i* 3.7:105–113 (November 1977), and Chu I-tsun, 85:1a–3b, 88:6b–7a. Scholars who questioned the authenticity of the *Documents* during this time included Chao Meng-fu (1254–1322), Wu Ch'eng (1247–1331), Cheng Yuan (fl. ca. 1481), and Mei Tsu (fl. ca. 1513), among others. Cf. Najita and Scheiner, eds., *Japanese Thought in the Tokugawa Period*, p. xi.

9. Shimada Kenji, *Chūgoku ni okeru*, pp. 230–299. See also Hsiao Kung-chuan's moving biography of Li Chih in MB, pp. 807–817. The best account of the T'ai-chou school in English remains Wm. T. de Bary, "Individualism and Humanitarianism in Late Ming Thought," *Self and Society in Ming Thought* (New York, 1970), pp. 157–225. See the attacks on Li Chih by Wang Fu-chih in Wang's *Tu T'ung-chien lun*, pp. 453–454, 1111. Ku Yen-wu's attack on Li Chih can be found in the *Jih-chih lu* (Taipei, 1974), pp. 540–541 (*chüan* 20). He bemoans the fact that Li Chih's works have still not all been destroyed. For Huang Tsung-hsi's critique, see *Ming-Ju hsueh-an* (Taipei, 1973), pp. 311–313 (*chüan* 32). For discussion, see Hamaguchi Fujio. "Shingaku seiritsu no haikei ni tsuite," *Tōhōgaku* 58:114–127 (July 1979).

10. Irene Bloom, "On the 'Abstraction' of Ming Thought: Some Concrete Evidence From the Philosophy of Lo Ch'in-shun," in de Bary and Bloom, eds., *Principle and Practicality: Essays in Neo-Confucianism and Practical Learning* (New York, 1979), p. 106. Cf. Shimada Kenji, *Chugoku ni okeru*, p. 232.

11. SKCSTM, 119:3b–5b (on Yang Shen), 119:12b–13a (on Yang Shen, Chiao Hung, and Fang I-chih). See Jung Chao-tsu, *Ming-tai ssu-hsiang-shih* (Taipei, 1969), pp. 270–283, for an account of Ch'en Ti (d. 1620) as a *k'ao-cheng* scholar. Cf. Arnold Thackray and Robert Merton, "On Discipline-Building: The Paradoxes of George Sarton," *Isis* 63:474 (1972). See also Edward Ch'ien, "Chiao Hung and the Revolt Against Ch'eng-Chu Orthodoxy," in Wm. T. de Bary

et al., *The Unfolding of Neo-Confucianism* (New York, 1975), pp. 271–303, Peterson, *Bitter Gourd,* p. 12, and Gillispie, p. 202.

12. Cf. Gay, pp. 127–203.
13. Nakamura Kyūshirō, "Shinchō gakujutsu shisō shi (1)," *Tō A kenkyū* 2.11:51 (November 1912). This change in exegesis can readily be seen in any chronological listing of Chinese texts related to the Classics written from the Han to the Ch'ing periods. Cf. Koita Natsujirō, "Shinchō kōkyogaku no haikei," *Kokumin seishin bunka* 1.1:33 (1935). For discussion, see Hayden White, *Tropics of Discourse: Essays in Cultural Criticism* (Baltimore, 1978), pp. 1–25. Cf. Harootunian, p. 84, and Kenneth Burke, *The Philosophy of Literary Form* (Berkeley, 1973), pp. 1–3.
14. Yamanoi Yū, "Min-Shin jidai ni okeru 'ki' no tetsugaku," *Tetsugaku zasshi* 46.711:82–103 (1951). See also Yamanoi's account in *Ki no shisō: Chūgoku ni okeru shizenkan to ningenkan no tenkai* (Tokyo, 1978), edited by Onozawa Seiichi et al., pp. 473–489.
15. Willard Peterson, "Fang I-chih: Western Learning and the 'Investigation of Things,'" in Wm. T. de Bary et al., *The Unfolding of Neo-Confucianism* (New York, 1975), pp. 378–380. See also Sakade Yoshinobu, "Hō Ichi no shisō," in *Min-Shin jidai no kagaku gijutsu shi* (Kyoto, 1970), pp. 95–102, and Bloom, p. 76.
16. Hu Wei's attack on the Neo-Confucian cosmograms, discussed in chapters 1 and 5, was an important example of this kind of research. See Arthur Waley, *The Analects of Confucius* (New York, n.d.), pp. 171–172.
17. SKCSTM, 119:16b–17a. The genre of *pien* and its offshoots (*pien-chieh* [analysis of scholia], *pien-cheng* [analysis of evidence], etc.) came into their own during the Ch'ing dynasty. See also E. D. Edwards, "A Classified Guide to the Thirteen Classes of Chinese Prose," *Bulletin of the School of Oriental and African Studies* 12:771–772 (1948). For the origins of the expression *shih-shih ch'iu-shih,* see the *Han-shu,* 5:2410 (53:1a), where it is said that "[Liu] Te, when he took the throne as King Hsien of Ho-chien in 155 B.C., restored scholarship and honored antiquity. He sought the truth in actual facts."
18. Yoshikawa Kōjirō, "Sen Ken'eki to Shinchō keigaku," *Kyōto daigaku bungakubu kenkyū kiyō* 9:22–23, 28 (1965). See also Ono

Kazuko, "Mimmatsu no kessha ni kan suru ichi no kōsatsu (jō)," *Shirin* 45.2:40–42 (March 1962), and William Atwell, "From Education to Politics: The Fu She," in Wm. de Bary et al., *The Unfolding of Neo-Confucianism,* pp. 348–349.

19. Uno Seiichi, "Gokei kara Shisho e—keigakushi oboegaki," *Tōyō no bunka to shakai* 2:6–13 (March 1952). See Hayashi Tomoharu, "Sōdai no shoin," p. 30, and SKCSTM, 35:1a–1b, 36:13b–14b. See also John Meskill, *Academies in Ming China: A Historical Essay* (Tucson, 1982), p. 24.

20. Miyazaki Ichisada, "Shisho kōshōgaku," *Ajia shi kenkyū,* vol. 4, pp. 379–382. See Louis Gallagher, tr., *China in the Sixteenth Century: The Journals of Matthew Ricci, 1583–1610* (New York, 1953), p. 95. For discussion, see Gerald Dunne, *Generation of Giants: The Story of the Jesuits in China in the Last Decades of the Ming Dynasty* (South Bend, 1962), pp. 27–43.

21. Yoshikawa Kōjirō, p. 81. See also Murayama Yoshihiro, "Yō Seikō no gakumon (ge)," *Kambungaku kenkyū* 9.22–23, 32–33 (1961).

22. Nivison, pp. 14–15. See Peterson, *Bitter Gourd,* p. 1, and Naitō Torajirō, *Shinchōshi tsūron* in vol. 8 of *Naitō Konan zenshū* (Tokyo, 1969–1974), pp. 355–356. See also Tu Wei-yun, "Huang Tsung-hsi yü Ch'ing-tai Che-tung shih-hsueh-p'ai chih hsing-ch'i (shang)," *Ku-kung wen-hsien* 2.3:7 (June 1971), and Ono Kazuko, "Jukyō no itanshatachi," *Taidō suru Ajia* (Tokyo, 1966), pp. 22–23. The quotation from Ku Yen-wu is cited and discussed in Ho Yu-sen, "Ku T'ing-lin te ching-hsueh," *Wen-shih-che hsueh-pao* 16:185 (1967). For the original, see *Ku T'ing-lin shih-wen chi* (Hong Kong, 1976), p. 62 (*chüan* 3). For Ch'ien Ta-hsin's remarks, see his *Shih-chia-chai yang-hsin lu* (Taipei, 1968), 18:19a. Cf. Yü Ying-shih, *Lun Tai Chen,* p. 189, and P'i Hsi-jui, *Ching-hsueh li-shih,* pp. 289–290.

23. Yü Ying-shih, "Ts'ung Sung-Ming Ju-hsueh te fa-chan lun Ch'ing-tai ssu-hsiang-shih," *Chung-kuo hsueh-jen* 2:26–37 (September 1970). Cf. Harootunian, pp. 66–67. See also Foucault, pp. 8–9, Hayden White, "Foucault Decoded," pp. 27–28, and Berger and Luckmann, p. 179.

24. See Frederic Wakeman's poignant account of the fall of Chiang-yin in 1645 to Manchu forces entitled "Localism and Loyalism During the Ch'ing Conquest of Kiangnan: The Tragedy of Chiang-yin" in Wakeman and Grant, eds., *Conflict and Control in Late*

Imperial China (Berkeley, 1975), pp. 43–85. Chia-ting was also razed by Manchu forces.

25. Nathan Sivin, "Wang Hsi-shan," *Dictionary of Scientific Biography* (New York, 1970–1978), vol. 14, p. 163. See also Edward Ch'ien, pp. 271–272, and Jonathan Spence, "Tao-chi, An Historical Introduction," *The Painting of Tao-chi, 1641–ca. 1720* (Ann Arbor, 1967), p. 17. For the impact on painting, see Michael Sullivan, "Art and Politics in Seventeenth-Century China," *Apollo* 103. 107:231–235 (March 1976).

26. Ku Yen-wu, *Jih-chih lu,* pp. 540–541. The passage quoted is translated in Nelson Wu, "Tung Ch'i-ch'ang (1555–1636): Apathy in Government and Fervor in Art," in Wright and Twitchett, eds., *Confucian Personalities* (Stanford, 1962), pp. 279–280. For the original, see Huang Tsung-hsi, *Ming-Ju hsueh-an,* p. 144 (*chüan* 16).

27. Yen Yuan, *Ssu-shu cheng-wu* (Corrections of errors on the Four Books), 1:2b, in *Yen-Li ts'ung-shu* (Taipei, 1965), 1:47. See also Ono Kazuko, "Gan Gen no gakumon ron," *Tōhōgaku hō* 41: 469–487 (1964), ECCP, p. 914, and *Yen-Li ts'ung-shu,* 1:199ff.

28. See SKCSTM, 97:9b–11b, especially 11a.

29. Sivin, "Wang Hsi-shan," p. 163. See also ECCP, p. 45, Okada Takehiko, "Chō Yōen to Riku Futei," *Teoria* 9:1–14 (December 1965), and Hiraoka Takeo, *Keisho no dentō* (Tokyo, 1951), pp. 372–425. See William Dolby, *A History of Chinese Drama* (New York, 1976), p. 127.

30. Wm. Theodore de Bary, "Chinese Despotism and the Confucian Ideal: A Seventeenth-Century View," in John K. Fairbank, ed., *Chinese Thought and Institutions* (Chicago, 1957), pp. 165–168. This critique materialized in Huang's *Ming-i tai-fang lu* (Record of the wait for a call to official service written in a period of darkness). The passage translated is from *Li-chou i-chu hui-k'an* (*hsia*), *Ming-i tai-fang lu* (Taipei, 1969), pp. 1b–2a.

31. Henderson, p. 20, and Peterson, *Bitter Gourd,* p. 10n. In addition, for the generation of 1644 there was the established ideology of *pu erh ch'en* (a servant of only one dynasty) that forbade one who had been an official—even a subject—of one dynasty to serve another. See also Sivin, "Wang Hsi-shan," p. 163, and Yü Ying-shih, *Lun Tai Chen,* p. 130n.

32. Mao Ch'i-ling, *Hsi-ho ho-chi* (K'ang-hsi edition, ca. 1699), *ts'e* 75:1:1a–6b.

33. Arthur Waley, *Yuan Mei: Eighteenth Century Chinese Poet* (Stanford, 1970), p. 66, and Peterson, *Bitter Gourd,* p. 166. See also Kung-chuan Hsiao, *Rural China: Imperial Control in the Nineteenth Century* (Seattle, 1967), pp. 184–258.

34. Nakamura Kyūshirō, "Shinchō gakujutsu shisō shi (3)," pp. 40–42. Cf. Yamanoi Yū, "Mimmatsu Shinsho ni okeru keisei chiyō no gaku," *Tōhōgaku ronshū* 1:136–150 (February 1954), "Kō Sōgi no gakumon: Mingaku kara Shingaku e no ikō ichi yōsō," *Tōkyō Shinagaku hō* 3:31–50 (1957), and "Ko Enbu no gakumon kan: 'Mingaku kara Shingaku e no tenkan' no kanten kara," *Chūō daigaku bungakubu kiyō* 35:67–93 (1964).

35. Yamanoi, "Mimmatsu Shinsho shisō ni tsuite no ichi kōsatsu," *Tōkyō Shinagaku hō* 11:37–54 (1965).

36. Yü, "Some Preliminary Observations," pp. 105–146. Cf. Merton, pp. 180–185, for a discussion of the support science received before it was recognized as an important endeavor in its own right.

37. Yamanoi Yū, "Min-Shin no tetsugaku to shuyō," *Rekishi kyōiku* 2.11:82–88 (November 1954). See also Henderson, pp. 4, 19–20, and Yü Ying-shih, *Lun Tai Chen,* p. 19. Moral cultivation remained an important undercurrent, however. In the 19th century, reemphasis on moral philosophy revived interest in self-cultivation, as demonstrated in the careers of K'ang Yu-wei and Liang Ch'i-ch'ao (see chapter 6).

38. Henderson, pp. 32, 51–52, 150, 187–206.

39. *Shu-cheng,* 1:7a, 1:10b, 8:10b, 8:31a. Reading *shih* as "concrete" and *hsu* as "speculative." See also Tai Chün-jen, *Yen-Mao ku-wen Shang-shu kung-an* (Hong Kong, 1963), pp. 58–59, and Hu Shih, "The Scientific Spirit and Method in Chinese Philosophy," in C. A. Moore, ed., *The Chinese Mind* (Honolulu, 1967), pp. 104–131.

40. On Yao Chi-heng, see Murayama Yoshihiro, "Yō Seikō no gakumon (ge)," p. 29. See also Yü Ying-shih, *Lun Tai Chen,* pp. 17–18, *Tai Chen wen-chi,* p. 76, and Tuan Yü-ts'ai, *Ching-yun-lou chi,* in *Tuan Yü-ts'ai i-shu* (Taipei, 1977), 11:40b.

41. Cf. Thomas Kuhn, *The Essential Tension,* pp. 118–119.

42. Sivin, "Wang Hsi-shan," p. 163. See also Nivison, p. 14, and John Gray, "Historical Writing in Twentieth-Century China: Notes on Its Background and Development" in Beasley and Pulleyblank, eds., *Historians of China and Japan* (Oxford, 1961), p. 197.

43. For Juan Yuan's remarks, see *Yen-ching-shih chi* (Taipei, 1964), 2: 505. Tuan Yü-ts'ai's assessment is from his *Ching-yun-lou chi,* 9:38a. Chiang Fan, for example, gave Yen Jo-chü and Hu Wei first and second place in his *Kuo-ch'ao Han-hsueh shih-ch'eng chi.* For Chuang Shu-tsu's connection to the Ch'ang-chou scholars, see Naitō Torajirō, "Shina gakumon no kinjō," *Naitō Konan zenshū,* vol. 6, pp. 51–52, and Chang Shou-an, "Kung Ting-an yü Ch'ang-chou Kung-yang-hsueh," *Shu-mu chi-k'an* 13.2:4 (September 1979). Cf. Ishiguro Nobutoshi, "Kyō Jichin to *Shunjū* Kuyōgaku—keigaku o chūshin to shite," *Aichi kyōiku daigaku kenkyū hōkoku* 24:3 (March 1975).

44. Hou Wai-lu, 1:365–366. Wang Ming-sheng, a follower of Hui Tung, also noted this difference. Cf. ECCP, p. 698, and Koita Natsujirō, pp. 34–35, 38. Chiao Hsun's remarks are from his *Tiao-ku chi,* 2:104–105 (*chüan* 7).

45. Fumoto Yasutaka, *Sō Gen Min Shin kinsei Jugaku hensen shiron* (Tokyo, 1976), pp. 133–167.

46. Fang Tung-shu was effusive in his praise for Wang Yin-chih's *k'ao-cheng* studies. See Fang's *Han-hsueh shang-tui,* 2B:10b, 2B:14a–17a, and Hu Shih, "Ch'ing-tai hsueh-che te chih-hsueh fang-fa," *Hu Shih wen-ts'un* (Taipei, 1968) 1:401–402. Fang's *Han-hsueh shang-tui* was composed of quotations from *k'ao-cheng* scholars followed by arguments refuting their anti-Sung-Learning stance. See also SKCSTM, 118:43b–44b.

47. Henderson, pp. 91–93. See also Gray, pp. 186–197.

48. For Tai Chen's and Ch'ien Ta-hsin's remarks, see Fang Tung-shu, *Han-hsueh shang-tui,* 2B:1a. See also Ch'ien Ta-hsin, *Ch'ien-yen T'ang wen-chi,* 3:348–349. See Ho Yu-sen, "Juan Yuan te ching-hsueh chi ch'i chih-hsueh fang-fa," *Ku-kung wen-hsien* 2.1:26–33 (December 1970), and Hou Wai-lu, 1:542–577, for a detailed discussion of Juan's textual research.

49. Nathan Sivin, "Copernicus in China," *Colloquia Copernica II: Études sur l'audience de la théorie héliocentrique* (Warsaw, 1973, p. 72, and Kondo Mitsuo, "Shinchō keishi ni okeru kagaku ishiki,"

Nihon Chūgoku gakkai hō 4:99, 106 (1952). See also SKCSTM, 107:1a–2a, 107:10a–11a.

50. The quotation is from Sivin, "Copernicus," pp. 99–100. See Leung Man-kam, pp. 61, 67–79, 169. Juan's questions are summarized from his *Yen-ching-shih chi,* 3:129–130. Cf. Needham, *Science and Civilization in China,* 3:175n. Wu Lan-hsiu's treatise can be found in *Hsueh-hai T'ang chi* (Canton, 1838) II, 10:1a–58b. For student essays on astronomy and mathematics, see III, 5:32a–34a; IV, 3:9a–11b; IV, 14:9a–34b. See Ulrich Libbrecht, *Chinese Mathematics in the Thirteenth Century: The Shu-shu chiu-chang of Ch'in Chiu-shao* (Cambridge, Mass., 1973), pp. 61–63. See also Yao Nai's Preface to Hsieh Ch'i-k'un's *Hsiao-hsueh k'ao* (Taipei, 1969), pp. 5a–6a.

51. My findings are based on a careful reading of the *Documents,* philology, bibliography, encyclopedias, and astronomy and mathematics subsections of the SKCSTM. In order to summarize the results, I focus here only on the *Documents* section because I have found it representative and adequate to serve as a good example of the kind of evaluation that made itself felt among the editors and their staff. In the discussion that follows the citations from the SKCSTM will be given in parentheses in the text itself.

52. Yü Ying-shih, *Lun Tai Chen,* pp. 7, 83, 90, 104. Ch'ien's and Chi Yun's opinions are given in a letter to Tai Chen from Chang Hsueh-ch'eng, who praised Tai for his important philosophical discoveries. See also pp. 38–41, 139–144, Shimada Kenji, "Rekishi teki risei hihan—'Rikkei minna shi' no setsu—," *Iwanami kōza: tetsugaku* 4:126–128 (1969), and Shimada, "Shō Gakusei no ichi," pp. 519–521. For Chang's quotation, see *Chang-shih i-shu,* 3:149 (*chüan* 18), translated by Nivison in *Chang,* p. 51. Cf. Tu Wei-yun, *Ch'ing Ch'ien-Chia shih-tai chih shih-hsueh yü shih-chia* (Taipei, 1962), p. 1.

53. See Juan Yuan's Preface to Ch'ien Ta-hsin's *Shih-chia-chai yang-hsin lu,* pp. 1a–2a. See also Paul Demiéville, "Chang Hsueh-ch'eng and His Historiography," in Beasley and Pulleyblank, eds., *Historians of China and Japan* (Oxford, 1961), pp. 167–168, and Nakamura Kyūshirō, "Shinchō gakujutsu shisō shi (4)," p. 43. Cf. Kung Tzu-chen's mention of the ten major fields of evidential studies in his account of Juan Yuan's distinguished career in *Kung*

Tzu-chen ch'üan-chi (Shanghai, 1975), pp. 225–230. For Chiao Hsun's fears, see *Tiao-ku chi,* 2:109 (*chüan* 8). In the discussion that follows, I will not repeat any account of the precise scholarship discussed in detail in later chapters. See also Yü Ying-shih, *Lun Tai Chen,* "Hsu" (Introduction), p. 5.

54. Tuan Yü-ts'ai, *Ching-yun-lou chi,* 12:47a–52b. See also Ts'ao Yang-wu, "Pien-wei-hsueh shih," *Ku-shih-pien* (Peking and Shanghai, 1926–1941), vol. 2, pp. 388–416, and Liang Ch'i-ch'ao, *Ku-shu chen-wei chi ch'i nien-tai* (Taipei, 1973), pp. 30–57.

55. For Chiang's comment, see Lun Ming, "Hsu-shu-lou tu-shu chi," *Yen-ching hsueh-pao* 3:482 (1928). See also Chou Yü-t'ung, *Ching chin-ku-wen hsueh,* pp. 49–51, Ku Chieh-kang, *Han-tai hsueh-shu-shih lueh* (Taipei, 1972), pp. 154, and Noel Barnard, "The Nature of the Ch'in 'Reform of the Script' as Reflected in Archaeological Documents Excavated Under Conditions of Control," in *Ancient China: Studies in Early Civilization* (Hong Kong, 1978), pp. 181–213.

56. Gray, p. 196, and SKCSTM, 49:31b–32a. See also *Tsou-p'ing hsien-chih,* 1836: 17:35a, Yabuuchi Kiyoshi, "Min-Shin jidai no kagaku gijutsu shi," *Min-Shin jidai no kagaku gijutsu shi* (Kyoto, 1970) pp. 21–25, and ECCP, p. 637.

57. Yeh Te-hui, *Ts'ang-shu shih-yueh,* in *Kuan-ku T'ang so-chu-shu* (1902 Changsha edition), pp. 9b–10a, and translated in Achilles Fang, "Bookman's Decalogue by Yeh Te hui," *HJAS* 13:150–151 (1950). For an account of the effort to reconstruct pre-Han texts, see Jeffrey Riegel, "Some Notes on the Ch'ing Reconstruction of Lost Pre-Han Philosophical Texts," *Selected Papers in Asian Studies* 1:172–185 (1976), and ECCP, p. 550.

58. Nivison, pp. 156, 164. Cf. Yü Ying-shih, *Lun Tai Chen,* pp. 70–71. Chang, as Yü points out, nevertheless favored a comprehensive synthesis for historical writing and research. See p. 64.

59. Wang Ming-sheng, "Hsu" (Introduction), in *Shih-ch'i-shih shang-ch'ueh,* pp. 2b–3a. See also Yü Ying-shih, *Lun Tai Chen,* pp. 38–39. For imperially sponsored histories in Peking, see chapter 3.

60. Wang Ming-sheng, "Hsu," in *Shih-ch'i-shih shang-ch'ueh,* pp. 1a–2a. See also Tu Wei-yun, *Ch'ing Ch'ien-Chia shih-tai,* pp. 13–48, 99–121, and Naitō Torajirō, *Shina shigaku shi,* in *Naitō Konan zenshū,* vol. 11, pp. 334–336. Cf. Liang Ch'i-ch'ao, *Chung-kuo chin san-pai-*

nien hsueh-shu shih (Taipei, 1955), pp. 291–292, and Koyasu Shichishirō, "Chō Yoku no shōgai to sono shigaku shisō ni tsuite," *Shigaku kenkyū* 3.41:93–95 (October 1950).

61. Tu Wei-yun *Ch'ing Ch'ien-Chia,* pp. 43–44. See also Ch'ien Ta-hsin, *Ch'ien-yen T'ang wen-chi,* 2:224–225 (*chüan* 16).

62. See Chao I, *Erh-shih-erh-shih cha-chi* (Taipei, 1974), pp. 418–419, 616, 629–658, and Chao's "Hsiao yin" (Brief introduction), p. 4 for the translated passage. Cf. Koyasu Shichishirō, "Chō Yoku no shōgai," pp. 95–96.

63. Lu Wen-ch'ao, 4:327 (*chüan* 23), Wang Ming-sheng, "Hsu," pp. 2a, 2b, and Ch'ien Ta-hsin, "Hsu" (Introduction), in *Nien-erh-shih k'ao-i* (Shanghai, 1935–1937), p. 1. See also Tu Wei-yun, *Ch'ing Ch'ien-Chia,* pp. 8–10.

64. Tu Wei-yun, *Ch'ing Ch'ien-Chia,* pp. 10–11.

65. Nakamura Kyūshirō, "Shinchō gakujutsu shisō shi (2)," p. 22. See also Juan Chih-sheng, "Hsueh-an t'i-ts'ai yuan-liu ch'u-t'an," *Shih-yuan* 2:57–75 (October 1971), and Tu Wei-yun, *Ch'ing Ch'ien-Chia,* pp. 5, 59. The *Sung-Yuan hsueh-an* was supplemented in a follow-up collection completed in 1841.

66. Tu Wei-yun, *Ch'ing Ch'ien-Chia,* pp. 7, 53–58, 90–97, Hou Wai-lu, 1:428–444, and Nivison, pp. 60–64.

67. Tu Wei-yun, ibid., pp. 67–90, Yü Ying-shih, *Lun Tai Chen,* pp. 45–81, and Nivison, pp. 172–173, 186, 220, 227ff, 297.

68. Kondo Mitsuo, "Sen Daikin no bungaku," *Tōkyō Shinagaku hō* 7:31 (1976). See also *Ch'ing-shih lieh-chuan* (Taipei, 1962), 69:38a, and Juan Chih-sheng, pp. 67–68.

69. See Albert Mann, "Cheng Ch'iao: An Essay in Re-evaluation," in Buxbaum and Mote, eds., *Transition and Permanence: Chinese History and Culture* (Hong Kong, 1972), pp. 23–57, especially 29 and 48n. See also Nivison, *passim,* and Jiro Numata, "Shigeno Yasutsugu and the Modern Tokyo Tradition of Historical Writing," in *Historians of China and Japan,* pp. 264–287. I am in the process of gathering materials for a broader study of the impact of Ch'ing *k'ao-cheng* in Korea and Japan.

70. Tu Wei-yun, *Ch'ing Ch'ien-Chia,* pp. 3–8, 13–18.

71. Wang Chung, *Shu-hsueh, pu-i* (supplement) (Taipei, 1970), 5b–8a. See Hou Wai-lu, 1:524, Nivison, p. 227, and Liang Ch'i-ch'ao, *Hsueh-shu-shih,* pp. 224–247. See also Ho Yu-sen, "Ku T'ing-lin

te ching-hsueh," pp. 194–195, and Angus C. Graham, *Later Mohist Logic, Ethics, and Science,* (Hong Kong, 1978), p. 70.

72. Wang Chung, *Shu-hsueh, nei-p'ien* (inner chapters) (Taipei, 1970), 3:1a–4a. See Hou Wai-lu, 1:480–484. Chang Hui-yen (1761–1802), Wang Nien-sun (1744–1832), Pi Yuan, Sun Hsing-yen (1761–1802) and Lu Wen-ch'ao all made important contributions to the rehabilitation of the *Mo-tzu* text, which had been almost entirely neglected for two thousand years. See ECCP, pp. 43, 624, 678, 829, and Nivison, pp. 260–262. Weng's remarks are from his *Fu-ch'u-chai wen-chi* (1877 edition), 15:9a. For Fang Tung-shu's defense, see *Han-hsueh shang-tui,* 2A:23b–24a, and 2A:32a–34a. See also Demiéville, "Chang Hsueh-ch'eng and His Historiography," p. 185, and SKCSTM, 107:3b–5a.

73. On the earliest uses of *Tao-t'ung,* see James T.C. Liu, "How Did a Neo-Confucian School Become the State Orthodoxy," p. 490n, and Ch'ien Ta-hsin, *Shih-chia-chai yang-hsin lu,* 18:10a–10b. See Shimada Kenji, "Rekishi teki risei hihan," pp. 140–141, 151. See also Takada Atsushi, "Shō Gakusei no rekishi shisō ni tsuite," pp. 73, 87, Hou Wai-lu, 1:465–466, and Nivison, pp. 147–150.

74. Liu Feng-lu, "Hsu" (Introduction), in *Ch'un-ch'iu Kung-yang ching Ho-shih shih-li* (HCCC), 1280:2b. See also Lu Pao-ch'ien, *Ch'ing-tai ssu-hsiang-shih* (Taipei, 1978), pp. 221–269, especially 248ff. Cf. Urabe Masanobu, "Chūgoku ni okeru taisei henkaku no ronri (jō)," *Tōyō gakujutsu kenkyū* 10.1:129–133 (April 1971). See also Nivison, pp. 148, 281–283.

75. Sivin, "Copernicus in China," pp. 63–75, 89–92. See also Hashimoto Keizō, "*Rekishō kōsei* no seiritsu," in *Min-Shin jidai no kagaku gijutsu shi,* pp. 49–92, and Libbrecht, p. 44.

76. Hashimoto, ibid., pp. 62–68. This failure in the Jesuit transmission of European science has been documented by Nathan Sivin in his "Copernicus in China," pp. 63–103. See also Willard Peterson, "Western Natural Philosophy Published in Late Ming China," *Proceedings of the American Philosophical Society* 117.4:295–322 (August 1973).

77. See Tai Chen, *Tung-yuan chi* (SPPY edition), 5:2a–3a, 5:8b–10a, and Tai's account in his review of the *Chou-pei suan-ching* for the SKCSTM, 106:2a–5a, especially 4a. See also the *Shang-shu t'ung-chien* (Taipei, 1966), p. 1. This question has been discussed in de-

tail by Kondo Mitsuo, "Shinchō keishi ni okeru kagaku ishiki," pp. 97–110.

78. Ch'ien Ta-hsin, *Ch'ien-yen T'ang wen-chi* 3:335 (*chüan* 23), and Juan Yuan, *Yen-ching-shih chi* 3:94–95. See also Sivin, "Copernicus," p. 99, Henderson, pp. 213ff, and Tu Wei-yun, *Ch'ing Ch'ien-Chia*, pp. 3–4.

79. Yabuuchi Kiyoshi, *Chūgoku no kagaku to Nihon* (Tokyo, 1978), pp. 162–163. Astronomy, however, was always applied to practical affairs, and mathematics in China never entirely transcended its applications.

80. Hu Shih, "Chih-hsueh te fang-fa yü ts'ai-liao," *Hu Shih wen-ts'un*, vol. 3, pp. 115–122. Hu takes a much more critical stand toward *k'ao-cheng* scholarship in this 1928 essay than in his earlier more positive account entitled "Ch'ing-tai hsueh-che te chih-hsueh fang-fa," vol. 1, pp. 383–412, completed in 1921.

81. Kondo Mitsuo, "Shinchō keishi," p. 110. Cf. Henderson, pp. 212–217, and de Bary et al., *Sources of Chinese Tradition,* 1:563–564. My thanks to Nathan Sivin for his advice on this problem. He has argued in "Wang Hsi-shan," pp. 159–168, that a scientific revolution of sorts did take place in 17th-century China.

3: The Professionalization of Lower Yangtze Academics

1. See Skinner, *The City,* pp. 268–269. See also Susan Jones, "Scholasticism and Political Thought," pp. 12–13, and Thomas Kuhn, *The Essential Tension,* pp. 294–295.

2. Merton, pp. 275–283, 228–253. For discussion, see H. F. Kearney, "Puritanism, Capitalism, and the Scientific Revolution," *Past and Present* 28:81–101 (July 1964).

3. *Hsueh-hai T'ang chih* (Hong Kong, 1964), p. 38b. See also Fujitsuka Chikashi, pp. 395–398, Tilemann Grimm, "Academies and Urban Systems in Kwangtung," in Skinner, ed., *The City,* pp. 489–490. and my "The Hsueh-hai T'ang," pp. 51–82.

4. Hamaguchi Fujio, "Hō Tōju no *Kangaku shōda* o megutte," *Taitō bunka daigaku Kangaku kaishi* 15:74–89, and Cheuk-woon Taam, pp. 73–74. See also Ho Yu-sen, "Juan Yuan te ching-hsueh chi ch'i chih-hsueh fang-fa," pp. 19–26.

5. See the "Table of Contents" to the HCCC. See also Hashimoto

Shigebumi, "Shinchō *Shōsho* gaku," *Kambungaku kōza* 4:10–27 (1933).

6. Included in the HCCC were works by Chuang Ts'un-yü (1719–1788), K'ung Kuang-sen (1752–1786), Liu Feng-lu (1776–1829), and Ling Shu (1775–1829). See my "The Hsueh-hai T'ang," pp. 63–65, and Fumoto Yasutaka, pp. 144–177.

7. Wang Hsien-ch'ien's editorial policy for the HCCCHP was modeled on Juan Yuan's criteria for the HCCC, and he included works by authors in the HCCC that were not included in the latter collection.

8. By "literati" is meant those members of the Chinese gentry who through demonstrated literary qualifications maintained their status in the elite class of traditional China. I have included as literati those scholars who had close family members who had passed the examinations and had entered China's upper social group within two previous generations. None of the scholars studied were purchased degree-holders or gentry who received their position through inheritance. The biographies of the 39 whose backgrounds were clearly literati make no mention of predecessors who achieved gentry status by these two other routes. Chung-li Chang rejects the term "literati" and uses "gentry" instead, because "literati" does not express the social, economic, and political power of this group. But for the focus of this volume, "literati," with its implied emphasis on scholarship, seems better suited for the men discussed here. Without wishing to be carried far afield by the debate on the definition and composition of the elite classes in traditional Chinese society, I would only emphasize that all definitions are based on criteria that must include the degree of success on the imperial examination system. For discussion, see Chung-li Chang, *The Chinese Gentry,* pp. xix–xx, Max Weber, *The Religion of China* (New York, 1954), pp. 107–141, Ping-ti Ho, *The Ladder of Success,* pp. 37–41, and Hsiao-tung Fei, *China's Gentry: Essays on Rural-Urban Relations* (Chicago, 1953), pp. 17–32.

9. Silas Wu, *Passage to Power,* p. 5, and Ono Kazuko, "Jukyō no itanshatachi," pp. 8–11. See also Ping-ti Ho, *The Ladder of Success,* pp. 71–86, and Maurice Freedman, *Chinese Lineage and Society: Fukien and Kwangtung* (New York, 1971), pp. 97–117. For a Marxist analysis that explicitly links the new ideas to a new social

class, see Shang Yueh, *Chung-kuo tzu-pen chu-i kuan-hsi fa-sheng chi yen-pien te ch'u-pu yen-chiu* (Peking, 1956), pp. 257ff.

10. Yamanoi Yū, "*Mōshi jigi soshō* no seikaku," *Nihon Chūgoku gak-kai hō* 12:126 (1960). See also Peterson, *Bitter Gourd,* p. 154.

11. Koyasu Shichishirō, pp. 90–95, and Peterson, ibid., pp. 166–167. See also Tu Wei-yun, *Ch'ing Ch'ien-Chia,* pp. 1–7.

12. Thomas Kuhn, *The Essential Tension,* pp. 110–120. See also Joseph Ben-David, "Scientific Growth: A Sociological View," *Minerva* 3:455–476 (1964). See Wakeman, *The Fall of Imperial China,* pp. 20–24.

13. Norman Storer and Talcott Parsons, "The Disciplines as a Differentiating Force," in Montgomery, ed., *The Foundations of Access to Knowledge* (Syracuse, 1968), pp. 101–120, and Ben-David, "Scitific Growth," p. 459.

14. See, for example, the essays in John Jackson, ed., *Professions and Professionalization* (Cambridge, 1970), *passim.* For a review of the literature, see C. Turner and M.N. Hodge, "Occupations and Professions," in ibid., pp. 23–33, Morris Cogan, "Toward a Definition of Profession," *Harvard Educational Review* 23:33–50 (1953), and Howard Becker, "The Nature of a Profession," *Education for the Professions* (Chicago, 1962), pp. 27–46.

15. Howard Vollmer and Donald Mills, eds., *Professionalization* (Englewood Cliffs, 1966), pp. vii–viii, 1–2.

16. See Eliot Freidson, *Profession of Medicine: A Study of the Sociology of Applied Knowledge* (New York, 1970), pp. xii–xvii, 77–82.

17. Jackson, pp. 1–15.

18. See Turner and Hodge, p. 32. For the problem of expertise in Chinese medicine, see Nathan Sivin, "Social Relations of Curing in Traditional China: Preliminary Considerations," *Nihon ishigaku zasshi* 23.4:1–7 (October 1977).

19. Vollmer and Mills, p. 2.

20. Freidson, pp. 25, 82, 369, and Ben-David, *The Scientist's Role in Society: A Comparative Study* (Englewood Cliffs, 1971), p. 82. Ben-David notes that in 17th-century France, royal recognition was given to the exact sciences under the condition that the empirical and experimental methods employed in science would not be diffused to politics, religious matters, or social questions.

21. Cf. Everett Mendelsohn, "The Emergence of Science as a Profession

in Nineteenth-Century Europe," in Karl Hill, ed., *The Management of Scientists* (Boston, 1964), pp. 3–48. See also my "Ch'ing Dynasty 'Schools' of Scholarship," pp. 1–44.

22. See William Goode, "Community Within a Community: The Professions," *American Sociological Review* 22:194–200 (April 1957), and Ben-David, "Professions in the Class System of Present-Day Societies: A Trend Report and Bibliography," *Current Sociology* 12.3:251 (1963).

23. Kessler, "Chinese Scholars and the Early Manchu State," *HJAS* 31:200 (1971).

24. Hellmut Wilhelm, "The *Po-hsueh Hung-Ju* Examination of 1679," *Journal of the American Oriental Society* 71:61–65 (1951).

25. On Sung Lao, see ECCP, pp. 689–690, and on Ts'ao Yin, see Jonathan Spence, "Tao-chi, An Historical Introduction," p. 16.

26. Teng Chih-ch'eng, *Ch'ing-shih chi-shih ch'u-pien* (Shanghai, 1965), 1:364, and Lynn Struve, "The Uses of History in Traditional Chinese Society: The Southern Ming in Ch'ing Historiography," (PhD dissertation, University of Michigan, 1974), pp. 141–144.

27. See Hsu's collected essays entitled *Tan-yuan wen-chi* (Ch'ing K'ang-hsi edition), 14:26a–26b, 36:37a. See also Naitō Torajirō, *Shina shigaku shi*, p. 317.

28. ECCP, p. 909.

29. *Te-ch'ing hsien hsu-chih*, 1808: 9:3b. See also Yen, *Shu-cheng*, 8: 13a, Naitō, *Shina shigaku shi*, pp. 302, 318–319, and ECCP, p. 522.

30. Hsieh Kuo-chen, *Ming-Ch'ing chih chi tang-she yun-tung k'ao* (Shanghai, 1934), pp. 137–144. See also Struve, "Ambivalence and Action: Some Frustrated Scholars of the K'ang-hsi Period," in Spence and Wills, eds., *From Ming to Ch'ing* (New Haven, 1979), p. 353, and ECCP, pp. 310–311. Hsu's political battles with Li Kuang-ti (1642–1718) in Peking forced the move to Soochow.

31. *T'ai-yuan hsien chih*, 1826: 10:33a–34a. See also Naitō, *Shina shigaku shi*, p. 319 and my "Geographical Research in the Ming-Ch'ing Period," *Monumenta Serica* 35, forthcoming (1981–1983).

32. Hsu was influenced by Yen Jo-chü's research on the *Documents*. See Hsu, *Tan-yuan wen-chi*, 18:21a–26b. Cf. Yen, *Shu-cheng*, 2:1a–2a.

33. Ch'üan Tsu-wang, *Chi-ch'i-t'ing chi* (Shanghai, 1929), 8:16a, and translated in Struve, "Ambivalence and Action," pp. 351–352.

34. Chang Hsueh-ch'eng, *Wen-shih t'ung-i,* p. 308. I have followed the translation in Nivison, pp. 5–6, 7n.

35. Hayashi, "Shinchō no shoin," p. 179, and Tu Wei-yun, *Hsueh-shu yü shih-pien,* pp. 117–130.

36. ECCP, pp. 93–94, 276. See also Wu Che-fu, "The Development of Books in China, Part II," *Echo* 5.7:58 (July 1975), and R. C. Rudolph, "Chinese Movable Type Printing in the 18th Century," in Kaizuka Shigeki, ed., *Silver Jubilee Volume of the Zinbun-kagaku-kenkyuso* (Kyoto, 1954), pp. 317–318. The encyclopedia was revised for political, not scholarly reasons. On *Shih-lu,* see Endymion Wilkinson, *The History of Imperial China: A Research Guide* (Cambridge, Mass., 1973), pp. 65–68.

37. Kuo Po-kung, *Ssu-k'u ch'üan-shu tsuan-hsiu k'ao* (Peking, 1937), p. 227, and Lun Ming, "Hsu-shu-lou tu-shu chi," p. 461.

38. Kuo Po-kung, pp. 60–69. See also Chi Yun, p. 69, and Guy, *passim.*

39. Kawata Teiichi, "Shindai gakujutsu no ichi sokumen," *Tōhōgaku* 57:103–104 (January 1979).

40. ECCP, pp. 198–199, and Kurahashi Takeshirō, "Shinchō shōgaku shiwa (ichi)," *Kangakkai zasshi* 10.3:4–8 (December 1942). See also Leung Man-kam, p. 39.

41. Nivison, pp. 31–32, 39–40. See also Kawata Teiichi, "Shindai gaku-jutsu no ichi sokumen," pp. 84–105, especially 88, 104, and ECCP, pp. 185, 199, 825–826, and Satō Shinji, "Kō Ryōkitsu no shisō teki seikaku," *Academy* 9:120 (January 1955).

42. ECCP, p. 624.

43. Nivison, pp. 97–98, 202ff.

44. ECCP, p. 515, Nivison, pp. 100–101, 205.

45. Naitō, *Shina shigaku shi,* p. 317. See Nivison, pp. 206, 258, and ECCP, pp. 140, 156, 505, 624.

46. ECCP, pp. 144, 175, 676, 736. See also Leung Man-kam, pp. 41–43, and Juan, *Yen-ching-shih chi* 2:681–682.

47. ECCP, pp. 399–402, 736, 869–870. See Juan Yuan, ibid., 2:681–682, and Sun Hsing-yen et al., "Ku-ching ching-she t'i-ming-pei-chi," *Ku-ching ching-she wen-chi* (Taipei, 1966), p. 2. See also A. von Rosthorn, "The *Erh-ya* and Other Synonymicons," *Journal of the Chinese Language Teachers Association* 10.3:140 (October 1975), and Taam, pp. 74–75.

48. ECCP, pp. 137–138, 144, 238, 400–401, 736. See also *Hsueh-hai*

T'ang chi, I, 16:18a–19a, and Leung Man-kam, pp. 258–259.

49. Yü Ying-shih, "Some Preliminary Observations," p. 113. See also *Kung Tzu-chen ch'üan-chi,* pp. 346–347, and Hamaguchi Fujio, "Hō Tōju no *Kangaku shōda* o megutte," pp. 73–89.

50. Juan Yuan, "Hsu" (Introduction) in Chiang Fan, *Kuo-ch'ao Han-hsueh shih-ch'eng chi,* pp. 1a–1b.

51. Nivison, pp. 38, 106.

52. Frederic Wakeman, "The Price of Autonomy: Intellectuals in Ming and Ch'ing Politics," *Daedalus* 101.2:35–70 (Spring 1972). Cf. Ben-David, *The Scientist's Role in Society,* pp. 46–54, and "Scientific Growth," p. 460. For discussion of the role of Sung academies in the emergence of Neo-Confucian discourse, see Linda Walton-Vargö, "Education, Social Change, and Neo-Confucianism in Sung-Yuan China: Academies and the Local Elite in Ming Prefecture (Ningpo)," (PhD dissertation, University of Pennsylvania, 1978), pp. 58–128, 186–237.

53. See Hayashi Tomoharu, "Tō-Sō shoin no hassei to sono kyōiku," *Gakushūin daigaku bungakubu kenkyū nempō* 2:133–156 (1953), and his "Gen-Min jidai no shoin kyōiku," *Kinsei Chūgoku kyōiku kenkyū,* (Tokyo, 1958), pp. 3–23. See also Ping-ti Ho, *The Ladder of Success,* pp. 197–203, and Meskill, *Academies in Ming China, passim.*

54. John Meskill, "Academies and Politics in the Ming Dynasty," in Charles Hucker, ed., *Chinese Government in Ming Times: Seven Studies* (New York, 1969), pp. 149–174. See also Atwell, "The Fu She," pp. 333–367, and Hucker, "The Tung-lin Movement of the Late Ming Period," pp. 132–162. Cf. Ku Chieh-kang, "A Study of Literary Persecution During the Ming," pp. 254–311, and Wakeman, "The Price of Autonomy," pp. 41–55.

55. For a balanced discussion of *she* scholarship, see Ono Kazuko, "Mimmatsu Shinsho ni okeru chishikijin no seiji kōdō," *Sekai no rekishi 11: Yuragu Chūka teikoku* (Tokyo, 1961), pp. 87–88, 105–106, and her "Mimmatsu no kessha ni kan suru ichi kōsatsu (jō)," pp. 38–42, 55–59. See Ōkubo Eiko, "Mimmatsu doku-shojin kessha to kyōiku katsudō," in Hayashi Tomoharu, ed., *Kinsei Chūgoku kyōiku kenkyū,* p. 206, and Atwell, "The Fu She," p. 349. See also Yamanoi Yū, "Kō Sōgi no gakumon," pp. 31–50, and "Ko Enbu no gakumon kan," pp. 67–93, Yü Ying-shih,

"Tsung Sung-Ming Ju-hsueh te fa-chan lun Ch'ing-tai ssu-hsiang-shih," pp. 19–41, and Chu T'an, "Ming-chi Hangchow Tu-shu She k'ao," *Kuo-hsueh chi-k'an* 2.2:264–265, 282 (1929).

56. Hsieh Kuo-chen, p. 220, and Ono Kazuko, "Mimmatsu no kessha," p. 57, and her "Mimmatsu Shinsho ni okeru," pp. 102–106. For a detailed discussion of these policies, see Ono Kazuko, "Shinsho no shisō tōsei o megutte," *Tōyōshi kenkyū* 18.3:99–123 (December 1959).

57. Ono Kazuko, "Shinsho no shisō tōsei," p. 347, and Wu Hung-i, *Ch'ing-tai shih-hsueh ch'u-t'an* (Taipei, 1977), pp. 19–22. See also Hsieh Kuo-chen, pp. 208–213. Cf. Goodrich, *The Literary Inquisition of Ch'ien-lung,* pp. 75–76.

58. Li Yuan-keng, "Wang She hsing-shih k'ao," *Kuo-ts'ui hsueh-pao* 71: 5b–6a, 9b–10a (September 1910). See also the biography of Tu Chün in Li Yuan-tu, *Kuo-ch'ao hsien-cheng shih-lueh* (SPPY edition), 48:3b. Tu also was a visitor at Yen Hsiu-ling's home during that time. See also Yen Jo-chü, *Ch'ien-ch'iu cha-chi* (Taipei, 1973) 1:38b–39b, 1:48a–48b.

59. Ono Kazuko, "Shinsho no Kōkeikai ni tsuite," *Tōhōgaku hō* 36: 633–661 (1964), and Ho Yu-sen, "Huang Li-chou yü Che-tung hsueh-shu," *Shu-mu chi-k'an* 7.4:15 (March 1974).

60. Huang Tsung-hsi, *Huang Li-chou wen-chi* (Peking, 1959), p. 199. See also ECCP, p. 801, Ono Kazuko, "Kōkeikai," pp. 639–643, and Leung Man-kam, pp. 91–92.

61. Uno Seiichi, "*Shurai* Ryū Kin gisakusetsu ni tsuite," pp. 237–249, and Ono Kazuko, "Kōkeikai," pp. 650–656. On the *Ming History,* see Lynn Struve, "Uses of History in Traditional Chinese Society," pp. 139–192.

62. Wan Ssu-t'ung, "Ku-wen *Shang-shu* pien erh" (Discerning the Old Text *Documents,* Part 2), in *Ch'ün-shu i-pien* (1816 edition), 1: 16a–17a. See Ono Kazuko, "Kōkeikai," pp. 656–658.

63. Henderson, pp. 115–116. See Huang's "Hsu" (Introduction) in the 1796 edition of the *Shu-cheng,* p. 2b. See also James Legge, *The Shoo King or the Book of Historical Documents* (Taipei, 1972), p. 61, and Ono Kazuko, "Kōkeikai," pp. 659–660. On the *jen-hsin Tao-hsin* debate, see Yen Jo-chü, *Shu-cheng* (HCCCHP edition), 8:28b, and Huang's preface included in the 1796 Tientsin edition of Yen's *Shu-cheng,* pp. 2b–3a. I have discussed this issue at greater

length in a paper presented in the fall of 1981 to the Regional
Seminar in Neo-Confucianism at Columbia University. A revised
version of that paper, entitled "Philosophy Vs. Philology: The *Jen-hsin Tao-hsin* Debate," appears in *T'oung Pao* 69.4&5:175–222 (1983).

64. Ono Kazuko, "Shinsho no shisō tōsei o megutte," p. 340. For the
impact on schools in Kiangnan, see Lawrence Kessler, *K'ang-hsi
and the Consolidation of Ch'ing Rule, 1661–1684* (Chicago, 1976)
pp. 37–38, and Tilemann Grimm, "Some Remarks on the Suppression of *Shu-yuan* in Ming China," pp. 8–16. Ogawa Yoshiko
has studied in some detail the phenomenal rise in number of
i-hsueh during the Ch'ing. See her "Shindai ni okeru gigaku setsuritsu no kiban," in Hayashi Tomoharu, ed., *Kinsei Chūgoku
kyōiku kenkyū* (Tokyo, 1958), pp. 275–308. See also Hayashi
Tomoharu, "Shinchō no shoin kyōiku," pp. 179–180, and Sheng
Lang-hsi, *Chung-kuo shu-yuan chih-tu* (Taiwan, 1977), pp. 132–133.

65. Hayashi Tomoharu, "Shinchō no shoin," pp. 181–191. See also
Sheng Lang-hsi, pp. 154–157, Kung-chuan Hsiao, *Rural China*, pp.
235–240, Grimm, "Academies and Urban Systems in Kwangtung,"
pp. 488–490, and Skinner, *The City*, p. 257. For an account of the
outcry against the academies oriented to the examination system,
see Wolfgang Franke, *The Reform and Abolition of the Traditional Chinese Examination System* (Cambridge, Mass., 1960),
pp. 19–27, and Ch'en Tung-yuan, "Ch'ing-tai chih k'e-chü yü chiao-
yü," *Hsueh-feng* 3.4:45–52 (May 1933).

66. Ch'en Tung-yuan in his article "Ch'ing-tai shu-yuan feng-ch'i chih
pien-ch'ien," *Hsueh-feng* 3.5:17–18 (June 1933), and Sheng
Lang-hsi, p. 157, single out the 19th-century Ku-ching ching-she
and the Hsueh-hai T'ang as the models for this third type of
academy.

67. Liu I-cheng, "Chiang-su shu-yuan chih ch'u-kao," *Kuo-hsueh t'u-
shu-kuan nien-k'an* 4:61–63 (1931). See also *Ch'ang-chou fu
chih*, 1886: 15:13a–13b, *Wu-chin Yang-hu hsien ho-chih*, 1886:
12:43a–46b, and ECCP, p. 550. On Li Chao-lo, see Wei Yuan,
Ku-wei T'ang nei-wai-chi (Taipei, 1966), pp. 541–548 (4:27a–
30b).

68. Liu I-cheng, pp. 56–58, 63–70. See *Chiang-yin hsien chih*, 1878:
5:19a, 23b, and *Wu hsien chih*, 1933: 27:1a. See also ECCP,

pp. 152–153, 593, 805, 828. On Wang Chün, see *Ch'ing-shih lieh-chuan,* 71:42b, and Ch'ien Ta-hsin, *Ch'ien-yen T'ang wen-chi,* 3:353 (*chüan* 24), and 6:671–672. On Ch'ien Ta-hsin's contributions as director of Tzu-yang Academy, see "Chu-t'ing chü-shih nien-p'u hsu-pien" (Continuation to Ch'ien Ta-hsin's chronological biography), pp. 1a–1b, appended to Ch'ien's *Shih-chia-chai yang-hsin lu.*

69. Liu I-cheng, pp. 51–53. See also Ping-ti Ho, *The Ladder of Success,* p. 202, and "The Salt Merchants of Yang-chou," p. 165n, ECCP, pp. 75, 144, 153, 528, 675–676, 783, 868, 900, Ch'en Tung-yuan, "Ch'ing-tai chih k'e-chü yü chiao-yü," p. 51, and Chang Shun-wei, *Ch'ing-tai Yang-chou hsueh-chi* (Shanghai, 1962), p. 210. See Wang Chung, *Shu-hsueh* (*wai-p'ien*), 1:9b, for the quotation. On Ch'en Tsu-fan, see Ch'ien Ta-hsin, *Ch'ien-yen T'ang wen-chi,* 5:595–598 (*chüan* 38).

70. ECCP, pp. 129, 141, 550, 677, 807. See Ch'en Tung-yuan, "Ch'ing-tai chih k'e-chü," p. 51, and Leung Man-kam, pp. 54–55. For Lu Wen-ch'ao's account of Tzu-yang and Ch'ung-wen in Hangchow, see *Pao-ching T'ang wen-chi,* 4:342–344 (*chüan* 25). Lu stressed that Chu Hsi studies were initially very important at Tzu-yang.

71. Juan Yuan, *Yen-ching-shih chi,* 2:505. See Cheuk-woon Taam, p. 89n, Sun Hsing-yen et al., "Ku-ching ching-she t'i-ming-pei-chi," p. 2, and Chang Yin, "Ku-ching ching-she ch'u-kao," *Wen-lan hsueh-pao* 2.1:39–41 (March 1936). For discussion, see Sivin, "Copernicus in China," p. 99. See also Jones and Kuhn, "Dynastic Decline and the Roots of Rebellion," in John Fairbank, ed., *The Cambridge History of China* (Cambridge, 1978), vol. 10, pp. 107–144.

72. See, for example, the series of essays on Sung-Learning topics such as *hsing* (nature), *ch'ing* (emotions), and *ko-wu* (the investigation of things) in the *Ku-ching ching-she wen-chi,* pp. 357–367. Essays on Han dynasty schools of scholarship are on pp. 321–333. Technical and astronomical topics are discussed on pp. 29–56. See also ECCP, pp. 418, 676–677. For an account of Mei Tsu's work, see Chu I-tsun, 88:6b–7a, and SKCSTM, 12:14b–15b.

73. *Ku-ching ching-she wen-chi,* pp. 313–333. The rediscovery of Han dynasty *chia-fa* (schools system) was regarded as the key to understand Han dynasty exegesis of the Classics.

74. For an account of the Hsueh-hai T'ang and its role in Cantonese

academics, see my "The Hsueh-hai T'ang and the Rise of New Text Scholarship," pp. 51–82. Juan Yuan's remarks are cited in the *Hsueh-hai T'ang chih,* p. 7b.

75. Liu Po-chi, *Kuang-tung shu-yuan chih-tu* (Hong Kong, 1958), pp. 310–311, 329, and Ting Wen-chiang, *Liang Jen-kung hsien-sheng nien-p'u ch'ang-pien ch'u-kao* (Taipei, 1972), 1:13.

76. Both Ch'en Ch'iao-ts'ung (1809–1869) and Yü Yueh (1821–1907) wrote works by this title and both were included in the HCCCHP collection. It is unclear which work is being referred to.

77. Jung Chao-tsu, "Hsueh-hai T'ang k'ao," *Ling-nan hsueh-pao* 3.4:20 (June 1934). The examination is reproduced on the page opposite p. 1 in Jung Chao-tsu's "Hsueh-hai T'ang k'ao." For discussion of the Hsueh-hai T'ang's library, see Leung Man-kam, pp. 277–280. I would like to thank Hua-yuan Li Mowry of Dartmouth College for her help in translating portions of the examination.

78. Cf. R. P. Dore, "The Legacy of Tokugawa Education," in Marius Jansen, ed., *Changing Japanese Attitudes Toward Modernization* (Princeton, 1965), pp. 109, 131. See Koita Natsujirō, pp. 42–43, and Nishi Junzō, "Tai Shin no hōhō shiron," *Tōkyō Shina-gaku hō* 1:131 (June 1955).

79. Hayashi Tomoharu, "Shinchō no shoin kyōiku," p. 189. Cf. Ben-David, "Scientific Growth," pp. 459–462. See also Ch'ien Ta-hsin's *Chu-t'ing jih-chi ch'ao* (Taipei, 1971), *passim,* but especially the "Afterword" by Ch'ien Tien, p. 113.

80. Wakeman, *The Fall of Imperial China,* pp. 22–23, and Ping-ti Ho, *The Ladder of Success,* pp. 168–221. See also Chung-li Chang, *The Chinese Gentry,* pp. 99–100, and Lawrence Kessler, *K'ang-hsi and the Consolidation of Ch'ing Rule, 1661–1684,* pp. 117–124.

81. Wakeman, *The Fall,* pp. 30–31, Nivison, p. 8, and Schwartz, "Fore-word," p. xviii.

82. See Nivison, pp. 52, 82–89, 96, Gray, pp. 196–197, and ECCP, pp. 152–154.

83. Wakeman, *The Fall,* p. 31. See ECCP, pp. 97–98, 152–154, 203–204, 276, 457, 900, and *Ch'ing-shih lieh-chuan,* 68:47a–47b. See also Chung-li Chang, *The Chinese Gentry,* p. 217, and *The Income of the Chinese Gentry* (Seattle, 1962), pp. 92–93.

84. Hashimoto Keizō, "Bai Buntei no rekisangaku," pp. 497–514, and Wang P'ing, "Ch'ing-ch'u li-suan-chia Mei Wen-ting," *Chin-tai-*

shih yen-chiu-so chi-k'an (Taipei, 1971), p. 314. On Yao Chi-heng, see Murayama Yoshihiro, "Yō Seikō no gakumon (chū)," pp. 37–38. Cf. Liang Ch'i-ch'ao, *Ku-shu chen-wei chi ch'i nien-tai,* pp. 36–37. See also ECCP, pp. 137–138, 140, 144, 357, 505, 814.

85. ECCP, pp. 324, 783, 811.

86. Ibid., pp. 243–244, 676, 696, and Nivison, pp. 30, 79, 216. See also Yü Ying-shih, *Lun Tai Chen,* pp. 31–32.

87. Chung-li Chang, *The Income of the Chinese Gentry,* pp. 7–42, 94, 111, 113–114, T'ung-tsu Ch'u, *Local Government in China Under the Ch'ing* (Stanford, 1973), pp. 22–32, and Leung Man-kam, p. 38. See also Susan Jones, "Finance in Ningpo: The 'Ch'ien Chuang,' 1750–1880," in W. E. Willmot, ed., *Economic Organization in Chinese Society* (Stanford, 1972), p. 49n, and William Atwell, "Notes on Silver, Foreign Trade, and the Late Ming Economy," *Ch'ing-shih wen-t'i* 3.8:1–33 (December 1977). On clan and merchant support for schools, see Evelyn Rawski, *Education and Popular Literacy,* pp. 54–80, Ōkubo Eiko, *Min-Shin jidai shoin no kenkyū,* pp. 221–361, and Ping-ti Ho, "The Salt Merchants of Yang-chou," p. 165, and *The Ladder of Success,* pp. 194–203.

88. Ping-ti Ho describes Wang Hui-tsu's career as a legal secretary in *The Ladder of Success,* pp. 292–294. See also Chung-li Chang, *The Income of the Chinese Gentry,* pp. 75, 81–87, and Taam, p. 87n.

89. Ben-David, *The Scientist's Role in Society,* pp. 21–74, especially 28ff, 50. One should also note the contribution of the traditional Confucian academy system to the reform of the school system in the late 19th century. Both the Hsueh-hai T'ang and Ku-ching ching-she remained important academic institutions until 1903 when they were abolished. See Hayashi Tomoharu, "Shinchō no shoin kyōiku," pp. 191–196, and Chang Yin, pp. 19–20.

90. See Harcourt Brown, *Scientific Organizations in Seventeenth-Century France, 1620–1680* (Baltimore, 1934), *passim;* R. Fox, "Scientific Enterprise and the Patronage of Research in France, 1800–1870," *Minerva* 11:442–473 (1973); Francis Johnson, "Gresham College: Precursor of the Royal Society," in Philip Wiener and Aaron Noland, eds., *Roots of Scientific Thought: A Cultural Perspective* (New York, 1958), pp. 328–353; and Martha Ornstein, *The Role of Scientific Societies in the Seventeenth Century* (Chicago, 1928), *passim.*

4: Scholarship, Libraries, and Book Production

1. Storer and Parsons, "The Disciplines as a Differentiating Force," pp. 119–120.
2. Eisenstein, "The Advent of Printing and the Problem of the Renaissance," *Past and Present* 45:19–89 (November 1969). See also her important *The Printing Press as an Agent of Change: Communications and Cultural Transformations in Early-Modern Europe,* vol. 1 (New York, 1979), pp. 3–159.
3. See for example Denys Hay, "Literature: The Printed Book," in G. R. Elton, ed., *The New Cambridge Modern History* (Cambridge, 1958), vol. 2, pp. 359–386.
4. Lucien Febvre and Henri-Jean Martin, *The Coming of the Book: The Impact of Printing, 1450–1800* (Highlands, N.J., 1976), pp. 10–12. See also Marshall McLuhan, *The Gutenberg Galaxy: The Making of Typographical Man* (Toronto, 1962), p. 124, A. R. Hall, "Science," in G. R. Elton, ed., *The New Cambridge Modern History,* vol. 2 (Cambridge, 1958), p. 389, and Denys Hay, "Fiat Lux," in J. Carter and P. Muir, eds., *Printing and the Mind of Man* (New York, 1967), pp. xxii–xxiv.
5. See Thomas Carter, *The Invention of Printing in China and Its Spread Westward* (New York, 1955), *passim,* and Kwang Tsing Wu, "The Development of Printing in China," *T'ien Hsia Monthly* 3:137–160 (September 1936). For T'ang and Sung developments in printing, see Kwang Tsing Wu, "Scholarship, Book Production, and Libraries in China," pp. 1, 62–83, 97–115. For Ming printing, see Wu's article "Ming Printing and Printers," *HJAS* 7:203–260 (1943).
6. Hayashi Tomoharu, "Tō-Sō shoin no hassei to sono kyōiku," pp. 141–144. See also Achilles Fang, tr., "Bookman's Decalogue by Yeh Teh-hui," *HJAS* 13:147 (1951), and Carter, pp. 67–96. Sung academies had libraries averaging 10,000 *chüan* of books, according to Walton-Vargö, pp. 246–247.
7. Kwang Tsing Wu, "Ming Printing," pp. 232–233, 251–256. See also Hu Ying-lin, *Shao-shih shan-fang pi-ts'ung* (Shanghai, 1958), pp. 55–57.
8. Sakai Tadao, "Shindai kōshōgaku no genryū," *Rekishi kyōiku* 5.11:30–34 (1957), and Sakai, "Confucianism and Popular Educa-

tional Works," in de Bary et al., *Self and Society in Ming Thought,* pp. 331–341.

9. See Thackray and Merton, p. 479. See also Merton, *The Sociology of Science,* p. 464.

10. MB, p. 645, and Kwang Tsing Wu, "Scholarship, Book Production," pp. 207–208.

11. Cheuk-woon Taam, pp. 4–5. Kenneth Starr in "An 'Old Rubbing' of the Later Han *Chang Chien pei,*" in David Roy and T.H. Tsien, eds., *Ancient China: Studies in Early Civilization* (Hong Kong, 1978), pp. 283–304, discusses the place of rubbings in China's aesthetic traditions. Cf. Hay, "Fiat Lux," pp. xxii–xxiii, for discussion of the same phenomenon in Renaissance Europe.

12. *Chinese Collections in the Library of Congress,* 2:473–474. For discussion of Ming libraries, see Ch'en Teng-yuan, *Ku-chin tien-chi chü-san k'ao* (Shanghai, 1936), pp. 310–318. See also Kwang Tsing Wu, "Scholarship, Book Production," pp. 198–199. For an account of the SKCS's solicitation of books, see Guy, chapter 3.

13. *Chinese Collections in the Library of Congress,* 2:473, ECCP, pp. 230–231, 400, and Ch'en Teng-yuan, pp. 534–535. See also Ch'ien Ta-hsin, *Ch'ien-yen T'ang wen-chi,* 4:366–367 (*chüan* 25). For an account of Juan's official tenure in Chekiang, see chapter 3.

14. Kwang Tsing Wu, "Scholarship," p. 178, and ECCP, p. 565. See also Cheuk-woon Taam, pp. 10–11.

15. Wu, ibid., pp. 179–180. See also Yoshikawa Kōjirō, pp. 22–23, 28.

16. Achilles Fang, "Bookman's Manual," p. 224. See also Wang Ming-sheng, "Hsu" (Introduction), in *Shih-ch'i-shih shang-ch'ueh,* p. 1a. See ECCP, p. 783, and Cheuk-woon Taam, p. 12.

17. ECCP, pp. 118, 157. See also Ch'en Teng-yuan, pp. 322–323.

18. Cheuk-woon Taam, pp. 48–49, and ECCP, pp. 183–184.

19. Tu Wei-yun, "Huang Tsung-hsi yü Ch'ing-tai Che-tung shih-hsueh-p'ai chih hsing-ch'i," p. 7. See also Ch'en Teng-yuan, pp. 319–320, Swann, p. 372, ECCP, p. 356, Huang Tsung-hsi, "Ch'uan-shih-lou ts'ang-shu chi," *Lo Hsueh-t'ang hsien-sheng ch'üan-chi* (Taipei, 1970), pp. 5863–5865, and Yves Hervouet, ed., *A Sung Bibliography* (Hong Kong, 1978), p. 56.

20. ECCP, pp. 76–77. See also Lu Wen-ch'ao, 4:339 (*chüan* 25). Sun's

work is translated by Achilles Fang and entitled "Bookman's Manual by Sun Ts'ung-t'ien," pp. 215–260. See also Cheuk-woon Taam, pp. 54–59.

21. Murayama Yoshihiro, "Yō Seikō no gakumon (jō)," pp. 77–78, and ECCP, p. 811. See also Taam, pp. 69–70, and Wong Lok Ping, "Lu Wen-ch'ao *Ching-tien shih-wen Mao-shih yin-i k'ao-cheng* ting-pu," *Journal of Oriental Studies* (Hong Kong) 8.2:289–301 (July 1970).

22. Swann, pp. 363–390. Probably not even a majority of libraries permitted the lending of books. For discussion, see Ch'en Teng-yuan, pp. 406–418. For an outline of the regulations at the Hsueh-hai T'ang's library in Canton, see Leung Man-kam, pp. 277–278.

23. See Swann, pp. 365, 383–385, and ECCP, pp. 276, 549, 810.

24. Swann, pp. 366–377.

25. ECCP, pp. 605–606, 612, 810, 867–868, 877, and Ch'en Teng-yuan, pp. 331–333. See also Swann, pp. 380–382, and my "The Hsueh-hai T'ang and the Rise of New Text Scholarship in Canton," pp. 51–82.

26. Swann, p. 387, Ch'en Teng-yuan, pp. 348–349, and Tu Wei-yun, *Hsueh-shu,* p. 134. See also ECCP, p. 613, Leung Man-kam, pp. 261–264, and Sohn Pow-key, "Early Korean Printing," *Journal of the American Oriental Society* 79:96–103 (1959).

27. Arthur Hummel, "Ts'ung-shu," *Journal of the American Oriental Society* 61:40–46 (1941). See also Kwang Tsing Wu, "Ming Printing," p. 217n.

28. Hummel, ibid., pp. 40–45. See also Alexander Wylie, *Notes on Chinese Literature* (Shanghai, 1867), pp. 255–271, for a list of the contents of many of the most important collectanea printed during the Ming and Ch'ing.

29. Tu Wei-yun, *Hsueh-shu,* p. 133, and Rudolph, "Chinese Movable Type Printing," p. 317. See also Fujitsuka Chikashi, p. 14, Wang Yeh-ch'iu, *Liu-li-ch'ang shih-hua* (Hong Kong, 1979), pp. 14–29, and ECCP, p. 183.

30. Spence, "The Wan-li Period Vs. the K'ang-hsi Period: Fragmentation Vs. Reintegration?" in Christian Murck, ed., *Artists and Traditions: Uses of the Past in Chinese Culture* (Princeton, 1976), p. 147. On the Liu-li-ch'ang, see Fujitsuka Chikashi, pp. 20–21.

See also Tu Wei-yun, *Hsueh-shu,* p. 132, ECCP, p. 175, and Ch'en Teng-yuan, p. 338.

31. ECCP, p. 175, and Leung Man-kam, pp. 51–52.

32. Cheuk-woon Taam, p. 49. See also Ch'ien's "Hsu" (Introduction) to his *Nien-erh-shih k'ao-i,* p. 1a, dated 1780.

33. ECCP, p. 340, and Ch'en Teng-yuan, pp. 341–342. See also Tu Wei-yun, *Hsueh-shu,* p. 132.

34. ECCP, p. 331, and Fujitsuka Chikashi, pp. 27–44. I am indebted to Gari Ledyard of Columbia University for his criticisms of an earlier draft.

35. Fujitsuka Chikashi, pp. 6–48. See also Gari Ledyard, "Korean Travellers in China Over Four Hundred Years, 1488–1887," *Occasional Papers on Korea* 2:1–42 (March 1974).

36. Fujitsuka Chikashi, pp. 36–44, 104–118. See also Hae-jong Chun, "Sino-Korean Tributary Relations in the Ch'ing Period," in John Fairbank, ed., *The Chinese World Order* (Cambridge, Mass., 1968), pp. 90–111, Roy Miller, "Some Japanese Influences on Chinese Classical Scholarship of the Ch'ing Period," *Journal of the American Oriental Society* 72:56–57 (1952), and SKCSTM, 33:30b–34a. I am presently collecting materials for a broader study of this interesting process of cultural interchange.

37. Cheuk-woon Taam, pp. 21–22, and Wing-tsit Chan, "The *Hsing-li ching-i* and the Ch'eng-Chu School of the Seventeenth Century," in de Bary et al., *The Unfolding of Neo-Confucianism,* pp. 543–547. See also Ssu-yü Teng and Knight Biggerstaff, *An Annotated Bibliography of Selected Chinese Reference Works* (Cambridge, Mass., 1971), pp. 94–96, M.R. Guignard, "The Chinese Precedent," in Febvre and Martin, *The Coming of the Book,* p. 75, and Rudolph, pp. 317–326.

38. Fujitsuka Chikashi, p. 22, and ECCP, p. 121. See also Ch'en Teng-yuan, pp. 134–139, Kuo Po-kung, pp. 164–165, and ECCP, pp. 159–160. See Guy, the concluding chapter, for an account of the inquisition.

39. Cheuk-woon Taam, pp. 36–37, ECCP, pp. 121–122, 677, 815, and Ch'en Teng-yuan, pp. 136–137. See also Tu Wei-yun, *Hsueh-shu,* p. 136, and Leung Man-kam, pp. 68–69.

40. Eisenstein, "The Advent of Printing," pp. 24, 84–85. See Wang

Ming-sheng, *Shih-ch'i-shih shang-ch'ueh,* 1:1b. Cf. Tu Wei-yun, *Hsueh-shu,* pp. 140–141. For a discussion of some of the most essential catalogs used, see Wylie, pp. 74–80. For a sample of the contents of some of the extant catalogs themselves, see Lo Chen-yü's *Yü-chien-chai ts'ung-shu,* in *Lo Hsueh-t'ang hsien-sheng ch'üan-chi* (Taipei, 1970).

41. Lo Ping-mien, "Chang Shih-chai te chiao-ch'ou lun chi ch'i yen-pien," *Hsin-Ya shu-yuan hsueh-shu nien-k'an* 8:77–95 (1966), and Nivison, pp. 29, 56–59, 65n, 77–81, 285.

42. Achilles Fang, "Bookman's Decalogue," pp. 151–153. See also Teng and Biggerstaff, p. 22, and Edwards, pp. 772–773.

43. Teng and Biggerstaff, pp. 41–43, and SKCSTM, 85:20a–21a. See also Nivison, pp. 258–259.

44. See T. H. Tsien, *Written on Bamboo and Silk,* pp. 14–15, Jesse Shera, "An Epistemological Foundation for Library Science," in Edward Montgomery, ed., *The Foundations of Access to Knowledge* (Syracuse, 1968), pp. 14–21, and Robert Sokol, "Classification: Purposes, Principles, Progress, Prospects," in P. N. Johnson-Laird and P. C. Wason, eds., *Thinking: Readings in Cognitive Science* (Cambridge, 1977), pp. 194–195.

45. Mann, pp. 40–43.

46. Kwang Tsing Wu, "Scholarship, Book Production," p. 257, and Ch'ien Ta-hsin, *Ch'ien-yen T'ang wen-chi,* 4:461–462 (*chüan* 29). For discussion, see Tsuen-hsuin Tsien, "A History of Bibliographic Classification in China," *The Library Quarterly* 22.4: 312–314 (October 1952).

47. SKCSTM, 41:28b, 86:46b, 106:2a. Epigraphical texts that dealt with ancient writing forms, however, were included in the paleography section of the *hsiao-hsueh* subdivision. Those that contained only lists and charts were placed in the repertories of science.

48. Ibid., 40:1a–1b, 40:25b.

49. Ch'ien Ta-hsin, *Ch'ien-yen T'ang wen-chi,* 3:350–351 (*chüan* 24).

50. SKCSTM, 117:1a–32b. See also Guy, chapter 6.

51. Sun Hsing-yen, *Sun-shih tz'u-t'ang shu-mu,* "Hsu," (Shanghai, 1935), pp. 1–3. See also Tsuen-hsuin Tsien, "A History of Bibliographic Classification in China," p. 316.

52. Chu Yun's remarks are from Chiang Fan's *Kuo-ch'ao Han-hsueh shih-ch'eng chi*, 6:6a.
53. Achilles Fang, "Bookman's Decalogue," pp. 147–148. Cf. Eisenstein, *The Printing Press as an Agent of Change*, 2:684.

5: Channels of Scholarly Communication in Kiangnan

1. Thackray and Merton, p. 473.
2. Cf. Thomas Kuhn, *The Structure of Scientific Revolution* (Chicago, 1970), p. 37, and Said, "Linguistics and the Archaeology of Mind," p. 108.
3. Cf. Thomas Kuhn, *The Essential Tension*, pp. 318–319.
4. Liang Ch'i-ch'ao, *Intellectual Trends in the Ch'ing Period* (Cambridge, Mass., 1959), p. 69. See also Koita Natsujirō, p. 42.
5. See SKCSTM, 118:43b–44b. See also Bloom's "On the 'Abstraction' of Ming Thought," pp. 72–73, and Tu Wei-yun, *Hsueh-shu*, p. 140. For Ku Yen-wu's interest in Wang Ying-lin, see Ho Yu-sen, "Ku T'ing-lin te ching-hsueh," pp. 204–205.
6. See, for example, the *Chu-tzu yü-lei* (Conversations with Master Chu [Hsi] classified topically) (Taipei reprint of 1473 edition), and Wang Yang-ming's *Ch'uan-hsi lu* in *Wang Yang-ming ch'üan-chi* (Taipei, 1973). Achilles Fang, "Bookman's Manual," p. 219 notes how the bibliophile Sun Ts'ung-t'ien (ca. 1680–1749) used the notebook form. See Tu Wei-ming, "'Inner Experience': The Basis of Creativity in Neo-Confucian Thinking," in Murck, ed., *Artists and Traditions*, p. 11, and Ono Kazuko, "Jukyō no itanshatachi," pp. 22–25.
7. Tu Wei-yun, *Hsueh-shu*, p. 140.
8. Willard Peterson, "The Life of Ku Yen-wu (1613–1682), Part II," *HJAS* 29:201–212 (1969). Fang I-chih (1611–1671) also collected data this way. See Sakade Yoshinobu, "Hō Ichi no shishō," p. 108.
9. Peterson, ibid., pp. 212–213. See also Yen Jo-chü, *Ch'ien-ch'iu cha-chi*, 5:1a–40b, and SKCSTM, 119:17a.
10. Yen Jo-chü, *Shu-cheng*, 6A:22b, and SKCSTM, 119:20b. See also Liang Ch'i-ch'ao, *Intellectual Trends*, p. 71, and Wang Ming-sheng, *I-shu pien* (Taipei, 1976), particularly the prefaces.

11. Liang Ch'i-ch'ao, *Intellectual Trends,* p. 70. See also Koita Natsu-jirō, p. 42.

12. Yen Jo-chü, *Shu-cheng,* 1:5a–6a. See also Koita Natsujirō, p. 45, and Hashimoto Shigebumi, "Shinchō *Shōsho* gaku," p. 11.

13. Yen Jo-chü, *Shu-cheng,* 1:2b. Cf. Michael Loewe, *Crisis and Conflict in Han China: 104 B.C. to A.D. 9* (London, 1974), pp. 37–90.

14. Yen Jo-chü, *Shu-cheng,* 1:2b.

15. Ibid., 2:3a–3b. Ch'ien Mu argues that Yen took the question up again because of some damaging arguments Mao Ch'i-ling had leveled at Yen's earlier writings. See Ch'ien Mu, *Chung-kuo chin san-pai-nien hsueh-shu-shih* (Taipei, 1972), p. 251.

16. Yen Jo-chü, *Shu-cheng,* 2:3b–4b.

17. Yen Jo-chü, *Shu-cheng,* 2:47b–48a. Burton Watson translates the passage from the *Hsun-tzu* as follows: "Hence the Classic of the Way says, 'There should be a fearfulness in the mind of man; there should be subtlety of vision in the mind of Tao.' One must have the enlightenment of a gentleman before he can comprehend the signs of such fearfulness and subtlety." See *Hsun Tzu: Basic Writings* (New York, 1963), p. 131. For the original, see *Hsun-tzu yin-te* (Taipei, 1966), 81:21:54. On the debate, see my "Philosophy Vs. Philology," pp. 175–222.

18. Yen Jo-chü, *Shu-cheng,* 1:36b.

19. Ibid. Yen made the same statistical calculations for the *Li-chi* with comparable results. See 1:37a–37b.

20. Henderson, p. 27. Not all Sung Confucians regarded *li* as numinous, however.

21. Sivin, "Wang Hsi-shan," pp. 159–168. See also Hashimoto Keizō, "Bai Buntei no rekisangaku," p. 500, and Henderson, ibid., pp. 174–175.

22. Henderson, p. 171. See also Hou Wai-lu, 1:499–507.

23. Chiao Hsun, 4:202 (*chüan* 13), and Juan Yuan, *Yen-ching-shih chi,* 1:105–107. Cf. Steven McKenna and Victor Mair, "A Reordering of the Hexagrams of the *I Ching,*" *Philosophy East and West* 29.4:424 (October 1979), and Henderson, p. 171. For Juan's praise of Chiao Hsun's analysis of the *Changes* see Hou Wai-lu, 1:507.

24. Kondo Mitsuo, "Tai Shin no *Kōko kizu* ni tsuite–Kagaku shisoshi teki kōsatsu," *Tōhōgaku* 11:6–7 (1955).

25. Ibid., pp. 9–21. See also Leung Man-kam, p. 15.

26. Kondo Mitsuo, "Tai Shin no *Kōko kizu* ni tsuite," p. 20.

27. Sivin, "Wang Hsi-shan," pp. 163–165. See also Kondo Mitsuo, "Shinchō keishi ni okeru kagaku ishiki," pp. 97–110.

28. Ku Yen-wu, *Ku T'ing-lin shih-wen chi,* p. 137. Translated in ECCP, p. 424. See also Peterson, "The Life of Ku Yen-wu, Part II," p. 210n.

29. Kondo Mitsuo, "Sen Daikin no bungaku," pp. 25, 31. See also Kondo's "Kei Tō to Sen Daikin," *Yoshikawa hakusei taikyū kinen Chūgoku bungaku ronshū* (Tokyo, 1968), pp. 715–716, and Nivison, pp. 227–228.

30. Murayama Yoshihiro, "Yō Seikō no gakumon (jō)," pp. 83–85.

31. Yen Jo-chü, *Shu-cheng,* 8:1a–46b.

32. SKCSTM, 12:25a–26a.

33. Hao Chang, *Liang Ch'i-ch'ao,* pp. 21–22. See Sun Hsing-yen, *Shang-shu chin-ku-wen chu-shu* (Taipei, 1967), *passim,* but especially the "Hsu" (Introduction), pp. 1–3, and "Fan-li" (Format), pp. 1–3, and Tu Wei-yun, *Ch'ing Ch'ien-Chia,* p. 38.

34. Nivison, p. 155n. See also Chang Hsueh-ch'eng's *Chang-shih i-shu,* 5:102–103 (*chüan* 29).

35. SKCSTM, 37:14a–14b, 87:4b, and 136:21b, 26a.

36. ECCP, p. 421. Tu Wei-yun, *Ch'ing Ch'ien-Chia,* pp. 11–12, gives a comprehensive list of such supplements. See also Nivison, pp. 195, 216.

37. Tsuen-hsuin Tsien, *Bamboo and Silk,* p. 64, and Rudolph, "Preliminary Notes on Sung Archaeology," *Journal of Asian Studies* 22:169–177 (1963). See also Wang Kuo-wei, "Archaeology in the Sung Dynasty," in C. H. Liu, tr., *Chinese Journal of Arts and Sciences* 6:222–231 (1927), and Kwang Tsing Wu, "Scholarship, Book Production," p. 105.

38. Sir Percivel David, tr., *Chinese Connoisseurship, The Ko Ku Yao Lun: The Essential Criteria of Antiquities* (London, 1971), pp. liv–lix. See MB, pp. 1296–1297, and Chuang Shen, "Ming Antiquarianism, An Aesthetic Approach to Archaeology," *Journal of Oriental Studies* 8:63–82 (1970).

39. Rudolph, "Preliminary Notes," pp. 171–172, and Kwang Tsing Wu, "Scholarship, Book Production" p. 106n.

40. Ku Yen-wu's remarks are from his "Hsu" (Introduction) to the *Ch'iu-*

ku lu in *T'ing-lin hsien-sheng i-shu hui-chi* (Shanghai, 1888), p. 1a, translated in Wm. T. de Bary et al., *Sources of Chinese Tradition,* 1:555. See Tsuen-hsuin Tsien, *Bamboo and Silk,* p. 80. See also *T'ai-yuan hsien chih,* 1826: 10:33b, and Murayama Yoshihiro, "Yō Seikō no gakumon (chū)," p. 39.

41. See ECCP, pp. 183, 807, 857, Hu Shih, "Ch'ing-tai hsueh-che te chih-hsueh fang-fa," p. 403, Ch'ien Ta-hsin, *Ch'ien-yen T'ang wen-chi,* 4:367 (*chüan* 25), and L. Wieger, *Chinese Characters* (New York, 1965), pp. 5–9.

42. Tsuen-hsuin Tsien, *Bamboo and Silk,* pp. 61, 73–79. See also ECCP, pp. 244, 624.

43. Ch'ien Ta-hsin, *Ch'ien-yen T'ang wen-chi,* 4:365–366 (*chüan* 25), and Lothar Ledderhose, *Die Siegelschrift (Chuan-shu) in der Ch'ing-zeit: Ein Beitrag zur Geschichte der Chinesischen Schriftkunst* (Wiesbaden, 1970), pp. 57–64. See also Tseng Yu-ho Ecke, *Chinese Calligraphy* (Philadelphia, 1971), Illustration No. 85, Chu Chia, *Shu-hsueh chien-shih* (Hong Kong, 1975), pp. 105–137, and ECCP, pp. 611, 716.

44. Ledderhose, *Mi Fu,* pp. 7–12, and Wen C. Fong, "Archaism as a 'Primitive' Style," in Murck, ed., *Artists and Traditions,* pp. 89–93.

45. Shen Fu et al., *Traces of the Brush: Studies in Chinese Calligraphy,* (New Haven, 1977), pp. 43–55, and Ledderhose, *Mi Fu,* pp. 9, 57.

46. Shen Fu, *Traces,* pp. 44–52, and Ledderhose, *Mi Fu,* p. 12.

47. T.C. Lai, *Chinese Calligraphy: An Introduction* (Seattle, 1974), p. 179. See Ecke, No. 85, and Marilyn and Shen Fu, *Studies in Connoisseurship,* pp. 40–45.

48. T.C. Lai, p. 184. For K'ang's account of the Monument School, see his *Kuang I-chou shuang-chi* (Shanghai, 1916), pp. 9–10. On Teng's importance, see Ledderhose, *Die Siegelschrift,* pp. 70–83. On K'ang Yu-wei's calligraphy, see Shen Fu, *Traces,* pp. 137–138, 290, 301n. See also ECCP, pp. 42, 140, 677, and Chu Chia, pp. 120–121.

49. Juan Yuan, *Yen-ching-shih chi,* 2:553–559. See also Ledderhose, *Die Siegelschrift,* pp. 152–211. See also Shen Fu, *Traces,* p. 5.

50. See ECCP, p. 154, and Fumoto Yasutaka, pp. 156–158. For a comprehensive list of *nien-p'u* written by Ch'ing scholars, see Liang Ch'i-ch'ao, *Hsueh-shu-shih,* pp. 325–336. On genealogies, see Johanna Meskill, "The Chinese Genealogy as a Research Source,"

in Maurice Freedman, ed., *Family and Kinship in Chinese Society* (Stanford, 1970), pp. 140–143.

51. It was as staff members on the *Ta-Ch'ing i-t'ung-chih* project that Yen Jo-chü and Hu Wei met and began their close friendship discussed in chapter 3. See Hsia Ting-yü, "Te-ch'ing Hu Ch'u-ming hsien-sheng nien-p'u," *Wen-lan hsueh-pao* 2.1:8 (1936).

52. ECCP, pp. 167–168, and Kondo Mitsuo, "Shinchō keishi ni okeru kagaku ishiki," p. 102. See also Yabuuchi Kiyoshi, "Tai Shin no rekisangaku," p. 31.

53. Sun Ts'ung-t'ien, *Ts'ang-shu chi-yao*, in *Shu-ku ts'ung-ch'ao* (1871 edition), pp. 11a–12b. The passage is translated by Achilles Fang in "Bookman's Manual by Sun Ts'ung-t'ien," pp. 234, 258–259n. See also ECCP, pp. 676, 910–911.

54. Yuan Mei, *Hsiao-ts'ang shan-fang shih-wen chi* (SPPY edition), 31:7b–8a. Translated in Arthur Waley, *Yuan Mei: Eighteenth Century Chinese Poet,* p. 163.

55. For the different positions Yen and Mao each took, see SKCSTM, 12:25a–31a. See Mao Ch'i-ling, *Hsi-ho ho-chi (shu-mu),* 7:5b–6a, for the quotation.

56. Mao Ch'i-ling, *Hsi-ho ho-chi (shu-mu),* 5:1a–3b.

57. Mao Ch'i-ling, *Ku-wen Shang-shu yuan-tz'u,* "Hsu" (Introduction), pp. 1a–2b, and Yen Jo-chü, *Shu-cheng,* 8:41b, 8:9b. See also Murayama, "Yō Seikō (chū)," p. 41.

58. See *Yen-Li ts'ung-shu,* p. 376, and Yen Jo-chü, *Shu-cheng,* 8:39b. See also Murayama Yoshihiro, "Yō Seikō no gakumon (chū)," pp. 40–42, and Ch'ien Mu, "Tu Chang Mu chu Yen Ch'ien-ch'iu nien-p'u," *Shu-mu chi-k'an* 10.1:6 (June 1976).

59. Mao Ch'i-ling, *Hsi-ho ho-chi (shu-mu),* 7:13b–14b. Mao's mention of Huang's suspicions most likely is a reference to Huang's preface to Yen's *Shu-cheng* cited in chapter 3.

60. In Hang Shih-chün's 1724 afterword included in the 1796 edition of the *Shu-cheng,* Hang wrote: "When Mr. [Yen] lived in Wu-lin, he met and discussed the Old Text *Documents* with Mr. Mao. They did not agree, and [Mao] Hsi-ho returned and wrote his [*Ku-wen Shang-shu*] *yuan-tz'u.* Mr. [Yen] returned and wrote this book." See p. 1a.

61. Nivison, p. 106, and Waley, *Yuan Mei,* p. 112. See also Edwards, pp. 776–777.

62. See, for example, the letters to Shao Chin-han included in Chang Hsueh-ch'eng, *Wen-shih t'ung-i*, pp. 290–298. See Nivison, pp. 41, 49, 107n, 142–143, 201–202, and Kawata Teiichi, "Shindai gakujutsu no ichi sokumen," pp. 91–93, for discussion. See also Liang Ch'i-ch'ao, *Intellectual Trends*, p. 72, Tu Wei-yun, *Ch'ing Ch'ien-Chia*, p. 37, and Yü Ying-shih, *Lun Tai Chen*, pp. 5–14, 31–32, 45–53, 83ff. Ch'ien Ta-hsin's correspondence with Tai Chen, Tuan Yü-ts'ai, and others is included in *Ch'ien-yen T'ang wen-chi*, 5:518–522 (*chüan* 33). See also Lu Wen-ch'ao, *Pao-ching T'ang wen-chi*, 4:263–305 (*chüan* 29–31). Tuan Yü-ts'ai carried on an extensive correspondence that focused on the technical aspects of reconstructing ancient pronunciation (see further below). See Tuan's *Ching-yun-lou chi*, *chüan* 6. See also his extensive correspondence with Ku Kuang-ch'i in *chüan* 11–12.

63. SKCSTM, 118:44b. See Nakumura Kyūshirō, "Shinchō gakujutsu shisō shi (4)," p. 44. See also *Ch'ing-shih lieh-chuan*, 69:29a. The cumulative results in Ming-Ch'ing geographical research has been discussed in my "Geographical Research in the Ming-Ch'ing Period," *Monumenta Serica* 35 forthcoming (1981–1983).

64. Fumoto, pp. 288–289.

65. SKCSTM, 86:37b, 46a, 106:48b. See also Wang P'ing, p. 323, ECCP, p. 569, and *Ch'ing-shih lieh-chuan*, 69:38a. See ECCP, p. 336, and R.P. Kramers, *K'ung Tzu Chia Yü: The School Sayings of Confucius* (Leiden, 1950), pp. 33, 164, 192–195.

66. For examples of the praise of discoveries, see SKCSTM, 11:25a, 11:27b, 14:4b, 14:6a, 14:29a, 40:20b, 41:34b, 42:34a, 42:43a, 42:53a, 106:10b, 106:17a, 106:26b, 106:47a, 106:50b. 107:18a, 107:23b. These citations are only a brief sample taken from the *Shang-shu*, *Hsiao-hsueh*, and Astronomy and Mathematics subsections. On the impact of Tuan Yü-ts'ai's research, see ECCP, p. 783. On Chiao Hung, see SKCSTM, 86:4b.

67. Shao Ch'ang-heng, "Ch'uan-shih-lou chi," *Lo Hsueh-t'ang hsien-sheng ch'üan-chi*, p. 5870. The quotations from Chang Hsueh-ch'eng can be found in Chang, *Wen-shih t'ung-i*, p. 41, and *Chang-shih i-shu*, 5:102–103 (*chüan* 29). See the translation in Nivison, p. 182. See also Yü Ying-shih, *Lun Tai Chen*, pp. 38–41, 139–144, Demiéville, "Chang Hsueh-ch'eng and His Historiography," p. 183, and Tu Wei-yun, *Ch'ing Ch'ien-Chia*, pp. 68–69.

68. Hui Tung, *Ku-wen Shang-shu k'ao,* in HCCC, 351:17a–17b. The same cumulative results could be shown for eighteenth-century research on the *Changes, Poetry,* or *Spring and Autumn Annals* Classics.

69. Hashimoto Shigebumi, "Shinchō *Shōsho* gaku," pp. 16–23, and Ku Kuo-shun, "Ch'ing-tai *Shang-shu* chu-shu k'ao (shang)," *Nü-shih chuan-hsueh pao* 10:163–167 (Taipei, 1978).

70. Hashimoto Shigebumi, ibid., pp. 23–27, and Ku Kuo-shun, pp. 169–171. See also Ku's "Ch'ing-tai *Shang-shu* chu-shu k'ao (hsia)," 11:220–221 (1979). For the list of books in Sun Hsing-yen's family library, see his *Sun-shih tz'u-t'ang shu-mu,* pp. 3–4.

71. Chou Yü-t'ung, *Ching chin-ku-wen hsueh,* pp. 28–29, and ECCP, p. 98, See also Liu Feng-lu's preface to the *Shang-shu chin-ku-wen chi-chieh* (Taipei, 1977), pp. 1–3. I am indebted to several conversations with Liu Yü-yun in Taiwan for my understanding of the complicated relations between Old Text philology and New Text Confucianism.

72. Wei Yuan, *Ku-wei T'ang nei-wai-chi,* pp. 310–311, (*wai-chi,* 1:63b–64a), and *Wei Yuan chi,* 1:109–119.

73. Hou Wai-lu, 2:597, and Lun Ming, pp. 505–506. Shao I-ch'en was an advocate of Sung Learning, and he saw in the later 25 chapters doctrines that provided textual support for the Neo-Confucian position. See Ku Kuo-shun, "Ch'ing-tai *Shang-shu* (shang)," pp. 182–183.

74. Hashimoto Shigebumi, "Shin Ju to banshutsu kobun *Shōsho* no sakusha ni tsuite," *Kangakkai zasshi* 2.1:86–92 (August 1934). See Liu Feng-lu, *Tso-shih ch'un-ch'iu k'ao-cheng* (HCCC collection), 1294:1a, 1295:4b–5a. See also Henri Maspero, "La composition et la date du *Tso tchouan,*" *Melanges Chinois et buddhiques* 1:139–154 (1931–1932), and Wei Yuan, *Wei Yuan chi,* 1:119–121.

75. For discussion, see Chang Shih-lu, *Chung-kuo yin-yun-hsueh shih (hsia),* vol. 2 (Taipei, 1975), pp. 261–323. See also Liang Ch'i-ch'ao, *Hsueh-shu-shih,* pp. 214–223, and *Chinese Collections in the Library of Congress,* 2:654–656. On the *Shuo-wen,* see Winston Lo, p. 3.

76. Winston Lo, pp. 9–10. See also Hervouet, pp. 55–56.

77. Kwang Tsing Wu, "Scholarship, Book Production," p. 28. See also

Wong Lok Ping, "Lu Wen-ch'ao *Ching-tien shih-wen Mao-shih yin-i k'ao-cheng* ting-pu," pp. 289–301, and T.H. Tsien, *Bamboo and Silk,* p. 24.

78. Ch'ien Ta-hsin, *Ch'ien-yen T'ang wen-chi,* 4:416 (*chüan* 27), Chang Shih-lu, pp. 362–365, and SKCSTM, 41:46b, 42:27a. See also Jung Chao-tsu, *Ming-tai ssu-hsiang-shih,* pp. 279–280, and Hu Shih, "The Scientific Spirit," pp. 123–125.

79. MB, pp. 182–183. See also ECCP, pp. 233, 423–424, 522, and SKCSTM, 41:15a–15b (for the critique of Tai Chen). For further discussion, see Sivin, "Copernicus in China," pp. 91ff, and SKCSTM, 42:32b–33b.

80. Chang Shih-lu, pp. 263–267. See also SKCSTM, 42:42a–43a, 44:49a, and Ma Yü-tsao, "Tai Tung-yuan tui-yü ku-yin-hsueh te kung-hsien," *Kuo-hsueh chi-k'an* 22:207–208 (December 1929).

81. Bernhard Karlgren, *Grammata Serica* (Taipei, 1966), p. 1, and "On the Script of the Chou Dynasty," *Bulletin of the Museum of Far Eastern Antiquities* 8:177–178 (1936).

82. SKCSTM, 42:47b–52a, and Ma Yü-tsao, "Tai Tung-yuan," pp. 208–209.

83. SKCSTM, 44:50a–50b.

84. Chang Shih-lu, p. 268, and SKCSTM, 42:45a–45b.

85. *Tai Chen wen-chi,* pp. 68, 75–77, and Chang Shih-lu, pp. 270–277. P'i Hsi-jui, p. 331 also discusses this research.

86. *Tai Chen wen-chi,* pp. 91–92, and Ma Yü-tsao, pp. 210–220, 227–228, 235. See also Chang Shih-lu, pp. 272–277, 281–294, ECCP, pp. 829–830, and Kinoshita Tetsuya, "Tai Shin no ongaku—sono taishō to ninshiki," *Tōhōgaku* 58:128–142 (July 1979).

87. See Hu Shih, "The Scientific Spirit," pp. 126–127. Cf. John Green, "The History of Science and the History of Linguistics," in Dell Hymes, ed., *Studies in the History of Linguistics* (Blooming-ton, 1974), pp. 487–501.

88. Cf. Merton, pp. 302, 322–323, 349, 371–376. See also Leung Man-kam, pp. 261–266.

89. Wang Ming-sheng, "Hsu," in *Shih-ch'i-shih shang-ch'üeh,* pp. 3b–4a. See also Juan Yuan, *Ch'ou-jen chuan,* "Fan-li" (Taipei, 1962), pp. 1–5. Cf. Merton, pp. 298–322, 371–412.

90. See ECCP, p. 772, and Ch'ien Ta-hsin, *Ch'ien-yen T'ang wen-chi,* 3:341 (*chüan* 24).

91. P'i Hsi-jui, p. 284. For an account of the near loss of Mei Tsu's manuscripts, see SKCSTM, 12:15b.
92. ECCP, pp. 772, 776, and *Chinese Collections in the Library of Congress,* 1:364.
93. For Weng's attack, see *Ch'ing-shih lieh-chuan,* 68:50b. See also *Lun Ming,* pp. 457–511, for an account of the backlash against Yen Jo-chü.
94. Hu Shih, "A Note on Ch'üan Tsu-wang, Chao I-ch'ing, and Tai Chen," in Arthur Hummel, ed., *Eminent Chinese of the Ch'ing Period* (Taipei, 1972), pp. 970–971. See also Hu Shih's more definitive account recently published in Shanghai entitled *"Shui-ching chu* chiao-pen te yen-chiu," *Chung-hua wen-shih lun-ts'ung* (Shanghai, 1979), pp. 145–220.
95. ECCP, pp. 76–77, and Hu Shih, "A Note," pp. 974–975. See also SKCSTM, 69:4b–6b.
96. Hu Shih, "A Note," pp. 971–977. Kwang Tsing Wu and Fang Chao-ying accept Wei's and Chang's assessment of Tai's plagiarism. See ECCP, pp. 77, 205, and Ch'ien Ta-hsin, *Ch'ien-yen T'ang wen-chi,* 4:449 (*chüan* 29).
97. ECCP, pp. 140, 277.
98. Joseph Levenson, "Liao P'ing and the Confucian Departure From History," in Denis Twitchett and Arthur Wright, eds., *Confucian Personalities* (Stanford, 1962), pp. 318–319. The text of the letter can be found in Ch'ien Mu, *Hsueh-shu-shih,* pp. 646–647. I have not located the original. See also Liang Ch'i-ch'ao, *Intellectual Trends,* p. 92.
99. Yü Ying-shih (*Lun Tai Chen,* pp. 185–196) rejects the claim and contends that circumstances in China and Japan were sufficiently analogous to allow for the independent convergence of Confucian research in both countries. See also Yoshikawa Kōjirō, "Itō Jinsai," p. 29. This issue is briefly discussed in chapter 3, but it deserves more detailed study.
100. *Shu-cheng,* 6A:9a–9b, 6A:18a–18b, 6A:21a, and Henderson, pp. 65–73. See Hashimoto Keizō, "Bai Buntei no rekisangaku," pp. 500–503, and Sivin, "Copernicus in China," pp. 71–75, and "Wang Hsi-shan," pp. 159–168. See also SKCSTM, 106:1a–1b, 106:16a.
101. *Ku-ching ching-she wen-chi,* "Hsu," p. 1.

102. *Shu-cheng,* 8:10b and 8:14a, and Leung Man-kam, pp. 73–74.

6: Denouement

1. Yü Ying-shih, *Lun Tai Chen,* pp. 83–147, especially 110–114.
2. Yü Ying-shih, "Some Preliminary Observations," pp. 114–115. See Chang Hsueh-ch'eng's *Wen-shih t'ung-i,* pp. 51–53, and Chi Yun, p. 35. See also my "Ch'ing Dynasty 'Schools' of Scholarship," pp. 1–44.
3. Chuang Yu-k'e, *Mu-liang tsa-chuan* in *Chuang Ta-chiu hsien-sheng i-chu* (Ch'ang-chou, 1930), 1:1a.
4. See my "The Hsueh-hai T'ang and the Rise of New Text Confucianism," pp. 59–60, 63–65. Juan's comments on Chuang Ts'un-yü are cited in his "Hsu" to Chuang's *Wei-ching-chai i-shu* (Yang-hu, Kiangsu, 1882), pp. 1a–1b. For Kung Tzu-chen's remarks, see *Kung Tzu-chen ch'üan-chi,* pp. 225–230. See also Juan Yuan, *Yen-ching-shih chi,* 1:32.
5. For discussion, see Kuhn, *Rebellion and Its Enemies,* pp. 37–38, 51. See also Nomura Kōichi, "Shimmatsu Kuyōgakuha no keisei to Kō Yūi gaku no rekishi teki igi (ichi)," *Kokka gakkai zasshi* 71.7:25–34 (July 1957), Susan Naquin, *Millenarian Rebellion in China: The Eight Trigrams Revolt of 1813* (New Haven, 1976), *passim,* and Jones and Kuhn, pp. 107–162.
6. John K. Fairbank, *Trade and Diplomacy on the China Coast* (Stanford, 1969), pp. 39–73. See also Frederic Wakeman, "The Huang-ch'ao ching-shih wen-pien," *Ch'ing-shih wen-t'i* 1.10:8–22 (1969), and ECCP, p. 102. For discussion, see Hou Wai-lu, 1:376–379, 389–392, 473–476.
7. Peter Mitchell, "The Limits of Reformism: Wei Yuan's Reaction to Western Intrusion," *Modern Asian Studies* 6.2:175–204 (1972). See also Ōtani Toshio, "Gi Gen keisei shisō kō," *Shirin* 54.6:33–71 (November 1971); Frederic Wakeman, "The Canton Trade and the Opium War," in Fairbank, ed., *Cambridge History of China,* vol. 10, pp. 182–184; Liang Ch'i-ch'ao, *Intellectual Trends,* pp. 88–95, which established this influential point of view; and Philip Huang, *Liang Ch'i-ch'ao and Modern Chinese Liberalism* (Seattle, 1972), pp. 16–19.

8. James Polachek, "Literati Groups and Group Politics in Nineteenth-Century China," (PhD dissertation, University of California, 1977), pp. 2–3.

9. Yang Hsiang-k'uei, "Ch'ing-tai te chin-wen ching-hsueh," pp. 177–209. Huang Chang-chien, pp. 49–87, argues that K'ang Yu-wei did not fully recognize these differences either.

10. Kung Tzu-chen, pp. 346–347. On Liu Feng-lu's interests in political and institutional reform, see his *Ch'un-ch'iu Kung-yang ching Ho-shih shih-li,* 1280:1a–9b.

11. Ishiguro Nobutoshi, p. 2. See also Usami Kazuhiro, "Kyō Jichin shisō shiron," *Chūgoku kankei ronsetsu* 17.1A: 549–557 (1975), Takemura Noriyuki, "Kenryū jidai to Kyō Jichin," *Chūgoku bungaku ronshū* 6:46–59 (1977), and Dorothy Borei, "Eccentricity and Dissent: The Case of Kung Tzu-chen," *Ch'ing-shih wen-t'i* 3.4:50–62 (December 1975). Cf. Hou Wai-lu, 2:609–642. The quotation can be found in *Kung Tzu-chen ch'üan-chi,* p. 5.

12. See Jones and Kuhn, pp. 148–156, for a discussion of Wei Yuan "as an exemplar of statecraft and New Text studies." See also Ho Yu-sen, "Ch'ing-tai Han-Sung chih cheng p'ing-i," *Wen-shih-che hsueh-pao* 27:106–109 (December 1978), Peter Mitchell, "A Further Note on the HCCSWP," *Ch'ing-shih wen t'i* 2.3:40–46 (1970), and the *Huang-ch'ao ching-shih wen-pien* (Taipei, 1964), *chüan* 1–6, and 2:1a–1b, 2:5b–6b.

13. Wei Yuan, *Ku-wei T'ang nei-wai-chi,* p. 542 (*wai-chi,* 4:27b).

14. Ho Yu-sen, "Ch'ing-tai Han-Sung chih cheng p'ing-i," pp. 111–112, and Sakade Yoshinobu, "Gi Gen shisō shiron," pp. 33–52. See also Jones and Kuhn, p. 150, and Harold Kahn, *Monarchy in the Emperor's Eyes: Image and Reality in the Ch'ien-lung Reign* (Cambridge, Mass., 1971), pp. 48–50. For T'ao Chu's praise for Wang Ming-sheng, see T'ao's 1829 Preface to Wang's *I-shu pien* (Taipei, 1976), pp. 1a–2a. On the *Hai-kuo t'u-chih,* see Jane Leonard, "Wei Yuan and Images of the *Nan-yang,*" *Ch'ing-shih wen-t'i* 4.1:23–57 (June 1979), and my "Geographical Research in the Ming-Ch'ing Period," *Monumenta Serica* 35 (1981–1983).

15. Jones and Kuhn, pp. 151–154, Nomura Kōichi, pp. 34–61, and Hao Chang, "On the *Ching-shih* Ideal in Neo-Confucianism," *Ch'ing-shih wen-t'i* 3.1:57 (November 1974). See also Satō Shinji,

"Gi Gen no gakumon to shisō," *Chūgoku koten kenkyū* 12:24–40 (December 1964).

16. Jones and Kuhn, p. 157, Kuhn, *Rebellion and Its Enemies,* p. 47, and Charlton Lewis, *Prologue to the Chinese Revolution: The Transformation of Ideas and Institutions* in *Hunan Province, 1891–1907* (Cambridge, Mass., 1976), pp. 10–11. See also Hamaguchi Fujio, "Hō Tōju no Kangaku hihan ni tsuite," *Nihon Chūgoku gakkai hō* 30:165–178 (1978).

17. Fang Tung-shu, *Han-hsueh shang-tui,* 1:21a–21b, 2A:1a, and 2A:16b.

18. Fang, *Han-hsueh shang-tui,* 2A:42b. See Peter Fay, *The Opium War, 1840–1842* (Chapel Hill, 1975), pp. 47–48, and Hsin-pao Chang, *Commissioner Lin and the Opium War* (New York, 1964), pp. 20–21. For discussion, see Hamaguchi Fujio, "Hō Tōju no Kangaku hihan," pp. 172–176. Cf. Frederic Wakeman, "The Canton Trade and the Opium War," pp. 178–185, Jonathan Spence, "Opium Smoking in Ch'ing China," in Wakeman and Grant, eds., *Conflict and Control,* pp. 143–173, and Leung Man-kam, pp. 202–213. Juan Yuan's buying of time in 1821 has been the basis for the accusation that his anti-opium policies in Canton were never designed to be implemented very thoroughly. The fact that part of the funding for the Hsueh-hai T'ang came from the senior hong merchant (Howqua) has been cited as evidence of the political influence of the hong merchants on opium policy in the period before Lin Tse-hsu's arrival in Canton.

19. Fang Tung-shu, *I-wei-hsuan wen-chi,* 4:9a. See also Leung Man-kam, pp. 234–236, 281–282, Arthur Waley, *The Opium War Through Chinese Eyes* (Stanford, 1958), pp. 20, 77–78, and Suzuki Chūsei, "Shimmatsu jōgai undō no kigen," *Shigaku zasshi* 67.10:12–14 (October 1953). See also Leung Man-kam, p. 103, and T'ang Chün-i, *Chung-kuo jen-wen ching-shen chih fa-chan* (Taipei, 1974), pp. 37–38. My thanks to R. Po-chia Hsia of Columbia University for the latter citation.

20. Yü Ying-shih, "Some Preliminary Observations," pp. 112–114. See *Hsueh-hai T'ang chi,* I, 2:6a–10b, 6:28a–29b.

21. For discussion of Juan Yuan's interests in Sung Learning, see Ho Yu-sen, "Juan Yuan te ching-hsueh," pp. 19–20. On Ch'en Li's

position, see Wang Tsung-yen, *Ch'en Tung-shu hsien-sheng nien-p'u* (Hong Kong, 1964), pp. 62–63, and Ch'en Li, *Tung-shu tu-shu chi* (Taipei, 1970), p. 253 (*chüan* 21). For an account of the eclectic movement in Canton, see Fumoto Yasutaka, *Sō Gen Min Shin kinsei Jugaku,* pp. 290–223. See also Ch'ien Mu, *Chu-tzu hsin hsueh-an* (Taipei, 1971), 5:266–341.

22. See Tseng Kuo-fan's afterword to T'ang Chien's (1778–1861) *Ch'ing hsueh-an hsiao-chih,* pp. 1–2. See also William Ayers, *Chang Chih-tung and Educational Reform in China* (Cambridge, Mass., 1971), pp. 50–62, Ho Yu-sen, "Ch'ing-tai Han-Sung chih cheng p'ing-i," pp. 9–12, and Liu Kwang-ching, "The Ch'ing Restoration," in Fairbank, ed., *Cambridge History of China,* vol. 10, p. 489.

23. Canton's wealth was based on foreign trade. For Hunan's economic growth, see Evelyn Rawski, *Agricultural Change and the Peasant Economy of South China* (Cambridge, Mass., 1972), pp. 101–138, 159–163.

24. Skinner, *The City,* p. 228, and Table 1 on p. 213. See also Ho Ping-ti, *Studies on the Population of China, 1368–1953* (Cambridge, Mass., 1959), pp. 153–158, 275, 285.

25. Yeh-chien Wang, "The Impact of the Taiping Rebellion on Population in Southern Kiangsu," *Harvard University Papers on China* 19:120–158 (1964).

26. Ibid., pp. 129–131, 149–151, and Miyazaki Ichisada, "Mindai So-Shō chihō no shidaifu to minshū," p. 248. See also Kuhn, *Rebellion and Its Enemies,* pp. 180–188, and Paul Cohen, *Between Tradition and Modernity: Wang T'ao and Reform in Late Ch'ing China* (Cambridge, Mass., 1974), pp. 32–34.

27. Hu Shih, *Tai Tung-yuan te che-hsueh* (Taipei, 1967), p. 175. For an account of the Taiping impact on libraries in Kiangnan, see Ch'en Teng-yuan, pp. 233–248. See also Cohen, *Between Tradition and Modernity,* pp. 165–166.

28. Achilles Fang, tr., "Bookman's Decalogue," pp. 133, 139, and Cheuk-woon Taam, pp. 63–64. See also ECCP, pp. 539, 638, 700, 726, 822, Ch'en Teng-yuan, pp. 237–238, and Chang Yin, p. 47.

29. Kondo Mitsuo, "Ō Chū to *Kokushi Jurinden kō,*" *Jimbun kagaku ronshū* 3:67 (1964). See also Mote, "A Millennium of Chinese Urban History," pp. 39–42, Polachek, "Gentry Hegemony: Soo-

chow in the T'ung-chih Restoration," in Wakeman and Grant, eds., *Conflict and Control in Late Imperial China* (Berkeley, 1975), p. 235, and ECCP, p. 479.

30. ECCP, pp. 36, 98, 624, and Nivison, p. 280.
31. Mary Wright, *The Last Stand of Chinese Conservatism: The T'ung-chih Restoration, 1862-1874* (Stanford, 1957), pp. 129-133. See also Hu Shih, *Tai Tung-yuan te che-hsueh,* p. 175, and ECCP, p. 342. The Hsueh-ku T'ang developed into the Kiangnan Provincial Library in the 20th century.
32. ECCP, pp. 91, 198, and the 1861 "Hou-hsu" (Later Preface) to the HCCC, pp. 20a–20b.
33. On the 19th-century growth of Shanghai into a major metropolis, see John Fairbank, "The Creation of the Treaty System," *Cambridge History of China,* vol. 10, pp. 237-243.
34. Hu Shih, *The Development of the Logical Method in Ancient China* (Shanghai, 1922), p. 8. See also his "The Scientific Spirit," pp. 128-131.
35. Herrlee Creel, *The Birth of China: A Study of the Formative Period of Chinese Civilization* (New York, 1937), p. 22. See also ECCP, pp. 517, 827, and Li Chi, *Anyang* (Seattle, 1977), pp. 7-8.
36. ECCP, p. 678, and Li Chi, *Anyang,* pp. 3-13. Jesuit impact has been documented in Sivin, "Copernicus in China," pp. 63-122. See also Demiéville, "The First Philosophic Contacts Between Europe and China," pp. 84-86.

Bibliography

Adshead, S.A.M. "The Seventeenth Century General Crisis," *Asian Profile* 1.2:271–280 (October 1973).

Aoki Masaru 青木正児. *Shindai bungaku hyōronshi* 清代文學評論史 (History of Ch'ing literary criticism). *Aoki Masaru zenshū* 全集 (Complete works of Aoki Masaru). Tokyo, Kyoritsusha, 1969.

Atwell, William. "From Education to Politics: The Fu She," *The Unfolding of Neo-Confucianism*. Wm. T. de Bary et al. New York, Columbia University Press, 1975.

——. "Notes on Silver, Foreign Trade, and the Late Ming Economy," *Ch'ing-shih wen-t'i* 3.8:1–33 (December 1977).

Auerbach, Erich. *Mimesis: The Representation of Reality in Western Literature*. Translated by Willard Trask. Princeton, Princeton University Press, 1968.

Ayers, William. *Chang Chih-tung and Educational Reform in China*. Cambridge, Harvard University Press, 1971.

Balazs, Étienne. *Chinese Civilization and Bureaucracy*. Translated by H. M. Wright. New Haven, Yale University Press, 1964.

Barnard, Noel. "The Nature of the Ch'in 'Reform of the Script' as Reflected in Archaeological Documents Excavated Under Conditions of Control," *Ancient China: Studies in Early Civilization*. Eds., David Roy and T. H. Tsien. Hong Kong, Chinese University Press, 1978.

Becker, Howard. "The Nature of a Profession," *Education For the Professions*. Chicago, University of Chicago Press for the National Society for the Study of Education, 1962.

Ben-David, Joseph. "Professions in the Class System of Present-Day Societies: A Trend Report and Bibliography," *Current Sociology* 12.3:246–330 (1963).

——. "Scientific Growth: A Sociological View," *Minerva* 3:455–476 (1964).

——. *The Scientist's Role in Society: A Comparative Study*. Englewood Cliffs, N. J., Prentice-Hall, 1971.

Berger, Peter and Thomas Luckmann. *The Social Construction of Reality: A Treatise in the Sociology of Knowledge*. New York, Doubleday, 1966.

Bloom, Irene. "On the 'Abstraction' of Ming Thought: Some Concrete Evidence From the Philosophy of Lo Ch'in-shun," *Principle and Practicality: Essays in Neo-Confucianism and Practical Learning*. Eds., Wm. T. de Bary and Irene Bloom. New York, Columbia University Press, 1979.

Borei, Dorothy. "Eccentricity and Dissent: The Case of Kung Tzu-chen," *Ch'ing-shih wen-t'i* 3.4:50–62 (December 1975).

Brown, Harcourt. *Scientific Organizations in Seventeenth-Century France, 1620–1680*. Baltimore, Williams & Wilkins Co., 1934.

Burke, Kenneth. *The Philosophy of Literary Form*. Berkeley, University of California Press, 1973.

Cahill, James. *Fantastics and Eccentrics in Chinese Painting*. New York, Asia Society, 1967.

——. *Parting at the Shore: Chinese Painting of the Early and Middle Ming Dynasty, 1368–1580*. New York, Weatherhill, 1978.

Cammann, Schuyler. "The Evolution of Magic Squares in China," *Journal of the American Oriental Society* 80:116–124 (1960).

Carter, Thomas. *The Invention of Printing in China and Its Spread Westward*. New York, Columbia University Press, 1955.

Chan, Wing-tsit. "The *Hsing-li ching-i* and the Ch'eng-Chu School of the Seventeenth Century," *The Unfolding of Neo-Confucianism*. Wm. T. de Bary et al. New York, Columbia University Press, 1975.

——, tr. *A Source Book in Chinese Philosophy*. Princeton, Princeton University Press, 1963.

——, tr. *Reflections on Things at Hand*. New York, Columbia University Press, 1967.

——, tr. *Instructions for Practical Living and other Neo-Confucian Writings by Wang Yang-ming*. New York, Columbia University Press, 1963.

Ch'ang-chou fu chih 常州府志 (Gazetteer of Ch'ang-chou Prefecture), 1886 edition.

Chang, Carsun. *The Development of Neo-Confucian Thought, Volume 2*. New York, Bookman Assoc., 1962.

Chang, Chung-li. *The Chinese Gentry: Studies on Their Role in Nineteenth-Century Chinese Society*. Seattle, University of Washington Press, 1967.

——. *The Income of the Chinese Gentry*. Seattle, University of Washington Press, 1962.

Chang, Hao. *Liang Ch'i-ch'ao and Intellectual Transition in China, 1890–1907*. Cambridge, Harvard University Press, 1971.

——. "On the *Ching-shih* Ideal in Neo-Confucianism," *Ch'ing-shih wen-t'i* 3.1:36–61 (November 1974).

Chang Hsieh-chih 張諧之. *Shang-shu ku-wen pien-huo* 尚書古文辯惑 (Exposé concerning the Old Text *Documents*). 1904 Ch'ien-hsiu ching-she edition.

Chang, Hsin-pao. *Commissioner Lin and the Opium War*. New York, Norton & Co., 1964.

Chang Hsueh-ch'eng 章學誠 . *Wen-shih t'ung-i* 文史通義 (General meaning of literature and history). Taipei, Han-shang ch'u-pan-she, 1973.

——. *Chang-shih i-shu* 章氏遺書 (Bequeathed writings of Chang Hsueh-ch'eng). 8 vols. Shanghai, Commercial Press, 1936.

Chang Ping-lin 章炳麟 . *Kuo-hsueh kai-lun* 國學概論 (Overview of our nation's learning). Taipei, Ho-Lo t'u-shu ch'u-pan-she, 1974.

Chang Shih-lu 張世祿 . *Chung-kuo yin-yun-hsueh shih (hsia)* 中國音韻學史(下) (History of Chinese phonology, Vol. 2). Taipei, Commercial Press, 1975.

Chang Shou-an 張壽安 . "Kung Ting-an yü Ch'ang-chou Kung-yang-hsueh" 龔定菴與常州公羊傳 (Kung Tzu-chen and the Ch'ang-chou *Kung-yang* school), *Shu-mu chi-k'an* 書目季刊 13.2:3–21 (September 1979).

Chang Shun-wei 張舜微 . *Ch'ing-tai Yang-chou hsueh-chi* 清代揚州學記 (Record of Yangchow scholarship in the Ch'ing period). Shanghai, Jen-min ch'u-pan-she, 1962.

Chang Yin 張鑑 . "Ku-ching ching-she ch'u-kao" 詁經精社初稿 (Preliminary draft of a gazetteer of the Ku-ching ching-she), *Wen-lan hsueh-pao* 文闌學報 2.1:1–47 (March 1936).

Chao I 趙翼 . *Erh-shih-erh-shih cha-chi* 二十二史劄記 (Notation book to the *Twenty-two Dynastic Histories*). Taipei, Kuang-wen shu-chü, 1974.

Chaves, Jonathan, tr. *Pilgrim of the Clouds: Poems and Essays By Yuan Hung-tao and His Brothers.* New York, Weatherhill, 1978.

Ch'en Li 陳澧 . *Tung-shu tu-shu chi* 東塾讀書記 (Ch'en Li's reading notes). Taipei, Commercial Press, 1970.

Ch'en Teng-yuan 陳登原 . *Ku-chin tien-chi chü-san k'ao* 古今典籍聚散考 (Inquiry into the collection and dispersion of books in ancient and modern times). Shanghai, Commercial Press, 1936.

Ch'en Tung-yuan 陳東原 . "Ch'ing-tai chih k'e-chü yü chiao-yü" 清代之科舉與教育 (Education and the examination system in the Ch'ing period), *Hsueh-feng* 學風 3.4:19–52 (May 1933).

——. "Ch'ing-tai shu-yuan feng-ch'i chih pien-ch'ien" 清代書院風氣之變遷 (Changes in Ch'ing dynasty academy practices), *Hsueh-feng* 3.5:15–20 (June 1933).

Cheng, Chung-ying, tr. *Tai Chen's Inquiry Into Goodness.* Honolulu, East-West Center Press, 1971.

Chi Yun 紀昀. *Chi Hsiao-lan shih-wen-chi* 紀曉嵐詩文集 (Collected essays and poetry of Chi Yun), Hong Kong, Kuang-chih shu-chü, n.d.

Ch'i Ssu-ho 齊思和 . "Wei Yuan yü wan-Ch'ing hsueh-feng" 魏源與晚清學風 (Wei Yuan and Late Ch'ing intellectual currents), *Yen-ching hsueh-pao* 燕京學報 39:177–226 (1950).

Chiang Fan 江藩 . *Kuo-ch'ao Han-hsueh shih-ch'eng chi* 國朝漢學師承記 (Record of Han-Learning masters in the Ch'ing dynasty). SPPY edition.

Chiang Yee. *Chinese Calligraphy: An Introduction to Its Aesthetics and Technique.* Cambridge, Harvard University Press, 1973.

Chiang-yin hsien chih 江陰縣志 (Chiang-yin county gazetteer). 1878 edition.

Chiao Hsun 焦循. *Tiao-ku chi* 雕菰集 (Collected writing from [the Studio of] Engraved Bamboo). 6 vols. Shanghai, Commercial Press, 1936.

Ch'ien, Edward. "Chiao Hung and the Revolt Against Ch'eng-Chu Orthodoxy," *The Unfolding of Neo-Confucianism.* Wm. T. de Bary et al. New York, Columbia University Press, 1975.

Ch'ien Mu 錢穆. *Chung-kuo chin san-pai-nien hsueh-shu-shih* 中國近三百年學術史 (Intellectual history of China during the last 300 years). 2 vols. Taipei, Commercial Press, 1972.

——. "Chu-tzu yü chaio-k'an-hsueh" 朱子與校勘學 (Chu Hsi and collation scholarship). *Hsin-ya hsueh-pao* 新亞學報 2.2:87–113 (February 1957).

——. "Tu Chang Mu chu Yen Ch'ien-ch'iu nien-p'u" 讀張穆著閻潛邱年譜 (Upon reading Chang Mu's chronological biography of Yen Jo-chü), *Shu-mu chi-k'an* 書目季刊 10.1:3–10 (June 1976).

——. *Chu-tzu hsin hsueh-an* 朱子新學案 (New studies of Master Chu [Hsi]). 5 vols, Taipei, San-min shu-chü, 1971.

Ch'ien Ta-hsin 錢大昕. *Ch'ien-yen T'ang wen-chi* 潛研堂文集 (Collected essays of the Hall of Subtle Research). 8 vols. Taipei, Commercial Press, 1968.

——. *Nien-erh-shih k'ao-i* 廿二史考異 (Examination of variances in the Twenty-two Dynastic Histories). Shanghai, Commercial Press, 1935–1937.

——. *Shih-chia-chai yang-hsin lu* (Record of self-renewal from the Ten Yokes Study). Taipei, Kuang-wen Reprint, 1968.

——. *Chu-t'ing jih-chi ch'ao* 竹汀日記鈔 (Copy of Ch'ien Ta-hsin's diary). Taipei, Kuang-wen Reprint, 1971.

Ch'in-ting Wu-ying-tien chü-chen-pan ch'eng-shih 欽定武英殿聚珍版程式 (Imperial Printing Office manual for movable type). Peking, Imperial Printing Office, 1776.

Chinese Collections in the Library of Congress. Compiled by P. K. Yu. 3 vols. Washington, D.C., Center for Chinese Research Materials, 1974.

Ch'ing-shih lieh-chuan 清史列傳 (Collection of Ch'ing dynasty biographies). Taipei, Chung-hua shu-chü, 1962.

Chou Yü-t'ung 周予同. *Ching chin-ku-wen hsueh* 經今古文學 (Study of the New and Old Text Classics). Taipei, Commercial Press, 1967.

Chu Chia 祝嘉. *Shu-hsueh chien-shih* 書學簡史 (Condensed history of calligraphy). Hong Kong, Chung-hua shu-chü, 1975.

Chu I-tsun 朱彝尊. *Ching-i k'ao* 經義考 (Critique of classical studies). SPPY edition.

Chu T'an 朱偰. "Ming-chi Hangchow Tu-shu She k'ao" 明季杭州讀書社考 (Analysis of the Ming-dynasty society of book-readers in Hangchow), *Kuo-hsueh chi-k'an* 國學季刊 2.2:261–285 (1929).

Chu-tzu yü-lei 朱子語類 (Conversations with Master Chu [Hsi] classified topically). 1473 edition. Taipei, Cheng-chung shu-chü reprint.

Ch'u, T'ung-tsu. *Local Government in China Under the Ch'ing*. Stanford, Stanford University Press, 1973.

Ch'üan Tsu-wang 全祖望. *Chi-ch'i-t'ing chi* 鮚埼亭集 (Collection from the Room on Chi-ch'i Mountain). Shanghai, Commercial Press, 1929.

Chuang Shen. "Ming Antiquarianism, An Aesthetic Approach to Archaeology," *Journal of Oriental Studies* 8:63–82 (1970).

Chuang Yu-k'e 莊有可. *Mu-liang tsa-tsuan* 慕良雜纂 (Miscellaneous collection in adoration of goodness). *Chuang Ta-chiu hsien-sheng i-chu* 莊大久先生遺著 (Bequeathed writings of Chuang Yu-k'e). Ch'ang-chou, Chuang Family Publication, 1930.

Chun Hae-jong. "Sino-Korean Tributary Relations in the Ch'ing Period," *The Chinese World Order: Traditional China's Foreign Relations*. Ed., John Fairbank. Cambridge, Harvard University Press, 1968.

Cogan, Morris. "Toward a Definition of Profession," *Harvard Educational Review* 23:33–50 (1953).

Cohen, Paul. "Ch'ing China: Confrontation With the West, 1850–1900," *Modern East Asia: Essays in Interpretation*. Ed., James Crowley. New York, Harcourt, Brace, & World, 1970.

——. *Between Tradition and Modernity: Wang T'ao and Reform in Late Ch'ing China*. Cambridge, Harvard University Press, 1974.

Creel, Herrlee. *The Birth of China: A Study of the Formative Period of Chinese Civilization*. New York, Ungar Pub. Co., 1937.

David, Sir Percival, *Chinese Connoisseurship, the Ko Ku Yao Lun: The Essential Criteria of Antiquities*. London, Faber, 1971.

de Bary, Wm. T. "Chinese Despotism and the Confucian Ideal: A Seventeenth-Century View," *Chinese Thought and Institutions*. Ed. John Fairbank, Chicago, University of Chicago Press, 1957.

—— et al. *Self and Society in Ming Thought*. New York, Columbia University Press, 1970.

—— et al. *Sources of Chinese Tradition*. 2 vols. New York, Columbia University Press, 1964.

—— et al. *The Unfolding of Neo-Confucianism*. New York, Columbia University Press, 1975.

Demiéville, Paul. "Chang Hsueh-ch'eng and His Historiography," *Historians of China and Japan*. Eds., W. G. Beasley and E. G. Pulleyblank. Oxford, Oxford University Press, 1961.

——. "The First Philosophic Contacts Between Europe and China," *Diogenes* 58:75–103 (Summer 1967).

Dolby, William. *A History of Chinese Drama*. New York, Barnes and Noble, 1976.

Dore, Ronald. "The Legacy of Tokugawa Education," *Changing Japanese Attitudes*

Toward Modernization. Ed., Marius Jansen. Princeton, Princeton University Press, 1965.

Dunne, Gerald. *Generation of Giants: The Story of the Jesuits in China in the Last Decades of the Ming Dynasty.* South Bend, University of Notre Dame Press, 1962.

Ecke, Tseng Yu-ho. *Chinese Calligraphy.* Philadelphia, David Godine, 1971.

Edwards, E.D. "A Classified Guide to the Thirteen Classes of Chinese Prose," *Bulletin of the School of Oriental and African Studies* 12:770–788 (1948).

Eisenstein, Elizabeth. "The Advent of Printing and the Problem of the Renaissance," *Past and Present* 45:19–89 (November 1969).

——. *The Printing Press as an Agent of Change: Communications and Cultural Transformations in Early-Modern Europe.* 2 vols. New York, Cambridge University Press, 1979.

Eliot, T. S. "What is a Classic?" in *On Poetry and Poets.* New York, Noonday Press, 1961.

Elman, Benjamin. "Yen Jo-chü's Debt to Sung and Ming Scholarship," *Ch'ing-shih wen-t'i* 3.7:105–113 (November 1977).

——. "The Hsueh-hai T'ang and the Rise of New Text Scholarship in Canton," *Ch'ing-shih wen-t'i* 4.2:51–82 (December 1979).

——. "Ch'ing Dynasty 'Schools' of Scholarship," *Ch'ing-shih wen-t'i* 4.6:1–44 (December 1981).

——. "From Value to Fact: The Emergence of Phonology as a Precise Discipline in Late Imperial China," *Journal of the American Oriental Society* 102.3:493–500 (July-October 1982).

——. "Philosophy Vs. Philology: The *Jen-hsin Tao-hsin* Debate." *T'oung Pao* 69.4 & 5:175–222 (1983).

——. "Geographical Research in the Ming-Ch'ing Period," *Monumenta Serica,* forthcoming, 35 (1981–1983).

Fairbank, John. *Trade and Diplomacy on the China Coast.* Stanford, Stanford University Press, 1969.

——. "The Creation of the Treaty System," *The Cambridge History of China,* Vol. 10, Part I. Ed., Fairbank. Cambridge, Cambridge University Press, 1978, pp. 213-263.

Fang, Achilles, tr. "Bookman's Decalogue by Yeh Te-hui," *HJAS,* 13:132–173 (1950).

——, tr. "Bookman's Manual by Sun Ts'ung-t'ien," *HJAS* 14:215–260 (1951).

Fang Tung-shu 方東樹 . *Han-hsueh shang-tui* 漢學商兌 (An assessment of Han Learning). Taipei, Kuang-wen shu-chü Reprint, 1963.

——. *I-wei-hsuan wen-chi* 儀衛軒文集 (Collected writings from the studio of Fang Tung-shu). 1868 Anhwei edition inscribed by Li Hung-chang 李鴻章 (1823–1901) and compiled by Fang Tsung-ch'eng 方宗誠 (1818–1888).

Fay, Peter. *The Opium War, 1840–1842.* Chapel Hill, University of North Carolina Press, 1975.

Febvre, Lucien and Henri-Jean Martin. *The Coming of the Book: The Impact of Printing, 1450-1800*. Translated by David Gerard. Atlantic Highlands, N.J., Humanities Press, 1976.

Fei, Hsiao-t'ung. *China's Gentry: Essays in Rural-Urban Relations*. Chicago, University of Chicago Press, 1953.

Feuerwerker, Albert. *State and Society in Eighteenth-Century China; The Ch'ing Empire in Its Glory*. Ann Arbor, Center for Chinese Studies, University of Michigan, 1976.

Fong, Wen C. "Archaism as a 'Primitive' Style," *Artists and Traditions: Uses of the Past in Chinese Culture*. Ed., Christian Murck. Princeton, Princeton University Press, 1976.

Foucault, Michel. *The Archaeology of Knowledge*. Translated by A.M. Sheridan Smith. New York, Pantheon Books, 1972.

Fox, R. "Scientific Enterprise and the Patronage of Research in France, 1800–1870," *Minerva* 11:442-473 (1973).

Franke, Wolfgang. *The Reform and Abolition of the Traditional Chinese Examination System*. Cambridge, East Asian Research Center, Harvard University, 1960.

Freedman, Maurice. *Chinese Lineage and Society: Fukien and Kwangtung*. New York, Humanities Press, 1971.

Freidson, Eliot. *Profession of Medicine: A Study of the Sociology of Applied Knowledge*. New York, Dodd, Mead, & Co., 1970.

Fu I-ling 傅衣凌 . *Ming-tai Chiang-nan shih-min ching-chi shih-t'an* 明代 江南市民經濟試談 (Examination of the Kiangnan urban economy in the Ming period). Shanghai, Jen-min ch'u-pan-she, 1957.

Fu, Marilyn and Shen Fu. *Studies in Connoisseurship: Chinese Paintings from the Arthur M. Sackler Collection in New York and Princeton*. Princeton, Princeton Arts Museum and others, 1973.

Fu, Shen, in collaboration with Marilyn Fu, Mary Neil, and Mary Clark. *Traces of the Brush: Studies in Chinese Calligraphy*. New Haven, Yale University Art Gallery, 1977.

Fujitsuka Chikashi 藤塚鄰 . *Shinchō bunka tōden no kenkyū* 清朝文化 東伝 の 研究 (Research on the eastward transmission of Ch'ing dynasty culture). Tokyo, Kokusho kankōkai, 1975.

Fumoto Yasutaka 麓保孝 . *Sō Gen Min Shin kinsei Jugaku hensen shiron* 宗元明清近世儒學變遷史論 (Historical essays on changes in Sung, Yuan, Ming, and Ch'ing early modern Confucianism). Tokyo, Kokusho kankōkai, 1976.

Furth, Charlotte. "The Sage As Rebel: The Inner World of Chang Ping-lin," in *The Limits of Change: Essays on Conservative Alternatives in Republican China*. Ed., Furth. Cambridge, Harvard University Press, 1976.

Gallagher, Louis, S.J., tr. *China in the Sixteenth Century: The Journals of Matthew Ricci, 1583-1610*. New York, Random House, 1953.

Gay, Peter. *The Enlightenment: An Introduction. The Rise of Modern Paganism.* New York, Norton & Co., 1966.

Gillispie, Charles. *The Edge of Objectivity: An Essay in the History of Scientific Ideas.* Princeton, Princeton University Press, 1960.

Goode, William. "Community Within a Community: The Professions," *American Sociological Review* 22:194-200 (April 1957).

Goodrich, Luther C. *The Literary Inquisition of Ch'ien-lung.* Baltimore, Waverly Press, 1935.

—— et al. *Dictionary of Ming Biography 1368-1644.* 2 vols. New York, Columbia University Press, 1976.

Graham, Angus C. *Later Mohist Logic, Ethics, and Science.* Hong Kong, Chinese University Press, 1978.

Gray, Jack. "Historical Writing in Twentieth-Century China: Notes on its Background and Development," *Historians of China and Japan.* Eds., W.G. Beasley and E.G. Pulleyblank. Oxford, Oxford University Press, 1961.

Green, John. "The History of Science and the History of Linguistics," *Studies in the History of Linguistics.* Ed., Dell Hymes. Bloomington, Indiana University Press, 1974.

Grimm, Tilemann. "Academies and Urban Systems in Kwangtung," *The City in Late Imperial China.* Ed., G. Wm. Skinner. Stanford, Stanford University Press, 1977.

——. "Some Remarks on the Suppression of *Shu-yuan* in Ming China," *International Conference of Orientalists in Japan: Transactions* 2:8–16 (1957).

Guignard, M.R. "The Chinese Precedent," *The Coming of the Book.* Lucien Febvre and Henri-Jean Martin. Atlantic Highlands, N.J., Humanities Press, 1976.

Guy, Kent. "The Scholar and the State in Late Imperial China: The Politics of the *Ssu-k'u ch'üan-shu* Project." PhD dissertation, Harvard University, 1981.

Haeger, John. "The Intellectual Context of Neo-Confucian Syncretism," *Journal of Asian Studies* 31:499-513 (1972).

Hall, A.R. "Science," *The New Cambridge Modern History. Volume II: The Reformation, 1520-1559.* Ed., G.R. Elton. Cambridge, Cambridge University Press, 1958.

Hamaguchi Fujio 濱口富士雄 . "Hō Tōju no *Kangaku shōda* o megutte" 方東樹の漢學商兌を繞って (On Fang Tung-shu's *An Assessment of Han Learning*), *Taitō bunka daigaku Kangaku kaishi* 大東文化大學漢學会誌 15:73-89 (n.d.).

——. "Hō Tōju no Kangaku hihan ni tsuite" 方東樹の漢學批評 について (Concerning Fang Tung-shu's criticism of Han Learning), *Nihon Chūgoku gakkai hō* 日本中國學会報 30:165-178 (1978).

——. "Shingaku seiritsu no haikei ni tsuite" 清學成立の背景 について (Concerning the background to the formation of Ch'ing scholarship), *Tōhōgaku* 東方学 58:114-127 (July 1979).

Bibliography

Han-shu 漢書 (History of the Former Han dynasty). Pan Ku 班固 . 7 vols. Taipei, Shih-hsueh ch'u-pan-she, 1974.

Harootunian, H.D. "The Consciousness of Archaic Form in the New Realism of Kokugaku," *Japanese Thought in the Tokugawa Period*. Eds., Najita Tetsuo and Irwin Scheiner. Chicago, University of Chicago Press, 1978.

Hashimoto Keizō 橋本敬造 . "Bai Buntei no rekisangaku" 梅文鼎の 曆算學 (Mei Wen-ting's calendrical studies), *Tōhōgaku hō* 東方学 報 41:491–518 (1970).

——. "Rekishō kōsei no seiritsu" 曆象考成の成立 (The origin of the *Compendium of Observational and Computational Astronomy*). *Min-Shin jidai no kagaku gijutsu shi*. Eds., Yabuuchi Kiyoshi and Yoshida Mitsukuni. Kyoto, Institute for Humanistic Studies, 1970.

Hashimoto Shigebumi 橋本成文 . "Shin Ju to banshutsu kobun *Shōsho no sakusha ni tsuite*" 清儒と晚出古文尚書の作者に就 りて (Concerning the author of the later version of the Old Text *Documents* and Ch'ing Confucians), *Kangakkai zasshi* 漢學會雜誌 2.1:86–92 (August 1934).

——. "Shinchō *Shōsho* gaku" 清朝尚書學 (Ch'ing-dynasty studies of the *Documents*), *Kambungaku kōza* 漢文學講座 4:1-49 (1933).

Hay, Denys. "Literature: the Printed Book," *The New Cambridge Modern History*, Vol. 2. Ed., G.R. Elton. Cambridge, Cambridge University Press, 1958.

——. "Fiat Lux," *Printing and the Mind of Man*. Eds., J. Carter and P. Muir. New York, Holt, Rinehart & Winston, 1967.

Hayashi Tomoharu 林友春 . "Shinchō no shoin kyōiku" 清朝の書院 教育 (Academy education in the Ch'ing dynasty), *Gakushūin daigaku bugakubu kenkyū nempō* 學習院大學文學部研究年報 6:177-197 (1959).

——. "Tō Sō shoin no hassei to sono kyōiku" 唐宋書院の發生 とその教育 (The development of T'ang and Sung academies and their education), *Gakushūin daigaku bungakubu kenkyū nempō* 2:133–156 (1953).

——. "Gen Min jidai no shoin kyōiku" 元明時代の書院教育 (Academy education in the Yuan and Ming era) *Kinsei Chūgoku kyōiku kenkyū* 近世中國教育研究 (Research on education in early modern China). Ed., Hayashi Tomoharu. Tokyo, Kokutosha, 1958.

Henderson, John. "The Ordering of the Heavens and the Earth in Early Ch'ing Thought." PhD Dissertation, University of California, Berkeley, 1977.

Hervouet, Yves, ed. *A Sung Bibliography*. Hong Kong, Chinese University Press, 1978.

Hiraoka Takeo 平岡武夫 . *Keisho no dentō* 經書の傳統 (The tradition of the Confucian Canon). Tokyo, Iwanami shoten, 1951.

Ho, Ping-ti. "The Salt Merchants of Yang-chou: A Study of Commercial Capitalism in Eighteenth-Century China," *HJAS* 17:130-168 (1954).

——. *The Ladder of Success in Imperial China.* New York, Wiley & Sons, 1962.

——. *Studies on the Population of China, 1368–1953.* Cambridge, Harvard University Press, 1959.

Ho Yu-sen 何佑森 . "Ku T'ing-lin te ching-hsueh" 顧亭林的經學 (Ku Yen-wu's classical scholarship), *Wen-shih-che hsueh-pao* 文史哲學報 16:183–205 (1967).

——. "Juan Yuan te ching-hsueh chi ch'i chih-hsueh fang-fa" 阮元的經學及其治學方法 (Juan Yuan's classical scholarship and his methods of scholarship), *Ku-kung wen-hsien* 故宮文獻 2.1:19–34 (December 1970).

——. "Huang Li-chou yü Che-tung hsueh-shu" 黃梨洲與浙東學術 (Huang Tsung-hsi and Che-tung scholarship), *Shu-mu chi-k'an* 書目季刊 7.4:9–16 (March 1974).

——. "Ch'ing-tai Han-Sung chih cheng p'ing-i" 清代漢宋之爭平議 (An evaluation of the Han-Sung debate in the Ch'ing Period), *Wen-shih-che hsueh-pao* 文史哲學報 27:97–113 (December 1978).

Hou Wai-lu 侯外廬 . *Chin-tai Chung-kuo ssu-hsiang hsueh-shuo shih* 近代中國思想學說史 (History of modern Chinese thought and theories). 2 vols. Shanghai, Sheng-huo shu-tien, 1947.

Hsia Ting-yü 夏定域 . "Te-ching Hu Ch'u-ming hsien-sheng nien-p'u" 德清胡朏明先生年譜 (Chronological biography of Mr. Hu Wei), *Wen-lan hsueh-pao* 文瀾學報 2.1:1–40 (1936).

Hsiao, Kung-chuan. *Rural China: Imperial Control in the Nineteenth Century.* Seattle, University of Washington Press, 1967.

——. *A Modern China and a New World: K'ang Yu-wei, Reformer and Utopian.* Seattle, University of Washington Press, 1975.

Hsieh Ch'i-k'un 謝啟昆 . *Hsiao-hsueh k'ao* 小學考 (Critique of classical philology). Taipei, Kuang-wen Reprint of 1887 Edition, 1969.

Hsieh Kuo-chen 謝國楨 . *Ming-Ch'ing chih chi tang-she yun-tung k'ao* 明清之際黨社運動考 (Analysis of party and society movements in the Ming-Ch'ing period). Shanghai, Commercial Press, 1934.

Hsu Ch'ien-hsueh 徐乾學 . *Tan-yuan wen-chi* 憺園文集 (Literary collection from the Garden of Contentment). Ch'ing, Kuan-shan T'ang 冠山堂 edition.

Hsu Tsung-yen 許宗彥 . "Hsu" 序 (Introduction). *Ku-ching ching-she wen-chi*, pp. 1–2.

Hsueh-hai T'ang chi 學海堂集 (Collected writings from the Hsueh-hai T'ang). Juan Yuan et al. Canton, Hsueh-hai T'ang, 1st series 1825, 2nd series 1838, 3rd series, 1859, 4th series 1886.

Hsueh-hai T'ang chih 學海堂志 (Gazetteer of the Hsueh-hai T'ang). Lin Po-t'ung 林佰桐 et al. Hong Kong, Tung-Ya hsueh-she, 1964.

Hsun-tzu yin-te 荀子引得 (Concordance to the *Hsun-tzu*). Taipei, Ch'eng Wen Reprint, 1966.

Hu Shih 胡適 . "K'e-hsueh-te ku-shih-chia Ts'ui Shu" 科學的古史家崔述 (The scientific historian of ancient China—Ts'ui Shu). *Ts'ui Tung-pi i-shu* 崔東壁遺書 (Ts'ui Shu's bequeathed works). Compiled by Ku Chieh-kang 顧頡剛 . Shanghai, Ya-tung t'u-shu-kuan, 1936, Vol. 2, pp. 1–176.

———. "Ch'ing-tai hsueh-che te chih-hsueh fang-fa" 清代學者的治學方法 (Methods of scholarship used by scholars in the Ch'ing period). *Hu Shih wen-ts'un* 胡適文存 (Abiding essays by Hu Shih). 4 vols. Taipei, Yuan-tung t'u-shu kung-ssu, 1968, Vol. 1, pp. 383–412.

———. "Chih-hsueh te fang-fa yü ts'ai-liao" 治學的方法與材料 (Methods of scholarship and source materials). *Hu Shih wen-ts'un,* Vol. 3, pp. 109–122.

———. "Weng Fang-kang yü Mo-tzu" 翁方綱與孟子 (Weng Fang-kang and Mo-tzu). *Hu Shih wen-ts'un,* Vol. 3, pp. 598–599.

———. *Tai Tung-yuan te che-hsueh* 戴東原的哲學 (Tai Chen's philosophy). Taipei, Commercial Press, 1967.

———. *The Development of the Logical Method in Ancient China.* Shanghai, Oriental Book Co., 1922.

———. "A Note on Ch'üan Tsu-wang, Chao I-ch'ing, and Tai Chen," *Eminent Chinese of the Ch'ing Period.* Ed., Arthur Hummel. Taipei, Ch'eng Wen Reprint, 1972.

———. "The Scientific Spirit and Method in Chinese Philosophy," *The Chinese Mind.* Ed., C. A. Moore. Honolulu, University of Hawaii Press, 1967.

———. "*Shui-ching chu chiao-pen te yen-chiu*" 水經注校本的研究 (Research on the collation of the notes to the *Classic of Waterways*). *Chung-hua wen-shih lun-ts'ung* 中華文史論叢 (Shanghai, 2nd series, 1979).

Hu Ying-lin 胡應麟 . *Shao-shih shan-fang pi-ts'ung* 少室山房筆叢 (Collected notes from the Mountain Hut of Few Rooms). Shanghai, Chung-hua shu-chü, 1958.

Huang Chang-chien 黃彰健 . "Ching chin-ku-wen hsueh wen-t'i hsin-lun (shang)" 經今古文學問題新論上 (New views on questions concerning the study of New and Old Text Classics), *Ta-lu tsa-chih* 大陸雜誌 58.2:49–87 (February 1979).

Huang-ch'ao ching-shih wen-pien 皇朝經世文編 (Collected writings on statecraft during the Ch'ing dyansty). Eds., Ho Ch'ang-ling 賀長齡 and Wei Yuan 魏源 . 8 vols. Taipei, Shih-chieh shu-chü, 1964.

Huang-Ch'ing ching-chieh 皇清經解 (Ch'ing exegesis of the Classics). Eds., Juan Yuan 阮元 et al. 20 vols. Taipei, Fu-hsing Reprint, 1961.

Huang, Pei. *Autocracy at Work: A Study of the Yung-cheng Period, 1723–1735.* Bloomington, Indiana University Press, 1974.

Huang, Philip. *Liang Ch'i-ch'ao and Modern Chinese Liberalism.* Seattle, University of Washington Press, 1972.

Huang Tsung-hsi 黃宗羲 *Huang Li-chou wen-chi* 黃梨洲文集

(Huang Tsung-hsi's collected essays). Peking, Chung-hua shu-chü, 1959.

——. *Ming-Ju hsueh-an* 明儒學案 (Studies of Ming Confucians). Taipei, Shih-chieh shu-chü, 1973.

——. "Ch'uan-shih-lou ts'ang-shu chi" 傳是樓藏書記 (Record of the library known as the Pavilion for the Transmission of the Truth). Lo Chen-yü, *Lo Hsueh-t'ang hsien-sheng ch'üan-chi* 3.14:5863-5865.

——. *Li-chou i-chu hui-k'an* 梨洲遺著彙刊 (Composite edition of Huang Tsung-hsi's bequeathed writings). 2 vols. Taipei, Lung-yen ch'u-pan-she, 1969.

Hucker, Charles. "The Tung-lin Movement of the Late Ming Period," *Chinese Thought and Institutions.* Ed., John Fairbank. Chicago, University of Chicago Press, 1957.

Hui Tung 惠棟. *Ku-wen Shang-shu k'ao* 古文尚書考 (Analysis of the Old Text *Documents*). HCCC collection.

Hummel, Arthur. "Ts'ung-shu," *Journal of the American Oriental Society* 61:71–76 (1941).

——, ed. *Eminent Chinese of the Ch'ing Period.* Taipei, Ch'eng Wen Reprint, 1972.

Ishiguro Nobutoshi 石黒宣俊. "Kyō Jichin to *Shunjū* Kuyōgaku—keigaku o chūshin to shite" 龔自珍と春秋公羊學 ── 經學を中心として ── (Kung Tzu-chen and *Ch'un-ch'iu Kung-yang* studies—From the perspective of classical studies), *Aichi kyōiku daigaku kenkyū hōkoku* 愛知教育大学研究報告 24:1-12 (March 1975).

Jackson, John A., ed. *Professions and Professionalization.* Cambridge, Cambridge University Press, 1970.

Johnson, Francis. "Gresham College: Precursor of the Royal Society," *Roots of Scientific Thought: A Cultural Perspective.* Eds., Philip Wiener and Aaron Noland. New York, Basic Books, 1958.

Jones, Susan Mann. "Scholasticism and Political Thought in Late Eighteenth-Century China," *Ch'ing-shih wen-t'i* 3.4:28–49 (December 1975).

——. "Finance in Ningpo: The 'Ch'ien Chuang,' 1750–1880," *Economic Organization in Chinese Society.* Ed., W. E. Willmot. Stanford, Stanford Univeristy Press, 1972.

—— and Philip Kuhn. "Dynastic Decline and the Roots of Rebellion," *The Cambridge History of China,* Vol. 10, Part 1. Ed. John Fairbank, Cambridge, Cambridge University Press, 1978.

Juan Chih-sheng 阮芝生. "Hsueh-an t'i-ts'ai yuan-liu ch'u-t'an 學案體裁源流初探 (Preliminary inquiry into the history of scholarship form), *Shih-yuan* 史原 2:57–75 (October 1971).

Juan Yuan 阮元. *Yen-ching-shih chi* 揅經室集 (Collection from the Studio for the Investigation of Classics). 3 vols. Taipei, Shih-chieh shu-chü, 1964.

——. *Ch'ou-jen chuan* 疇人傳 (Biographies of mathematical astronomers). 2 vols. Taipei, Shih-chieh shu-chü, 1962.

——. "Hsu" 序 (Introduction). *Wei-ching-chai i-shu* 味經齋遺書 (Bequeathed writings from the Study of Appealing Classics). Chuang Ts'un-yü 莊存與 . 1882 Yang-hu, Kiangsu, edition.

Jung Chao-tsu 容肇祖. *Ming-tai ssu-hsiang-shih* 明代思想史 (History of thought in the Ming period). Taipei, K'ai-ming shu-tien, 1969.

——. "Hsueh-hai T'ang k'ao" 學海堂考 (Analysis of the Hsueh-hai T'ang), *Ling-nan hsueh-pao* 嶺南學報 3.4:1–147 (June 1934).

Kahn, Harold. *Monarchy in the Emperor's Eyes: Image and Reality in the Ch'ien-lung Reign.* Cambridge, Harvard University Press, 1971.

K'ang Yu-wei 康有為 . *K'ung-tzu kai-chih k'ao* 孔子改制考 (Confucius as reformer). Peking, Chung-hua shu-chü, 1958.

——. *Kuang I-chou shuang-chi* 廣藝舟雙輯 (Enlargement of [Pao Shih-ch'en's] collection of parallel comments on the vessels of artistic expression). Shanghai, Kuang-i shu-chü, 1916.

Karlgren, Bernhard. "On the Script of the Chou Dyansty," *Bulletin of the Museum of Far Eastern Antiquities* 8:157–178 (1936).

——. *Grammata Serica.* Taipei, Ch'eng Wen Reprint, 1966.

Kawata Teiichi 河田悌一 . "Shindai gakujutsu no ichi sokumen" 清代學術の一側面 (Sidelights on scholarship in the Ch'ing period), *Tōhōgaku* 東方學 57:84–105 (January 1979).

——. "Dōjidaijin no nemuri—Shō Gakusei no Tai Shin kan" 同時代人の眼—章學誠の戴震觀 (The sense of contemporaries for each other—Chang Hsueh-ch'eng's view of Tai Chen), *Chūgoku tetsugaku shi no tembō to mosaku* 中國哲學史の展望と摸索 (Prospects and directions in the history of Chinese philosophy). Compiled by the Committee in Commemoration of Professor Kimura Eiichi 木村英一 Tokyo, Sōbunsha, 1976.

——. "Shimmatsu no Tai Shin zō—Ryū Shibai no bai" 清末の戴震像—劉師培の場合 (The image of Tai Chen in the late Ch'ing—The case of Liu Shih-p'ei). *Tōyōgaku ronshū* 東洋學論集 (Collected essays on Eastern studies). Compiled by the Committee in Commemoration of Professor Mori Mikasaburō 森三樹三郎 . Kyoto, Hōyū shoten, 1979.

Kearney, H. F. "Puritanism, Capitalism, and the Scientific Revolution," *Past and Present* 28:81–101 (July 1964).

Kelley, Donald. *Foundations of Modern Historical Scholarship: Language, Law, and History in the French Renaissance.* New York, Columbia University Press, 1970.

Kermode, Frank. *The Classic: Literary Images of Permanence and Change.* New York, Viking Press, 1975.

Kessler, Lawrence. "Chinese Scholars and the Early Manchu State," *HJAS* 31:179–200 (1971).

——. *K'ang-hsi and the Consolidation of Ch'ing Rule, 1661-1684.* Chicago, University of Chicago Press, 1976.

Kinoshita Tetsuya 木下鐵矢 . "Tai Shin no ongaku—sono taishō to ninshiki" 戴震の音學その對象と認識 (Tai Chen's phonology—Its objectives and realizations), *Tōhōgaku* 東方學 58:128-142 (July 1979).

Koita Natsujirō 小糸夏次郎 . "Shinchō kōkyogaku no haikei" 清朝考據學の背景 (The background of evidential research studies in the Ch'ing dynasty), *Kokumin seishin bunka* 國民精神文化 1.1:30-49 (1935).

Kondo Mitsuo 近滕光男 . "Kangaku shijoki no bunshō" 漢學師承記の文章 (The composition of *The Record of Han-Learning Masters*), *Jimbun ronkyū* 人文論究 (Hokkaido University) 17:1-24 (June 1957).

——. "Ō Chū to *Kokushi Jurinden kō*" 汪中と国史儒林伝稿 (*Draft Biographies of Confucians in Ch'ing History* and Wang Chung), *Jimbun kagaku ronshū* 人文科學論集 (Hokkaido University) 3:64-89 (1964).

——. "Kei Tō to Sen Daikin" 惠棟と錢大昕 (Hui Tung and Ch'ien Ta-hsin). *Yoshikawa hakusei taikyū kinen Chūgoku bungaku ronshū* 吉川博士退休記念中國文學論集 (Studies in Chinese literature dedicated to Dr. Yoshikawa [Kōjirō] on his 65th birthday). Tokyo, Chikuma shobō, 1968.

——. "Sen Daikin no bungaku" 錢大昕の文學 (Ch'ien Ta-hsin's literature), *Tōkyō Shinagaku hō* 東京支那學報 7:18-34 (1961), and 8:60-76 (1962).

——. "Shinchō keishi ni okeru kagaku ishiki—Tai Shin no hokkyoku senki shiyū kai o chūshin to shite" 清朝經師における科學意識—戴震の北極睿機四澈解を中心として—(The scientific consciousness of Ch'ing classicists—A focus on Tai Chen's explication of the rotation of the celestial North Pole), *Nihon Chūgoku gakkai hō* 日本中國學會報 4:97-110 (1952).

——. "Tai Shin no *Kōko kizu* ni tsuite—Kagaku shisōshi teki kōsatsu" 戴震の考工記図について — 科學思想史的考察 (Concerning Tai Chen's drawings for the "Record of Technology"—A Study from the viewpoint of the history of scientific thought), *Tōhōgaku* 東方學 11:1-22 (1955).

Koyasu Shichishirō 宇安七四郎 . "Chō Yoku no shōgai to sono shigaku shisō ni tsuite" 趙翼の生涯とその史學思想について (Chao I's life and his historical thought), *Shigaku kenkyū* 史學研究 3.41:85-100 (October 1950).

Kracke, E. A., Jr. "Sung Society: Change Within Tradition," *Enduring Scholarship Selected from the Far Eastern Quarterly—The Journal of Asian Studies 1941-1971.* Ed., John Harrison. Tucson, University of Arizona Press, 1972.

Kramers, R.P. *K'ung Tzu Chia Yü: The School Sayings of Confucius.* Leiden, E.J. Brill, 1950.

Kratochvil, Paul. "Traditions in Chinese Linguistics Fact or Fiction?" *Cahiers de linguistique Asie Orientale* 1:17–30 (March 1977).

Ku Chieh-kang 顧頡剛 et al. *Ku-shih-pien* 古史辨 (Debates on ancient history). 7 vols. Peking and Shanghai, Chih-ch'eng yin-shu-kuan, 1926–1941.

——. *Han-tai hsueh-shu shih lueh* 漢代學術史略 (Intellectual history of the Han period, A summary). Taipei, Yuan-ta yin-shu-ch'ang Reprint, 1972.

——. "A Study of Literary Persecution During the Ming." Translated by L.C. Goodrich. *HJAS* 3:254–311 (1938).

Ku Kuo-shun 古國順 . "Ch'ing-tai *Shang-shu* chu-shu k'ao (shang, hsia)" 清代尚書著書考(上,下)(Analysis of works on the *Documents* in the Ch'ing, 1 and 2), *Nü-shih chuan-hsueh pao* 女師專學報 (Taipei), 10:145–237 (1978), 11:177–271 (1979).

Ku-ching ching-she wen-chi 詁經精舍文集 (Prose collection of the Ku-ching-she). Eds., Juan Yuan 阮元 et al. Taipei, Commercial Press, 1966.

Ku Yen-wu 顧炎武 . *Jih-chih lu* 日知錄 (Record of knowledge gained day by day). Taipei, P'ing-p'ing ch'u-pan-she, 1974.

——. *Ku T'ing-lin shih-wen chi* 顧亭林詩文集 (Ku Yen-wu's collected essays and poems). Hong Kong, Chung-hua shu-chü, 1976.

——. *Ch'iu-ku lu* 求古錄 (Record of the search for antiquity). *T'ing-lin hsien-sheng i-shu hui-chi* 亭林先生遺書彙輯 (Composite collection of Ku Yen-wu's bequeathed writings). Shanghai, Chiao-ching shan-fang edition, 1888.

Kuei Chuang 歸莊 . *Kuei Chuang chi* 歸莊集 (Collected writings of Kuei Chuang). 2 vols. Peking, Chung-hua shu-chü, 1962.

Kuhn, Philip. *Rebellion and Its Enemies in Late Imperial China: Militarization and Social Structure, 1796–1864.* Cambridge, Harvard University Press, 1970.

Kuhn, Thomas. *The Structure of Scientific Revolutions.* 2nd edition. Chicago, University of Chicago Press, 1970.

——. *The Essential Tension: Selected Studies in Scientific Tradition and Change.* Chicago, University of Chicago Press, 1977.

Kung Tzu-chen 龔自珍 . *Kung Tzu-chen ch'üan-chi* 全集 (Complete works of Kung Tzu-chen). Shanghai, Jen-min ch'u-pan-she, 1975.

Kuo Po-kung 郭伯恭 . *Ssu-k'u ch'üan-shu tsuan-hsiu k'ao* 四庫全書纂修考 (Study of the compilation of the SKCS). Peking, Commercial Press, 1937.

Kurahashi Takeshirō 倉石武四郎 . "Shinchō shōgaku shiwa (ichi)" 清朝小學史話(一)(Discussion of the history of philology in the Ch'ing dynasty [1], *Kangakkai zasshi* 漢學會雜誌 10.3:1–15 (December 1942).

Lai, T.C. *Chinese Calligraphy: An Introduction.* Seattle, University of Washington Press, 1974.

Ledderhose, Lothar. *Mi Fu and the Classical Tradition of Chinese Calligraphy.* Princeton, Princeton University Press, 1979.

——. *Die Siegelschrift (Chuan-shu) in der Ch'ing-zeit: Ein Beitrag zur Geschichte der chinesischen Schriftkunst.* Wiesbaden, Franz Steiner, 1970.

Ledyard, Gari. "Korean Travellers in China Over Four Hundred Years, 1488–1887," *Occasional Papers on Korea* 2:1–42 (March 1974).

Legge, James, tr. *The Four Books.* New York, Paragon Book Reprint Corp., 1966.

——, tr. *The Shoo King or The Book of Historical Documents.* Taipei, Wen-shih-che ch'u-pan-she Reprint, 1972.

Leonard, Jane, "Wei Yuan and Images of the *Nan-yang*," *Ch'ing-shih wen-t'i* 4.1:23–57 (June 1979).

Leslie, Donald. "Local Gazetteers," *Essays on the Sources for Chinese History.* Eds., Donald Leslie, Colin Mackerras, & Wang Gungwu. Columbia, University of South Carolina Press, 1973.

Leung Man-kam. "Juan Yuan (1764–1849): The Life, Works, and Career of a Chinese Scholar-Bureaucrat." PhD dissertation, University of Hawaii, 1977.

Levenson, Joseph. *Confucian China and Its Modern Fate: A Trilogy.* Berkeley, University of California Press, 1968.

——. "Liao P'ing and the Confucian Departure From History," *Confucian Personalities.* Eds., Arthur Wright and Denis Twitchett. Stanford, Stanford University Press, 1962.

Lévy, André. "Un Document sur la querelle des anciens et des modernes *More Sinico*," *T'oung Pao* 54:251–274 (1968).

Lewis, Charlton. *Prologue to the Chinese Revolution: The Transformation of Ideas and Institutions in Hunan Province, 1891–1907.* Cambridge, Harvard University Press, 1976.

Li Chi. *Anyang.* Seattle, University of Washington Press, 1977.

Li Chih 李贄 . *Ts'ang-shu* 藏書 (A book to be hidden away). Peking, Chung-hua shu-chü, 1959.

Li Yuan-keng 李元庚 . "Wang She hsing-shih k'ao" 望社姓氏考 (Studies of the participants in the Wang She), *Kuo-ts'ui hsueh-pao* 國粹學報 71 (September 1910): 1a–10b (shih-p'ien wai 史篇外).

Li Yuan-tu 李元度 . *Kuo-ch'ao hsien-cheng shih-lueh* 國朝先正事略 (Survey of earlier upright scholars of the Ch'ing dynasty). SPPY edition.

Liang Ch'i-ch'ao 梁啟超 . *Ku-shu chen-wei chi ch'i nien-tai* 古書真偽 及其年代 (Authenticity and dating of ancient works). Taipei, Chung-hua shu-chü, 1973.

——. *Chung-kuo chin san-pai-nien hsueh-shu-shih* 中國近三百年學術史 (Intellectual history of China during the last 300 years). Taipei, Chung-hua shu-chü, 1955.

——. *Intellectual Trends in the Ch'ing Period.* Translated by Immanuel Hsu. Cambridge, Harvard University Press, 1959.

Libbrecht, Ulrich. *Chinese Mathematics in the Thirteenth Century: The Shu-shu chiu-chang of Ch'in Chiu-shao*. Cambridge, MIT Press, 1973.

Liu Feng-lu 劉逢祿. *Shang-shu chin-ku-wen chi-chieh* 尚書今古文集解 (Collected notes to the New and Old Text *Documents*). 2 vols. Taipei, Commercial Press, 1977.

——. *Ch'un-ch'iu Kung-yang ching Ho-shih shih-li* 春秋公羊經何氏釋列 (Explication of the precedents in Master Ho [Hsiu's] *Kung-yang* Classic of the *Ch'un-ch'iu*). HCCC collection.

——. *Tso-shih ch'un-ch'iu k'ao-cheng* 左氏春秋考證 (Evidential analysis of *Master Tso's Spring and Autumn Annals*). HCCC collection.

Liu I-cheng 柳詒徵. "Chiang-su shu-yuan chih ch'u-kao" 江蘇書院志初稿 (Preliminary draft of a gazetteer of Kiangsu academies), *Kuo-hsueh t'u-shu-kuan nien-k'an* 國學圖書館年刊 4:1–112 (1931).

Liu, James T. C. "How Did a Neo-Confucian School Become the State Orthodoxy?," *Philosophy East and West* 23.4:483–505 (1973).

——. *Ou-yang Hsiu: An Eleventh-Century Neo-Confucianist*. Stanford, Stanford University Press, 1967.

Liu Kwang-ching. "The Ch'ing Restoration," *The Cambridge History of China,* Vol. 10, Part 1. Ed., John Fairbank, Cambridge, Cambridge University Press, 1978.

Liu Po-chi 劉伯驥. *Kuang-tung shu-yuan chih-tu* 廣東書院制度 (The academy system in Kwangtung). Hong Kong, Chi-sheng Book Co., 1958.

Lo Chen-yü 羅振玉. *Yü-chien-chai ts'ung-shu* 玉簡齋叢書 (Collectanea from the study of precious texts). *Lo Hsueh-t'ang hsien-sheng ch'üan-chi* 羅雪堂先生全集 (Complete writings of Mr. Lo Chen Yü). Taipei, Wen-hua chu-pan kung-ssu, 1970, 3:14, etc.

Lo Ping-mien 羅炳綿. "Chang Shih-chai te chiao-ch'ou lun chi ch'i yen-pien" 章實齋的校讐論及其演變 (Chang Hsueh-ch'eng's theories of bibliography and their development), *Hsin-Ya shu-yuan hsueh-shu nien-k'an* 新亞書院學術年刊 8:77–95 (1966).

Lo, Winston, "Philology, An Aspect of Sung Rationalism," *Chinese Culture* 17.4:1–26 (December 1976).

Loewe, Michael. *Crisis and Conflict in Han China: 104 B.C. to A.D. 9.* London, Allen & Unwin, 1974.

Lu Hsiang-shan 陸象山. *Hsiang-shan ch'üan-chi* 象山全集 (Lu Hsiang-shan's complete works). SPPY edition.

Lu Pao-ch'ien 陸寶千. *Ch'ing-tai ssu-hsiang-shih* 清代思想史 (History of thought in the Ch'ing period). Taipei, Kuang-wen shu-chü, 1978.

Lu Wen-ch'ao 盧文弨. *Pao-ching T'ang wen-chi* 抱經堂文集 (Collected writings from the Hall for Cherishing the Classics). Shanghai, Commercial Press, 1937.

Lun Ming 倫明. "Hsu-shu-lou tu-shu chi" 續書樓讀書記 (Reading notes from the Pavilion of Continuous Books), *Yen-ching hsueh-pao* 燕京學報 3:457–511 (1928).

Lun-yü yin-te 論語引得 (Concordance to the *Analects*). Taipei, Ch'eng Wen Reprint, 1966.

Lung Mu-tsun 龍木勛 . "Lun Ch'ang-chou tz'u-p'ai" 論常州詞派 (On the Ch'ang-chou school of Tz'u), *T'ung-sheng* 同聲 1.10:1–20 (September 1941).

Ma Yü-tsao 馬裕藻 . "Tai Tung-yuan tui-yü ku-yin-hsueh te kung-hsien" 戴東原對於古音學的貢獻 (Tai Chen's contribution to the study of ancient pronunciation), *Kuo-hsueh chi-k'an* 國學季刊 2.2:205–235 (December 1929).

McKenna, Stephen and Victor Mair. "A Reordering of the Hexagrams of the *I Ching*," *Philosophy East and West* 29.4:421–441 (October 1979).

Mackerras, Colin. *The Rise of the Peking Opera, 1770–1870: Social Aspects of the Theatre in Manchu China.* Oxford, Clarendon Press, 1972.

McLuhan, Marshall. *The Gutenburg Galaxy: The Making of Typographical Man.* Toronto, University of Toronto Press, 1962.

Mann, Albert. "Cheng Ch'iao: An Essay in Re-evaluation," *Transition and Permanence: Chinese History and Culture.* Eds., David Buxbaum and Frederick Mote. Hong Kong, Cathay Press, 1972.

Mao Ch'i-ling 毛奇齡 . *Hsi-ho ho-chi* 西河合集 (Combined collection of Mao Ch'i-ling). Compiled by Li Kung 李塨 et al. K'ang-hsi edition, ca. 1699.

——. *Ku-wen Shang-shu yuan-tz'u* 古文尚書冤詞 (In defense of the Old Text *Documents*). *Hsi-ho ho-chi* collection.

Maruyama, Masao. *Studies in the Intellectual History of Tokugawa Japan.* Translated by Mikiso Hane. Princeton, Princeton University Press, 1974.

Maspero, Henri. "La Composition et la date du *Tso tchouan*," *Mélanges Chinois et buddhiques* 1:137–215 (1931–1932).

Mei, Tsu-lin and Jerry Norman. "The Numeral 'Six' in Old Chinese," *Studies in General and Oriental Linguistics.* Eds., Roman Jacobson and Shigeo Kawamoto. Tokyo, TEC Co., 1970.

Mendelsohn, Everett. "The Emergence of Science as a Profession in 19th-Century Europe," *The Management of Scientists.* Ed., Karl Hill. Boston, Beacon Press, 1964.

Merton, Robert. *The Sociology of Science: Theoretical and Empirical Investigations.* Ed., Norman Storer. Chicago, University of Chicago Press, 1973.

Meskill, Johanna. "The Chinese Genealogy as a Research Source," *Family and Kinship in Chinese Society.* Ed., Maurice Freedman. Stanford, Stanford University Press, 1970.

Meskill, John. "Academies and Politics in the Ming Dynasty," *Chinese Government in Ming Times: Seven Studies.* Ed., Charles Hucker. New York, Columbia University Press, 1969.

——. *Academies in Ming China: A Historical Essay.* Tucson, University of Arizona Press, 1982.

Metzger, Thomas. *The Internal Organization of the Ch'ing Bureaucracy: Legal, Normative, and Communication Aspects.* Cambridge, Harvard University Press, 1973.

——. "The Organizational Capabilities of the Ch'ing State in the Field of Commerce: The Liang-Huai Salt Monopoly, 1740–1840," *Economic Organization in Chinese Society*. Ed., W. E. Willmot. Stanford, Stanford University Press, 1972, pp. 9–45.

——. *Escape From Predicament: Neo-Confucianism and China's Evolving Political Culture*. New York, Columbia University Press, 1977.

Miller, Roy A. "Some Japanese Influences on Chinese Classical Scholarship of the Ch'ing Period," *Journal of the American Oriental Society* 72:56–67 (1952).

Mitchell, Peter. "The Limits of Reformism: Wei Yuan's Reaction to Western Intrusion," *Modern Asian Studies* 6.2:175–204 (1972).

——. "A Further Note on the HCCSWP," *Ch'ing-shih wen-t'i* 2.3:40–46 (1970).

Miyazaki Ichisada 宮崎市定 . "Min-Shin jidai no Soshū to keikōgyō no hattatsu" 明清時代の蘇州と輕工業の発達 (Development of light industry and Soochow in the Ming-Ch'ing period). *Ajia shi kenkyū* アジア史研究 (Researches on Asian history). Kyoto, Tōyōshi kenkyūkai, 1964, Vol. 4, pp. 306–320.

——. "Mindai So-Shō chihō no shidaifu to minshū" 明代蘇頌地方の士大夫と民衆 (Local gentry and the common people in Ming-period Soochow and Sung-chiang), *Shirin* 史林 33.3:219–251 (June 1954).

——. "Tōyō no Renaissance to Seiyō no Renaissance" 東洋のルネッサンスと西洋のルネッサンス (The Eastern Renaissance and the Western Renaissance), *Shirin* 25.4:465–480 (1942) and 26.1:69–102 (1943).

——. "Shisho kōshōgaku" 四書考證学 (Evidential research studies of the Four Books). *Ajia shi kenkyū*, Vol. 4, pp. 379–387.

Mote, Frederick. "A Millennium of Chinese Urban History: Form, Time, and Space Concepts in Soochow," *Rice University Studies* 59.4:33–65 (Fall 1973).

——. "The Arts and the 'Theorizing Mode' of the Civilization," *Artists and Traditions: Uses of the Past in Chinese Culture*. Ed., Christian Murck. Princeton, Princeton University Press, 1976.

Murayama Yoshihiro 村山吉広 . "Yō Seikō no gakumon (jō, chū, ge)" 姚際恒の学問 (Yao Chi-heng's scholarship, 1–3), *Kambungaku kenkyū* 漢文学研究 7:77–94 (1959), 8:34–46 (1960), and 9:15–35 (1961).

Naitō Torajirō 内藤虎次郎 . "Shina gakumon no kinjō" 支那学問の近状 (Recent state of Chinese scholarship). *Naitō Konan zenshū* 湖南全集 (Complete works of Naitō Torajirō). 13 vols. Tokyo, Chikuma shobō, 1969–1974, Vol. 6, pp. 48–66.

——. *Shinchōshi tsūron* 清朝史通論 (Outline of Ch'ing History). *Naitō Konan zenshū*, Vol. 8.

——. *Shina shigaku shi* 支那史学史 (History of Chinese historiography). *Naitō Konan zenshū*, Vol. 11.

Najita, Tetsuo and Irwin Scheiner, eds. *Japanese Thought in the Tokugawa Period:*

Methods and Metaphors. Chicago, University of Chicago Press, 1978.

Nakamura Kyūshirō 中村久四郎 . "Shinchō gakujutsu shisō shi" 清朝 學術思想史 (History of thought and scholarship in the Ch'ing dynasty), *Tō A kenkyū* 東亞研究 (1) 2.11:49–53 (November 1912); (2) 2.12:20–26 (December 1912); (3) 3.1:38–42 (January 1913); (4) 3.2:42–47 (February 1913); (5) 3.5:9–15 (May 1913); (6) 3.8:30–40 (August 1913).

Nakayama, Shigeru. *A History of Japanese Astronomy.* Cambridge, Harvard University Press, 1969.

Naquin, Susan. *Millenarian Rebellion in China: The Eight Trigrams Uprising of 1813.* New Haven, Yale University Press, 1976.

Needham, Joseph et al. *Science and Civilization in China.* 5 vols. Cambridge, Cambridge University Press, 1954– .

Nishi Junzō 西順藏 . "Tai Shin no hōhō shiron" 戴震の方法試論 (Analysis of Tai Chen's methods), *Tōkyō Shinagaku hō* 東京支那学報 1:130–145 (June 1955).

Nivison, David. *The Life and Thought of Chang Hsueh-ch'eng (1738–1801).* Stanford, Stanford University Press, 1966.

Nomura Kōichi 野村浩一 . "Shimmatsu Kuyōgakuha no keisei to Kō Yūi gaku no rekishi teki igi (ichi)" 清末公羊学派の形成と康有為学の歴史的意義 (一) (The formation of the Late Ch'ing *Kung-yang* school and the historical significance of K'ang Yu-wei [1]), *Kokka gakkai zasshi* 國家学會雑誌 71.7:1–61 (July 1957).

Numata Jiro. "Shigeno Yasutsugu and the Modern Tokyo Tradition of Historical Writing," *Historians of China and Japan.* Eds., W.G. Beasley and E.G. Pulleyblank. Oxford, Oxford University Press, 1961.

Ogawa Yoshiko 小川嘉子 . "Shindai ni okeru gigaku setsuritsu no kiban" 清代における義学設立の基盤 (The basis for the establishment of charity schools in the Ch'ing period). *Kinsei Chūgoku kyōiku kenkyū* 近代中国教育研究 (Research on education in early modern China). Ed., Hayashi Tomoharu. Tokyo, Kokutosha, 1958.

Okada Takehiko 岡田武彦 . "Chō Yōen to Riku Futei" 張楊園と陸桴亭 (Chang Li-hsiang and Lu Shih-i), *Teoria* テオリア 9:1–30 (December 1965).

Ōkubo Eiko 大久保英子 . "Mimmatsu dokushojin kessha to kyōiku katsudō" 明末読書人結社と教育活動 (Societies of intellectuals in the late Ming and educational behavior). *Kinsei Chūgoku kyōiku kenkyū* 近世中國教育研究 (Research on education in early modern China). Ed., Hayashi Tomoharu. Tokyo, Kokutosha, 1958.

——. *Min-Shin jidai shoin no kenkyū* 明清時代書院の研究 (Research on academies in the Ming-Ch'ing period). Tokyo, Kokusho kankōkai, 1976.

Ono Kazuko 小野和子 . "Mimmatsu no kessha ni kan suru ichi kōsatsu (jō & ge)" 明末の結社に関する一考察（上下） (Overview

of late Ming societies, 1 and 2), *Shirin* 史林 45.2:37–67 (March 1962) and
45.3:67–92 (May 1962).

——. "Mimmatsu Shinsho ni okeru chishikijin no seiji kōdō" 明末清初に
おける知識人の政治行動 (Political behavior of in-
tellectuals in the late Ming and early Ch'ing), *Sekai no rekishi 11: Yuragu
Chūka teikoku* 世界の歴史 11：ゆうぐ中華帝國
(History of the world, volume 11: Decline of imperial China). Tokyo, Chikuma
shobō, 1961.

——. "Shinsho no shisō tōsei o megutte" 清初の思想統制をめぐっ
て (Thought control in the early Ch'ing), *Tōyōshi kenkyū* 東洋史
研究 18.3:99–123 (December 1959).

——. "Gan Gen no gakumon ron" 顔元の學問論 (Yen Yuan's view of
learning), *Tōhōgaku hō* 41:467–490 (March 1970).

——. "Shinsho no Kōkeikai ni tsuite" 清初の講經會について
(Concerning the Society for the Discussion of the Classics in the early Ch'ing),
Tōhōgaku hō 36:633–661 (1964).

——. "Jukyō no itanshatachi" 儒教の異端者たち (Heterodox Confucian scholars). *Taidō suru Ajia* 胎動するアジア (Asia in transition). Ed., Matsumoto Sannosuke 松本三之介 . Tokyo, Heibonsha,
1966.

Onozawa Seiichi 小野決精一 et al., eds. *Ki no shisō: Chūgoku ni okeru
shizenkan to ningenkan no tenkai* 氣の思想・中國における自
然観と人間観の展開 (The idea of Ch'i: The develop-
ment of a view of nature and man). Tokyo, Tokyo University Press, 1978.

Ornstein, Martha. *The Role of Scientific Societies in the Seventeenth Century.*
Chicago, University of Chicago, 1928.

Ōtani Toshio 大谷敏夫 . "Gi Gen keisei shisō kō" 魏源經世思想
考 (Analysis of Wei Yuan's statecraft ideas), *Shirin* 史林 54.6:33–75
(November 1971).

Peterson, Willard. "The Life of Ku Yen-wu (1613–1682)," *HJAS* 28:114–156
(1968), 29:201–247 (1969).

——. "Fang I-chih: Western Learning and the 'Investigation of Things.'" *The
Unfolding of Neo-Confucianism.* Wm. T. de Bary et al. New York, Columbia
University Press, 1975.

——. "Western Natural Philosophy Published in Late Ming China," *Proceedings
of the American Philosophical Society* 117.4:295–322 (August 1973).

——. *Bitter Gourd: Fang I-chih and the Impetus For Intellectual Change.* New
Haven, Yale University Press, 1979.

P'i Hsi-jui 皮錫瑞 . *Ching-hsueh li-shih* 經學歷史 (History of classical
studies). Annotated by Chou Yü-t'ung 周予同 . Hong Kong, Chung-
hua shu-chü, 1961.

Polachek, James. "Literati Groups and Group Politics in Nineteenth-Century
China." PhD dissertation, Berkeley, University of California, 1977.

——. "Gentry Hegemony: Soochow in the T'ung-chih Restoration," *Conflict and Control in Late Imperial China*. Eds., Frederic Wakeman and Carolyn Grant. Berkeley, University of California Press, 1975.

Pulleyblank, Edwin G. "Neo-Confucianism and Neo-Legalism in T'ang Intellectual Life, 755–805," *The Confucian Persuasion*. Ed., Arthur Wright. Stanford, Stanford University Press, 1960.

Rawski, Evelyn. *Education and Popular Literacy in Ch'ing China*. Ann Arbor, Center for Chinese Studies, University of Michigan, 1979.

——. *Agricultural Change and the Peasant Economy of South China*. Cambridge, Harvard University Press, 1972.

Riegel, Jeffrey. "Some Notes on the Ch'ing Reconstruction of Lost Pre-Han Philosophical Texts," *Selected Papers in Asian Studies* 1:172–185 (1976).

Rosthorn, A. von. "The *Erh-ya* and Other Synonymicons," translated by Ernst Wolff, *Journal of the Chinese Language Teachers Association* 10.3:137–145 (October 1975).

Rudolph, R.C. "Chinese Movable Type Printing in the Eighteenth Century," *Silver Jubilee Volume of the Zinbun-kagaku-kenkyuso*. Ed., Kaizuka Shigeki. Kyoto, Institute of Humanistic Studies, 1954.

——. "Preliminary Notes on Sung Archaeology," *Journal of Asian Studies* 22:169–177 (1963).

Said, Edward. *Orientalism*. New York, Vintage Books, 1979.

——. *Beginnings: Intention and Method*. Baltimore, Johns Hopkins University Press, 1975.

——. "Linguistics and the Archaeology of Mind," *International Philosophical Quarterly* 11.1:104–134 (March 1971).

Sakade Yoshinobu 坂出祥神 . "Gi Gen shisō shiron" 魏源思想試論 (Analysis of Wei Yuan's thought), *Kaitoku* 懷德 35:33–52 (1964).

——. "Hō Ichi no shisō" 方以智の思想 (Fang I-chih's thought), *Min-Shin jidai no kagaku gijutsu shi*. Eds., Yabuuchi and Yoshida. Kyoto, Institute of Humanistic Studies, 1970.

Sakai Tadao 酒井忠夫 . "Shinchō kōshōgaku no genryū" 清朝考證學の源流 (Origins of Ch'ing evidential research scholarship), *Rekishi kyōiku* 歷史教育 5.11:28–34 (1957).

——. "Confucianism and Popular Education Works," *Self and Society in Ming Thought*. Wm. T. de Bary et al. New York, Columbia University Press, 1970.

Satō Shinji 佐藤震二 . "Gi Gen no gakumon to shisō" 魏源の學問と思想 (Wei Yuan's learning and thought), *Chūgoku koten kenkyū* 中國古典研究 12:24–40 (December 1964).

——. "Kō Ryōkitsu no shisō teki seikaku" 洪亮吉の思想の性格 (The structure of Hung Liang-chi's thought), *Academy* アカデミ 9:119–148 (January 1955).

Schirokauer, Conrad. "Neo-Confucianism Under Attack: The Condemnation of *Wei-hsueh*," *Crisis and Prosperity in Sung China*. Ed., John Haeger. Tucson, University of Arizona Press, 1975.

Schneider, Lawrence. *Ku Chieh-kang and China's New History*. Berkeley, University of California Press, 1971.

Schwartz, Benjamin. "Foreword," *Intellectual Trends in the Ch'ing Period*. Liang Ch'i-ch'ao, pp. xi–xxii.

Scott, Sir William H. "Yangchow and Its Eight Eccentrics," *Asiatische Studien* 1-2:1–19 (1964–1965).

Shang-shu t'ung-chien 尚書通檢 (Concordance to the *Documents*). Compiled by Ku Chieh-kang 顧頡剛. Taipei, Chinese Materials and Research Aids Service Center Reprint, 1966.

Shang Yueh 尚鉞. *Chung-kuo tzu-pen chu-i kuan-hsi fa-sheng chi yen-pien te ch'u-pu yen-chiu* 中國資本主義關係發生及演變的初步研究 (Preliminary studies of the appearance and development related to Chinese capitalism). Peking, San-lien shu-tien, 1956.

Shao Ch'ang-heng 邵長蘅. "Ch'uan-shih-lou chi" 傳是樓記 (Record of the Pavilion for the Transmission of Truth). *Lo Hsueh-t'ang hsien-sheng ch'üan-chi*. Lo Chen-yü. 3.14:5868–5871.

Sheng Lang-hsi 盛朗西. *Chung-kuo shu-yuan chih-tu* 中國書院制度 (The system of academies in China). Ching-mei, Taiwan, Hua-shih ch'u-pan-she, 1977.

Shera, Jesse, "An Epistemological Foundation for Library Science," *The Foundations of Access to Knowledge*. Ed., Edward Montgomery. Syracuse, Syracuse University Press, 1968.

Shimada Kenji 島田虔次. *Chūgoku ni okeru kindai shii no zasetsu* 中國に於ける近代思惟の挫折 (The frustration of modern thought in China). Tokyo, Chikuma shobō, 1970.

——. "Rekishi teki risei hihan–'Rikkei minna shi' no setsu" 歷史的理性批評 — 六經皆史の説 — (Criticism of historical reason—The theory that 'the Six Classics are all Histories'), *Iwanami kōza: tetsugaku* 岩波講座哲學 4:123-157 (1969).

——. "Shō Gakusei no ichi" 章學誠の位置 (Chang Hsueh-ch'eng's position), *Tōhōgaku hō* 東方學報 41:519-530 (March 1970).

Sivin, Nathan. "Wang Hsi-shan," *Dictionary of Scientific Biography*. 15 vols. New York: Scribner's Sons, 1970–1978, Vol. 14, pp. 159–168.

——. "Copernicus in China," *Colloquia Copernica II: Études sur l'audience de la théorie héliocentrique*. Warsaw, Union Internationale d'Historie et de Philosophie des Sciences, 1973.

——. "Social Relations of Curing in Traditional China: Preliminary Considerations," *Nihon ishigaku zasshi* 日本醫學雜誌 23.4:1-28 (October 1977).

Skinner, G. William, ed. *The City in Late Imperial China*. Stanford, Stanford University Press, 1977.

——. *Marketing and Social Structure in Rural China*. Reprinted from *Journal of*

Asian Studies 24.1:3–43 (November 1964), 2:195–228 (February 1965); 3:363–399 (May 1965).

Skinner, Quentin. *Foundations of Modern Political Thought.* 2 vols. Cambridge, Cambridge University Press, 1979.

Sohn Pow-key. "Early Korean Printing," *Journal of the American Oriental Society* 79:96–103 (1959).

Sokol, Robert. "Classification: Purposes, Principles, Progress, Prospects," *Thinking: Readings in Cognitive Science.* Eds., P.N. Johnson-Laird and P.C. Wason. Cambridge, Cambridge University Press, 1977.

Spence, Jonathan. "Chang Po-hsing and the K'ang-hsi Emperor," *Ch'ing-shih wen-t'i* 1.8:3–9 (1968).

——. "Opium Smoking in Ch'ing China," *Conflict and Control in Late Imperial China.* Eds., Wakeman and Grant. Berkeley, University of California Press, 1975.

——. "The Wan-li Period Vs. the K'ang-hsi Period: Fragmentation Vs. Reintegration?" *Artists and Traditions: Uses of the Past in Chinese Culture.* Ed., Christian Murck. Princeton, Princeton University Press, 1976.

——. "Tao-chi, An Historical Introduction," *The Painting of Tao-chi, 1641–ca. 1720.* Ann Arbor, Museum of Art, University of Michigan, 1967.

Ssu-k'u ch'üan-shu tsung-mu 四庫全書總目 (Catalog of the complete collection of the four treasuries). Chi Yun 紀昀 et al. 10 vols. Taipei, I-wen yin-shu-kuan Reprint, 1974.

Starr, Kenneth. "An 'Old Rubbing' of the Later Han *Chang Ch'ien pei*," *Ancient China: Studies in Early Civilization.* Eds., David Roy and T.H. Tsien. Hong Kong, Chinese University Press, 1978.

Storer, Norman and Talcott Parsons. "The Disciplines as a Differentiating Force," *The Foundations of Access to Knowledge.* Ed., Edward Montgomery. Syracuse, Syracuse University Press, 1968.

Struve, Lynn. "Uses of History in Traditional Chinese Society: The Southern Ming in Ch'ing Historiography." PhD dissertation, University of Michigan, 1974.

——. "Ambivalence and Action: Some Frustrated Scholars of the K'ang-hsi Period," *From Ming to Ch'ing: Conquest, Region, and Continuity in Seventeenth-Century China.* Eds., Jonathan Spence and John Wills. New Haven, Yale University Press, 1979.

Sullivan, Michael. "Art and Politics in Seventeenth-Century China," *Apollo* 103.170:231–235 (March 1976).

Sun Hsing-yen 孫星衍 et al. "Ku-ching ching-she t'i-ming-pei-chi" 詁經精舍題名碑記 (Inscriptional list of scholars and degree holders at the Ku-ching ching-she). *Ku-ching ching-she wen-chi*, pp. 1–6.

——. *Shang-shu chin-ku-wen chu-shu* 尚書今古文注疏 (Notes and annotations to the New and Old Text *Documents*). Taipei, Commercial Press, 1967.

——. *Sun-shih tz'u-t'ang shu-mu* 孫氏祠堂書目 (Catalog for the temple collection of the Sun lineage). Shanghai, Commercial Press, 1935.

Sun Ts'ung-t'ien 孫從添 . *Ts'ang-shu chi-yao* 藏書記要 (Bookman's manual). *Shu-ku ts'ung-ch'ao* 述古叢鈔 (Collectanea of works from [the Study] of Discourse on Antiquity). Compiled by Liu Wan-jung 劉晚榮 1871 Ts'ang-hsiu T'ang 藏脩堂 edition.

Suzuki Chūsei 鈴中正 . "Shimmatsu jōgai undō no kigen" 清末攘外 運動の起原 (Origins of the antiforeign movement in the late Ch'ing), *Shigaku zasshi* 史學雜誌 67.10:1–29 (October 1953).

Swann, Nancy Lee. "Seven Intimate Library Owners," *HJAS* 1:363–390 (1936).

Ta-Ch'ing i-t'ung-chih piao 大清一統志表 (Tables for the comprehensive geography of the great Ch'ing realm). Compiled by Hsu Wu 徐午 et al. Taipei, Hsin wen-feng ch'u-pan Reprint of 1794 Edition, 1975.

Taam, Cheuk-woon. *The Development of Chinese Libraries Under the Ch'ing Dynasty, 1644–1911.* Taipei, CMT Reprint Series, 1977.

Tai Chen 戴震 . *Meng-tzu tzu-i shu-cheng* 孟子字義疏證 (Evidential analysis of the meanings of terms in the *Mencius*). Appended to *Tai Tung-yuan te che-hsueh.* Hu Shih, pp. 37–157.

——. *Tung-yuan chi* 東原集 (Tai Chen's collected writings). SPPY edition.

——. *Tai Chen wen-chi* 文集 (Tai Chen's essays). Hong Kong, Chung-hua shu-chü, 1974.

Tai Chün-jen 戴君仁 . *Yen-Mao ku-wen Shang-shu kung-an* 閻毛古文 尚書公案 (The case of Yen Jo-chü versus Mao Ch'i-ling on the Old Text *Documents*). Hong Kong, Chi Sheng Book Co., 1963.

T'ai-yuan fu chih 太原府志 (T'ai-yuan prefectural gazetteer). 1783 edition.

T'ai-yuan hsien chih 太原縣志 (T'ai-yuan county gazetteer). 1731 and 1826 editions.

Takada Atsushi 高田淳 . "Shō Gakusei no shigaku shisō ni tsuite" 章學誠 の史學思想について (Concerning Chang Hsueh-ch'eng's historical thought), *Tōyōgaku hō* 東洋學報 47.1:61–93 (June 1964).

Takemura Noriyuki 竹村則行 . "Kenryū jidai to Kyō Jichin" 乾隆 時代と龔自珍 (The Ch'ien-lung era and Kung Tzu-chen), *Chūgoku bungaku ronshū* 中國文學論集 6:46–59 (1977).

T'ang Chien 唐鑑 . *Ch'ing hsueh-an hsiao-chih* 清學案小識 (Condensed history of scholarship in the Ch'ing). Taipei, Commercial Press, 1975.

T'ang Chün-i 唐君毅 . *Chung-kuo jen-wen ching-shen chih fa-chan* 中國 文人精神之發展 (Development of the humanistic spirit in China). Taipei, Hsueh-sheng shu-chü, 1974.

Te-ch'ing hsien hsu-chih 德清縣續志 (Continuation to the Te-ch'ing county gazetteer). 1808 edition.

Teng Chih-ch'eng 鄧之誠 . *Ch'ing-shih chi-shih ch'u-pien* 清詩紀事初 編 (Preliminary accounts concerning Ch'ing poetry affairs). 2 vols. Shanghai, Chung-hua shu-chü, 1965.

Teng Shih-ju chuan-shu 鄧石如篆書 (Teng shih-ju's seal calligraphy). Peking, Wen-wu ch'u-pan-she, 1982.

Teng, Ssu-yü. "Wang Fu-chih's Views on History and Historical Writing," *Journal of Asian Studies* 28.1:111–123 (November 1968).

—— and Knight Biggerstaff. *An Annotated Bibliography of Selected Chinese Reference Works*. Cambridge, Harvard University Press, 1971.

Thackray, Arnold and Robert Merton. "On Discipline-Building: The Paradoxes of George Sarton," *Isis* 63:473–495 (1972).

Tillman, Hoyt. *Utilitarian Confucianism: Ch'en Liang's Challenge to Chu Hsi*. Cambridge and London, Council on East Asian Studies, Harvard University, 1982.

Ting Wen-chiang 丁文江 . *Liang Jen-kung hsien-sheng nien-p'u ch'ang-pien ch'u-kao* 梁任公先生年譜長編初稿 (First draft of a chronological biography of Liang Ch'i-ch'ao). 2 vols. Taipei, Shih-chieh shu-chü, 1972.

Tsang Lin 臧琳. *Ching-i tsa-chi shu-lu* 經義雜記敘錄 (Writings from the jottings on the meaning of the Classics). 2 vols. Taipei, Chung-ting wen-hua ch'u-pan kung-ssu, 1967.

Ts'ao Yang-wu 曹養吾 . "Pien-wei-hsueh shih" 辨僞學史 (History of forgery detection). *Ku-shih-pien* 古史辨 . Ku Chieh-kang et al. Vol. 2. Peking and Shanghai, 1926–1941, pp. 388–416.

Tsien, Tsuen-hsuin. "A History of Bibliographical Classification in China," *The Library Quarterly* 22.4:307–324 (October 1952).

——. *Written on Bamboo and Silk*. Chicago, University of Chicago Press, 1962.

Tsou-p'ing hsien chih 鄒平縣志 (Gazetteer of Tsou-p'ing county). 1836 edition.

Tu Ching-i. "The Chinese Examination Essay: Some Literary Considerations," *Monumenta Serica* 31:393–406 (1974–1975).

Tu, Wei-ming. "'Inner Experience': The Basis of Creativity in Neo-Confucian Thinking," *Artists and Traditions: Uses of the Past in Chinese Culture*. Ed., Christian Murck. Princeton, Princeton University Press, 1976.

Tu Wei-yun 杜維運 . *Hsueh-shu yü shih-pien* 學術與世變 (Scholarship and epochal change). Taipei, Huan-yü ch'u-pan-she, 1971.

——. "Huang Tsung-hsi yü Ch'ing-tai Che-tung shih-hsueh-p'ai chih hsing-ch'i (shang)" 黃宗義與清代浙東史學派之興起 (上) (Huang Tsung-hsi and the rise of the Che-tung historical school (1)), *Ku-kung wen-hsien* 故宮文獻 2.3:1–13 (June 1971).

——. *Ch'ing Ch'ien-Chia shih-tai chih shih-hsueh yü shih-chia* 清乾嘉時代之史學與史家 (Historians and historical studies in the Ch'ien-lung and Chia-ch'ing eras). Taipei, Wen-shih ts'ung-k'an, 1962.

Tuan Yü-ts'ai 段玉裁 . *Ching-yun-lou chi* 經韵樓集 (Collection from the Pavilion of Classical Rhymes). *Tuan Yü-ts'ai i-shu* 段玉裁遺書 (Bequeathed writings of Tuan Yü-ts'ai). 2 vols. Taipei, Ta-hua shu-chü Reprint, 1977.

——. *Shuo-wen chieh-tzu chu* 説文解字注 (Notes for the *Analysis of Characters as an Explanation of Writing* [by Hsu Shen]). Taipei, I-wen yin-shu-kuan Reprint, 1973.

——. *Tai Tung-yuan (Chen) hsien-sheng nien-p'u* 戴東原(震)先生年譜 (Chronological biography of Tai Chen). Taipei, Wen-hai ch'u-pan-she Reprint, n.d

Turner, C. and M.N. Hodge. "Occupations and Professions," *Professions and Professionalization*. Ed., John Jackson.

Uno Seiichi 宇野精一. "*Shurai* Ryū Kin gisaku setsu ni tsuite" 周禮劉歆 僞作説について (On the theory that Liu Hsin forged the *Rites of Chou*), *Tō A ronsō* 東亞倫叢 5:237–273 (1941).

——. "Gokei kara Shisho e—Keigakushi oboegaki" 五經から四書へ— 經學史覺書 (From the Five Classics to the Four Books—Notes on the history of classical studies), *Tōyō no bunka to shakai* 東洋の文化と 社會 2:1–14 (March 1952).

Urabe Masanobu 浦邊正信 . "Chūgoku ni okeru taisei henkaku no ronri" 中國における体制変革の論理 (The logic of change in the state system in China), *Tōyō gakujutsu kenkyū* 東洋学術 研究 10.1:156–172 (April 1971).

Usami Kazuhiro 宇佐美一博 . "Kyō Jichin shisō shiron" 龔自珍 思想試論(Analysis of Kung Tzu-chen's thought), *Chūgoku kankei ronsetsu shiryō* 中國關係論説資料 17. 1A:549–557 (1975).

Vollmer, Howard and Donald Mills, eds. *Professionalization*. Englewood Cliffs, N.J., Prentice-Hall, 1966.

Wakeman, Frederic. "The Canton Trade and the Opium War," *The Cambridge History of China*, Vol. 10, Part 1. Ed., John Fairbank. Cambridge, Cambridge University Press, 1978.

——. "The Price of Autonomy: Intellectuals in Ming and Ch'ing Politics," *Daedalus* 101.2:35–70 (Spring 1972).

——. "The Huang-ch'ao ching-shih wen-pien," *Ch'ing-shih wen-t'i* 1.10:8–22 (1969).

——. "Localism and Loyalism During the Ch'ing Conquest of Kiangnan: The Tragedy of Chiang-yin," *Conflict and Control in Late Imperial China*. Eds., Frederic Wakeman and Carolyn Grant. Berkeley, University of California Press, 1975, pp. 43–85.

——. *The Fall of Imperial China*. New York, Free Press, 1975.

Waley, Arthur. *The Opium War Through Chinese Eyes*. Stanford, Stanford University Press, 1958.

——. *Yuan Mei: Eighteenth Century Chinese Poet*. Stanford, Stanford University Press, 1970.

——. *The Analects of Confucius*. New York, Vintage Books, n.d.

Wallacker, Benjamin. "Han Confucianism and Confucius in Han," *Ancient China: Studies in Early Civilization*. Eds., David Roy and T.H. Tsien. Hong Kong, Chinese University Press, 1978.

Walton-Vargö, Linda. "Education, Social Change, and Neo-Confucianism in Sung-

Yuan China: Academies and the Local Elite in Ming Prefecture (Ningpo)."
PhD dissertation, University of Pennsylvania, 1978.

Wan Ssu-t'ung 萬斯同. *Ch'ün-shu i-pien* 羣書疑辨 (Doubts and criticism of various books). 1816 Kung-shih-t'ing 供石亭 edition.

Wang Chung 汪中. *Shu-hsueh* 述學 (Discourses on learning). Taipei, Kuang-wen shu-chü Reprint, 1970.

Wang Fu-chih 王夫之. *Tu T'ung-chien lun* 讀通鑑論 (On reading the *Comprehensive Mirror*). Peking, Chung-hua shu-chü, 1975.

Wang Kuo-wei. "Archaeology in the Sung Dynasty." Translated by C.H. Liu. *Chinese Journal of Arts and Sciences* 6:222–231 (1927).

Wang Ming-sheng 王鳴盛. *Shih-ch'i-shih shang-ch'ueh* 十七史商榷 (Critical study of the *Seventeen Dynastic Histories*). Taipei, Kuang-wen shu-chü Reprint, 1960.

——. *I-shu pien* 蛾術編 (Chapters on the antlike [accumulation] of scholarship). Taipei, Hsin-i shu-chü Reprint, 1976.

Wang P'ing 王萍. "Ch'ing-ch'u li-suan-chia Mei Wen-ting" 清初曆算家梅文鼎 (Mei Wen-ting—Early Ch'ing calendrical scientist). *Chin-tai-shih yen-chiu-so chi-k'an* 近代史研究所集刊 (Bulletin of the Institute of Modern History). Taipei, Academia Sinica, 1971.

Wang Tsung-yen 汪宗衍. *Ch'en Tung-shu hsien-sheng nien-p'u* 陳東塾先生年譜 (Chronological biography of Ch'en Li). Hong Kong, Commercial Press, 1964.

Wang Yang-ming 王陽明. *Ch'uan-hsi lu* 傳習錄 (Record of transmitted cultivation). *Wang Yang-ming ch'üan-chi* 全集 (Complete works of Wang Yang-ming). Taipei, K'ao-cheng ch'u-pan-she, 1973.

Wang Yeh-chien. "The Impact of the Taiping Rebellion on Population in Southern Kiangsu," *Harvard University Papers on China* 19:120–158 (1964).

Wang Yeh-ch'iu 王冶秋. *Liu-li-ch'ang shih-hua* 琉璃廠史話 (Historical account of the Liu-li-ch'ang). Hong Kong, San-kuan shu-tien, 1979.

Watson, Burton, tr. *Hsun Tzu: Basic Writings*. New York, Columbia University Press, 1963.

Weber, Max. *The Religion of China*. Translated by Hans Gerth. New York, Macmillan, 1954.

Wei Yuan 魏源. *Ku-wei T'ang nei-wai chi* 古微堂內外集 (Outer and inner collection from the Hall of Ancient Subtleties). Taipei, Wen-hai ch'u-pan-she, 1966.

——. *Wei Yuan chi* 集 (Wei Yuan's collection). 2 vols. Peking, Chung-hua shu-chü, 1976.

Weng Fang-kang 翁方綱. *Fu-ch'u-chai wen-chi* 復初齋文集 (Collection from the Studio of the Return to Beginnings). 1877 edition.

White, Hayden. "Foucault Decoded: Notes From Underground," *History and Theory* 12:23–54 (1973).

——. *Tropics of Discourse: Essays in Cultural Criticism*. Baltimore, Johns Hopkins University Press, 1978.

Wieger, L. *Chinese Characters*. New York, Paragon Book Reprint, 1965.

Wilhelm, Hellmut. "The *Po-hsueh Hung-Ju* Examination of 1679," *Journal of the American Oriental Society* 71:60–66 (1951).

Wilkinson, Endymion. *The History of Imperial China: A Research Guide*. Cambridge, Harvard University, East Asian Research Center, 1973.

Wong Lok Ping 黃六平 . "Lu Wen-ch'ao *Ching-tien shih-wen Mao-shih yin-i k'ao-cheng* ting-pu" 盧文弨經典釋文毛詩音義考證訂補 (Supplementary notes on Lu Wen-ch'ao's *Evidential Analysis of the Phonetics of the Mao Poetry in* [Lu Te-ming's] *Explanation of Primary Graphs in the Classics*), *Journal of Oriental Studies* (Hong Kong), 8.2:289–301 (July 1970).

Wright, Mary. *The Last Stand of Chinese Conservatism: The T'ung-chih Restoration, 1862–1874*. Stanford, Stanford University Press, 1957.

Wu Che-fu. "The Development of Books in China," *Echo* 5.6:21–37 (June 1975), 5.7:48–59 (July 1975).

Wu-chin Yang-hu hsien ho-chih 武進陽湖縣合志 (Combined gazetteer of Wu-chin and Yang-hu counties). 1886 edition.

Wu Ching-tzu. *The Scholars*. Translated by Yang Hsien-yi and Gladys Yang. New York, Grosset & Dunlap, 1972.

Wu hsien chih 吳縣志 (Gazetteer of Wu [Soochow] county). 1933 edition.

Wu Hung-i 吳宏一 . *Ch'ing-tai shih-hsueh ch'u-t'an* 清代詩學初探 (Preliminary discussion of poetics in the Ch'ing period). Taipei, Mu-t'ung ch'u-pan-she, 1977.

Wu, Kwang Tsing. "Scholarship, Book Production, and Libraries in China, 618–1644." PhD dissertation, University of Chicago, 1944.

———. "The Development of Printing in China," *T'ien Hsia Monthly* 3:137–160 (September 1936).

———. "Ming Printing and Printers," *HJAS* 7:203–260 (1943).

Wu, Nelson. "Tung Ch'i-ch'ang (1555–1636): Apathy in Government and Fervor in Art," *Confucian Personalities*. Eds., Arthur Wright and Denis Twitchett. Stanford, Stanford University Press, 1962.

Wu, Silas. *Passage to Power: K'ang-hsi and His Heir Apparent, 1661–1722*. Cambridge, Harvard University Press, 1979.

Wylie, Alexander. *Notes on Chinese Literature*. Shanghai, Presbyterian Mission Press, 1867.

Yabuuchi Kiyoshi 藪內清 . *Chūgoku no kagaku to Nihon* 中國の科學と日本 (Chinese science and Japan). Tokyo, Asahi Shinbunsha, 1978.

——— and Yoshida Mitsukuni 吉田光邦 , eds. *Min-Shin jidai no kagaku gijutsu shi* 明清時代の科學技術史 (History of science and technology in the Ming and Ch'ing periods). Kyoto, Research Institute for Humanistic Studies, 1970.

———. "Min-Shin jidai no kagaku gijutsu shi" 明清時代の科学技術史

(History of science and technology in the Ming and Ch'ing periods). *Min-Shin jidai no kagaku gijutsu shi*, pp. 1–26.

——. "Tai Shin no rekisangaku" 戴震の暦算学 (Tai Chen's calendrical studies). *Min-Shin jidai no kagaku gijutsu shi*, pp. 27–34.

Yamanoi Yū 山井湧 . "Mimmatsu Shinsho ni okeru keisei chiyō no gaku" 明末清初における經世致用の学 (Practical statecraft studies in the late Ming and early Ch'ing), *Tōhōgaku ronshū* 東方学論集 1:136–150 (February 1954).

——. "Min-Shin jidai ni okeru 'ki' no tetsugaku" 明清時代における気の哲学 (The philosophy of *ch'i* in the Ming-Ch'ing period), *Tetsugaku zasshi* 哲学雜誌 46.711:82–103 (1951).

——. "*Mōshi jigi soshō* no seikaku" 孟子字義疏証の性格 (The nature of Tai Chen's *Meng-tzu tzu-i shu-cheng*), *Nihon Chūgoku gakkai hō* 日本中國学会報 12:108–126 (1960).

——. "Min-Shin no tetsugaku to shuyō" 明清の哲学と修養 (Ming-Ch'ing philosophy and moral cultivation), *Rekishi kyōiku* 歴史教育 2.11:82–88 (November 1954).

——. "Kō Sōgi no gakumon—Mingaku kara Shingaku e no ikō no ichi yōsō" 黄宗義の学問—明学から清学への移行の一様相 (Huang Tsung-hsi's scholarship—An example of the shift from Ming learning to Ch'ing learning), *Tōkyō Shinagaku hō* 東京支那学報 3:31–50 (1957).

——. "Ko Enbu no gakumon kan—'Mingaku kara Shingaku e no tenkan' no kanten kara" 顧炎武の学問観—明学から清学への転換の観点から (Ku Yen-wu's scholarly position—A perspective from 'the transition from Ming learning to Ch'ing learning'), *Chūō daigaku bugakubu kiyō* 中央大学文学部紀要 35:67–93 (1964).

——. "Mimmatsu Shinso shisō ni tsuite no ichi kōsatsu" 明末清初思想についての一考察 (An overview of late Ming and early Ch'ing thought), *Tōkyō Shinagaku hō* 東京支那学報 11:37–54 (1965).

Yang Hsiang-k'uei 楊向奎 . "Ch'ing-tai te chin-wen ching-hsueh" 清代的今文經學 (Ch'ing dynasty New Text classical studies), *Ch'ing-shih lun-ts'ung* 清史論叢 1:177–209 (Peking, 1979).

Yeh Te-hui 葉德輝 . *Ts'ang-shu shih-yueh* 藏書十約 (Bookman's decalogue). *Kuan-ku T'ang so-chu-shu* 觀古堂所著書 (Writings from [Yeh Te-hui's] Hall for Observing Antiquity). 1902 Changsha edition.

Yen Jo-chü 閻若璩 . *Shang-shu ku-wen shu-cheng* 尚書古文疏證 (Evidential analysis of the Old Text *Documents*). *Huang-Ch'ing ching-chieh hsu-pien* 皇清經解續編 (Ch'ing exegesis of the Classics, supplement) collection. Eds., Wang Hsien-ch'ien 王先謙 et al. 20 vols. Taipei, Fu-hsing shu-chü. Reprint, 1972.

——. *Shang-shu ku-wen shu-cheng.* 1796 Tientsin edition.

——. *Ch'ien-ch'iu cha-chi* 潛邱劄記 ([Yen] Ch'ien-ch'iu's reading notes). *Ssu-k'u ch'üan-shu chen-pen* 四庫全書珍本 . Taipei, Commercial Press, 1973.

Yen-Li ts'ung-shu 顏李叢書 (Collectanea of Yen Yuan and Li Kung). 4 vols. Taipei, Kuang-wen shu-chü Reprint, 1965.

Yoshikawa Kōjirō 吉川幸次郎 . "Sen Ken'eki to Shinchō keigaku" 錢謙益と清朝經學 (Ch'ien Ch'ien-i and Ch'ing dynasty classical studies), *Kyōto daigaku bungakubu kenkyū kiyō* 京都大学文学部研究紀要 9:1–82 (1965).

———. "Itō Jinsai," *Acta Asiatica* 25:22–53 (1973).

Yü Ying-shih 余英時 . "Ch'ing-tai ssu-hsiang-shih te i-ko hsin chieh-shih" 清代思想史的一個新解釋 (A new interpretation of the history of thought in the Ch'ing period). *Chung-kuo che-hsüeh ssu-hsiang lun-chi Ch'ing-tai p'ien* 中國哲學思想論集清代篇 (Collected essays on Chinese philosophy and thought, Ch'ing period volume). Yü Ying-shih et al. Taipei, Mu-t'ung ch'u-pan-she, 1977.

———. "Ts'ung Sung-Ming Ju-hsüeh te fa-chan lun Ch'ing-tai ssu-hsiang-shih" 從宋明儒學的發展論清代思想史 (Discussion of Ch'ing history of thought from the perspective of the development of Sung-Ming Confucianism), *Chung-kuo hsüeh-jen* 中國學人 2:19–41 (September 1970).

———. *Lun Tai Chen yü Chang Hsüeh-ch'eng* 論戴震與章學誠 (On Tai Chen and Chang Hsüeh-ch'eng). Hong Kong, Lung-men shu-tien, 1976.

———. "Some Preliminary Observations on the Rise of Ch'ing Confucian Intellectualism," *Tsing Hua Journal of Chinese Studies* 11:105–146 (1975).

Yuan Mei 袁枚 . *Hsiao-ts'ang shan-fang shih-wen chi* 小倉山房詩文集 (Collected prose and poems from the hut on Mt. Hsiao-ts'ang). SPPY edition.

Glossary

(Names, Terms, and Book Titles Not in the Bibliography)

An-ting shu-yuan 安定書院

cha-chi ts'e-tzu 劄記冊子
Chang Ch'i-jan 張岐然
Chang Chih-tung 張之洞
Chang Hsieh-chih 張諧之
Chang Hui-yen 張惠言
Chang Mu 張穆
Chang Po-hsing 張伯行
Chang Shih-chün 張士俊
Ch'ang-chou 常州
Chao I 趙翼
Chao I-ch'ing 趙一清
Chao Ming-ch'eng 趙明城
Chao Yü 趙昱
Ch'ao Kung-wu 晁公武
Che-chiang chuan-lu 浙江磚錄
Che-hsi 浙西
Che-tung 浙東
Ch'en Ch'iao-ts'ung 陳喬樅
Ch'en Li 陳澧

Ch'en P'eng-nien 陳彭年
Ch'en Shou-ch'i 陳壽祺
Ch'en Ti 陳第
Ch'en Tsu-fan 陳祖范
Ch'en Tzu-lung 陳子龍
Cheng Ch'iao 鄭樵
Cheng Ho 鄭和
Cheng Hsiang 鄭庠
Cheng Hsuan 鄭玄
Cheng-jen shu-yuan 證人書院
cheng-ming 正名
Cheng Shih-t'ai 鄭世泰
Ch'eng-Chu 程朱
Ch'eng En-tse 程恩澤
Ch'eng I 程頤
Ch'eng Yao-t'ien 程瑤田
Chi Chen-i 李振宜
Chi-fu ts'ung-shu 畿輔叢書
Chi-ku ko 汲古閣
Chi-ku ko Shuo-wen ting
　　汲古閣說文訂
Chi-ku lu 集古錄

chi-shih pen-mo 紀事本末

Chi-shu yuan 藉書院

chi-wu ch'iung-li 即物窮理

Chi-yang shu-yuan 暨陽書院

ch'i 氣

Ch'i Shao-nan 齊召南

ch'i-t'ung 齊同

chia 家

chia-chieh 假借

chia-chieh-tzu 假借字

Chia-ch'ing 嘉慶

chia-fa 家法

Chia K'uei 賈逵

Chiang-ching hui 講經會

chiang-hsueh 講學

Chiang Sheng 江聲

Chiang Shih-ch'üan 蔣士銓

Chiang Yung 江永

Chiao-ch'ou t'ung-i 校讐通義

Chiao Hung 焦竑

chiao-k'an-hsueh 校勘學

Ch'ieh-yun 切韻

Ch'ien Ch'ien-i 錢謙益

Ch'ien Hsi-tso 錢熙祚

Ch'ien-lung 乾隆

Ch'ien Tien 錢坫

Ch'ien Tseng 錢曾

Chih-hsin chi 知新集

Chih-pu-tsu-chai ts'ung-shu
　　　　知不足齋叢書

chih-shih 指事

chih-yeh 枝葉

Chin Chien 金簡

Chin-ch'uan 金川

Chin Nung 金農

chin-shih 進士

chin-shih-hsueh 金石學

Chin-shih lu 金石錄

Chin-tai pi-shu 津逮秘書

chin-wen 今文

Chin-wen Shang-shu i-shuo k'ao
　　　　今文尚書遺説考

Ch'in Hui-t'ien 秦蕙田

ching 經

Ching-chi tsuan-ku 經籍纂詁

ching-hsueh 經學

Ching-hsun T'ang ts'ung shu
　　　　經訓堂叢書

ching-i 經義

Ching-i k'ao pu-cheng
　　　　經義考補正

Ching-tien shih-wen 經典釋文

Ching-yin shih-she 驚隱詩社

ch'ing 情

ch'ing ch'un-yin 輕脣音

ch'ing-t'an 清談

Chiu-chih 九執

Chiu wu-tai shih 舊五代史

Chou-i shu pu 周易述補

Chou-kuan pien-fei 周官辨非

Chou-li 周禮

Chou-pei suan-ching 周髀算經

Chou Yung-nien 周永年

Chu Ch'ao-ying 朱朝英

Chu Hsi 朱熹

Chu Kuei 朱珪

chu-shu 注疏

Chu-ting chü-shih nien-p'u hsu-pien
　　　　朱汀居士年譜續編

chu-tzu 諸子

chu-tzu-hsueh 諸子學

Chu Yun 朱筠

chuan-chu 轉注

chuan-k'e sheng 專課生

chuan-shu 篆書

Chuan yueh 傳曰

Ch'uan-hsi lu 傳習錄

Ch'uan-shih lou 傳是樓

chüan 卷

Ch'üan T'ang-shih 全唐詩

Chuang Shu-tsu 莊述祖

Chuang Ts'un-yü 莊存與

ch'ueh-ch'iu shih-chü 確求實據

Ch'un-ch'iu 春秋

Ch'un-ch'iu fan-lu 春秋繁露

Ch'un-ch'iu ta-shih piao
春秋大事表

Ch'ün-shu i-pien 羣書疑辨

Chung-fa 中法

Chung-hsueh 中學

Chung-shan shu-yuan 鍾山書院

Chung-shan cha-chi 鍾山劄記

Ch'ung-wen shu-yuan 崇文書院

Erh-ya 爾雅

fa ch'i chih 發其指

fa ch'ien-jen so wei fa
發前人所未發

fa-ming 發明

fan-ch'ieh 反切

Fan Ch'in 范欽

fan-li 凡例

Fan Mou-chu 范懋柱

Fang-ch'eng k'ao 方程考

fang-chih 方志

Fang I-chih 方以智

feng-ch'i 風氣

Feng Tung-fu 馮登府

Fo-tsang 佛藏

fu 賦

Fu Hsi 伏羲

fu-k'e sheng 附課生

fu-ku 復古

Fu Shan 傅山

Fu She 復社

Fu Sheng 伏勝

Fu-wen shu-yuan 敷文書院

Go-Mō jigi 論孟字義

Hai-kuo t'u-chih 海國圖志

Han-hsueh 漢學

Han-Ju t'ung-i 漢儒通義

Han-lin 翰林

Han Wu-ti 漢武帝

Hang Shih-chün 杭世駿

Ho Ch'ang-ling 何長齡

Ho Ch'o 何焯

Ho Hsiu 何休

Hong Tae-yong 洪大容

Hou Han-shu 後漢書

Hou-hsu 後序

hsi-fa 西法

Hsi-hu yin-she 西湖吟社

Hsi-yü 西域

hsiang-hsing 象形

hsiao hsi-yang 小西洋

hsiao-hsueh 小學

Hsiao-yin 小引

hsieh-sheng 諧聲

hsieh-yun 叶韻

hsien-t'ien 先天

hsin 心

hsin-hsing 心性

hsin-hsueh 心學

Hsin-hsueh wei-ching k'ao 新學偽經考

hsin Ju-hsueh 新儒學

hsin p'ing 心平

hsin-te 心得

hsing (poem, running script) 行

hsing (nature) 性

hsing chi li 性即理

hsing-li 性理

Hsing-li ching-i 性理精義

Hsing-ming ku-hsun 性命古訓

Hsu (Introduction) 序

hsu (empty, speculative) 虛

Hsu Kuang-ch'i 徐光啟

Hsu Nai-chi 許乃濟

Hsu Shen 許慎

hsu-t'an 虛談

Hsu Yu-jen 徐有壬

Hsu Yuan-wen 徐元文

hsueh-an 學案

hsueh-chang 學長

hsueh-cheng 學政

Hsueh-hai T'ang 學海棠

Hsueh-ku T'ang 學古堂

hsueh-shu 學術

Hsueh Ying-ch'i 薛應旂

hsun-ku 訓詁

Hsun-tzu 荀子

Hu Ch'ien 胡虔

Hu Lin-i 胡林翼

Hu-shih Yü kung t'u k'ao-cheng 胡氏禹貢圖考正

Hu Wei 胡渭

Hu Ying-lin 胡應麟

Hua-yen ching 華嚴經

Huai-nan-tzu 淮南子

Huang-ch'ao ching-shih wen-pien 皇朝經世文編

Huang-Ch'ing ching-chieh hsu-pien 皇清經解續編

Huang Ching-jen 黃景仁

Huang Chu-chung 黃居中

Huang-fu Mi 皇甫謐

Huang-Ming ching-shih wen-pien 皇明經世文編

Huang P'ei-lieh 黃丕烈

Huang P'eng-nien 黃彭年

Huang Po-chia 黃百家

Huang Yü-chi 黃虞稷

hui-i 會意

Hung Liang-chi 洪亮吉

Hung-wu 洪武

huo-chiao 活校

i ch'i ch'i 易其氣

i-chia chih hsueh 一家之學

i-chien 臆見

i-hsueh 義學

I-hsueh hsiang-shu lun 易學象數論

i-li (meanings & principles) 義理

I-li (Leftover chapters of the *Rites*) 遺禮

I-li (Decorum ritual) 儀禮

i-li chih-hsueh 義理之學

I-Mei 翼梅

I-nien lu 疑年錄

I-shih 繹史

i-shu 遺書

I-t'u ming-pien 易圖明辨

Itō Jinsai 伊藤仁齋

jen-hsin Tao-hsin 人心道心

jen-wu piao 人物表

Ju 儒

Ju-tsang shuo 儒藏説

kai-chih 改制

k'ai-shu 楷書

K'ang-hsi 康熙

K'ang-hsi tzu-tien 康熙字典

k'ao-cheng 考證

k'ao-cheng chih tzu 考證之資

K'ao-hsin lu 考信錄

k'ao-ku 考古

K'ao-kung chi 考工記

K'ao-kung chi t'u 考工記圖

K'ao-kung chi ch'e-chih t'u-chieh 考工記車制圖解

Kiangnan 江南

Kim Chong-hui 金正喜

Ko-ku yao-lun 格古要論

ko-wu 格物

kōshō 考證

Ku-chin t'u-shu chi-ch'eng 古今圖書集成

Ku-chin wei-shu k'ao 古今偽書考

Ku-ching ching-she 詁經精舍

ku-hsueh 古學

ku-hsun 古訓

ku-i 古義

Ku Kuang-ch'i 顧廣圻

ku-t'i 古體

Ku Tsu-yü 顧祖禹

Ku Tung-kao 顧棟高

ku-wen 古文

Ku-wen Shang-shu chuan-i 古文尚書撰異

Ku-wen Shang-shu k'ao-i 古文尚書考異

Ku-wen Shang-shu pien 古文尚書辨

Ku-wen Shang-shu t'iao-pien 古文尚書條辨

Ku wu ch'ing ch'un-yin shuo 古無輕脣音説

kuan-hsueh 官學

Kuang-hsu 光緒

Kuang-tung t'ung-chih 廣東通志

Kuang-yun 廣韻

Kuei Fu 桂馥

Kuei-ku-tzu 鬼谷子

K'un-chih chi 困知記

K'un-hsueh chi-wen 困學紀聞

kung 工

kung-sheng 貢生

Kung-yang chuan 公羊傳

Kung-yang chuan-chu yin Han-lü kao 公羊傳注引漢律考

k'ung 空

K'ung An-kuo 孔安國

K'ung Kuang-sen 孔廣森

K'ung-tzu chia-yü 孔子家語

k'ung-yen 空言

K'ung Ying-ta 孔穎達

Kuo-ch'ao ching-hsueh shih-ch'eng chi 國朝經學師承記

Kuo-ch'ao Sung-hsueh yuan-yuan chi 國朝宋學淵源記

Kuo P'u 郭璞

Kuo-shih ching-chi-chih 國史經籍志

Kuo-shih Ju-lin chuan 國史儒林傳

Kuo-tzu chien 國子監

Kuo-yü 國語

lei-shu 類書

li (principle) 理

li (rites) 禮

Li Chao-lo 李兆洛

Li-chi 禮記

Li-chi Cheng-tu k'ao 禮記鄭讀考

Li Ch'ing-chao 李清照

Li Ch'un 李惇

Li Fu 李紱

Li Fu-sun 李富孫

Li-hsiang k'ao-ch'eng 歷象考成

li-hsueh 理學

Li Hung-chang 李鴻章

Li Jui 李銳

Li Kuang-ti 李光地

Li Kung 李塨

Li Shan-lan 李善蘭

li-shu 隸書

Li-suan ch'üan-shu 曆算全書

Li Tao-nan 李道南

Li Tao-yuan 酈道元

Li Wen-tsao 李文藻

Liang-Han chin-shih chi 兩漢金石記

Liang Shang-kuo 梁上國

Liang Yü-sheng 梁玉繩

Liao P'ing 廖平

Lin Po-t'ung 林佰桐

Lin Tse-hsu 林則徐

Ling Shu 凌曙

Ling T'ing-k'an 凌廷堪

Lingnan 嶺南

Liu Chih-chi 劉知幾

Liu E 劉鶚

Liu Hsiang 劉向

Liu Hsien-t'ing 劉獻廷

Liu Hsin 劉歆

Liu-li-ch'ang 琉璃廠

Liu-li-ch'ang shu-ssu chi 琉璃廠書肆記

Liu Shih-p'ei 劉師培

liu-shu 六書

Liu T'ai-kung 劉台拱

Liu Te 劉德

Liu Tsung-chou 劉宗周

Lo Ch'in-shun 羅欽順

Lo Shih-lin 羅士琳

Lu Fa-yen 陸法言

Lu Hsin-yuan 陸心源

Lu Kung wang 魯恭王
Lu Lung-ch'i 陸隴其
Lu Te-ming 陸德明
Lü Liu-liang 呂留良
Lü-shih ch'un-ch'iu 呂氏春秋
Lung-ch'eng shu-yuan 龍城書院
Lung-ch'eng cha-chi
龍城劄記

Ma Su 馬驌
Ma Yueh-kuan 馬曰琯
Mao Chin 毛晉 (晉)
Mao I 毛扆
Mao-shih k'ao-cheng 毛詩考證
Mao-shih ku-yin k'ao 毛詩古音考
Mao Wan-ling 毛萬齡
Mei-hua shu-yuan 梅花書院
Mei Ku-ch'eng 梅穀成
Mei Tse 梅鷟
Mei Tsu 梅鷟
Mei Wen-ting 梅文鼎
Meng-tzu cheng-i 孟子正義
ming 命
ming-chiao 名教
Ming-i tai-fang lu 明夷待訪錄
Ming-shih 明史
ming-wu 名物
Mo-tzu 墨子
Mo Yu-chih 莫友芝
mu-lu-hsueh 目錄學
mu-yu 幕友

Nan-ch'ing shu-yuan 南菁書院
nei-p'ien 內篇

Nei-wu-fu 內務府
nien-p'u 年譜
Niu Shu-yü 鈕樹玉

Ou-lo-pa 歐邏巴
Ou-yang Hsiu 歐陽修

pa-ku 八股
Pai-ching jih-lu 拜經日錄
Pak Che-ga 朴齊家
Pan Ku 班固
pan-pen-hsueh 版本學
P'an Shih-ch'eng 潘仕成
p'ang-cheng 旁證
Pao Shih-ch'en 包世臣
Pao T'ing-p'o 鮑廷博
pei 碑
pei-hsueh 北學
pei-hsueh p'ai 碑學派
P'ei-wen yun-fu 佩文韻府
pen-cheng 本證
pen-i 本義
pi-li 比例
Pi Yuan 畢沅
piao 表
pien 辨
pien-cheng 辨證
pien-chieh 辨解
pien-wei 辨偽
p'ing ch'i hsin 平其心
P'ing-hua-chai 瓶花齋
po-hsueh 博學
po-hsueh hung-tz'u 博學宏詞

pu-cheng 補正

Pu-cheng Jih-chih lu 補正日知錄

pu erh ch'en 不二臣

pu ho hsun-ku 不合訓詁

pu-i 補遺

pu-shou 部首

p'u-hsueh 樸學

pukhak 北學

San-kuo-chih 三國志

San-kuo-chih chu-pu 三國志注補

San-kuo-chih pu-chu 三國志補注

san-shih 三世

shan-chang 山長

Shang-shan T'ang 上善堂

Shang-shu 尚書

Shang-shu cheng-i 尚書正義

Shang-shu chi-chu yin-shu 尚書集注音書

Shang-shu chin-ku-wen chi-chieh 尚書今古文集解

Shang-shu hou-an 尚書後案

Shang-shu ta-chuan ting-pen 尚書大傳定本

Shang-shu t'ung-i 尚書通義

Shang-shu yü-lun 尚書餘論

Shao Ch'ang-heng 邵長蘅

Shao Ch'i-tao 邵齊燾

Shao Chin-han 邵晉涵

Shao I-ch'en 邵懿辰

Shao Yung 邵雍

she 社

she-hsueh 社學

Shen Te-ch'ien 沈德潛

sheng-ching 聖經

sheng-lei 聲類

Sheng Pai-erh 盛百二

Sheng-wu chi 聖武記

sheng-yuan 生員

sheng-yun 聲韻

Shichikei Mōshi kōbun 七經孟子考文

Shigeno Yasutsugu 重野安繹

shih (literati) 士

shih (facts) 事

shih (concrete) 實

Shih-chi 史記

Shih-chi k'ao 史籍考

Shih-ching hsiao-hsueh 詩經小學

Shih-ching k'ao 石經考

Shih-ching k'ao-i 石經考異

shih-hsueh 實學

Shih-ku-wei 詩古微

Shih-lu 實錄

Shih-ming 釋名

Shih-san-ching chu-shu 十三經注疏

Shih-san-ching chiao-k'an chi 十三經校勘記

shih-shih ch'iu-shih 實事求是

Shih-t'ung 史通

shih-wen 時文

shih yü k'ao-cheng 失於考證

Shu-cheng 疏證

Shu-ku-wei 書古微

shu-mu 書目

shu-yuan 書院

Shu yueh 書曰

Shui-ching chu 水經注

Shui-ching chu shih 水經注釋

Shun-chih 順治

Shuo-wen chieh-tzu 說文解字

Shuo-wen ting ting 說文誆誆

Shuo-wen Tuan-chu ting-pu
說文段注誆補

sirhak 實學

ssu-chiao 死校

Ssu-k'u ch'üan-shu chien-ming mu-lu
四庫全書簡明目錄

Ssu-k'u ch'üan-shu tsung-mu
四庫全書總目

Ssu-ma Ch'ien 司馬遷

Ssu-ma Kuang 司馬光

ssu-pu 四部

Ssu-pu pei-yao 四部備要

Ssu-shu cheng-wu 四書正誤

Ssu-shu jen-wu k'ao 四書人物考

Ssu-shu shih-ti 四書釋地

Ssu-shu shih-ti pien-cheng
四書釋地辯證

Ssu-shu ta-ch'üan 四書大全

Su Shih 蘇軾

su-wang 素王

Sui-shu 隋書

Sun Ch'i-feng 孫奇逢

Sun Chih-tsu 孫志祖

Sun I-jang 孫詒讓

Sun Tsung-lien 孫宗濂

Sung Hsiang-feng 宋翔鳳

Sung-hsueh 宋學

Sung Lao 宋犖

Sung Lien 宋濂

Sung-shih 宋史

Sung-shih Sun Shih chuan shu-hou
宋史孫奭傳書後

Sung-Yuan hsueh-an 宋元學案

Ta-Ch'ing i-t'ung-chih 大清一統志

Ta-chuan 大傳

ta hsi-yang 大西洋

Ta-hsueh 大學

ta-i wei-yen 大義微言

Ta-t'ung shu 大同書

Ta Yü mo 大禹謨

T'ai chou 泰州

T'ai-p'ing yü-lan 太平御覽

T'ai shih 太誓

T'ang Chün-i 唐君毅

T'ang-Sung ts'ung-shu 唐宋叢書

Tao-ching 道經

Tao-chi 道濟

Tao-hsin 道心

Tao-hsueh 道學

Tao-kuang 道光

Tao-tsang 道藏

Tao-t'ung 道統

T'ao Chu 陶澍

Teng Shih-ju 鄧石如

t'i-chih 體制

t'iao-li 條理

t'ieh 帖

t'ieh-hsueh 帖學

tien-chih 典制

T'ien-i ko 天一閣

T'ien-wen suan-fa 天文算法

Ting chia 丁家

Ting Jih-ch'ang 丁日昌

ting-lun 定論

Ting Yen 丁晏

t'o-ku kai-chih 託古改制

tsa-chia 雜家

Tsang Yung 臧庸

Ts'ao Chao 曹昭

ts'ao-shu 草書

Ts'ao Yin 曹寅

Tseng Kuo-fan 曾國藩

Tso chuan 左傳

Tso Tsung-t'ang 左宗棠

Tsou Shan 鄒善

Ts'ui Mai 崔邁

Ts'ui Shu 崔述

ts'ung-shu 叢書

Tu Chün 杜濬

tu-shih chih i 篤實之遺

Tu-shu min-ch'iu chi
讀書敏求記

Tu-shu She 讀書社

Tu-shu tsa-chih 讀書雜誌

Tu Yü 杜預

t'u 圖

Tuan-shih Shuo-wen chiao-ting
段氏説文校定

t'uan-tz'u 彖詞

Tung Chung-shu 董仲舒

Tung-lin shu-yuan 東林書院

T'ung-chih 同治

T'ung-chih T'ang ching-chieh
通志堂經解

t'ung-sheng 童生

t'ung-shih 通史

Tzu-chih t'ung-chien 資治通鑑

tzu-jan chih chieh-hsien
自然之節限

Tzu-shuo 字説

Tzu-yang shu-yuan 紫陽書院

wai-chi 外集

wai-p'ien 外篇

Wan Ching 萬經

Wan Ssu-ta 萬斯大

Wan Yen 萬言

Wang An-kuo 王安國

Wang An-shih 王安石

Wang Ch'ang 王昶

Wang Ch'i-shu 汪啓淑

Wang Chün 王峻

Wang Chung 汪中

Wang Hsi-chih 王羲之

Wang Hsi-shan 王錫闡

Wang Hsien 汪憲

Wang Hsien-ch'ien 王先謙

Wang Hsien-chih 王獻之

Wang Hui 王翬

Wang Hui-tsu 汪輝祖

Wang I-jung 王懿榮

Wang Lun 王倫

Wang Mang 王莽

Wang Mao-hung 王懋竑

Wang Nien-sun 王念孫

Wang Po 王柏

Wang Shao-lan 王紹蘭

Wang She 望社

Wang Shih-to 汪士鐸

Wang Shu 王澍

Wang Su 王肅

Wang Tso 王佐

Wang Yin-chih 王引之

Wang Ying-lin 王應麟

Wei Chung-hsien 魏忠賢

wei-li 微理

wei-yen ta-i 微言大義

wen-chi 文集

wen-chien chih chih 聞見之知

Wen-hsuan-lou ts'ung-shu
文選樓叢書

Wen-lan ko 文瀾閣

wen-ta 問答

wen-tzu 文字

wen-tzu-hsueh 文字學

Wen-yuan ko 文淵閣

wu 物

Wu Ch'eng (Yuan) 吳澄

Wu Ch'eng (Ch'ing) 吳城

Wu Chih-chen 吳之振

Wu Ch'o 吳焯

Wu I 武億

Wu Lan-hsiu 吳蘭修

Wu-li hsiao-chih 物理小識

Wu-li t'ung-k'ao 五禮通考

Wu Ping-chien 伍秉鑑

wu so fa-ming 無所發明

Wu T'ang 吳棠

wu tsu-i tzu k'ao-cheng
無足以資考證

Wu-ying-tien 武英殿

Wu Yü 吳棫

Yamanoi Tei 山井鼎

yang-lien 養廉

Yang Shen 楊慎

Yang Shih 楊時

Yao Chi-heng 姚際恆

Yao Nai 姚鼐

yao-tz'u 爻詞

Yeh Shih 葉適

Yen Hsiu-ling 閻修齡

Yen K'o-chün 嚴可均

Yen-Li ts'ung-shu 顏李叢書

Yen-yu 延祐

Yen Yuan 顏元

Yin-hsueh wu-shu 音學五書

yin-i 音義

ying-Sung-ch'ao 影宋鈔

Yoshimune 吉宗

yu-wen 右文

Yü Hsiao-k'o 余蕭客

Yü kung 禹貢

Yü kung chui-chih cheng-wu
禹貢錐指正誤

Yü Li 郁禮

Yü Yueh 俞樾

yü-lu 語錄

Yuan-chien lei-han 淵鑑類函

Yuan Mei 袁枚

Yuan shan 原善

Yuan-shih 元史

"Yuan Tao" 原道

Yueh-hua shu-yuan 越華書院

Index

Index

Index

Index

Ta-Ch'ing i-t'ung-chih (continued)
geography of the great Ch'ing realm), 102–
103; collaboration on, 198
Ta-chuan (Great commentary), 209–210
Ta-hsueh (moral philosophy), 167
Ta-t'ung shu (The book of the great community; K'ang Yu-wei), 24
"Ta Yü mo" (Counsels of Yü the Great),
118; controversy over texts in, 178–179,
200
Taam, Cheuk-woon, 143
Tables (piao), for tabulation of data, 188
Tai Chen, 39, 44, 56, 58, 73, 75, 243; as
social critic, 17–22, 105; on philology and
the Tao, 29; and Han Learning, 59; on
purification of texts, 61–62; criticized by
editors of Ssu-k'u ch'üan-shu, 66; on
ancient texts, 69; on Western science, 80–
81, 83, 216; merchant origin of, 93, 95;
and Chu Yun, 106; teaching in Yangchow,
123; work on local gazetteers, 134; and
classification, 168; on application of
mathematics to ancient bells, 182–184; as
collaborator, 199; on phonology, 219–220;
on Classic of Waterways, 225; and Itō Jinsai, 227–228; attitude toward philosophy,
233
T'ai-chou school, 115; Ch'ing attacks on, 42;
strength of, 42–43; and philosophy of
ch'i, 44; merchant connections of, 95;
17th-century attacks on, 114
T'ai-p'ing yü-lan (Imperial encyclopedia of
the T'ai-p'ing reign period), 187
Taiping Rebellion, xvi, xvii, 2; and academic
patronage, 111; and numbers of licentiates,
130; impact of, 248–253; intellectual impact, 249–251; scholarship and the T'ung-
chih Restoration, 251–253
T'ang Chien, 20, 244
T'ang Chün-i, 245
T'ang dynasty, xx, 10, 40
T'ang-Sung ts'ung-shu (Collectanea of the
T'ang and Sung dynasties), 152
Tao: use of Classics for understanding of,
28–29; and the "Ta Yü mo," 179
Tao-ching (Classic of the Way), 179, 200
Tao-hsueh ("Studies of the Way"; "Studies
of the Tao"), 27, 43; and Neo-Confucianism, xx; Sung studies of, 41; based on li,
45; relation of Four Books to, 46; influence of Buddhism on, 48–49; promoted
by Hsu Ch'ien-hsueh, 102; criticism of,
129; k'ao-cheng scholars on, 156–157;
"dialogue records" of, 174
Tao-kuang Emperor, 244
Tao-t'ung: transmission of, 78, use of term,
79
T'ao Chu, 125, 241, 242

Taoism, 48; and Confucianism, 111
Teacher-pupil relationships, changes in,
128–129
Teaching, as career, 131–133
Teng Shih-ju, 193, 196
Texts, authenticity of, 68–70
Thackray, Arnold, 172
Thirteen Classics, 145
Tibetans, Manchu record of history of, 16
T'ien-i ko (Pavilion of Everything United
under Heaven), 109, 144–145, 146, 148,
158; catalog of, 145
Tillman, Hoyt, xx
Ting, Jih-ch'ang, 252
Ting Yen, 206
Tones, research on, 220
Tsang Lin, 93
Tsang Yung, 92, 93, 109, 110, 204; note-
books of, 176
Ts'ang-shu chi-yao (Bookman's manual;
Sun Ts'ung-t'ien), 147
Ts'ao Chao, 189
Ts'ao Yin, 101, 104
Tseng Kuo-fan, 242, 249, 251; pro-Sung
Learning, 247
Tsien, T. H., 167
Tso chuan (Tso's commentary), 179–180,
201, 211
Tso-shih ch'un-ch'iu k'ao-cheng (Evidential
analysis of Master Tso's Spring and
Autumn Annals; Liu Feng-lu), 59
Tso Tsung-t'ang, 122, 249
Tsou Shan, 51
Ts'ui Mai, 224
Ts'ui Shu, 32, 223
Tu-shu min-ch'iu chi (Record of an earnest
search in the interest of study; Ch'ien
Tseng), 146
Tu-shu She (Society of Book-Readers), 114
Tu-shu tsa-chih (Miscellaneous reading notes;
Wang Nien-sun), 176
Tu Wei-yun, 71, 75–76; on patronage, 104
Tuan-shih Shuo-wen chiao-ting (Collation
and emendation of Master Tuan's Shuo-
wen; Niu Shu-yü), 206
Tuan Yü-ts'ai, 18, 56, 123, 145, 155, 204,
227, 239; rejection of Sung Learning by,
58; on authenticity of texts, 68, 208–209;
early retirement of, 134; use of inscriptions by, 191, 194, 195; supplementary
studies of, 206; on phonology, 219–220;
on Han philology as narrow, 241
Tung Chung-shu, 210, 211
Tung-lin Academy, 14, 52, 113
T'ung-ch'eng "ancient prose" literary school,
234, 247
T'ung-chih Restoration, scholarship in, 251–
253

Index

Index

Harvard East Asian Monographs

46. W. P. J. Hall, *A Bibliographical Guide to Japanese Research on the Chinese Economy, 1958–1970*

47. Jack J. Gerson, *Horatio Nelson Lay and Sino-British Relations, 1854–1864*

48. Paul Richard Bohr, *Famine and the Missionary: Timothy Richard as Relief Administrator and Advocate of National Reform*

49. Endymion Wilkinson, *The History of Imperial China: A Research Guide*

50. Britten Dean, *China and Great Britain: The Diplomacy of Commerical Relations, 1860–1864*

51. Ellsworth C. Carlson, *The Foochow Missionaries, 1847–1880*

52. Yeh-chien Wang, *An Estimate of the Land-Tax Collection in China, 1753 and 1908*

53. Richard M. Pfeffer, *Understanding Business Contracts in China, 1949–1963*

54. Han-sheng Chuan and Richard Kraus, *Mid-Ch'ing Rice Markets and Trade, An Essay in Price History*

55. Ranbir Vohra, *Lao She and the Chinese Revolution*

56. Liang-lin Hsiao, *China's Foreign Trade Statistics, 1864–1949*

57. Lee-hsia Hsu Ting, *Government Control of the Press in Modern China, 1900–1949*

58. Edward W. Wagner, *The Literati Purges: Political Conflict in Early Yi Korea*

59. Joungwon A. Kim, *Divided Korea: The Politics of Development, 1945–1972*

60. Noriko Kamachi, John K. Fairbank, and Chūzō Ichiko, *Japanese Studies of Modern China Since 1953: A Bibliographical Guide to Historical and Social-Science Research on the Nineteenth and Twentieth Centuries, Supplementary Volume for 1953–1969*

61. Donald A. Gibbs and Yun-chen Li, *A Bibliography of Studies and Translations of Modern Chinese Literature, 1918–1942*

62. Robert H. Silin, *Leadership and Values: The Organization of Large-Scale Taiwanese Enterprises*

63. David Pong, *A Critical Guide to the Kwangtung Provincial Archives Deposited at the Public Record Office of London*

64. Fred W. Drake, *China Charts the World: Hsu Chi-yü and His Geography of 1848*

65. William A. Brown and Urgunge Onon, translators and annotators, *History of the Mongolian People's Republic*

66. Edward L. Farmer, *Early Ming Government: The Evolution of Dual Capitals*

67. Ralph C. Croizier, *Koxinga and Chinese Nationalism: History, Myth, and the Hero*

68. William J. Tyler, tr., *The Psychological World of Natsumi Sōseki*, by Doi Takeo